Good and Bad Power

GEOFF MULGAN

Good and Bad Power
The Ideals and Betrayals of Government

ALLEN LANE
an imprint of
PENGUIN BOOKS

ALLEN LANE

Published by the Penguin Group
Penguin Books Ltd, 80 Strand, London WC2R ORL, England
Penguin Group (USA) Inc., 375 Hudson Street, New York, New York 10014, USA
Penguin Group (Canada), 90 Eglinton Avenue East, Suite 700, Toronto, Ontario, Canada M4P 2Y3
(a division of Pearson Penguin Canada Inc.)
Penguin Ireland, 25 St Stephen's Green, Dublin 2, Ireland (a division of Penguin Books Ltd)
Penguin Group (Australia), 250 Camberwell Road,
Camberwell, Victoria 3124, Australia (a division of Pearson Australia Group Pty Ltd)
Penguin Books India Pvt Ltd, 11 Community Centre,
Panchsheel Park, New Delhi – 110 017, India
Penguin Group (NZ), cnr Airborne and Rosedale Roads, Albany,
Auckland 1310, New Zealand (a division of Pearson New Zealand Ltd)
Penguin Books (South Africa) (Pty) Ltd, 24 Sturdee Avenue,
Rosebank, Johannesburg 2196, South Africa

Penguin Books Ltd, Registered Offices: 80 Strand, London WC2R ORL, England

www.penguin.com

First published 2006
1

Copyright © Geoff Mulgan, 2006

The moral right of the author has been asserted

Set in 10.5/14pt PostScript Linotype Sabon
Typeset by Rowland Phototypesetting Ltd, Bury St Edmunds, Suffolk
Printed in Great Britain by Clays Ltd, St Ives plc

A CIP catalogue record for this book is available from the British Library

ISBN-13: 978-0-713-99882-5
ISBN-10: 0-713-99882-2

Contents

1 The Question of Good Power   1

2 The Origins of the State   14

3 Accelerated Evolution   28

4 The Servant State   43

5 The State as Possession   78

6 The Self-serving State   95

7 Moral Ends and Moral Means   127

8 Revolt and Revolution   149

9 Hot and Cold Democracy   161

10 Alienation and Cycles   196

11 Habit-forming Ethics   205

12 Civic Commitment   226

13 Unsettling Knowledge as a Source of Renewal   252

14 Could a Government Serve the Whole World?   272

15 Service to the Future   306

16 The State as a Work of Art   312

Summary of the Argument   318
Notes   323
Index   363

I

The Question of Good Power

'Any political system is an accident. It is an accumulation of habits, customs, prejudices, and principles that have survived a long process of trial and error and of ceaseless response to changing circumstances. If the system works well on the whole it is a lucky accident – the luckiest, indeed, that can befall a society, for all of the institutions of the society, and thus its entire character and that of the human types formed within it, depend ultimately on the government and the political order.'   Edward Banfield[1]

Over the last century governments have shown an unprecedented capacity for doing both good and evil. This is what makes them so fascinating. It is why so many people want to understand how they behave, how they think, how they change us and how they can be changed.

The playwright Samuel Beckett once wrote that 'the tears of the world are a constant quantity'. The implication is that there is little that governments, or indeed anyone else, can do to reduce human suffering. Yet seen through any historical lens this view, which seems so full of world-weary wisdom, turns out to be untenable. There have been times when most people could expect a reasonably happy life, and times when most could expect a vale of tears.[2]

What makes the difference? For any one of us the prospects of happiness will depend on such things as our genetic endowment, our character and relationships and where and in what circumstances we were born, as well as sheer luck.[3] But for the larger populations of cities or nations what matters most to human happiness is not the climate or the landscape, genes or national characters[4] but rather the quality of government in its widest sense, and the extent to which people can govern their own actions. People blessed with peace, order, equity and rights, and governed by benign rulers, stand a far better chance of living a good life, whatever their personal qualities. People living under dictators, without rights, laws or honest officials risk misery and suffering.[5]

That states matter to human happiness has been apparent ever since the first ones learned how to protect their cities and tax their people.[6] But it has become ever more obvious as states' capacity for both good and evil has grown; from Kyrgyzstan to Canada and Korea their qualities do more to determine people's well-being than oil, gold and diamonds (which have more often cursed their possessors than helped them[7]) and more than culture or religion (which turn out to be disappointingly unreliable explanations for anything to do with politics and governance[8]). According to the fullest analysis yet done of the many factors that explain widely varying levels of happiness in some fifty countries across the world, 'the effects of the quality of government on well-being were above and beyond the effects flowing through better education, higher incomes and better health, all of which were themselves dependent on the quality of government.'[9] Democracies outperform dictatorships, and states which fear the people are far more conducive to well-being than ones that are feared by them.

The most brilliant depiction of the difference between good power and bad power was produced at the dawn of the modern era by the painter Ambrogio Lorenzetti, in the two celebrated frescoes he painted for the Palazzo Pubblico in Siena. The frescoes set out allegories of good and bad government. The walls showing good government display two threads passing from a ruler, inspired by classical virtues, through the hands of the citizens, symbolizing a voluntary political order, to a figure representing judgement. There is a thriving town, with prosperous markets and citizens happily going about their business. Beyond the walls a carefully tended countryside is blooming. It is a vision of benign order, founded on reciprocity between rulers and ruled, on equity and concord. Facing it is the allegory of bad government. There a devilish figure rules; justice has been put aside, and plague, violence and famine have swept the land.

The frescoes are an argument and a vision. They represent an argument that the state should be ruled for the common good rather than by a monarch, and they represent, as a vision, the principles that the leaders and citizens of the city believed themselves to be living out in their republic, which was itself part of a vigorous civic movement across Italy which believed that the state's freedom rested on the freedom of its citizens.

Lorenzetti's confident celebration of good government in medieval Siena was to be mocked by history. Within a few years the Black Death arrived in the city, killing him and most of his family. Siena was subjected to repeated attacks, many encouraged by its great rival, Florence. The civic republic was replaced by tyranny. The benign order Lorenzetti had portrayed with such tenderness collapsed, and for many centuries the ideal of civic rule was seen as an anachronism.

The people of Siena thought that they had found an answer to the ancient question of what makes government good. This question has been the central issue of political philosophy for well over two thousand years, and insights can be found in the writings of Christians and Buddhists, Confucians and Muslims and liberals, socialists and conservatives.

What is striking about many of these writings is that the structure of the arguments has changed little over time. According to one side, good government depends on the best people with the best policies being put in charge. The best might be philosophers (depicted in Plato's *Republic*), or the ideally wise and virtuous (depicted in Aristotle's *Politics*), who provided a standard against which all other kinds of rule could be judged.

On the other side of the world, in India and China, similar claims were made. China was the first empire to move beyond the idea that rulers ruled solely because of divine sanction, birth or force of arms. By around 1000 BCE it had become accepted (at least in theory) that rulers should rule only because of their personal moral virtues. If they ceased to be virtuous their people would be entitled to depose them. Later, in India, similar arguments took hold in the vigorous republics

3

of the north, and the Buddha argued against there being any role for a god, or for birthright, in determining who should rule. Instead righteousness was the only valid basis for a ruler's authority.

But within each civilization thinkers also acknowledged that the virtue of individual leaders was rarely enough. Too much reliance on leaders' ethics involves what psychologists call the 'fundamental attribution error': the tendency wrongly to attribute behaviours to people's characters rather than to the situations they find themselves in. Aristotle argued that although the ruler's good character might be the single best guarantee of good government, it is also the least reliable since rulers are so often corrupted by power. Even the best can turn bad. In any case there would never be a simple causal link between leaders' personal qualities and their successes (George Schultz, the former US Secretary of State, wrote in his memoirs that he could never understand how President Reagan could know so little but achieve so much). So a better guarantee of good government was the rule of laws which could protect the community's wider interests, since no ruler, however intelligent, could design the laws in such a way that they would always favour his interests.[10] These laws might guarantee a division of powers of the kind seen in Republican Rome, where what to modern eyes looks like a bizarre confusion of institutions and functions competed so as to avoid the alternative of kingship. Laws might govern a confederation of cities. And laws might confer sovereignty or self-rule on the people, as in ancient Athens.

Two thousand years of subsequent history have done little to change the shape of these arguments. We still want good men and women to rule us and we still look to laws and structures to rein in the venal and corrupt (the British Prime Minister Harold Macmillan was once asked what the collective noun was for heads of governments: a 'lack' of principals was his reply).[11]

The fundamental tasks facing governments have also changed surprisingly little. Communities need states to protect them, to promote their welfare, to enforce justice and to uphold truth, and in carrying out these tasks contemporary states face some of the same ambiguities as their predecessors. All have to use force, and sometimes guile, to get their writ to run. All have to cultivate economic prosperity so that they can raise enough tax to pay for armies and roads, just like their predecessors millennia ago. All have to avoid overreaching themselves and meddling too much in the lives of the people they are meant to serve. And all have to remain legitimate while taking unpleasant actions: the novelist Carlos Fuentes' comment that politics is 'the art of swallowing toads without making a face' applies just as well to ancient monarchs as to modern Prime Ministers.

This book is interested both in what has changed and in what remains unchanged. It is concerned with morality in its widest sense: with the many ways in which the word 'should' comes into the business of government – what governments should do, how they should treat their citizens, when they should go to war, and when they should be honest or secretive, loyal or disloyal. And it is concerned with the many meanings that the word 'good' can have in relation to government.

To make sense of these questions I've drawn on many sources. The first source is literature. There is a vast literature on power, which it would take many lifetimes to absorb. I have had to be very selective. But I have deliberately drawn on ideas and literature from across the world, and from across many periods, rather than assuming that the modern West has a monopoly of wisdom about good government. There are risks in attempting to use such an extensive literature, and I don't doubt that some specialists will take issue with my interpretations of the sources that I have drawn on. But the justification for my approach is that it may reveal patterns that are otherwise invisible and, in a century when China and India are likely to reassert their traditional roles as leading powers, I doubt that it will long remain acceptable for western political thought to remain so oblivious to the insights that can be found in their traditions.

The second source is experience. I have worked as a local government official, an activist, an advocate, an employee of a parliament and, later, as an adviser to a Prime Minister and as a senior civil servant. I've also visited and worked for many governments around the world. I have seen very many lives changed for the better by governments, and I've worked with many honest and decent public servants. But I have also seen the darker, and drabber, sides of government. Governments can't help but see people as problems to be managed, and they can't help preferring passive gratitude to active scepticism.[12] They may have little in common with the cartoon caricatures that make up much of the description of government in literature, television and film, but most do have inbuilt biases in favour of the rich and powerful, and most do contain plenty of manipulators who love intrigue, who have lost whatever moral compass they may once have had, and who protect themselves with a steely cynicism.

Drawing both on written sources and direct experience, this book is an attempt to respond to a double revolution. The first revolution has transformed how nations are governed. Today there are no self-proclaimed empires, no philosopher kings and no aristocracies in the strict sense. Totalitarian regimes are a pale shadow of their former selves, and even military dictatorships are out of fashion. Instead there are well over a hundred democracies (including one, Bulgaria, which has for a time elected a former monarch), and quite a few genuine innovations in governance, like the novel hybrids of the European Union.

Compared to monarchy, fascism or communism the moral advantages of representative democracy are not hard to discern: although democracies contain plenty of lazy and self-serving bureaucrats most of the vices of power – from cruelty and greed to lies and violence – are at least partially held in check. But with the spread of democracy to regions as varied as Mongolia and Madagascar its tensions and moral contradictions have become more visible. As many of the ancient philosophers warned, democracy can easily descend into populism and prejudice and a search for real or imagined enemies. It can become a fig-leaf for oligarchs, masking profound inequalities of power. And it can all too easily sap its own energies, drifting into a sullen fatalism. A large majority of the world's population now believes that democracy is the best form of government; but almost equally large majorities believe that political leaders are unethical or dishonest, and in the mature democracies large minorities doubt whether their governments reflect the will of the people. Addressing these weaknesses and providing democracy with its own sources of renewable energy look set to be among the great tasks for this century, tasks for which history provides no obvious guides.

The other revolution is global. The sharply rising population densities that made states so essential in the Middle East's fertile crescent and eastern China five thousand years ago are now being matched by much greater interdependence on a global scale and a clutch of 'wicked' problems, from nuclear proliferation and climate change to poverty and virulent disease, that are unlikely to be resolved without authority at a global scale. Existing global institutions lack the power to do much about these problems, and are locked in a difficult struggle with superpowers that are doubtful of the very idea that they might subordinate themselves to international law. Finding ways to make and remake effective and legitimate global institutions looks set to be another great task for this century, and again it is one for which there are no obvious precedents.

I argue that the best way to understand government both within nations and globally is through the lens of service. Most western political theory starts from individuals, and then derives conclusions about how constitutions or governments should be organized either to promote individuals' rights or to protect them from each other. I am concerned with government as a relationship that we are born into, an imperfect and messy relationship which at best is one of service and at worst is one of domination and oppression. It is from this relationship that the state's powers derive, and it is the mutual dependence of rulers and ruled that gives all politics its distinctive hues. To ascribe laws and constitutions to god, or natural laws, or human nature, inevitably leads to confusion. Individual rights are not prior to government; instead they are comprehensible only as an aspect of the relationship that people have with governments, and like so many of our freedoms, they rest on the ability of governments to use force to defend them.

The idea that governments have a responsibility to serve the people can be traced far back through time, to Chinese notions of a 'mandate of heaven', Indian ideas of *rajadharma* (the moral duties of kings) and western arguments that power rests on the consent of the governed. But it is only in the last century that states have had the tools and techniques to act as genuine servants. One French historian wrote that 'nobody was governed before the later nineteenth century',[13] and it was only after states acquired the means to survey, monitor, direct and shape millions of people's daily lives that they could contemplate pensions systems and health services, police forces to keep order or regulators to keep air and water safe.

There is much to celebrate in these changes. But governments' roles as servants are fraught with ambiguities, and these ambiguities have become more acute as governments' powers have grown. Good governments are servants to the people who are their masters, but when they pass laws and collect taxes governments also act as masters to the people they serve. All governments have interests that are different from those of the public; all governments use methods that are necessarily impersonal, abstract and cold, almost the opposite qualities to those that we expect from a true servant; and all governments can, *in extremis*, suspend the rules that govern them. Exploring and understanding these ambiguities is the precondition for intelligent politics, whether one's goal is radical reform or conservative caution.

HOW TO THINK ABOUT POWER

Pascal described 'looking at pictures which are too near or too far away. There is just one indivisible point which is the right place.' In painting, he wrote, 'the rules of perspective decide it. But how will it be decided when it comes to truth and morality?'

This has been a constant problem for writers interested in power: how to get the right distance so as to understand underlying causes rather than surface phenomena. Much of the literature on power is flawed because of the limits of its perspective: the hagiographies and biographies of great men and women, and the self-justifying autobiographies usually stand too close, while the analyses that point to deep forces and ineluctable logics and the stories of betrayal and disillusion, conspiracy and courage usually stand too far back.

Much western political theory has sought a high vantage point, gazing down in search of an ultimate explanation of power: reason working its way through history, class conflict, human will or the drive for power, or some other collection of instincts. Much of it has been essentially deductive, attempting to derive conclusions about government and its morality from first principles. To modern readers it can come as a surprise to learn that in the seventeenth and eighteenth centuries it was widely believed that political theory and ethics were more surely grounded forms of knowledge than the natural sciences. But the arguments about governance that were made by the pioneers of modern political theory – like Thomas Hobbes or John Locke – were not based on observation or experiment. Instead they were deduced from the natural laws that God had embedded in the world, and these deductions were the basis for what was taken to be a science of human affairs.[14]

Most of the greatest thinkers about power, from Kautilya, Confucius and Aristotle through to Machiavelli, were more pragmatic than this, perhaps because they had served as advisers to rulers. According to tradition, Kautilya was not only the chief minister of the great Indian Emperor Chandragupta but also helped him to gain his throne.[15] The Buddha served as an adviser to Bimbisara, the ruler of Magadha, and was familiar with the great variety of states that existed in northern India at the time. Aristotle taught the young Alexander before he set off to conquer the world. Plato sought a prince, and was briefly, and unhappily, an adviser to the tyrant Dionysius. Confucius went in search of a prince but failed, lamenting at the end of his life: 'No intelligent ruler arises to take me as his master.' Machiavelli worked as an ambassador and as adviser to Piero Soderini of Florence (although his greatest writings date from his period of unemployment after the Medicis won power).

All of them had some feeling for the ambiguities of power, and this made them reluctant to rely too much on deductive reasoning. Then as now, the best political thinkers understood that politics rests on apparently paradoxical truths. Peace depends on war. Freedom on order. Stability on change. Liberty on violence. Security on fear. The greatest political thinkers therefore leavened abstract logic with observations of the messy turbulence of politics and power in the kingdoms and republics they saw around them.[16]

There are good reasons for doing this. Precisely because power is so inseparable from every other aspect of daily life, no single theoretical perspective will ever be adequate to explain it. Deduction can lead thought badly astray, and science cannot offer any wholly reliable explanations of the psychological complexity of real societies, the motivations of leaders, or the organizational dynamics of parties and states. There are simply too many variables and, as with other areas of social knowledge, whatever is learned itself becomes a factor in the object of study, so that like the physicist investigating the inner workings of the atom, each new observation of the workings of states itself changes the nature of the state.

Power is part of life, not separate from it. We all want others to do things for us, to love us or to obey. Every relationship has power in it: the relationship of parent and child, friend and friend, employer and worker, lover and lover.[17] This inherent complexity may be why there is no settled science of the state, and why the same state can during a single day act out many different theories: economic theories that emphasize class power, and the role of the state in upholding dominant interests; pluralist theories that emphasize the competition for power and public participation through political parties; or rationalist theories that explain the state's behaviour as a means to maximize the rewards for officials and their allies.[18]

It follows that the conditions for good government cannot be deduced logically from presumptions about human nature, universal rights or ideologies. Instead they have to be learned, painfully, from experience. We use the language of universals to make sense of these lessons, perhaps because it is too frightening to admit just how much of human affairs is improvised. But these abstract ideas are useful fictions, no more and no less. Rousseau put it well:

people begin by seeking rules, on which they ought to agree for the common good; and then they apply the term 'natural law' to the collection of these rules with no other proof than the good they feel would result from their universal practice.

So the answer to Pascal's question is that there is no right distance from which to view power. Too much closeness can be as disabling as too much distance. From afar power looks mysterious and full of conspiracies. From close up the people involved look reasonable, humane and constrained. From afar the powerful look untrammelled; yet the powerful are always acutely aware of their constraints. Both positions, the close and the distant, impose an excess of meaning on what is often chaotic, which is why the best vantage point may be with one foot inside and one outside – the vantage point of a long tradition of political philosophy, from Ibn Khaldun and Niccolò Machiavelli to Thomas More and Antonio Gramsci, which has sought to 'triangulate': to look head on but also sideways, from inside out and from outside in.

THE SHAPE OF THE ARGUMENT

This book begins by asking about the underlying character of the state. Chapter 2 looks at how states took shape, what made them grow or decline, and what was the basis of their power. I look at how they dealt with the 'problems of other people' – the unavoidable difficulties that arise when many people share the same space together – as well as how states served the warriors, families and cliques who stood at their apex. In Chapter 3 I show how the growth of new knowledge and the widening of connections greatly amplified states' power for good and evil.

I then turn in Chapter 4 to the moral quality of states, and ask how widely different societies have thought about what they should do and how they should serve their people. At first glance modern states have little in common with their sparse and spare predecessors, which could barely maintain a modicum of order, let alone contemplate vast social security systems. Yet some of the moral arguments that surround them are remarkably similar.

Next, in Chapters 5 and 6, I look at why so many states have merely paid lip service to moral goals. I examine how states have been captured by small groups, and why states' primary concern is their own survival. Chapter 7 probes the moral complexities of power: how we should think about moral principles, and how morality comes to bear on decisions about war and peace, tax and welfare. Chapter 8 describes the role of revolt as a force for moral improvement, and Chapter 9 explores precisely what it is about democracy that encourages good government.

In Chapter 10 I show that democracies, like all regimes, suffer from tendencies to decay and alienation, and the succeeding chapters address the necessary conditions for the renewal of good government: Chapter 11 describes how ethics are cultivated among leaders or officials; Chapter 12, the roles and responsibilities of the people themselves; Chapter 13, the contribution of open knowledge and argument; and Chapter 14, the role of other states and of global agencies in reinforcing good behaviour. Finally, Chapter 15 asks about the duties of governments to future generations, and Chapter 16 suggests how politics and governance might evolve in radically new directions, beyond the largely nineteenth-century western models with which the world has become so familiar.

Throughout I emphasize that it is in the everyday prose of service that the best qualities of government are made manifest (I have become suspicious of abstractions, grand words and stories, perhaps because of having had to write too many politicians' speeches). Many people still long for soaring rhetoric and beautiful ideals, but these are usually deceptions, throwbacks to an immature politics in which the public sits passive and admiring, bedazzled by the fineries of power, or hypnotized by revolutionaries. They are deceptions that have usually let people down, while the humbler prose of government has often served them well.

I also emphasize the vulnerability of good government. That democratic ideals of service are dominant today is more the result of good fortune – the victory of the democracies in wars both hot and cold – than of any underlying logic in human affairs. It is not hard to imagine scenarios in which powerful nations drift towards illiberal authoritarianism or worse. John Adams wrote only two centuries ago, in the early years of American independence, that 'democracy never lasts long. It soon wastes, exhausts, and murders itself. There never was a democracy yet that did not commit suicide.' Imperial ideologies, claiming rights to act which they deny to others, remain strong. Past history has shown many good governments consigned to the scrapheap by their own mistakes, or by the cunning of more ruthless neighbours.

History is one reason for being cautious. The other is that now, as in the past, many people have been attracted by the idea that morality is a costly luxury, a delusion for the naïve and soft-headed. President Mitterrand was once asked by his adviser Jacques Attali to define the most important quality in a leader: his answer was 'indifference'. Mitterrand took pleasure in being nicknamed 'the Florentine',[19] and stood in a long line of leaders who believed that power is its own justification and that values are nothing more than convenient garments to be worn or discarded at will. Talleyrand, the great surviver of the French revolutionary era, is sometimes taken as a model of this kind of flexibility. During France's 1830 July revolution he heard the sound of church bells signalling that the riots were over and turned to an assistant to say: 'We're winning.' 'Who are we?' the assistant asked. 'I'll tell you tomorrow,' Talleyrand replied.

This sort of cynicism is sometimes described as realism. But from the point of view of the public it is more like betrayal. True realism doesn't ignore morality. Instead it navigates the tensions between absolute moral principles and shifting social realities. Confucian thinkers, for example, often wrote about the need to balance 'right' with 'expediency' and Max Weber, one of the modern West's greatest thinkers about political power, wrote that there are only two mortal sins in politics: lack of realism and lack of responsibility for the consequences of decisions. This is why the morality of power is never solely a matter of principles and rules. It also involves judgements between equally unpalatable alternatives, and choices between alternative goods rather than between goods and bads.[20]

Good government is one of the very best things that can happen to any society. Contrary to conventional wisdom, I show that the business of government is becoming more moral, not less; that many governments are stumbling closer to an ideal of service that has been imagined for as long as states have existed but was rarely realized; and that, just as new knowledge has given governments vastly greater power, it has also made them more dependent, more accountable, and more embedded in their societies. But good government is also always fragile, always vulnerable to capture by special interests and self-serving elites, and always at risk of becoming detached from the people it is meant to serve and from ideals. Perhaps this uncertainty, which sits just behind the blithe confidence of official pronouncements and the bold façades of public buildings, is what makes government so fascinating. Perhaps, too, this is why so many commit their lives to bringing the reality closer to the ideal.

2

The Origins of the State

'You are the servant of the servants of God and not their master; you are the protector and not the owner of your people.' Admonition to Henry I of England, after his coronation

On Saturday 30 April 2005, nine million mobile phone users in Beijing received a text message. The message was from the police and read: 'Express patriotism rationally. Don't take part in illegal protests. Don't make trouble. Help by not creating trouble, love the nation by not breaking the law.' The message came after a period of street protests directed against the government in Japan and prompted by the publication of educational books there which made no mention of Japanese atrocities in China in the 1930s. The protests had been encouraged by the Chinese authorities. But it was now time to call a halt.

The message symbolized the complex position of the modern Chinese state: it was halfway between a command and an entreaty. It was an instruction but it also asked people to 'help'. It implored people to obey the law not through fear but through love.

The Chinese state is unique in the modern world, both because of its scale and because it holds a vast country together through a single political party which monopolizes political power while proclaiming in front of its headquarters that it exists to 'serve the people'. But the ambiguous tone of its message in April 2005 could stand for any modern state that is grappling with how simultaneously to be a servant and a master.

Today we live in a world dominated by states that claim rights over people: rights to command, to punish and to instruct. Although from a distance the world still looks as if it is made up of mountains and rivers, deserts and plains, dotted here and there with towns and cities shining light into the sky, every blade of grass, grain of sand and inch of tundra is now claimed by a sovereign power,[1] and which side of their borders you live on can be a matter of life and death. The historical record offers not a single example of a successful society of any size or density without highly organized, specialized functions of power, even though many, like the first colonists of Iceland and the USA, dreamed of creating a society without a state. It is a common optical illusion of a highly individualistic world that people see themselves as self-made and independent. The order that states provide is so taken for granted that we barely notice how much we are protected from gunmen and bandits, plagues and currency collapses, or consider why it is that we can fly from one continent to another, leave our savings in a bank or campaign against another state's misdemeanours. Yet by any past standards the most striking features of the modern world include not only its freedoms and prosperity but also the degree to which it is ordered and governed.

In this chapter I analyse the character of the states which we now depend on by looking at how their past illuminates their present: what needs did they serve, why did they evolve as they did, and how did they turn into purveyors of mass text messages and managers of pension systems and nuclear weapons?

THE ROOTS OF GOVERNMENT

Over many millennia of human history people lived without states, taxes, armies or officials. But the roots of government go deep. In 1945 the anthropologist George Murdock collated a celebrated list of universal cultural traits that were to be found in every one of the many hundreds of human societies documented by Yale University. The list included such things as weaving and sexual restrictions, but it also included government, law, penal sanctions, ethics and community organization. Murdock's list suggested that the ability to form rules and to govern is a universal human trait.

Archaeology confirms the point by demonstrating the antiquity of government and rule. The 32,000-year-old burials at Sungir in Russia, vastly older than the pyramids, are indicative. Amid extensive living areas, two graves contain the body of what is thought to have been a prince, with 4,900 beads, a decorated belt with 250 canine teeth from polar fox, an ivory statuette of a mammoth and an ivory lance, and the body of a girl, decorated with even more beads. Since it has been estimated that each bead might have taken forty-five minutes to prepare, a huge amount of labour was involved in burying two young people whose prestige must have come as much from their offices as from their achievements. From the very earliest times, it seems, human society was not only organized into the very extensive networks needed to gather these objects,[2] it also had hierarchy, differentiation and elites which could command the time of others.[3]

Much of the history of how loose-knit communities evolved into societies ruled by chiefs, and then into states and empires has been lost.[4] We lack hard evidence on whether states grew more because trade encouraged co-operation or because war gave people little choice but to arm themselves in bigger groups.[5] The later written records with which states described their own origins are of little help. The Sumerian records, for example, show kingship descending fully formed from the heavens, even though the archaeological evidence shows that councils of elders ruled before kings and that temples long pre-dated palaces.[6] What is clear, however, is that states appeared in tandem with surpluses. Once there were surpluses – particularly surpluses of food – someone needed to record, manage and distribute them. With control over surpluses came prestige and power, and so before long communities had to define who had power over whom, and as bands became tribes, and then nations, that power was amplified and given ever more sophisticated symbolic expression as the powerful claimed privileged access to the world of spirits and gods.[7]

From the earliest times these divisions of power were not accepted as natural. One of the hallmarks of the human imagination is that it can see power as artificial. Surpluses could be fought over and kings could be overturned. Rebellion, then as now, is as natural as obedience, and as soon as writing passed beyond the control of the state these ideas were articulated with great force, in descriptions of the people's right to revolt against bad rulers (by Mencius in ancient China and in parts of the *Mahabharata*), of kingship as part of the world of illusion (by Buddha in ancient northern India), and of the meek inheriting the earth (by Jesus in the ancient Middle East).[8]

THE STRUGGLES TO CAPTURE STATES

Vast energies have been devoted to capturing states and the surpluses they controlled, and much of history (and much of the best drama inspired by history) documents the intrigues and brutal struggles for state power.

The will for power and recognition is by no means universal. Machiavelli, whose writings are often invoked to support a cynical view of human motivation, believed that although among the 'grandi', the urban elites, it was easy to see 'a great desire to dominate others', most people's 'sole desire is not to be dominated; as a result their principal wish is to live freely', to enjoy 'the common benefit of a free way of life'.

But wherever population densities rose the struggle for surplus resources brought out the worst in people. Violence and conflict, ditches and walls, intimidation and rape, differentiated identities to mark out 'us' from 'them' are all being brought to light in the archaeology of the millennia before states emerged. Anyone who failed to grasp power risked being enslaved by others. Plunder and conquest offered more rewards than quiet cultivation, allowing the winners, who became chiefs, kings and emperors, to monopolize the biggest houses, the treasures of gold and precious stones, and the most beautiful women. The winners could spread their genes and their gods, and write the laws to reinforce the gradations of status that most suited them, defining who owed what to whom. The lucky losers became slaves; the unlucky ones were slaughtered. In every early civilization systematic inequalities were reinforced by the state, not least through intense efforts to show that hierarchies were natural.[9]

By the time states emerge from the mists of prehistory, most of the free-standing towns and cities that had carried civilization forward in an earlier phase – like the messy townscape of Çatal Hüyük in modern

Turkey, and more ordered cities like Jericho next to the Dead Sea –
had already been crushed or absorbed into larger kingdoms, which
were throwing themselves with gusto into warfare against their neighbours. These early states appear at times like criminal enterprises that
had found the ideal way of perpetuating and legitimizing themselves
since, by definition, whatever states do cannot be criminal. The winners' priority was usually to extract value: as much as possible, as
quickly as possible. The rulers were warriors, like Gilgamesh, the king
of Uruk, or the kings and princes that Homer described, and their
struggles to capture states dominate the histories of Babylon and
Assyria, the earliest Chinese records of the Shang and the Zhou, and
the Old Testament. To avoid constant war, these predatory rulers
sometimes came to agreements about boundaries, recognizing each
other's monopoly rights to dominate the people within their territories. But since honour among thieves is limited they could never
trust that treaties and promises would not be broken.

Five thousand years ago, a world where individual chiefs had to
build up their own wealth and prestige during their lifetime was
evolving into one where roles were clearly defined, recognized, and
passed on. New words were being used to describe kings and emperors, who had become ever more distant from the common people
and endowed with supernatural powers, rather than simply being first
among equals: Sumer's *en*, *ensi* and *lugal* (a word literally meaning 'big
man'), Egypt's *nswt* (or pharaoh), and Shang China's *wang* differed in
terms of their precise powers, yet were all comparable, and distinct
from the chiefs who went before them in their capacity to make laws,
and to command a bureaucracy.

The earliest states to appear in the historical record – from Sumer
and Egypt to China – can appear remarkably modern. Their work
revolved around records and statistics: clay tablets, wooden rods,
coloured and knotted strings. They were powers serving populations in a defined territory; they were recognized as the paramount
source of authority by most of the people within that territory;
they imposed binding rules; they were run by a specialized group of
officials and financed by taxes; and they were protected by another
specialized group who defended them and attacked others. They were
recognized by other states that shared these characteristics, and they

were identified with, at least by some of the population they ruled.

In ancient Sumeria, where the very earliest states emerged, some very modern features stand out. Despite the warrior values of the *Epic of Gilgamesh* the Sumerian city-states of the third millennium BCE were not built for conquest, though some did conquer others. Nor were they primarily designed to worship gods, though they did have temples. Instead they were essentially designed for sustenance and survival, distributing and storing grain, and recording in detail who got what and why. They were welfare states built on the new surpluses of agrarian society, under the grip of accountants and auditors, who stumbled into the invention of writing to keep records of who had paid taxes. The *en* was the leader of the bureaucracy and presided over a rigid hierarchy with some 130 specialized roles, mainly concerned with grain, textiles, metals and flocks, and set out in rank order in official documents. The literacy and numeracy on which the system depended were jealously guarded by scribes who secured their position in a quickly stratified class structure (although despite the great scale of cities like Uruk, half the size Rome was in 100 CE, there were relatively few signs of privately owned wealth, or separate residential areas for the wealthy).[10]

In the succeeding millennia many different forms of state took shape until, by the fifth century BCE, most of the forms of the state that we now know already existed: despotism, democracy, theocracy and oligarchy were already familiar, along with treaties and assemblies, bureaucracies and legislators. There were intensive, almost totalitarian, states (like Sparta) and democratic governments overseeing cosmopolitan freewheeling cities (like Athens). There were republics that were hostile to the very idea of kingship (like Rome, whose last king was deposed in 510 BCE), aristocratic republics (like the north Indian one where the Buddha was born in the sixth century BCE) and empires that believed their rulers to be gods (like Egypt). There were kingdoms in which church and state were intertwined (like the Jewish kingdoms). Sometimes states appear to have jumped into the historical record already fully formed. Ministerial roles in Zhou China (described in the 'Book of History'[11] at the end of the second millennium BCE) are easily recognizable: there were ministers for education, rites, war, punishments and economy, and a Prime Minister, not dissimilar to the twenty-first-century state (though now public relations has replaced rites). On the other side of the world, by the first century BCE, Rome had public infrastructures, competitive elections and propaganda, individual legal rights, job-creation schemes and a rough and ready welfare system.

These states often described themselves as bringing cosmic order in place of the chaos that existed both before them and beyond their borders. In the Indian tradition, for example, before government was instituted men were said to have lived in anarchy, reigned over by evil in a world where the strong destroyed the weak.

But in truth the new states delivered as much violence as they contained. One of Aesop's fables captures the point. The frogs are concerned about the chaos of their lives and send a deputation to Zeus asking him to give them a king ('Give us a king, give us a ruler'). Zeus throws down a log, and the frogs are at first impressed by the big splash it makes but are then disappointed when it issues no commands. A second deputation then goes to Zeus, pleading for him to send them a real king and prompting the annoyed god to give them a water snake as their ruler, which promptly proceeds to swallow his new subjects.

If the risks were high for people ruled over by states, they were also high for anyone nearby. Each time a strong state emerged the peoples living around it faced a simple choice: to form an alliance with it, copy it, or risk being swallowed up by it. Many of the peoples living close to early states chose to follow suit, in Mesopotamia and up the Tigris and Euphrates, in China around the Yellow River and the Yangtze, in the Levant, and in the Indus Valley.[12] Ever since, the character of states has been shaped by their dual nature – looking inwards to a territory and a people, and looking outwards to other states. And, ever since, states have been transformed by their response to other states, from Athens' responses to Sparta in the fifth century BCE to Japan's Meiji modernization in response to Commodore Perry's black ships in 1852–3.

THE NEED FOR STATES AND THE PROBLEMS CAUSED
BY OTHER PEOPLE

What needs did states meet? It is risky to interpret institutions functionally, as if they could only exist if they met an inescapable need. But states do not exist solely because some people found them a convenient way to exploit others.

Any community has to solve the 'problems of other people'. The most pressing is the threat of violence.[13] Murder rates in most past societies were dramatically higher than they are today. We may not be naturally murderous, but without severe punishments and restraints people do turn more quickly to the knife (or now the gun) to settle scores. Then there are conflicting interests. People may want the same land, the same goods or the same lovers. The more dense the society the more inescapable some of these conflicts are likely to be. Some can be dealt with by the ten commandments and their equivalents in other cultures, forbidding murder, theft or adultery. But others are less easy to prohibit through simple rules.

There are the problems of simple exploitation, for example where one farmer knows that others will have to maintain a shared irrigation system even if he does not, or where only one sibling bothers to look after an ageing parent. There are the problems that economists describe as 'externalities', the costs that some people impose on others: for example, pouring sewage into rivers used for drinking water (businesses are particularly prone to externalize costs in the pursuit of profit, which is why laws and regulations force them to look after their employees' safety or cut pollution). There are the many situations where what is rational for one person becomes irrational for the community as a whole – the various 'prisoners' dilemmas' (if I cheat and you don't, I gain; if we both cheat we both lose); the various 'tragedies of the commons' (in which individuals overuse a shared resource);[14] and the problems of public goods like clean air and defence.[15] Societies without rules and authority to solve these problems easily slide into an unhappy and grimly distrustful state, accumulating free-riders who take advantage of others, and who then elicit the resentment and bitterness to which human beings seem so well disposed.[16]

Communities also need to align their everyday behaviours and beliefs. Some of this happens naturally. We are reasonably good at aligning what we do with other people around us, picking up subtle social cues, for example about how to walk on busy pavements without knocking other people down. But large-scale co-ordination isn't automatic. Self-interest may drive people to co-operate in creating networks of irrigation, sharing scarce resources or keeping watch on each other's children. But often it takes an outside authority to set rules, or to encourage common mental models that make daily life easier: thereafter communities may be happier if everyone drives on the same side of the road, uses the same shape of electrical plugs, takes holidays on the same days, recognizes the same monies, obeys the same laws, shares a similar repertoire of social behaviours, or even speaks the same language, and often these depend on a state to impose them.

For all of this to happen communities need trust. From Confucius to Bertrand de Jouvenel, political philosophers have seen the promotion of trust as a primary task of the state. Laws, shared norms, shared languages and scripts can all contribute to trust, and make it possible for people to trade and exchange or to establish common projects over long stretches of time and space. In the modern era common standards and protocols (ranging from the technical rules governing how computers talk to each other, to the regulations banning incitements to hatred) have come to play a similar role. They provide some of the soft infrastructures on which human intercourse depends. Just as good fences make good neighbours, unambiguous rules make it easier for people to trust each other casually.[17] When the community is threatened, trust between members of the community may be decisive in helping it to survive. A society riven by mutual resentment and lacking any shared moral purpose starts from a huge defensive disadvantage.

Each of these types of problem – the problems of competing interests, co-ordination and trust – can be solved voluntarily without a state. For millennia people entrusted their most life-threatening and life-enhancing risks, such as getting married, having children, planting crops or migrating to a new territory, to social networks and organizations far removed from any state. Much of the machinery of the modern welfare state was created first in independent clubs and associations providing mutual support and insurance. But voluntarism has never been more than a very partial answer to the problems of other people. Even with the optimistic assumption that conflicting interests can be overcome, any voluntary agreement will be time consuming to reach and costly to enforce, and in very large communities dialogue and enforcement on such a scale is practically impossible. Without a state to arbitrate, communities tend to breed exploitation and cheating, particularly when people cannot check on others' behaviour, or when their interactions are limited in time.[18] Without a state there will be no records – clay tablets (as in Sumeria), scrolls (as in Rome), or cardboard files (Britain's great contribution to bureaucracy, invented in 1868) – to track who has paid their taxes or committed crimes. There may be an order of sorts, but it will be unbalanced and illegitimate by comparison with a social order held together by a state.[19]

VIOLENCE, MONEY AND TRUST

States exist both because they are useful to their rulers and because they can be useful to everyone else. This dual character – that of a master and that of a servant – is reflected in the sources of power which states have drawn on. The most visible source of power for any state is force, which has traditionally been seen as their most basic capacity (Max Weber defined states as monopolies of violence),[20] and as a decisive reason why states find it so hard to be moral.[21] Violence is usually a simpler and cheaper way to secure obedience than rewards. States certainly do everything they can to crush competing centres of military power, from rebel armies to terrorists, and traditionally rulers' sovereignty was most purely expressed in their power over the life and death of their people. In China, for example, the ruler's authority was based on 'ritually directed violence in the form of sacrifices, warfare and hunting'[22] – in other words the legitimized taking of life – and to this day the American President retains the right to pardon criminals on death row.

But Weber's definition of the state as an organization holding a monopoly of violence in a particular territory is misleading. Before the modern era no states possessed a monopoly in this sense. Beyond a few days' march from their capitals or army camps their reach was limited.[23] Most depended uneasily on governors, lords and vassals. The grandest empires were capable of vast works: pyramids, huge irrigation schemes, temples like Angkor Wat or cities like Teotihuacán, and elaborate networks of roads. But they couldn't easily mandate what should happen in a town a hundred miles from their capitals. China was one of the most intensively governed states, with a huge bureaucracy and secret police, but in the words of a very old saying 'the hills are high and the emperor is far away', and beneath the façade of dignified stability the country was at times a cauldron of rebellion (often with vast death tolls, like the 20 million who died in the nineteenth-century Taiping revolt). In Russia Peter the Great issued *ukases* (decrees) to his lords and officials, but once, in desperation, had to issue a *ukase* commanding them to obey all the other *ukases*. So the tools available to states were limited: they could fight, and build bridges and canals, and even design new religions. But they could do little to cure sickness, to stop riots, or to make more than a few people rich.

Only in relatively recent times have states even been able to maintain a rough monopoly of legitimate violence, with the help of extensive communications systems, roads and railways, and national police forces. In England, this was the great achievement of the Tudors, who demilitarized the great lords, forcing them to disband their armed retainers and to dismantle their fortresses (thereafter their applications for licences to crennellate their castles were refused). In France Louis XIII, on his minister Richelieu's advice, destroyed rebel lords' castles too. In the rest of Europe the state's monopoly of violence is usually dated to the Treaty of Westphalia in 1648, which abolished the private armies of counts and earls. As a result Weber's definition works better for the modern than the ancient world, and the *absence* of a monopoly of violence has indeed now become the best indicator that a state is failing. Weak states typically preside over higher levels of violence than strong ones, sometimes collaborating with the perpetrators, sometimes turning a blind eye (Sudan's government did all of these things with the Janjaweed militias that terrorized Darfur in the 2000s). Conversely the best mark of states with a high capacity to govern, and even more of democratic states, is that casual violence diminishes greatly, and control of violence has become a defining feature not just of nation states but also of transnational government (the most important provision of the UN Charter was the promise that it would criminalize acts of state aggression).

But violence is never enough. States' ability to sustain armies and police forces has always depended on money, or to be more precise, on their ability to command people's time. In Charles Tilly's words, 'almost all war-making states borrow extensively, raise taxes, and conscript the means of combat – including men – from reluctant citizens.'[24] In ancient times every state engaged in slavery and the trade in people – often the product of raiding a neighbour's territory to seize workers and wives. In Han China the peasants had to give one month each year to the Emperor. Absolutist France bequeathed us the word 'corvée', and conscription for armies (each young man giving two or three years of his life to the state) survives in many places to this day. In medieval Europe feudal obligation formalized the state's power over time into complex systems of duty. But just as ancient states lacked a monopoly over violence so did they also lack a monopoly power to tax. Instead both of these powers had to be bartered and exchanged for sanctioned autonomy. The satrap, governor and tax farmer were all proof that the state's monopoly was limited.

Taxes and corvées were ways of capturing and controlling surpluses. The food surpluses of the hydraulic civilizations of ancient Mesopotamia and Egypt provided the basis for empire,[25] and for the glittering extravagance of ziggurats and pyramids; the new technologies of the late medieval period generated the surpluses that paved the way for absolutism, with its ocean-going fleets and vast palaces; and the industrial revolution's even bigger surpluses made possible the new European empires and totalitarianism.

As states' control over violence grew so did their power over time. England's decisive step forward came when Henry VIII started to levy taxes for purposes other than warfare in 1540, and by the time of the Napoleonic Wars the British state was raising nearly a quarter of national income in taxes, far more than its enemy France. Modern rulers jealously guard their monopoly power to issue money, and the central bank sits alongside the military at the heart of the modern nation state. Time can be more easily controlled in labour markets where it is bought and sold impersonally, and taxes on income, sales and wealth achieve some of the same results as the corvée, so that in most developed societies two to three days each week are worked for the state (and much of childhood is co-opted by the state through compulsory education). In democracies this extraction is chosen not imposed, and richer countries raise proportionately more money from their citizens and businesses than poor ones – partly because richer people tend to want relatively more health and education, but also because, despite globalization and the Internet, richer states have learned better how to track down activities to tax. Nevertheless the sense of the state as an alien parasite remains strong, and bursts to the fore in moments of tax revolt (as in California in the 1970s), which are usually led not by the people paying the highest taxes but by the people who feel their incomes being most squeezed by tax.

Control over violence rests on control over time; but control over time also rests on something more basic. This is the ability to command, or attract, the thoughts and minds of others. Confucius wrote that every ruler needs arms, food and trust, but that if any of these had to be given up arms and food should be forfeited before trust, because once trust was lost there would be no arms or food anyway.[26] Power can be buttressed by fear but fear can never wholly substitute for trust, because there are never enough rulers on their own to terrorize the rest.

Governments need trust not just to survive, but also to do their day-to-day work. Without it laws will more often be evaded and broken, taxes will be harder to raise, and information will be harder to gather. Without trust it is impossible to delegate, and much of the business of government involves principals commissioning agents to do things for them and then trying to track which promises have been kept and who has turned out to be trustworthy.[27]

To foster trust states try to shape how people think. They have a special ability to influence minds, and the most enduring states (such as ancient Egypt or Imperial China) are marked out not by their technological or military prowess but by their ideological sophisti-

cation. They are the ones that succeeded in defining the most important categories that helped people to think: what is legal or illegal;
who belongs and who doesn't; what is or is not healthy, or natural,
or sacred.

These three sources of power – violence, money and trust – are
closely interlinked.[28] The control of violence depends on the control
of time and money, and the control of time and money depends on
trust, which is unavoidably moral in nature.

The three sources of power together underpin political power, the
sovereign power to impose laws, issue commands and hold together
a people and a territory. This power is nothing without force, money
and trust, but it presents itself as a different kind of power, a purer
power from which everything else derives. It concentrates force
through its armies,[29] concentrates resources through exchequers, and
concentrates the power to shape minds,[30] most recently through the
big systems of education and communication that are the twin glues
of modern nation states.[31]

Political power also converts one form of power to another. The
currency of legitimacy can be turned into money through taxation. Money can buy armies or it can be converted into respect and
authority, through palaces, awards and public monuments. It can be
used to lock in support through welfare and public programmes, or
through corporate subsidies. Sometimes money pays for deference:
the Mongols, for example, paid homage to Chinese emperors but
actually received a substantial pay-off in return – a protection racket
disguised as humility.[32]

Of the three sources of power the most important for sovereignty
is the power over thoughts that gives rise to trust. Violence can only
be used negatively; money can only be used in two dimensions, giving
and taking away. But knowledge and thoughts can transform things,
move mountains and make ephemeral power appear permanent.[33]

3

Accelerated Evolution

'To be GOVERNED is to be watched, inspected, spied upon,
directed, law-driven, numbered, regulated, enrolled, indoctri-
nated, preached at, controlled, checked, estimated, valued,
censured, commended, by creatures who have neither the right
nor the wisdom nor the virtue to do so.'

Pierre-Joseph Proudhon[1]

Many early modern thinkers were optimistic that the combination of
good government and human nature would make the world a better
place. Adam Smith wrote with blithe confidence that 'little else is
required to carry a state to the highest degree of opulence from the
lowest barbarism but peace, easy taxes, and a tolerable administration
of justice; all the rest being brought about by the natural course of
things.' For John Stuart Mill the recipe was somewhat different: better
government and property laws; the decay of superstition and growth
of mental activity; and hospitality to foreign arts (by which he meant
technology) and foreign capital. But he too saw progress as immanent
in the nature of the world, which was, after all, God's work.

Yet the evolution of states has been very uneven, with many
deviations and culs-de-sac. During some periods whole categories of
state – democracies and empires, theocracies and principalities – were
sent into oblivion, sometimes for ever, and sometimes until more
propitious conditions returned. The states of renaissance Europe were
not much more capable than those 1,500 years earlier around the
Mediterranean. Ming China was not obviously more advanced than
T'ang China. In some cases military genius could coincide with stunted

28

political imagination. States could be brilliant at conquest but poor at managing their new territories. Some ancient states were undoubtedly advanced by any standards. These are the words of Fa-Hian, a Buddhist pilgrim in the fifth century CE, writing about the Guptan Empire in India: 'The people are very well off, without poll tax or official restrictions . . . the kings govern without corporal punishment, criminals are fined according to circumstance . . . the kings' personal assistants have fixed salaries.' Occasional rulers like Ashoka a few centuries earlier in northern India stand out as beacons of enlightenment and moral clarity too, but they do so precisely because there is no pattern of evolution (and in Ashoka's case his empire crumbled quickly after his death in 232 BCE).

Such examples are rare, and more the result of luck than anything else. Benign rule was rarely rewarded in history, and in the ancient world, and again during the early modern period, republics and democracies tended to get swallowed up by their more militaristic neighbours. The highly competent army of a small state could be beaten by the incompetent and demoralized army of a large empire. The very qualities that led in one century to a glorious flowering of civilization might in another century become sources of torpor and intolerance. And there was never any guarantee that the qualities of a civilization would automatically be manifest in the qualities of its state. Samuel Finer wrote, for example, of the Islamic caliphate in the early Middle Ages that

as a despotic form of government many of its caliphs and the majority of its administrators both high and low, and reputedly many of its judges, seem self-serving . . . It is remarkable that so brilliant and creative a society could give rise to so impoverished a system of government.[2]

More recently, however, the picture has changed, decisively. The peculiarity of the last two centuries is that they have brought such unprecedented evolution in states' capacities to organize violence, money and trust. Social evolution is very different from biological evolution. The causes of mutations are very different, there is no equivalent of sexual recombination and intentions can be decisive. But the pace of change has accelerated, with faster generation of new possibilities, faster disposal of the failures and faster emulation of the successes. This evolution cannot easily be separated from the emergence of capitalism and a global economy and the spread of science and technology, which along with advances in government have contributed to a 50 per cent increase in body size in many areas of the world, a 100 per cent rise in life expectancy, and a measureless expansion of knowledge. But it is in the behaviour of states that both the best and the worst of modernity have been made manifest.

KNOWLEDGE AND CONNECTIONS

How did this change come about? The answer is that new knowledge changed government just as it changed science and industry. In politics as in other fields, all progress comes from new knowledge and ideas, particularly knowledge that is embedded in institutions, or that increases the rewards for co-operative behaviour.[3]

There had been many attempts in the distant past to establish a science of government. In China, Confucius in the fifth century BCE had advised on the need to 'approach a problem by seeking the widest differences of opinions and by making the most careful study of the facts in the spirit of absolute impartiality and unselfishness, and then to solve it moderately, practicably, and logically, in accordance with the best ethical rules.' A fourth-century BCE scholar, Shen Pu-hai, wrote a widely read book concerned with 'almost mathematical rigor, to describe the ways in which a ruler can maintain his position and cause his state to prosper by means of administrative technique and applied psychology',[4] and in 124 BCE an imperial university was founded to nurture the right knowledge, and values, in future officials.

But the application of new knowledge to government in Europe two thousand years later had far more impact because it went in tandem with other revolutions that allowed knowledge to grow cumulatively: the application of inductive reasoning; deliberate strategies to cultivate new scientific knowledge (all of the fundamental advances of information technology, for example, from the microchip to the world wide web were massively subsidized by states); the dramatic opening up of civic knowledge; and the accumulation of new knowledge about war (from dreadnoughts to cruise missiles). The pioneers of scientific government were less glamorous than the inventors of new weapons and gadgets, but they were no less influential, and their work transformed the moral potential of government as well as its dangers.

Frederick the Great in Prussia and Louis XIV in France actively encouraged radical administrative reformers, who, alongside their English counterparts, such as William Petty and William Paterson, founder of the Bank of England in the 1690s, introduced rationality and mathematics into the work of government in ways that have now become commonplace. Petty and John Graunt, for example, launched the 'invisible college' of political arithmetic, which ensured that statistics (derived from the German '*Staat*') provided the foundation stones for rational government. Others worked on new techniques for accounting, for raising taxes, and for moving and processing information. These new techniques treated people as categories, and they made states ever more impersonal and, literally, calculating in their concern for probabilities and distributions. But the pursuit of knowledge was also imbued with a mission of moral betterment. In the early eighteenth century Prussia established the principle that officials in the army, tax system, schools and the postal service had a duty to the people rather than to the feudal nobility. The 'cameralist' movement of reformers who thrived under Frederick William I and Frederick the Great aimed to advance the common happiness of the ruler and his subjects through rules and laws, and through 'meritocracy rather than noble birth, administrative science rather than feudal law, standardized principles rather than local particularity, and formalism and professionalism rather than traditionalism.'[5]

These many reforms transformed the daily business of governments, and made it possible for them to reach into every corner of life in large societies, well before the telegraph, the telephone, the satellite and the computer. They also made it possible for states to imagine new ambitions: eighteenth-century Prussian reformers even led sophisticated discussions of the contribution of different forms of spending to public well-being. A century later it was an expertise in statistics that allowed Florence Nightingale to make such a passionate case for sanitary reform, and since then it has been the advance of natural and social science that has helped states to protect people from poverty, to extend their lives, and dramatically to cut murder rates.[6] Knowledge and action did not come cheap. Instead they depended on armies of recorders, rule-makers and enforcers: the number of bureaucrats was 27,000 in Britain in 1821, 23,000 in Prussia and 8,000 in the USA, but sixty years later the figures had risen more than tenfold. Everything that we now associate with welfare and the services of a modern state depends on what by historical standards are vast powers of surveillance and action.[7]

Perhaps less predictably, new knowledge also changed the moral landscape of states. Enlightened reformers assumed that new knowledge would be an unambiguous good. But eating from the tree of knowledge makes life more complicated, and more morally anxious. There are, for example, no scientific answers to how modern states should cope with nuclear power, balancing the contribution to arresting climate change against the problems of disposing of waste, or the anxieties of the public, or how they should cope with much more easily managed personal data, balancing fears about lost privacy with the possible benefits of greater security and services better fitted to individual needs. Nor are there any simple answers to how they should prevent predictable harms, like those from smoking, or how they should regulate the unintended side effects of new technology, such as nanotechnology. It used to be said that if you gave a man a fish he would eat for a day, but that if you taught him to fish he would never go hungry; today it is said that if you teach a man to fish he will overfish. Knowledge is not always good. Ignorance may not be bliss but it is at least simpler.

The new knowledge that accelerated state evolution was amplified by multiplying connections. The spread of global empire was brutal and capricious ('so many cities razed, so many nations exterminated, so many peoples cut down by the sword and the richest and most beautiful part of the world overthrown for the sake of pearls and pepper', wrote Montaigne on the conquest of America). But it left a legacy of railways, shipping routes and transoceanic cables, radio transmitters and ports that transformed both the conquerors and the conquered with the greater flows of money, goods, people and ideas that came in their wake. One of the legacies was an increasingly organized global public opinion that campaigned against slavery and the worst excesses of imperialism ('Am I not a man and a brother' was the slogan of the world's first modern social movement to force moral principles on to recalcitrant statesmen).

Another legacy was the far quicker emulation of ideas. All past states watched their neighbours for useful lessons, but the pace of mutual inspiration or infection greatly accelerated in the nineteenth century. Universal male suffrage spread from France and Germany in 1870 to Switzerland in 1874, New Zealand in 1879, Spain in 1900, Sweden in 1909 and to Britain after 1918. Income tax was introduced in Britain in 1842 for the first time in peacetime, then in Sweden in 1861, Italy in 1864 and Japan in 1867.[8] Other innovations spread because governments faced parallel pressures. Social security spread from Bismarck's Germany via Lloyd George's Britain until almost every industrialized country followed suit, encouraged in part by fear of the growing labour movement. A century later a similar pattern could be seen in the spread of privatizations, contracting out, welfare reforms and environmental regulations.

Connections between states were encouraged in the nineteenth and twentieth centuries because they looked likely to increase states' powers. But they also changed states' moral environment, making them much more dependent on the actions of other states and on the beliefs of other citizens. Europe's leaders now know that their very survival depends on persuading sceptical states in other parts of the world to reduce their people's carbon emissions, just as their physical security depends on resolving the political problems that breed terrorism in distant places.

In a more connected world even the worst dictators feel impelled to maintain at least a pretence of legitimacy because of the high costs that come with being a pariah. The boycotts of apartheid South Africa in the 1980s eventually destroyed the confidence of the ruling elite, just as two decades later Robert Mugabe's Zimbabwe paid a high price for rough internal policies. Militarized Myanmar missed out on the boom that transformed much of its region at the end of the twentieth century. North Korea has survived in its impoverished state only because it has a powerful protector in Beijing.

Both of these forces for change – the advance of knowledge and the rise of global connections – changed the relationship between states and citizens and brought a new intensity of mutual dependence that marks out modern states from their predecessors. This mutual dependence had both malign and benign causes, and has had both malign and benign consequences. Its origins can be traced back to the peculiar circumstances of state competition in seventeenth- and eighteenth-century Europe, which made possible new ways of linking violence, money and trust. In this competition the more intensively governed states gained an advantage over their less governed rivals: they could put larger armies into the field, raise more money more sustainably, and motivate their troops to fight better. But there was a price to be paid for this success. Governing more intensively changed states' natures; it made them larger and more bureaucratic, but also, because of their need for tax revenues, more subject to the wishes of their citizens and more dependent on bargains struck with the people. Rulers were offered the chance of greater power but, paradoxically, only if they shared the power they already had with parliaments and, later, with the public (anyone who didn't matter for war – women or servants – had to wait).

Sweden and the Netherlands, which in the twentieth century became exemplary servant states, pioneered this new deal. At the beginning of the eighteenth century both kept over 5 per cent of their entire population under arms, a huge proportion by any standards.[9] Such large armies could only be sustained by very high levels of tax and these in turn were only possible once extensive rights had been conceded to peasants and burghers (Sweden's peasants, for example, had their own formally recognized parliamentary Estate). Britain had a different version of the deal, and married superior tax raising and debt creation with a powerful elected assembly, which was, in retrospect, greatly empowered relative to the king by the costly wars of the eighteenth century. The French Revolution took these arrangements to a new level, tying universal rights to a vast revolutionary army (the product of a revolution brought to a head by the *Ancien Régime*'s futile plea for more taxes). Each of these countries moved more quickly towards an ideal of service than others, using the language of rights to describe the ever more comprehensive bargains that were struck between states and their peoples.

Because the most dynamic states had adopted a strategy that involved widening the circle of power, others had no choice but to react. They wanted to match the prosperity and military edge of Britain and France, and to match their success in mobilizing their people in service to the nation, but without sharing power. Japan's strategy was the most overt, and a model of how to turn relative weakness into a strength. In the famous memorandum written by one of its ministers, Hotta Masayoshi, in 1857, the strategy was set out bluntly:

[to] copy the foreigners where they are at their best and so repair our own shortcomings, to foster our national strength and complete our armaments, and so gradually subject the foreigners to our influence until in the end all the countries of the world know the blessings of perfect tranquillity and our hegemony is acknowledged throughout the globe.

The governing strategies of Japan, Russia and Germany in the late nineteenth century emphasized technological mastery and industrial strength. As each tried to fashion a more efficient state from the top down, with minimal concessions to democracy (though more in the case of Germany), the moral claims of national and imperial identity served as a political glue,[10] and were propagated by newspapers and secondary schools, parades and pronouncements. The twentieth-century successors of the Meiji Emperor, Bismarck and the Tsars went even further, mobilizing the passions of the people against real and imagined enemies. Tsarism was succeeded by the mass mobilization of Stalinism; Bismarck by Hitler (who, like Stalin, used the mass political party as the vehicle to arouse the people's energies); and the technocratic Meijis were succeeded by the militarized frenzy of Japan in the 1930s.

It is comforting to believe that democracy was inherently superior to these alternatives. But there is no evidence for this. We know now that the militarized states of Stalinism, Nazism and Tojo-ism burned themselves out through overreach, self-deception and chronic waste. But there have been many times over the last century when these models appeared more dynamic, and more likely to set the tone for the future, than tired and divided democracies.

We live today in a world dominated by democracies not because history is deterministically guided by an inexorable logic, but mainly because democracies won the decisive wars. There are some plausible reasons why democracies might be better at war: they may have richer economies because fewer spoils are extracted by the state; they may be better able to create technologies with a free climate of scientific exploration; they may be better at motivating their troops. But none of these conditions is inevitable, and it is just as possible for democracies to be more divided, less willing to spend on defence than their enemies, and more likely to lose the wars that matter most.

SYSTEMS OF SERVICE: THE RISE OF DEMOCRATIC WELFARE CAPITALISM

In the early years of the twenty-first century democracies have more fluently mastered the connections between military force, money and trust than competing models. But one of the lessons of history is that relatively few types of regime survive for any length of time. Peace and stability are rare and fragile privileges. Only eight contemporary nations both existed in 1914 and have since then avoided the violent overthrow of their government. History has constantly winnowed the weak, and many fewer kinds of state exist today than are possible or have been attempted. There are now few totalitarian regimes, no 'night watchman' states (the minimal state favoured by nineteenth-century liberals), no empires in the classical sense, no communes or soviets. No states of any size or wealth fail to provide at least some welfare for their citizens, emergency health care or education. None directly sells the offices of state; none depends on slavery. There are no overt aristocracies (in the original sense), and no one in charge of a government calls himself Emperor.[11]

The dominant political ideas of the twenty-first century derive from the architecture of the French Revolution, which was derived in turn from English theorists: liberty (from state power), equality (through state power) and fraternity (which came to mean identification with national state power). Liberty took shape in the ideas of liberalism, absorbed into the common sense of modernity through free trade and the ubiquity of human rights. The idea of equality took its purest form in communism, which was defeated in 1989, but has been absorbed into the common sense of our age so that even reactionaries now support equal rights, equality before the law, equal votes and welfare. Fraternity was taken forward by nationalism, took extreme form in Fascism and Nazism, which were defeated in 1945, but has survived in a milder form as the glue for nation states.

The political imagination of the eighteenth century and before could not easily picture how ubiquitous, active and even competent states could become, or how much they could take on the qualities of a servant. But the ideas of liberty, equality and fraternity, amplified by the greater technical capacity of modern states, have directly shaped the dominant systems of service that define government in much of the world. The three together gave rise to modern representative democracy, which combines political liberty, equal votes and the fraternity of the nation state, simultaneously empowering citizens to remove bad governments, but also making them more dependent on the good sense of their peers. Well over a hundred nations have something akin to a working democracy. The crucial issue for the rulers of nations such as Russia, China or Saudi Arabia is how to contain democracy (for example, restricting it to very local elections), not whether to avoid it altogether. Ideas of liberty gave rise to the dominance of a capitalist market economy, which has become equally ubiquitous as the best way of creating wealth. Although capitalism takes many forms, and contains many flaws, there is no alternative economic system waiting in the wings. Fraternity and equality gave rise to welfare. All of the successful states have mutated into welfare providers in some form, replacing the roles played by families and communities to a degree scarcely imagined a century or two ago. The comment made by the English Liberal politician Sir William Harcourt in the 1890s – 'we are all socialists now' – is far more true today. Ironically, one of the major exceptions is China, which lacks the comprehensive welfare supports of its neighbours like Japan and Singapore.

These three systems have become standard partly because of the military and economic prowess of the nations that adopted them first, and partly because citizens living with them[12] tend to lead better lives, as measured by their material prosperity, their reported happiness, their life expectancy and their ability to put their trust in others.[13]

The world contains many different values, but there is nowhere on earth that does not value long life, prosperity and trust.

Each of the three systems is, at root, about service. The democratic government serves the people – and can be dismissed if it fails. Capitalist businesses serve consumers – who can take their custom elsewhere if they are unhappy in an economy that is ever more organized around services. The welfare state serves people's needs – for health, or security, or knowledge – and is legitimate only to the extent that it succeeds in doing so.

The mutual reinforcement of democracy, capitalism and socialism into a hybrid service-based democratic welfare capitalism was not anticipated. Few expected that the states that had for so long been the enemies of the poor could transform themselves into their friends. Yet as suffrage was widened in the late nineteenth and early twentieth centuries and thereafter, states' capacities evolved in tandem with the public's ability to make claims on them. In 1870 national states typically absorbed around 11 per cent of GDP in developed countries; by the mid-1930s that level had more than doubled, before another surge of growth in the 1950s took the averages up to 28 per cent in 1960 and 43 per cent in 1990, pulled forward by public demand for welfare and services. The biggest growth took place during the major wars, yet after the wars levels of spending never returned to the earlier levels.[14]

What systems thinkers describe as 'positive feedback loops' amplified these trends that have brought states into the sinews of life, as providers, regulators and observers. New knowledge and public health helped economies to grow, which then created new surpluses for states to spend; then, when states provided new services, they also created both beneficiaries and advocates, like the 35 million members of the American Association for Retired People who have fiercely, and successfully, protected their rights to healthcare and pensions from politicians seeking public spending cuts. Sometimes the feedback was negative. The most radical innovations – totalitarian party rule, cultural revolution and wholesale marketization – imploded. Many states taxed too heavily, and had to rein back; in Sweden the public sector's share of GDP peaked at around 67 per cent in the early 1980s (public finances have their own equivalent of the business cycle and need periodic crises to shed the more marginal programmes). Overblown missions also ran aground. The disappearance of war as a primary task for states encouraged some to declare war not on other states but on problems: drugs, cancer, poverty, crime or terrorism. These 'wars' share some of the emotions of conventional wars as they are announced with great fanfare and large budgets. But, unlike conventional wars, they have invisible enemies which change in shape and they are rarely won (indeed, it is sometimes unclear what winning such wars would look like).

In the latter years of the twentieth century states generally retreated from direct involvement in the economy as owners and planners. But even in those countries where attempts were made to shrink the state, a declining role in the economy was more than made up for by widening roles in care, education and health.[15] The tools used by governments have changed and now include more arm's-length regulation, more purchasing rather than direct provision of products and services, and more use of markets for everything from healthcare to pollution control alongside the traditional tools of law, tax and coercion.[16] Meanwhile many of the functions of states have moved upwards (to transnational bodies), downwards (to local government), or outwards (to the private sector and non-profit organizations). However, the basic principles of democratic welfare capitalism and of institutions founded on service rather than hierarchy or tradition have become even more dominant as a result of these changes.[17]

THE UNEVEN MORAL GEOGRAPHY OF THE WORLD

Tolstoy wrote that all happy families are happy in the same way and all unhappy ones are unhappy in different ways. Today nations are unhappy in surprisingly consistent ways. Some are unhappy because their states are too strong while their citizens are too weak. Countries like North Korea or Uzbekistan lack any serious ethos of service and anyone living in them risks a lesser life, less room to breathe, to create or even to love. Some nations are unhappy because their states have been captured by ruthless cliques. The worst – like Equatorial Guinea or Syria – behave at times like predatory criminal enterprises covered with a thin veneer of constitutional propriety, buttressed with the guns and technologies that are the black flowers of civilization.

Other nations are unhappy because their states are too weak. Fifty years ago the world's bleakest nightmares involved over-mighty governments, 'a boot stamping on a human face, forever' in Orwell's words. Today they are as likely to be nightmares about anarchy and chaos, a world beyond the control of governments. Many states, from Sudan to the Congo, Colombia to Afghanistan, are unable to protect their own citizens from poverty and war, or are becalmed in corrupted irrelevance.

None of these countries can confidently expect to escape their current condition. A celebrated piece of research in the 1990s[18] showed that over the preceding forty years the chances of achieving sustainable democracy were heavily dependent on income levels. In the poorest countries any moves towards democracy were likely to be short-lived; in countries with income levels near or above the average (US $6,000 in current prices) the transitions to democracy tended to be permanent. The implication was that so long as global economic growth continued, democracy would inevitably follow.

But the causal relationships have turned out to be more complex than this. According to more recent and extensive cross-national surveys there is some correlation between democracy and growth at low levels of development, but this becomes negative at middle incomes (perhaps because elites learn how to exploit nominally democratic party systems to capture resources for themselves – Pakistan and (pre-Lula) Brazil are good examples).[19] Large elites who are benefiting from growth rarely see much virtue in empowering the weak and poor to take their newfound wealth away from them (this is one of many reasons why China is unlikely to evolve in the near future into anything resembling a democracy).[20] There is also some evidence that the early stages of any move from authoritarianism to democracy are most likely to be associated with the worst excesses of violence, genocide and aggressive war; it is when the people become conscious of themselves as a people – and as a class or a race with power – that revenge is taken on others. So even if economic growth does make the journey to democracy more likely, the journey is likely to be bumpy.

When nations do evolve into mature democracies, history does not come to an end.[21] By most measures the citizens of the older democracies are happier than others but they still have a distinctive pattern of unhappiness. In a recent global survey of attitudes to power, large groups were found in the mature democracies who believed that elections in their countries were free and fair but did not believe that their country was ruled by the will of the people. The numbers were highest in the UK, Sweden, Denmark, France and the Netherlands. When asked to describe their government they most frequently used the label 'bureaucratic'.[22] In many of these countries the most democratic institutions are among the least trusted. This disillusion with democracy explains why election turnouts have begun to fall across the western world (though they are still rising elsewhere); likewise party membership, and why activist energies have moved away from parties and towards single issues (there has been a steady rise over the last thirty years in the proportion of the population who have taken part in a demonstration, a strike, a consumer boycott or a petition, at precisely the same time that the more conventional politics of parties and elections has been in decline).[23]

MORAL PROGRESS

Throughout the modern era commentators have forecast that states are, or soon would be, drained of moral content. This was the promise made by a long tradition of reformers, from the eighteenth-century Prussian cameralists to the twentieth-century proponents of modern public management. A recent example was Philip Bobbitt's claim that modern states are mutating into a 'market' state that 'is largely indifferent to the claims of justice, or for that matter any particular set of moral values'.[24]

These claims accurately echo the beliefs of some of the officials working within states, and they fit with the state's self-image as a rational, calculating machine. They also echo generations of critics' complaints about the cold, impersonal character of the modern state that locks people into its 'iron cage' of rationality.

Yet these arguments are strikingly at odds with what has happened. They miss the moral dimension of the service that is so central to democracy, to markets and to welfare. They are certainly at odds with how leaders as varied as George W. Bush and Nelson Mandela speak about their roles. They are at odds with the state's much greater capacities to carry out tasks that in everyday terms are moral ones (healing, caring, protecting), and also at odds with the much broader moral debate now common in democracies on everything from the ethics of childcare or abortion to research on stem cells, the nature of just war and the ethics of climate change.

It is true that the liberal democracies have sought to expand the scope for people to make their own moral choices and to control their own lives free from state interference.[25] But no states have found it possible to stand back from their own moral duties and judgements. Instead democracy has tended to draw them deeper into areas of moral argument and action, for example around the environment or rights to life or paedophilia, that were irrelevant to the daily life of states a century or two ago. And it has drawn them nearer to the ideals of service described by successive thinkers over the last few thousand years, whether judged by the ends to which they devote their resources, by the ethos with which they act, or by the outcomes they achieve.

4

The Servant State

Harun al-Rashid, the celebrated ruler who appears in the *Tales of a Thousand and One Nights*, reigned over an immense empire that stretched right across the Middle East and into Asia. He also won renown as a poet and a lover of scholarship. When he was declared Caliph, Harun opened the treasury and distributed prizes to his friends and relatives. He hoped to receive a visit from Sufyan, his former teacher. When Sufyan failed to appear he wrote him a letter and sent a messenger named Abbad to deliver it. Abbad found Sufyan sitting with his companions inside a mosque. When he presented him with the letter Sufyan refused to touch it and instead asked one of his companions to read it for him. The letter said: 'We await your coming to visit us; we are mindful of the friendship that binds us.'

Sufyan said to his companions: 'Write my answer on the back of the letter.' His disciples said, 'Master you must write to him on a fresh sheet.' 'On the back of the sheet,' he said again. He then dictated the following words: 'To Harun the misguided, deprived of the sweetness of the Koran. You have opened the treasury of the believers and distributed its funds to gratify your desires. Have you asked permission of those who fight on behalf of the faith? Have you asked permission of the widows and the orphans?' and so on in this manner, concluding: 'as for friendship, we have broken it off; no tie or affection binds us now. Do not write to us again; for if you do, we shall neither read your letter nor reply to it.'

After seeing this, Abbad went to the market, where he replaced his clothing with cheaper clothes. When he returned with the letter to al-Rashid, the Caliph understood the meaning of Abbad's change in appearance and cried out, 'The messenger has succeeded where his master has failed.' Abbad handed him the letter. When the Caliph read it he burst into tears and wept in the most piteous fashion. His courtiers said, 'Sufyan has demonstrated his impertinence; have someone fetch him here.' 'Silence,' said al-Rashid, 'for you are the ones who have misguided me.' Harun preserved Sufyan's letter and would take it out from time to time and read it.[1]

There are stories of this kind in many traditions, stories that tell of great rulers being humiliated by advisers or mystics who bring them down to earth.[2] Usually these stories describe them being reminded that they are servants – servants of ideals and servants of the community. There are very few traditions in which these ideals are completely absent: the Legalists in China, who won great influence in the last centuries BCE, were one of the rare exceptions, arguing to receptive emperors that everyone and everything should serve the state, and that brutal force should be used to punish a dumb, mischievous populace.

Harun's story should not be taken at face value; he was quite capable of ruthlessness as well as revenge (Saddam Hussein, who occasionally executed colleagues in the middle of meetings,[3] sometimes liked to compare himself to Harun, his most illustrious predecessor as ruler of Baghdad). But his story is a reminder that most states have claimed for themselves a moral role of service, duty, care and guardianship. In what follows I explore the character of this claim to service and show that beneath the glittering variety of rituals, pageants, declarations and pronouncements with which governments have embellished themselves, the claims to service have fitted into a broadly consistent structure that is as characteristic of modern Denmark or the United Nations Organization as it is of republican Siena or the Ottoman Empire.

THE RESPONSIBILITY TO PROTECT

The first moral claim that all states make is that they can protect people from harm. If they fail they forfeit their legitimacy. This is why in the past the responsibility to protect has overridden all other concerns, including everyday morality, easily justifying cruelty and deceit in the writings of Niccolò Machiavelli, Sun Tzu and Henry Kissinger.

This duty is at the heart of every state's implicit contract with its public. It gives any state an underlying character of harsh brutality, which appears at times of threat,[4] and it gives the guardians of this role a distinctively paranoid moral world view. The primacy of protection from harm also frames modern liberalism; in the writings of John Stuart Mill, the only justification for actions against others is self-protection and the only justifiable restraints on liberties are those that prevent harm to others.[5]

Protection matters because order and safety are essential not just for life to carry on but also for people to live well. The available data confirm that political stability and order, the rule of law and justice, are decisive to happiness. The lowest ever rate of national happiness was recorded in the Dominican Republic in the early 1960s after the assassination of President Trujillo at a time of chronic disorder.[6] The highest levels of recorded happiness are generally to be found in stable democracies like Norway, Switzerland and Denmark. It is hard to overestimate the value of strong, stable, protective and legitimate governance to human well-being.

States' capacity to protect people from harm varies greatly. Most states do all that they can to protect against aggression from other states. They are also generally vigilant against terrorism, which poses a less direct yet more unsettling challenge to states because its deliberate randomness challenges not only security, morale and mutual trust, but also, more subtly, people's confidence that the world is ordered and rational.

Until recently the extent of the protection states could offer was limited. Even ubiquitous policing is barely a century old in most countries, and only in very recent times have a minority of highly competent states been able to promise some protection from flows of drugs, organized crime or infectious diseases. Their success in doing so has ratcheted public expectations upwards, so that areas of life that used to be seen as subject to fate are now expected to be managed, including unsafe cars, dangerous technologies, intrusive messages directed to children and toxins in food. The expectation that states can protect us from risks now extends far beyond the nation's borders, and threats like climate change, economic downturns and epidemics – the many 'problems without passports' – have forced states to pool their sovereignty so that they can better protect their citizens.

Globalization has also prompted a changed view of responsibilities to protect individual citizens. In the nineteenth century imperial states often justified gunboat diplomacy by claiming to be protecting their citizens. Many of these claims were spurious, and there was little most states could realistically do to protect their citizens once they went beyond their borders. But in the modern world it has come to be assumed that states are responsible for protecting their people wherever they are. The Bali nightclub bombing in 2002, for example, prompted official inquiries to find who in the Australian government was to blame – it couldn't be the result simply of bad luck or factors outside government's control.

Many of the subtle dynamics of power arise from the duty of protection. From the start it justified states in becoming monopolists of force, yet this in turn made them a threat to their people. This is a tension captured well in Aesop's fable of the horse which is being attacked by the pig and asks for help from the man. The man says that he would like to help, but will have to harness the horse first (in other words, from the very beginning, freedom depends on subjection). Repeatedly dictators and would-be dictators have taken refuge in the claim that the community is under threat and that only they can protect it: having taken power, the protectors then become attackers. The exploitation of fears is a recurrent motif in political history: anxiety is the first refuge of the political scoundrel.[7] Goering advised that 'the people can always be brought to the bidding of the leaders . . . All you have to do is to tell them they are being attacked and denounce the pacifists for lack of patriotism', and Goebbels based his career on the idea that fear was the most powerful tool available to any state. Democratic leaders have also often manipulated fears. After the Irish Fenians set off bombs in London in 1867, for example, Prime Minister Disraeli advocated repealing habeas corpus, and (falsely) claimed that there were 10,000 armed Fenians in London waiting to strike.

Awareness of the potential risks involved in giving protectors unbounded power may explain why in the Chinese tradition there was such profound disdain for warriors, who were left out of the traditional list of the main classes, which included scholars, farmers, artisans and merchants. *Wu* or violence was inferior to, and anathema to, the *wei* of civilization, and had to be constantly kept in check (which helps to explain why so many non-Chinese rulers founded dynasties, ruling as warriors over Chinese scholar bureaucracies).[8]

In the West, similar anxieties repeatedly came to the surface. James Madison warned at the time of the American Revolution that 'the fetters imposed on liberty at home have ever been forged out of the weapons provided for defense against real, pretended, or imaginary dangers from abroad.' In the twentieth century alone some 170 million people are estimated to have been killed by their own governments: over 60 million in the USSR, 35 million in China under Mao and another 10 million by the Kuomintang, over 20 million by Germany, and 6 million by Japan – a far higher number than the 40 million killed by war during the same period. It is entirely appropriate that the word 'terrorism' was first used to describe violence by the state in revolutionary France (Robespierre in 1794 had claimed that virtue and terror are the 'springs of popular government', and that virtue without terror was powerless).

Since then state terrorism has been far more deadly than its non-state counterpart, whether promoted within borders (by the Cheka and its descendants, the NKVD and KGB, the South Africa Defence Force, or the Gestapo) or beyond national borders (by the CIA and KGB, the various terrorist clients of Iran and Syria or the assassins of Mossad). In the Marxist-Leninist tradition there was even pride in the state's capacity for harshness: Leon Trotsky once wrote a book justifying violence against a people by the state that was published in English as *In Defence of Terrorism*.

Many of the heroes of modern democracy dipped their hands in blood to preserve the state: Friedrich Ebert, the leader of Germany's Social Democrats, sent troops on to the streets of many cities in 1919 (and was denounced by the Spartacists as 'the mass executioner of the German proletariat'). De Gaulle faced down the Algerian rebels in 1961–2 and through guile and force extracted France from its colonial quagmire, and Churchill sent the troops to fight striking miners in Britain soon after the First World War. All justified their attacks on one part of the community as essential for the protection of the whole.

Just how far states should go to protect their community has always been a matter of judgement and proportion rather than absolute principle. Until modern times most of the world's republics and democracies were destroyed by their failure to protect themselves and their citizens. Liberal societies are always likely to be more vulnerable to external threats, precisely because they are the ones most likely to marginalize martial values. When in 1933 the students of Oxford University famously voted against fighting for king and country in a debate, Adolf Hitler duly took note. War ensued six years later and many of the same students fought – and died – for king and country. Republican France, which had suffered so much from war in 1870– 71 and 1914–18, was unwilling to countenance war in the 1930s, and disparaged the warmongers and re-armers with disastrous consequences. Most democracies have subsequently learned the lesson and taken care to train some young men and women to be ruthless killers, some to keep track of armaments and threats, and others to keep their antennae attuned to dangers and to specialize in paranoia (and the oldest democracy, Switzerland, has successfully turned defence into a shared responsibility of the state and the people).

The responsibility to protect brings with it other complex dynamics too. As we have seen, it makes rulers and ruled interdependent since rulers need people and money for their armies. And it creates wider obligations since, as Thomas Hobbes wrote in *Leviathan* over three hundred years ago, 'the weakest has strength enough to kill the strongest, either by secret machination or by confederacy with others', which means that the strongest have no choice but to care about the lives and needs of the weakest, and security is never solely a matter of guns and borders (especially in an age when states are grappling with radically new threats, from climate change to the risk of immensely dangerous technologies falling into the hands of terrorists).

So the responsibility to protect can be thought of as a deal. To the people, states make an offer (one that is not easily refused): an offer of order, predictability, reliability and prosperity in exchange for subservience, a minimum of loyalty, the payment of taxes and, at times, other duties. The deal is sustainable because the risks faced by the people and the risks faced by states overlap. For the citizen the greatest risks are those of disorder and violence, whether that violence comes from outside invaders or domestic criminals and bandits. For the state, likewise, the greatest risks to its power and prosperity come from disorder, whether the sources of that disorder are other states or its own people. Because these risks overlap there is always the basis for a social contract. But this contract can be profoundly unbalanced and every community has at times had to ask whether its fear of its rulers is greater than its fear of strangers.

THE RESPONSIBILITY FOR WELFARE

The second source of legitimacy for states has been welfare – a responsibility to promote well-being and reduce unnecessary suffering. Although families and communities have always looked after their own needs for care and welfare there is a very long history of state involvement in welfare in all its forms, including programmes to distribute food and alleviate poverty which can be found from third millennium BCE Sumer and Republican Rome to modern Brazil, and there are many examples throughout history of states that have presented themselves, and been presented by philosophers, not just as protectors but as promoters of well-being.

The conscious pursuit of happiness is one of the marks of civilizations that have grown beyond sheer survival. For Socrates, the 'aim in founding the commonwealth was not to make any one class especially happy but to secure the greatest possible happiness for the community as a whole.' Ashoka described himself in one of his edicts as desiring 'safety, self-control, justice and happiness for all beings'. The great Islamic philosopher Abu Nasr al-Farabi wrote in his classic tenth-century book on political philosophy, *The Perfect City*,[9] that 'happiness is the good desired for itself; it is never desired to achieve by it something else and there is nothing greater beyond it that a human being can achieve.' An influential Chinese thinker of the twelfth century, Ch'en Liang, argued in a similar vein the rightness of whatever 'satisfied the reasonable desires and needs of the people'.[10]

The West formalized these ideas a few centuries later. The US Declaration of Independence promised 'life, liberty and the pursuit of happiness' and the French constitution of 1793 committed the new nation to the statement that 'the purpose of society is the common happiness'. In Britain, the utilitarianism of Jeremy Bentham, who argued that the good state is one that achieves the greatest happiness of the greatest number (an ideal almost precisely opposite to that of *raison d'état*) had an extraordinary impact on rulers (and often disastrous consequences, as when it was applied by zealous British imperial reformers in India in the 1850s). More recently it has achieved influence indirectly through modern economics, which is now the lingua franca of the global elite. The small Asian state of Bhutan even committed its government to maximizing gross domestic happiness, an alternative to gross domestic product (GDP)(although whether its rules prescribing that all adults should wear the same kind of draughty tunic and banning tobacco actually succeed in promoting happiness remains unclear).

It is one thing to want to make people happy, it is another to succeed in doing so. For most states the starting point has been economic policy, with the mix of discipline and freedom that makes prosperity possible, providing and protecting money, defining and enforcing property rights, and overseeing the rules of trade and exchange. Some states administered economic life very directly: the temples in Sumer distributed grain in precisely calibrated rations; the European empires merged statecraft and exploitation in the East India Company, the Hudson's Bay Company and the Compagnie des Habitants; and twentieth-century states ran the great infrastructures of rail, electricity and telephones, as well as steel and coal. But generally states have not needed to command and direct economic activity. Another of Aesop's fables describes the sun and the wind competing over who could strip a shepherd boy of his cloak. The wind blows and the boy clutches it ever tighter. The sun shines, and he takes it off. The moral is that states do best when they go with the grain of self-interest, rather than using force and command.

Governments' economic roles are sometimes seen as protections for a negative liberty, a commitment to non-interference on the part of states that will otherwise choke off prosperity. But economic growth has always depended on more than unconstrained self-interest. The conditions for prosperity are not natural; they are deeply unnatural (which is why sustained growth has been so rare) and dependent on careful design and very active management. The great American jurist Oliver Wendell Holmes described it well in one of his pithiest and most elliptical epigrams: 'property, a creation of law, does not arise from value, although exchangeable, a matter of fact'. In other words, value does not pre-exist property rights, or the active role of the state; it arises from the very definition and enforcement of those rights. This is why in economic life, as in daily life, the idea of laissez-faire is a fiction – true laissez-faire would be anarchy in which the strong dominated the weak.

The responsibility for welfare brings states into fields where moral principles are unavoidably difficult – how to balance freedom and regulation, how much to provide in public goods or whether to be the protector and insurer of last resort. Some past rulers, like Ashoka more than two millennia ago, wished to provide health and education for their people, and there have been patchy traditions of health provision in the distant past which belie the modern assumption that ancient states were about nothing more than weapons and war. The great Buddhist philosopher Nagarjuna in the second century CE advised rulers to provide support for doctors and hospitals. One fifth-century visitor from China, Faxian, wrote in admiring detail about the public health care he saw in Pataliputra in northern India. Across much of the Muslim world extensive welfare was provided around mosques, paid for by alms. Renaissance Europe witnessed an extended argument about the balance between private charity and public obligations, and Erasmus and Juan Luis Vives were among the advocates of a greater role for secular authorities in caring for the poor and the sick.[11] England, for example, imposed a national framework of duties on local parishes between 1597 and 1601, along with a power for local authorities to levy taxes for poor relief. This was prompted in part by concerns about vagrancy at a time of social dislocation, but was also an attempt to realize Christian values. This early welfare state was not marginal. It covered some 8 per cent of the population by 1750 and 14 per cent by 1800, and the rising costs which resulted prompted ferocious debate both about how the burden could be contained and about how welfare could avoid giving the poor incentives to be idle.[12]

In the late eighteenth century more radical arguments for welfare gained ground. Condorcet argued that the gross inequalities of the era were the result of the 'imperfections of the social art', whose final end would be 'the abolition of inequality between nations' and 'the progress of equality within each nation'. Thomas Paine set out a detailed proposal for tax-funded social insurance to do away with poverty at roughly the same time. It was to be another century, however, before these ideas were put into practice. States were then dragged into welfare mainly because of demand from electors. As the mass of the population won the vote they used it to reject the limited liberalism of small states in favour of a state much more suited to their day-to-day needs: one providing pensions, doctors, schools and homes.[13] States learned that they couldn't aspire to military prowess or economic dynamism if their people were malnourished, illiterate or vulnerable to disease (four in ten recruits to the British Army in the late nineteenth century had to be rejected on grounds of ill health). So insurance was collectivized and pooled, and states evolved into a flotilla of curers, carers, therapists and regulators, some involved in the most intimate details of private life. Within the space of a century the typical employee of governments changed from being a soldier or official to become a carer, involved in direct, face-to-face service with the public.

Some of the hardest issues for any state concern equity and distribution, and how far they should go in equalizing incomes. As Amartya Sen has shown, famines like those in Ireland in the 1840s and Bengal in the 1940s were not primarily caused by shortages of food. They happened, and still happen, because some people lack property rights and purchasing power, which in turn usually reflect their lack of influence over the state. The five million or so who died of famine in southern India in 1877, for example, did so not because food was short but because the then Viceroy, Lord Lytton, ensured that grain continued to be exported to England and ordered his officials to 'discourage relief works in every possible way'.

Poverty is rarely natural; it usually also reflects conditions of power, which is why questions of distribution have so often dominated politics. But how far should the state go? If the state's job is to maximize well-being, economic theory and psychological evidence both show that the happiness gained by a poor family from additional income is greater than for a rich one: relative levels matter and although an increase in one person's income may make them happier it can make other people more envious and dissatisfied with their lot.[14] Just how inequality affects life satisfaction is to some extent culturally determined; for example, it appears to have much more effect in Europe than in the USA, either because Europeans favour more equal societies, or because the (largely incorrect) perception of higher levels of social mobility in the US reduces the unhappiness caused by inequality.[15] But the strong implication is that any duty to promote material welfare has to entail substantial redistribution from the rich to the poor.

The responsibility for welfare is tightly linked to the responsibility to protect. In both areas the state's role has been to reduce risks, particularly in those fields where individuals cannot protect or insure themselves. In the US, for example, government has at various times insured against unemployment, sickness in old age, crop failure, floods, fire, bank failure and inflation.[16] In all of these cases common welfare depends on either a social or a political sense of common identity or interest. In some countries people's willingness to pay for the welfare of others is adversely affected by levels of migration: more diverse societies can be less solidaristic than homogeneous ones. But where there are strong parties and movements of the Left even diversity seems to have little impact on willingness to share.[17]

Government involvement in welfare has been encouraged by what could be called 'generous politics' – the attempts to extend to strangers the kindness and generosity which people display to their friends and family. It lies at the heart of the message of the Christian New Testament, in much of the Koran, and of what came to be the political Left. It is a dream of compassion, intimacy and care taken to a much larger scale through the state, and it has had a significant effect on state behaviour: according to one well-researched estimate, electorates in some developed countries are willing to forego between a quarter and a third of their income to achieve a more equitable distribution,[18] which helps to explain the ubiquity of redistribution, from India's support for the lowest castes, to Europe's 'structural programmes' for the poorest rural and urban areas, and America's welfare for poor families.

The responsibility to protect and the responsibility for welfare come together in relation to the environment. People have made lives in an extraordinary range of environments, from the Arctic to the Sahara, without any help from the state. In each they have found a way to live with an ecosystem, and sometimes to shape it, and become acutely dependent on its twists and turns. But in the most heavily populated areas states have been closely involved in managing environments – promoting irrigation, building canals, or planting forests to prevent erosion. Failure to manage vital environments has been one of the common causes of state collapse, from Uruk in Iraq whose once-fertile lands were reduced to desert, to the Akkadian Empire (where by 2000 BCE the earth had 'turned white') and the great empires of central America. Athens' great ruler Solon in the sixth century BCE banned food exports and the cultivation of steep slopes in a desperate attempt to arrest erosion, and many others earned their legitimacy through the vigour with which they built or maintained systems of irrigation. It was in response to the hellish unregulated growth of cities in the nineteenth century that the paraphernalia of modern planning and public health grew up, and it is in the slums of Mexico City, Mumbai or Lagos that the absense of an active state makes so many people's lives so vulnerable to crime, poverty and disease.

If part of the state's role has been to protect people from the risks of a malign environment, its other role has been to make people happier by cultivating a better one. We associate the good life with abundant trees and beautiful landscapes, cities full of parks and piazzas, and modern states have seen fit to provide public parks and protected wildernesses, as well as art galleries and concert halls. A third of the landmass of Australia and New Zealand, the USA and Canada is managed directly or indirectly by government as national parks of various kinds for this reason, and wealthy states spend generously on the public spaces of their great cities, iconic buildings and public art.[19]

THE RESPONSIBILITY FOR JUSTICE

The third consistent source of legitimacy for states is justice – punishing criminals and resolving conflicts. The earliest states dispensed a violent and unequal justice, primarily designed to protect the rich and powerful from the far more numerous poor and weak. One of the first and most resonant pieces of political philosophy is a fragment from the Greek poet Pindar. 'The law,'[20] he wrote, 'sovereign of all, of mortals and immortals, leads with the strongest hand, justifying the most violent.' In other words, at the birth of the state, violence and the law were fused.

Yet all rulers have also presented themselves as the servants of a more universal justice. Hammurabi, the great lawmaker of the ancient Middle East, claimed to have derived his laws from the sun god who saw everything that humans did. For Aristotle, the ability to distinguish good and bad, just and unjust, distinguished humans from the other animals, and found its greatest expression in a state which could distinguish between good and evil. As states formalized the justice that had previously been organized informally by elders it became a distinct arm of government, free from, and at times superior to, executive power. It became impersonal, cool and blind (as in the iconography of a blindfolded figure holding scales), and able to listen (*audi alteram partem* – the legal principle of hearing the other side).

The meaning of justice, and of the state's role in promoting it, has depended on context and culture. The guiding principle of Roman law was that each should be given their due (*ius suum cuique*) and that what effects everyone should be approved by everyone (*quod omnes tangit, ab omnibus approbetur*). In other words, no one's interests should be ignored, and no one should be subject to anyone else. The idea that the law should be even handed galvanized later rebels, including the leaders of England's Peasants' Revolt in 1381, who demanded the right to stand up in court and speak out against anyone who wronged them, even if that someone was their lord and master.

In India an opposite principle was embodied in the 'Laws of Manu', which four thousand years ago prescribed the very different duties and rights governing its hierarchy of castes, and in China the Emperor dispensed justice without any notion that those on the receiving end had rights. Indeed the Legalists admonished rulers 'to use the full severity of the law against the unfilial and the unfraternal', believing that 'the virtue of the rulers was manifested as much in their righteous punishments as in the power of their moral influence'[21] (and in sixteenth-century England William Tyndale justified the claim that it 'is better to have a tyrant as thy king than a shadow: a passive king who does nought himself' on the grounds that 'a tyrant though he do wrong to the good, punishes the vile').

In early modern Europe the struggles over justice prepared the way for democracy and rights. When Frederick the Great wanted to extend the gardens of his palace near Berlin, Sans Souci, he is said to have asked a miller who owned a mill overlooking the extension to sell it. The miller replied that he wanted to keep it for his children. The King said he could take it without compensation, to which the miller replied, 'Yes majesty, if our courts did not exist.' The mill still stands overlooking Sans Souci as a symbol of subordination of royalty to law.

The scope of state justice was traditionally limited to acts of violence, property, family and resources (one of the Polynesian words for law means 'relating to water', a vital area of contention in the distant past and probably in the future). Yet in the western world, and through its influence globally, the scope for justice has expanded to include social justice, global justice, gender justice, intergenerational justice, discrimination and the state's own procedures. Many more areas of life have been opened up to an essentially moral public argument,[22] particularly in common-law systems, where judges have sought to find the unarticulated underlying principles behind particular laws and recast their role as being about guarding principles, rather than simply enforcing the policies that issue forth from legislatures and kings.[23]

Justice has generally been a monopoly of the state, sometimes shared with religions, but its resilience has often depended on the people. Solon's law in ancient Athens, for example, required anyone who did not take sides in a civil war to be punished – a law intended to ensure that the whole of society used its weight to pacify warring factions.

Today many countries continue to resist a fully professionalized justice system, and hold on to the use of lay magistrates and juries made up of citizens as a protection against tyranny.

THE RESPONSIBILITY FOR TRUTH AND KNOWLEDGE

The fourth source of legitimacy has been the state's claim to uphold the truths and knowledge vital to the community's survival. Originally the truths that mattered concerned the cosmos, the climate, hunting grounds or competing tribes (knowledge that reduced the uncertainty of the environment and widened the scope for human sovereignty). Later kings drew legitimacy from their own godlike character, and carried out rituals to maintain order in the world and to reinforce religious truths.

Akbar in sixteenth-century India was probably the first great leader to promote reason as the highest value of his state, at a time when Islam had much to teach Christianity about tolerance and enlightenment. During the eighteenth and nineteenth centuries many western governments legitimized themselves by reference to knowledge and reason, with constitutions founded on truths that are taken 'to be self-evident' (including the preamble to the failed early twenty-first-century European Constitution, which acknowledged the primacy of reason). The various professions of engineering, urban planning and public health were corralled around the state, and new curriculums systematized what children needed to know.

Many of the claims made by states were fallacious, self-serving and hypocritical. Talleyrand enjoyed the cynicism of his comment that 'the truth is whatever is plausibly asserted and confidently maintained'. It is said that if you torture the data enough it will confess to anything. Mao and Kim-Il Sung were not content to be the greatest statesmen and poets in human history: they also had to be the greatest scientists (regardless of nature – one of the slogans of the Cultural Revolution proclaimed 'However much we can dream the land will yield').

The Nazis and (for a brief period) the Stalinists stand out for the degree to which they instrumentalized truth. Goebbels went furthest: 'If you tell a lie big enough and keep repeating it, people will eventually

57

come to believe it', explaining with even greater candour why it was 'vitally important for the State to use all its powers to repress dissent; for the truth is the mortal enemy of the lie – and thus by extension – the truth is the greatest enemy of the State.'

Such brusque cynicism was unsustainable, however. Governors need an authority for their authority,[24] and that has to come from a claim to truth. A state which did not bother to make any pretence to truth (and even the Nazis laid claim to some truths about history, genetics and identity) would be capable of regulating the day-to-day conduct of teachers, police officers, doctors and officials only through fear.[25]

THE MEANING OF SERVICE

Many virtues matter to states, including consistency and reliability, courage and foresight. But the four claims to legitimacy – protection, welfare, justice and truth – stand out as forming a consistent ethical architecture and a continuous thread, at least of ideals, from the very earliest recorded states to the present day. Together they make up the order that states promise: an order that is safe and prosperous, just and true. Few, if any, states have made no claims in these four areas. Even though they have been reached through many different philosophical paths (widely different societies can agree much more easily on the practical expressions of service than they can on the underlying rationales) there is an unmistakeable common pattern. So, for example, King Ur-Nammu of Ur, who reigned around 2100 BCE, promised his people that he would 'establish equity in the land and banish malediction, violence and strife', as well as upholding the religious duties of the state and promulgating laws. (The rulers of Sumeria were portrayed on seals, sculptures and vases as warriors, sources of fertility and as dispensers of justice.) Two thousand years later in India, around 300 BCE, the first great realist political theorist, Kautilya, adviser to the Mauryan emperor, described the duties of the ruler in his book the *Arthashastra* in much the same ways. He wrote of these as including protection of the state from external aggression; safeguarding the welfare of the people; and maintenance of law and order within the state. He presented these as ethical duties, aspects of *rajadharma*, the *dharma* or moral duties of kings, and described them as rooted in the very nature of the universe. They could also be justified in terms of self-interest because when an 'unjust king is attacked his people will either topple him or go over to the enemy'.

Two thousand years later in the modern era, governments in the West generally describe their duties in very similar terms, promising security, prosperity and welfare, justice and knowledge in the forms of science and education. Election battles often turn on an argument between the primacy of protection and the primacy of welfare (ancient Athens faced similar choices: when new silver was discovered Themistocles argued that it should be used to build 200 warships, while others wanted to distribute 10 drachmas to every family), and occasionally opposition parties try to make elections turn on questions of truth.

The four sources of legitimation correspond, broadly, with ministerial roles and departmental structures (defence and policing; welfare and health; justice; communications and education), and with the professions most associated with states – soldiers and police, doctors and social workers, regulators and economists, lawyers and judges, scientists and academics. Each profession also has its own stated ideals of service, its restraints on the abuse of power (like doctors' Hippocratic oath), and its own longstanding arguments about whether professional knowledge is a possession to be exploited or a gift to be shared.

At a more profound level the four correspond with aspects of human nature: the drive for survival; the drive for happiness; the deep-seated dispositions towards justice and fairness (and resentment of free-riders, exploiters and bullies); and the apparently universal drive to learn. They also correspond with the ethical syndromes or outlooks that underpin many societies. These include the guardian syndrome of protection; the utilitarianism of maximizing the welfare of the greatest number, in which ends often justify means; the proceduralism of law, in which the process matters more than the ends; and the scientific reasoning of universities. Each of these syndromes has a distinct view of moral questions, yet in the day-to-day workings of a community they complement each other.

Most states' claims to legitimacy have been much more cosmetic than real. But their pervasiveness over time and space confirms that although the character of states has changed hugely, as power has become syndicated, professionalized, distributed and networked, the fundamental needs of human communities have not.[26]

What, then, is the nature of the service that states provide? An ideal of service can be found in many cultures. At root it means taking the person being served as the ultimate end, understanding, anticipating and meeting their needs quietly, and with humility. It involves an ability to listen and understand (St Francis asked God to 'grant that I may not seek so much to be understood as to understand'). It seems to be rooted in the care and nurture of children that families provide, and, perhaps even more, in the care for the sick and elderly that marks out human civilization from the rest of nature.

In private life service is personal. In public life it is universal, spread fairly across all citizens. For governments the ideal is to govern in the common interest rather than in the ruler's own interests. To Plato and Aristotle this ideal of communal service defined the very essence of what government was for. It justified the rigours of guardian training described in *The Republic*, which were designed to suppress any vestige of self-interest and encourage the guardians to find fulfilment in the welfare of the whole community. For Aristotle 'the correct forms of government are those in which the one, the few or the many govern with a view to the common interest: but the governments which rule with a view to the private interest whether of the one, or of the few, or of the many are deviations.'[27]

The Romans took these arguments a step further. Service for them implied a universal set of claims, a commitment to the needs of everyone, the whole rather than just its parts. Cicero wrote that 'anyone who looks after the interests of only one part of a citizen body while neglecting the rest, introduces into a city the most pernicious element of all, namely sedition and discord.'[28] The key to civic harmony was to give precedence to the ideal of the common good, with magistrates looking 'after the welfare of the whole body politic, never allowing themselves to care only for one part of the citizens while betraying the rest'. In the modern West, too, the idea of the public good contains within it the notion that there are some needs and rights so important that they must be guaranteed for everyone and provided equitably.

Other traditions contain similar ideas. Chinese political philosophy has been concerned with the contrast between the collective good or public interest – *kung* – and the private interest – *ssu*. The virtuous ruler is the one who serves the collective good, and who does what is right rather than what is only advantageous (*i* rather than *li*).[29] Within Islam the concepts of *maslaha* (public interest) and *siyasah* (public policy) played some of the same roles.

Good servants take what they need, not what they can get away with.[30] Since anyone in a position of power faces temptations to exploit their power to secure wealth, such self-discipline has been rare in the past. It is a measure of moral progress that our rulers now usually take salaries significantly lower than their counterparts in other sectors (British Prime Ministers, for example, earn a third of the salary of the head of the BBC and far less than business leaders or successful lawyers), and we look unfavourably on the leader who leaves office with Swiss bank accounts and suspiciously lucrative directorships (and a host of rules ensure that self-interest is contained, including restraints on partisan appointments, corporate donations to political campaigns, and public spending unfairly directed to areas of electoral support).

Good servants also account for their actions. Many civilizations punished rulers who failed in their duties, or sacrificed them to appease angry gods. Yoruba kings in West Africa were killed or expected to commit suicide if they were defeated in battle. Others sought to cultivate humility in their rulers: Sumerian kings had their faces slapped once a year by the high priest,[31] and Roman victors parading through the streets were famously accompanied by a slave whispering in their ear 'Remember that you are mortal'. Today the equivalent is the ritual humiliation of the public inquiry or the hustings.

A good servant is discrete, limited and restrained, often the very opposite of the bragging, exhibitionist state. There have been many descriptions of an ideal of quiet service in government – from Lao Tzu's descriptions of the best leader as the one who leaves the people believing 'we did it ourselves' to Marcus Aurelius' accounts of stoical humility – but there have been equally many examples of states which overreached, meddled and interfered, or sucked dry their people's capacity to act.

This takes us to the vexed question of how states should exercise self-restraint, which has become one of the most difficult questions of modern political philosophy and practice, because there is no simple zero-sum calculus between states and societies, as if a bigger state automatically entails a weaker society (though this was a popular view in the nineteenth century and again in the 1980s). It matters more how governments behave than how big they are. Big governments can leave their citizens stronger. Small ones can leave them weaker. Retreating governments are often replaced not by vigorous civic activity but by organized crime, as the states of the former Soviet Union learned in the 1990s, and many US cities in the decade before. The critical issue is whether states create additional value for their public, turning the powers and resources they take into things that are truly useful,[32] or whether, in the end, they destroy value. Either way, even the most competent need to cull themselves regularly, to strip away past programmes and activities, lest they crowd out their citizens.

This issue has become more difficult over time because the things that matter most to people cannot be provided by states to passive citizens. They are more like joint productions. States cannot make economies prosper without the energy and enterprise of their people. Nor can they educate people unless the people wish to learn, or make them healthy if they don't wish to be. The implication, however, is that if governments want to serve the people and provide them with what they want, they also have to subtly change the way people think and act. David Hume once wrote that 'all plans of government which suppose great reformation in the manners of mankind are plainly imaginary', yet in the two centuries after he wrote this, mankind's manners were reformed to an extraordinary degree, whether in personal hygiene and diet, in work habits or family life, in leisure or in beliefs. The dramatic advances achieved in life expectancy in the nineteenth and twentieth centuries, for example, depended as much on changes in public behaviour as they did on new services and regulations. They were surprisingly little affected by economic growth, and more recent evidence confirms that improvements to health tend to precede economic growth rather than following it.[33] The nation states of the late nineteenth and twentieth centuries were unashamed about the need to change the habits of their people, cultivating discipline, order, temperance and patriotism. Today that smacks of Big Brother. But any state which is serious about well-being cannot wholly ignore questions of behaviour, and many of the actions they take to 'reform the manners of mankind' leave people stronger, not weaker.

The precise ways in which states should act as self-restrained servants differ according to the field. For example, in relation to protection and justice the risks of excessive state power are particularly great, but so are the risks of society organizing itself. A society with a thousand police forces is likely to be more dangerous than a society with only one, so long as it is suitably hemmed in with rules. In relation to welfare and knowledge the risks of excessive state action are less immediate, but these are both fields where societal self-organization is generally a good thing and where an overactive state can leave people overdependent.

These are some of the reasons why the perpetual debate about the size of the state has been so sterile. A French economist, Pierre Paul Leroy-Beaulieu, calculated in 1888 that a modern state could not sustainably extract more than 12–13 per cent of GNP, and parallel arguments were made when state spending reached 20, 30, 40 and 50 per cent of GDP.[34] Whatever level had been reached was 'proved' to be an absolute limit. Clearly there must be some economic as well as political limits. It is self-evident that overreach is unwise, and that a state which did everything would have removed all moral agency from its citizens, and crowded out private initiative. But an active state can increase people's moral autonomy if they are made healthier, more knowledgeable or more mobile, or released from the constraints of poverty and oppression, and a state that never stretches itself will tend to stagnate. This is why, despite many attempts, no one has been able to show an inverse correlation between the size of states and the dynamism of their economies or societies. What states do, and how well they do it, matters much more than their size.

The philosopher Michael Oakeshott famously said that there is nothing so morally debilitating as to take on an impossible task. Yet for states to have the power to act in the face of evident suffering and to fail to do so may be just as morally damaging. Leaders are poor servants if they only follow, or if they treat the public with such deference that they dare not change them. They may serve best not just through providing services but also by changing the community's self-image, its aspirations and its sense of possibility.[35]

SOCIAL CONTRACTS

Ideas of service rest on metaphors with which people make sense of the relationship between states and people. In China, the state was likened to the head of a family, providing safety, welfare and moral guidance to a people generally seen as intellectual and moral inferiors. Subservience to the state was something people were born into.

In the West the favoured moral metaphors have been very different. The most influential has been the metaphor of the contract voluntarily agreed between citizens, and between citizens and the state. This is often imagined happening in an ancient village or on a desert island. But one of the clearest examples of how such a contract could be made can be found in the history of Ivan IV of Russia. After years of rule that had been hampered by the resistance of the boyar aristocrats, Ivan abdicated in the depths of the winter of 1564/5, leaving Moscow to take up residence in a small village. As he had expected, panic took hold of the city after he had left because the public were terrified about the prospect of chaos and oppression by the boyars. Ivan agreed to return only if he was given absolute power. Within a few weeks he had it, begged to return by the terrified people of Moscow for whom anything was preferable to the greed of the boyars and the savagery of the Tatars.

Thomas Hobbes provided a theoretical explanation of why this happened. Man begins his life free, he argued, but comes up against other men – other men who are vicious, murderous and untrustworthy, just as he is. To survive, all men therefore have to agree to surrender their sovereignty so that together they 'become a single person that goes by the name of a city or a republic', and which then protects them against threats.

But this social contract cannot hold through voluntary agreement alone. Instead, a sovereign, someone standing above and apart from the community, is needed to enforce it. After such an enforcer is appointed, there is no easy way for the community to rein them in (as the Russians soon learned under Ivan as he earned his epithet 'the Terrible'); hence the unavoidable logic, as Hobbes saw it, that takes you from the social contract to the all-powerful ruler who you are duty-bound to obey. Since the greatest danger for anyone is anarchy and chaos, obedience is the only rational basis on which to run a society. The contract is not wholly one-sided: if the ruler fails to protect you, you are entitled to rebel. But in the normal run of daily life your duty is to do what you are told.

John Locke, and many others after him, took an almost opposite view. For them the greatest danger was abuse of power by the state rather than anarchy. Their contract was therefore both more explicit and more equal. It drew on the natural laws that God had planted into the world, and included the right to life, property and freedoms. The contract had to be consented to in order to be meaningful (and if individuals chose to reject the terms of the contract the world was full of 'vacant places' where they could go). But it was likely to be consented to because it provided the best protection for people's property. Because people were naturally good, and in a state of nature under God had lived in 'peace, goodwill, mutual assistance and preservation', the state could reign lightly.

These social contract stories[36] are like the origin myths that many societies use to make sense of their past and future. They are of limited use as history. They leave many out of the contract, such as slaves and women, and those without property. As Edmund Burke pointed out, they also exclude the dead and the unborn. None confers any rights or claims on people living beyond the borders of the state (until very recently political theory effectively treated every society as a closed, largely self-sufficient entity). But these attempts to define a primordial social contract (and the related attempts to imagine what the state would look like if it was negotiated from scratch)[37] provide a compelling way of thinking about service and how to reduce the stark imbalance between big states and small people.

THE MUTUAL DEPENDENCE OF STATES AND PEOPLES

Why are ideals of good power common across so many different eras and cultures? It is possible that they are true archetypes, written into our genetic make-up, or at the very least carried across long distances of time by the power of cultural memory. Many societies have recognized a similar moral logic: the idea that any exercise of power brings with it moral obligations, so that the dependence and vulnerability of people on the receiving end of power is matched by the responsibility of those exercising that power. This principle may apply to parents in families, managers in organizations, landlords and employers, and to political and official leaders in states. The greater the dependence, the greater the implied moral responsibility.

An alternative explanation for the ubiquity of these ideas of service is that states had no choice but to accept the moral implications of their power because of their dependence on the people they ruled. States depend on the compliance of their officials, soldiers and agents, and when they cease obeying the state's power soon crumbles. The same relationship exists between employer and employees, the former at times utterly dependent on the latter as trade unions discovered. This mutual dependence was once celebrated in carnivals where roles were reversed, and today is marked at election times when powerful leaders are briefly turned into humble supplicants.

All predators depend on their prey, but in relation to power the dependence is more subtle. Hegel wrote about this mutual dependence brilliantly in his description of the dialectic of the master and the slave. The world began, he wrote, with war between people and a struggle not just for things but also for recognition. The struggle was bitter and when it was over the winners became masters and the losers became slaves. But in Hegel's argument people are only truly formed as free subjects of history by their experience of working to shape the world, grappling with the difficult nature of real things. So victory has a paradoxical effect: the winner's reward for being a master is that he no longer has to work. But the luxuries of power and leisure make him ever less a free subject, and over time his will atrophies because he has nothing to struggle against. The slave, by contrast, remains active and, through his work on the world, realizes an ever fuller and freer identity. Over time the master becomes more dependent on him, while the slave grows in self-consciousness until he overthrows the master, setting in motion a cycle which then repeats itself, until ultimately, through revolution, a new state emerges in which every citizen is recognized.[38]

Something of this pattern can be seen in the way that rulers who depended on soldiers to sustain them in power became vulnerable to being deposed by them. This happened repeatedly in ancient Rome, Byzantium and medieval Europe; more recently, civilian leaders found themselves beholden to the military in the many new nations that emerged from the ashes of colonialism in the 1960s and 1970s. Even the most developed democracies are not immune to these risks. President Eisenhower warned in the 1950s that the USA was creating a 'military-industrial complex' with undue power and influence over politics; as a former soldier he was peculiarly well-placed to know.

Many ruses have been used to contain this dangerous dependence. States have showered the military with prestige, pay and honours, or hemmed them in with constitutional limits. Byzantine emperors surrounded themselves with foreign bodyguards, the Varangians, who were wholly dependent on them, and many political leaders feel safest with advisers whose careers are solely dependent on their patronage. Some leaders ruthlessly destroyed their vanguard troops so as to stay one step ahead of any threat. Ibn Saud, who ruled Saudi Arabia from the 1920s to 1953, destroyed the *Ikhwan* warriors who had helped him unite his kingdom. Hitler slaughtered the SA leadership in the 'Night of the Long Knives' once they had served their purpose in winning him power.

The more that anyone accumulates, land or weapons, soldiers or cities, the more they depend on others to manage and supervise their possessions. A great emperor might appear omnipotent, but as his empire expanded he was likely to become ever more dependent on the people and institutions he ostensibly controlled – the agencies and departments, scribes and soldiers. He could accept this dependence by becoming just one of the functionaries of a specialized division of labour, a servant alongside other servants, but not surprisingly many rulers became bitter about the constraints they lay under.

Greater power could also, paradoxically, bring greater vulnerability. The first emperor of a unified China, Qin Shi Huang, in the second century BCE, is a case in point: having conquered all his enemies with extraordinary cunning he became terrified of assassins, and retreated ever deeper into his palace, never sleeping in the same room twice. When he travelled he did so incognito. Power passed to his ministers and eunuchs and by the time he died, travelling anonymously around his newly conquered provinces, he was emperor in name only.

HAPPINESS AND UNCHANGING NEEDS

Moral logic, and the interdependence of rulers and ruled, help to explain why ideas of good power have been so consistent across time and space. But the other explanation for the ubiquity of these ideas is that the needs of human communities have changed relatively little. Despite longer lives, greater wealth and greater freedom, there has been relatively little change in how people want to live (and the ideas of philosophers and prophets from more than two thousand years ago, including Buddha, Jesus, Confucius and Lao Tze, have not been superseded, or rendered obsolete).

The philosopher Robert Nozick once asked how the same good life could ever be right for a human race composed of people as different as Marilyn Monroe and Albert Einstein, Ludwig Wittgenstein and Louis Armstrong. Any single view of the good life, he argued, and certainly one imposed by the state, must inevitably be oppressive. The best that we can hope for is a society in which everyone is given as much freedom as possible to define the good life for themselves. The role of the state is therefore to expand this realm as much as possible, partly through guaranteeing the order which makes choice possible and partly through putting in place the legal and other means for people to shape their own lives. Jeremy Bentham reached a roughly similar conclusion as he developed the theory of utilitarianism. 'The request which agriculture, manufacture and commerce present to governments', he wrote, 'is as modest and reasonable as that which Diogenes made to Alexander: "stand out of my sunshine". We have no need of favour. We require only a secure and open path.' Subsequently, this has become the defining spirit of modern liberalism.[39]

The idea that human needs are infinitely varied, and that the mark of a civilization's progress is the degree to which people are free to make their own lives, is undoubtedly compelling, especially given states' past propensity for oppression. But it explains surprisingly little about why states take the shape they do, or what free people actually ask of their states. The principle of individual choice sits precariously on the uneven surfaces of daily life where people's choices are intimately interconnected. Many freedoms, like the freedom to travel, or to borrow money safely, are utterly dependent on states' ability to impose rules. Daily well-being rests on our confidence that risks such as crime or epidemics are handled collectively, since there are few credible ways for them to be handled by individuals alone. More subtly, much of our day-to-day freedom depends on how well states have socialized other people, made them law-abiding, tolerant of strangers, or literate. And if it is right that people should be free to choose their own lives and share in decisions that affect them, it follows that people should have some influence on each other's choices rather than being seen as self-sufficient atoms.[40]

The consistency over time of thinking about the responsibilities of government reflects a simple truth which points in a very different direction from Robert Nozick. People's basic physical needs for food, shelter, water and safety are universal (and missing for much of the world's population). When poor people are empowered to make claims on the state these are the things they usually demand first. Even once basic biological needs have been met, perceptions of the good life have differed little across very different times and very different places. The meanings generated by cultures are limitless, and often appear divergent. Yet all that we know from history, anthropology and psychology suggests that although the variety of human aspirations is vast, it is neither infinite nor random. There are consistent patterns in what people want, and in what tends to make them happy, and these correlate closely with the responsibilities of the state for protection and welfare.

These factors are now well attested by social science,[41] with the help of extensive cross-national and time-series analyses of well-being based, among other things, on surveys asking people how contented they are with their lives.[42] This data points to a limited number of needs and wants that have shaped the behaviour of billions of people in very diverse societies. I have already mentioned some of the most basic ones, which give shape to the ways in which states have legitimated themselves – the needs for material goods, health, protection and a benign environment.

Other near universal needs are less directly linked to the responsibilities of states, but these too help to explain why ideas of service are so consistent. One is the need for family. Throughout history the great majority of people have chosen to live in families. Their shape has varied hugely. They have sometimes been extended, sometimes nuclear, have sometimes combined three or more generations, and sometimes involved polygamy and polyandry. But the family unit has provided emotional sustenance and support of many different kinds – far more than any other institution.[43] Another is the need for community. People need to live in society, in contact with friends and acquaintances. Social connections support our health, our resilience to shocks, and our sense of self. For most people isolation is deeply damaging, which is why the village, town and city have always pulled people in. Beyond the family, the community provides recognition, meaning and opportunities. Like the family it can at times oppress and divide, but it provides the order that we need to have a fair chance of thriving.[44]

Spiritual needs are also near universal across cultures and times, as are the tensions between the spiritual dimension of life and the ties of family and community. The great prophets often began their careers by rejecting their families and friends. But a spiritual understanding of transcendence, of connectedness, and awe in face of the universe, has been made manifest in the churches, temples and mosques that are found at the heart of every community. These symbolize the search for fundamental truths that lie behind the clutter of daily life (as the medieval Christian mystic Meister Eckhart said, God is not found in the soul by adding anything, but by a process of subtraction), and there are strong correlations between adherence to a religion and reported life satisfaction.[45]

Finally, there is evidence of a consistent need for what can loosely be called autonomy, or self-rule: the absence of external powers that dominate us. This is not a modern invention; it seems, rather, to be part of our make-up. There is strong evidence that people low in hierarchies suffer from greater stress than those at the top, and that this in turn reduces their life chances.[46] Exercising a wider span of control makes us feel more alive. This does not imply that everyone wants to invent for themselves a new identity and to treat their life as a work of art in a world of limitless freedom. Autonomy is better understood in negative terms – what we want is the absence of bullying and bossing. The pervasiveness of revolts against oppression throughout history, and more recently the ability of democracy to take root in cultures as varied as Taiwan and India, Turkey and Mexico, confirms that this hunger for autonomy is not a peculiar concern of the liberal West.

The work of the Swiss theorist Bruno Frey[47] and his colleagues suggests that the exercise of sovereignty is good for us: more direct forms of democracy can make people happier, partly because the very act of participation and engagement is valuable, partly because in democracies the actions of governments are more likely to be aligned with what people want. The same patterns appear true in the workplace where satisfaction and control are closely linked; as Marx wrote in the *Grundrisse*, the problem of industrial society is not too much work but too much work which is controlled by others – truly free and fulfilling work is work undertaken for its own sake, free from 'external urgencies'.

HUMAN NEEDS AND THE ROLE OF THE STATE

That people's needs are consistent across time and space does not automatically justify any role for the state. But the consistency of human needs explains much about the shape states have taken, as does the fact that states have become fairly competent at helping people to live a good life. Some needs depend very directly on states. Safety depends on police forces and regulations, health on publicly regulated clean water and publicly funded doctors, prosperity on intelligent monetary policies, and a benign environment on public spending and rules to outlaw pollution.

Even the most intimate relationships can be influenced by states. North Korea organized mass weddings; the state of Utah permitted polygamy; and a clutch of European countries has now legalized same-sex partnerships. Elsewhere, the design of benefits and tax systems has undoubtedly influenced relationships, and some countries, such as Finland and Denmark, have seen quite sharp turnarounds in marriage rates and birthrates that are at least partly explicable as the results of public policy.

Governments can also have some influence, albeit usually indirect, on free time and leisure, gardening and membership of clubs, all of which correlate with reported happiness. The strength of communities can be strongly influenced by planning policies, the positioning of roads and the organization of schools. Governments cannot make people believe in a deity, but the spiritual life can be assisted by allowing religions to function, giving them economic advantages and respect. Governments cannot directly shape people's sense of sovereignty, but it can be influenced by constitutions and by the climate of freedom and tolerance they encourage.

In all of these areas the balance of power and responsibility between states and their societies is open to constant argument. For example, the care of souls was a collective responsibility for the Catholic Church in the Middle Ages, but is now much more of a private concern in societies like Britain where religious adherence is both weak and fragmented. The care of bodies was a private concern then, but is now generally treated as a public responsibility. Families used to be seen as entirely private, but have been increasingly subjected to public action to protect children, punish domestic violence, or teach parents how to look after their children. Egged on by television, families have also happily made themselves publicly visible in ways that would have seemed bizarre to past generations.

Most political leaders understand the importance of these fundamental and ever-present needs almost intuitively. Yet one of the stranger features of the twentieth century was the oblivious disregard by two of its dominant ideologies – communism and pro-market neoliberalism – of these shapers of well-being. Marxism-Leninism was wilfully hostile to the family and spiritual life, and at best negligent towards the environment. Although Marx's ideal (described in *The German Ideology*) was a future in which '[I may] hunt in the morning, fish in the afternoon, rear cattle in the evening, criticise after dinner, just as I have a mind, without ever becoming hunter, fisherman, herdsman or critic',[48] in some societies Marxist-Leninists sought to obliterate not only the family, community and the environment, but also religion and material provision.

Liberalism has often been suspicious of the pull of the archaic ties of community, god and family, and capitalism has for two hundred years been attacked for its spiritual hollowness, and its tendency to squeeze time and energy out of the family and community and into work and commercialized leisure. The single-minded emphasis on material prosperity of the neoliberalism of the 1980s and 1990s limited its influence as a political project, and made it necessary for the Thatcherites and Reaganites to tie it, often uneasily, to a socially conservative stance on the family, nation and religion.

Both ideologies promised the good life, but through a fundamental deception. Communism promised the achievement of human freedom and potential, but asked that these be suspended in the interim. The market economy, by contrast, as Adam Smith argued eloquently in *The Wealth of Nations*, has always been based on the deceitful nature of an invisible hand that can work wonders in creating prosperity but also encourages people to labour in order to gain essentially worthless things, 'trinkets and baubles' as he put it, that do not make them happy. Neither side had much to say about service. Instead their intellectual energies were devoted to ferocious arguments about means (rights and ownership, markets and constitutional processes) rather than ends.

THE FAMILY AS METAPHOR

I have described the moral structure of a state's duties to its citizens, and suggested that these are grounded in universal needs, reaching back well beyond the origins of the state. Here I want to suggest an even more basic origin for these duties. The claims made by states mainly derive from ideas about the family. What this means has changed as families have become more equal, open and democratic. But our basic metaphors and mental frameworks come from the parental role of protection, support and care, and the most basic responsibility we ask of leaders is that they exercise a duty of care.

This is easily apparent at a superficial level, since the language of states has always borrowed freely from the language of family life. States are founded by fathers of the nation; patriots are believers in the fatherland; the citizens form a brotherhood; rulers can be Uncle Joe (Stalin) or a Big Brother; the sons and daughters of the nation are sent to war by Uncle Sam while Mother Russia and Mother India suffer with and nurture their people. Ancient China was thought of as *Kuo-chia*, a family state.

But the links go deeper. Family relationships are the primordial unconscious origin of many metaphysical ideas – who am I, where do I belong, how should I behave, and whom should I obey? Even in the most advanced societies, families continue to be where children learn most about morality: how to share; what constitutes a just distribution; who has power; who has rights. The clues to any society's relationship with power can be found in the sometimes visible, sometimes hidden, curriculum that is learned in the family and in childhood, imbibed with the mother's milk in an institution that, like the state, protects the weak but formalizes their submission to the strong.

These links between families and states become even more apparent if we look at the close correlation between the limited number of family forms – extended or nuclear, egalitarian or authoritarian – and the equally limited number of forms of governance. According to the work of Emmanuel Todd,[49] communism thrived best in those areas where egalitarian family forms predominated, nationalism in areas where the authoritarian family was the norm. England's individualist market economy, and its assertive democratic culture, drew on family structures in which children were rather more independent (albeit of a still-dominant father), but not equal. German families were traditionally authoritarian, based on the submission of children to the father's will, and indifferent to equality. The Russian family 'combines equality and discipline, parity between brothers and obedience to the father'. There are similarities between the kin structures of China and Russia – a strong feeling of brotherhood, a great capacity to assimilate, and a refusal to believe that people are fundamentally different. In regions with authoritarian family structures and inequality between children, such as Ireland, Belgium and Japan, by contrast people are more likely to see differences where they don't exist.[50]

The imagination of states is not comprehensible without some grasp of the family ideals that they have in mind. Indeed, these various traditions have crystallized into the dominant visions of the family that shape much of the political landscape of the western world. George Lakoff has shown how much of the morality of states and politicians is comprehensible only in the light of idealized family forms.[51] These do not correspond to actual families; nor is there any clear evidence of a link between styles of parenting and the ideologies that children adopt. But they provide the underlying glue for the political positions people adopt, and that states then try to embody, and they provide the metaphorical framework through which the primary colours of vernacular politics are organized.

Conservative politics derives from many different intellectual traditions that have, respectively, advocated a strong order to rein in innately evil human nature or small government to let people get on with their lives without interference, or markets to let people trade freely or nations to embody identity and belonging. But these all fit together in the underlying model of a strict father in a nuclear family taking responsibility for protecting the family, setting rules and enforcing them alongside a mother responsible for care. Through respect and obedience children learn self-discipline and self-reliance, and essential truths about the world that, in time, enable them to become independent. Competition then rewards the hard-working and self-disciplined whose pursuit of self-interest benefits everyone, and it is through competition that we learn who has been moral and self-disciplined. In this view wrongdoing should be punished, and not just because of the deterrent effects of punishments; indeed, it is immoral for anyone with authority not to do so. By the time children reach adulthood their characters have been formed, and are unlikely to be reformed. But thereafter the right combination of incentives and punishments can achieve almost anything. Power and authority exist in a hierarchy (from God through leaders to adults to children and, ultimately, to nature). Each layer of the hierarchy has responsibilities to those lower down, just as a parent has responsibilities to a child. The central metaphor in this morality is moral strength – being upright, standing up to evil forces, and cultivating toughness.

Progressive politics has drawn on a similarly diverse set of currents, from arguments that benign human nature needs to be set free from restraints, through advocacy of a transforming state to achieve equity, to claims that the marginalized need to be directly empowered. Again, however, all of these fit together in, and are explained in part by, an idea about families – in this case the idea of a nurturing family, based on love and empathy. Through love and nurture children become self-disciplined and responsible, and empathetic to others. Obedience grows from respect, and communication. Children need to be protected from harms – crime, drugs, or toxic chemicals – but they are also taught to question, and learn that two wrongs do not make a right. The goal of life is to be fulfilled. Nurturing is internalized into the child, who becomes generous and supportive of others. Morality is founded on empathy.

These contrasting visions help to explain why otherwise incompatible elements tend to cluster together in political programmes: conservatism's love of the strong state alongside hostility to regulation; progressive politics' support for rights to abortion combined with active state intervention to prevent child abuse. They also help to explain competing governing philosophies. The conservative view sees the state as a strict, tough but caring father; the progressive view sees the state at its best as a nurturing mother. At root the conservative view prioritizes protection, justice as punishment for the wicked rather than as a means to achieve outcomes, and truths that are fixed and eternal. The progressive view prioritizes welfare, judges justice by the outcomes it achieves, and generally regards social and moral truths as provisional discoveries.

Political ideas that appear rational and sophisticated are often built out of simple emotions. This is both their power and their danger. The simple emotions include care for friends and family; fear of violence; sadness at the suffering of loved ones, and each of these can motivate the very best actions. But political concepts – and institutions – achieve much of their traction by focusing and channelling these simple emotions in other directions. They work through extension and metaphor, until often the sources of the ideas are quite unrecognizable, as otherwise decent people kill, maim or torture in the name of love of friends or family. Many studies of genocide and war have confirmed this: the first steps on a moral slide are often guided by the best intentions of ordinary people wanting to protect their families, advance freedom, or achieve the brotherhood of man.

5

The State as Possession

'Most of the time the things that benefit a prince harm his city,
while the things that benefit the city harm the prince.'

Machiavelli

Election nights can be moments of great drama, when powerful people are subjected to an unpredictable vortex of anger and hope, resentment and calculation. In the most exciting ones the governing parties are humiliated at the polls. Usually, soon after the loser concedes defeat, the victorious new leader comes to wave from the balcony or a stage, bathed in the glow of electric lights and the adoring screams of the crowd, before being pulled into a revolving door of television interviews. The script is usually the same: he (it usually is) talks about how humbled he feels; about the great honour of being able to serve the people; about how he will serve all the people, including those who voted for the other side. All around the adrenaline of victory courses through people's veins like a drug.

The next morning another script takes over behind the scenes. A blitz of phone calls begins. A new team moves into government offices, almost like a *coup d'état* (in the USA several thousand political appointments are made immediately after a Presidential election victory, including ambassadorships and regulators). The new ministers and advisers are fawned over by anxious and obsequious officials. The party funders begin to get their payback; party loyalists get the jobs they have been waiting for; and the wheels start turning that in a few months or years will deliver the vested interests their laws and subsidies.

Every democratic government shares this ambiguous character, and is simultaneously a servant of the many and a servant of the few. All governments have incentives to reward most the people who can do most to keep them in power, with tax cuts and subsidies, legal protections and privileges. In the words of the economist Douglass North: 'In some cases this means that the government is, in effect, a kleptocracy; in other cases it means that the government will cartelise economic activity in favour of politically influential parties.'[1] Either way the public's interests come second.

These deals and paybacks are reminders of the state's history as a private possession of predatory rulers. Many states have identified with predators – the wolf in Rome, the lion in England, the eagle in America and Germany. Some of the public titles used by states have frozen private roles from the past, like the terms 'Privy Council' and 'Privy Seal'. 'Marshal' meant the keeper of the royal mares; 'constable' referred to the keeper of the royal stables – and all monarchs fought against the rest of their governments to channel money for their own purposes.[2] In Britain public servants are still formally described as servants of the crown (the government describes itself as HMG: 'Her Majesty's Government'), in practice answering to the current political rulers rather than, as in other traditions, to the people.

When Karamzin, the author of one of the first multi-volume histories of Russia, was asked to summarize its message he was able to do so in only one word: 'Voruiut' (they steal).[3] Its rulers were little more than thieves, shameless in their use of the state to enrich themselves. States were, and still are, fought over precisely because their powers are so useful. Even stable democratic states reflect deals and settlements between conflicting groups of families, classes and ethnicities that usually continue, albeit sublimated into new forms. In societies riven by communal conflicts great energies are directed to the capture of state power so that it can be used to settle scores.

Many recent rulers revelled in their own variants of this distinction between insiders and outsiders, us and them. Nationalist leaders rarely pretended to represent the minorities unlucky enough to be inside their borders. Class warriors brought their own divides. Lenin wrote that 'what is ethical is what serves the interests of the proletariat', and rejected the idea that the state might have any duties towards others (including most of the peasants).[4] Even liberal democratic political theory justifies a not dissimilar stance: if politics is seen as a competition between parties and interests, the victors are entitled to the spoils (subject only to a few legal protections for minorities).

One of the common cyclical patterns in Chinese history has some parallels in modern democracies. It starts with a new dynasty conducting a census to determine tax obligations. Later, local elites struggle to secure tax exemptions, whether through 'the destruction of tax registers, official connivance or legal falsification',[5] which inevitably results in ever higher burdens on the remaining taxpayers (particularly the peasantry). Ultimately, when the burden is unbearable, the peasants revolt and the dynasty collapses. Similar accretions of special privileges in modern states are equally likely to lead first to stagnation and then to revolt.

Charles Tilly has described the emergence of the modern state in Europe between the sixteenth and the nineteenth centuries very much as a story of capture:

across much of the continent bourgeois landlords were expelling hunters, fishers, gatherers, herders and householders from their increasingly enclosed properties, merchants were collaborating with officials in freeing food markets from local controls, and employers were liberating themselves from customary forms of hiring and payment; government officials not only supported these efforts but also expanded taxation, conscription and registration of populations . . . all these changes generated scattered attacks: pulling down of enclosures, killing of forbidden game, sniping at forest guards, mobbing of tax collectors, driving off census takers, roughing up of police and more.[6]

But because centralized, organized and cohesive minorities will always defeat disorganized majorities these stratagems to expand state power generally worked. Marx characterized the state as the executive committee of the bourgeoisie. He may have underestimated the autonomy of the state, but he had identified a fundamental truth: that behind the neutral, abstract language of governance, law was serving a minority class interest. The crudest sign of this capture is the diversion of resources into the pockets of the privileged. A third of the average Kenyan's daily budget today has to be spent on bribery[7] and corruption is one of the factors most closely associated with public unhappiness in comparative surveys of national well-being.[8] But privileged flows of money from taxpayers to particular groups are also common in societies without overt corruption, for example in the form of subsidies and protections for industries like aerospace, nuclear power and agribusiness (and, some might add, the remarkable capture of arts spending by elites).

Machiavelli exaggerated for effect in the epigraph at the beginning of this chapter, but even the best-intentioned leaders are likely to have interests at variance with the people they serve, interests which will divert them from their moral duties. They may wish to give favours to their friends and their supporters. They may want to give in to the temptations of corruption, the money and sex that power makes available, using their position to satisfy their own desires. They may subordinate the public interest to their private interest. They may want to hide the truth about their own failings, mistakes and internal conflicts.

Several traditions of political theory have argued that this is the only meaningful prism through which to understand politics. Writing in the turbulent interwar years in Germany, the influential theorist Carl Schmitt described the state as at heart about the conflict between friends and enemies. No political order, he wrote, could be universal, however liberal, universal and democratic its claims. It had to take sides. Libertarian philosophers like Ludwig von Mises and Bertrand de Jouvenel presented modern states as direct descendants of the near-criminal predatory enterprises that bequeathed to history such marvellous monuments as the Kremlin, Versailles or the Taj Mahal,[9] even if in the twentieth century they were more likely to be captured by working-class movements and mass parties than by imperial dynasties.

As we have seen, states are captured because they control surpluses. These surpluses make art and civilization possible, but they also breed corruption, since they offer a short-cut to wealth. Spoils spoil. Large surpluses in capital cities tend to corrupt politics since the games that are played in and around rulers' courts and their modern equivalents provide a more direct route to wealth and prestige than hard work. For the same reason the existence of spoils encourages war. Big states with large surpluses at the centre generally found it hard to rein in ambition, and so became a danger to their own people. From the twelfth century to the nineteenth, when Germany was divided into principalities, duchies and kingdoms, the Germans participated in only 13 wars, compared to Denmark's 15, Sweden's 24, Austria's and Russia's 40, France's 42, Britain's 44 and Spain's 48. The small countries saw little advantage in war. Within a century of unification, however, Germany had passed through war with Denmark, Austria, France and then two world wars, urged on by a succession of war-hungry leaders.[10]

The dynamics of power in autocracies revolve around surpluses, and how they are shared out with a relatively small group, including the leaders of the military, the civil service, and those in charge of the communications and information infrastructure, and the economic commanding heights. Everyone within the ruling circle has an interest in keeping that circle as small as possible (Ferdinand Marcos, the Philippines' ruler in the 1970s and 1980s, eventually lost power because so many members of the elite had been excluded from this magic circle), and in poor countries, autocrats face acute personal political risks if they dissipate resources away from the powerful few to the powerless many.[11]

Autocracies are relatively straightforward cases. Most seek to extract as much wealth from their people as they can get away with, and claim only a thin veneer of service. Some, like Sani Abacha, who ruled Nigeria between 1993 and 1998, become so consumed by greed that even their supporters feel the need to depose them. (It is widely assumed that Abacha's mysterious death at the hands of a prostitute was as much the result of poisoning as the equally mysterious death a few weeks later in prison of his arch-rival Abiola, who posed just as much of a threat to the ruling military elite.[12]) over a decade later, despite the trappings of democracy, fewer than one in ten Nigerians believe that their country is ruled by the will of the people.[13]

In democratic polities the differences of interest between rulers and ruled are more subtle. Ultimate power rests with the voters, who can eject their rulers, and this tends to foster dynamism, since parts of ruling groups will often see advantage in making an alliance with an excluded group (much of the history of democracy involves just such shifts – for example when the British Tories reached out to working-class voters in the nineteenth century, when the Labour Party reached out to the middle classes in the 1990s or, more recently, when the US Republicans reached out to Hispanics). But even in democracies similar patterns of capture are common. The arithmetic of electoral systems guarantees that very large minorities, and often a majority, are ruled by people they did not vote for.

Even when states try to serve all the people some have to command others, to take taxes from unwilling citizens and to impose punishments. There have been many attempts to blunt this sharp inequality, for example with juries made up of ordinary citizens and term limits for leaders. At the extreme it is possible to have leaders so weak that they are almost indistinguishable from the led, and some republics and communes have sought to recapture what they saw as a lost Elysian equality. But even in such societies, and even in brief periods of revolutionary fervour, some hold specialized offices responsible for exercising power over others, while others receive and obey. This is why the ideal of service is always vulnerable to compromise or betrayal.

Within all states, however democratic they may seem, there are also likely to be privileged channels of access to power. These can be seen most clearly at the points of connection between systems, where organized interests seek to entrench advantages, often away from the public gaze. Political and party finance is one key to bypassing the electorate. Follow the money and you soon discover where influence lies. (The US tax code is a good case in point, full of special provisions for strong interests. An extreme example is the special provision made for just one family, the Gallo family of winemakers.[14]) Even political parties that ostensibly represent the poor can become reliant on the rich. The US Democrats are now heavily dependent on the ultra rich and have more electoral support among millionaires than the Republicans. Barely a quarter of the funding for the 2004 Kerry Presidential campaign came from small donations of $200 or less. In the UK, funding for the Labour Party has rapidly shifted from trade unionists to business leaders, while across Europe a succession of centre-left parties have received funding, sometimes secretly, from wealthy businesses.

Many of the scandals of the democratic world – including those that tarnished the reputations of Mitterrand and Bettino Craxi of Italy in the 1980s, Kohl, Gonzalez and John Major in the 1990s, and Lula of Brazil in the 2000s – have revolved around finance, fuelled by the escalation of political funding not just in the US (where the last Presidential election involved spending of almost $4 billion) and Europe but also in countries like Brazil and India. Tony Blair's first crisis in office came when the Formula One racing tycoon Bernie Ecclestone gave the ruling Labour Party £1 million – no one could believe that this signalled a sudden political conversion and was unconnected to the struggles underway on banning cigarette companies from sports sponsorship. In later years the scarcely concealed sale of peerages to wealthy party donors, and the appointment of the party's top donor – Lord Sainsbury – to ministerial office, did little to restore the British public's confidence.

In the US the beneficiaries of the intimate ties between money and politics have successfully resisted campaign finance reform, and twisted the system into one where it is now virtually impossible for anyone other than the rich or the patronized to stand for high office. Roosevelt had warned in 1936 that 'Government by organized money is just as dangerous as Government by organized mob': what would he say today?

The control of public and media space is another short-cut through which private power tries to capture the state, since it provides the one resource – attention – which is most valuable for elected politicians. Media magnates like Beaverbrook, Hearst and Murdoch can, with skill, exercise huge power over politicians hungry for attention and validation. The apotheosis of this trend has been the career of Silvio Berlusconi, who, with cavalier disregard for inconvenient laws, used the media and business as the base for an assault on state power, and then used state power to reinforce his dominance in the media (and, as he said to his adviser, Marcelle Dell'utri, 'if something is not on television it doesn't exist').

Any interest which monopolizes a scarce asset such as airtime, capital, specialized labour or the approval of a larger foreign state, can leverage that into extra power. Equally, any interest that is particularly dependent on state largesse is likely to work hard to protect its privileges: extractive industries, export industries, arms industries and regulated utilities all tend to be eager to find an inside track.

The importance of these links can be gauged by the numbers of lobbyists and intermediaries employed to manage them, specialists in trying to capture the state. Most work secretly, and when their works are exposed their clients suffer. Their job is to skew the terms of law and regulation and to shape the public agenda – how society thinks about itself, its tasks and choices. Subtle tools can be used to shape climates of opinion (sponsoring research, financing foundations and universities), or to head off threats (committees that take minutes and last for years, cosmetic consultations, hired experts to muddy the water on controversial issues, not to mention more basic strategies like the selective privatization of public issues).[15] When brought out into the open the characteristic arguments they make on behalf of the interests they serve take the form 'despite everything you need us more than we need you' (reminding us of the comment attributed to Fidel Castro that the only thing worse than being exploited by multinational corporations is not being exploited by them).

These are some of the ways that elected leaders come to be captured. But they also live with a more basic division from the people they serve in that they are bound to prioritize their prospects for survival and re-election.[16] Indeed, many of the moral dilemmas of modern leaders revolve around this issue: how far should they go to retain power? Should they accept illegal payments (like Mitterrand); authorize burglaries (like Nixon); arrest and put on trial their potential successors (like Mahathir in Malaysia); or renege on their promises (like most)?

The imperative of survival can be all consuming. For political parties it easily becomes an end in itself rather than a means to other ends, and some of the longest surviving political parties (like Walpole's Whigs in early eighteenth-century Britain or the Japanese Liberal Democrats in the second half of the twentieth century) have become little more than vehicles for re-election, changing their own social allegiances according to circumstance, and redefining their primary allegiances, which usually correlate with their sources of funding. One British Labour minister commented in the late 1990s that his party, which had been created to serve the poor but had become ever more dependent on wealthy donors, was 'intensely relaxed about people getting filthy rich', reminding one of Groucho Marx's comment that of course he had principles, and 'if you don't like these ones I have plenty more'.

So political leaders face a constant challenge. To survive they need to be able to present themselves simultaneously as loyal servants of their core constituency and as servants of the public and the nation as a whole. George W. Bush, for example, has had to present himself both as a committed champion of the Christian Right and as a man of the mainstream. Naturally the two may pull in opposite directions, and part of the skill of the politician lies in obscuring the tensions (and avoiding the problems faced by a German Social Democrat leader, whose description of foreign investors as 'locusts' made it from a party meeting into the mainstream media). This is not always a matter of malevolence or deceit, though many of the methods used can be unethical. The craft of holding complex and fractious societies together involves guile: leaders have to appear to give more to their supporters than they really do; they have to learn how to divide and rule; how to cover over imperfections with inflated rhetoric; how to galvanize group identity against enemies, particularly when times are hard; how to broadcast achievements, however minor; how to cover up internal divisions and uncertainties; and how to cultivate ambiguity where interests and ideals are irreconcilable.

Seen in this light there is less of a break between dictatorships and monarchies on the one hand and democracies on the other. In both there is a gap between those with power and those without, even if the gap may be much diminished in democracy. In both the rulers need at least some popularity, and to win the love of the people, even if democratic leaders are both less loved and less hated – and less likely to be the object of exuberant rapture or terror than Stalin, Mao and Hitler were.

Both democracies and dictatorships draw on the public aspiration for harmony and unity. This aspiration fuels nationalisms. It lies behind the communist brotherhood of man and the feminist sisterhood, and inspired the Swedish social democratic *folkhemmet*, which portrayed society as the people's home, and the contemporary aspiration of many young Muslims for a return to the caliphate or Hindu politicians' advocacy of a utopian 'Ram-raj'; all embody this mystic dimension of politics. Yet, the division of labour between rulers and ruled makes some tension unavoidable, and has led many traditions, particularly progressive ones, to experience moments of profound disenchantment as their leaders appeared to betray, to be co-opted or to serve themselves rather than the cause.

For the officials who run the state machine another set of divisions and inequalities come into play. Officials may be as keen to capture state power, or to share in surpluses, as the authorities they ostensibly serve. Many emperors fought battles for power as well as money with their own officials. The Persian monarch Chosroes I in the sixth century CE was reputed to have said that a kingdom would only thrive if its ruler could curb his officials' rapacity and allow farming and crafts the room to flourish and thus generate the taxes on which the state depended.

The etymology of the names for officials retains the pretence that they are only advisers and implementers of their masters' commands: the word 'mandarin' comes from the Sanskrit *mantrin*, an adviser; the word 'vizier' came from the Arabic *wazir*, literally the carrier (one who carries the burden of office). In a modern civil service there is supposed to be a clear distinction between the role of officials who advise and implement, and elected ministers who decide.

But all real bureaucracies are adept not only at advice but also at decisions and actions, and sometimes at conspiracy. Sir George Murray, the head of the British Treasury in 1908, wrote on Treasury headed notepaper to a leading opposition politician (the former Prime Minister Lord Rosebery) inciting him to oppose his own Chancellor's budget. In one letter he described his minister, Lloyd George, as his 'Welsh goat, who feeds happily out of my hand'.[17] Every official cadre that claims to act in the public interest also serves its own interests, even if only subconsciously. De Tocqueville wrote that unless they were bent to the ruler's will bureaucracies were 'apt to become a power absolute and apart', and a century later the great English political thinker G. D. H. Cole wrote, at a time when he knew that he was losing the argument, that 'democratic control through Parliament is little better than a farce' and that 'the collective state would be the earthly paradise of bureaucracy'.[18] In the last decades of the twentieth century, 'public choice' theory grew up to challenge that earthly paradise, with an elaborate account of the many ways in which officials might try to maximize their power and money, often behind a veil of public service, and of how they might be held in check.

These accounts of cynical grasping public servants offer only a partial truth. Many of the civil servants who came through Oxbridge in the UK, the École Nationale d'Administration in France and Tokyo University in Japan, saw themselves as servants of a deeper public interest than grasping politicians, and they described themselves, rather like some aristocracies, as stabilizers or shock absorbers against overheated democracy who therefore kept government closer to the true interests of the people.[19]

But there can be little doubt that officials do have interests different both from the public and from political leaders. Four thousand years of subsequent history are prefigured in the reform tablets of Uruinimgina in Sumeria around 2000 BCE, which describe a newly established ruler winning legitimacy by putting to rights a ruling administrative class that had abused its power, stolen donkeys and sheep, given short rations and exacted illegal payments.

The many inequalities that derive from the partial or captured nature of the state and its bureaucracy reinforce, and are reinforced by, inherent biases in the actions of states. One is the bias in favour of order, since order is the common claim of each of the four responsibilities of service described in the previous chapter. To be in favour of order rather than chaos tends to bias states in favour of the powerful, and in favour of old power against insurgents (the exceptions, when states have deliberately sided against order – like Mao's launch of the Cultural Revolution – stand out precisely because they are so exceptional). This bias in favour of order ties states to existing hierarchies. It is why early modern police forces so often protected employers and so rarely protected employees, and why armies generally side with dominant ethnic groups not minorities.[20] Another is the bias in favour of economic inequalities, which derives from the close-knit nature of many elites and the fact that the greatest beneficiaries of any economic system will have the most resources to influence government. Just as important, the resources of greatest value to government (tax revenues, people, information) flow from the very systems that generate these inequalities. Challenging the systems that give states their surpluses invariably involves disruption to these flows and so is another threat to order.

The many 'feedback loops' that reinforce these biases guarantee that inequalities can become deeply embedded. Many survive apparently brusque changes of regime. A good contemporary example is the struggle between competing oligarchs in the Ukraine after the 'orange revolution' of 2004, a popular revolution that turned out to be little more than a supporting chorus for one part of the elite in its battles with others (symbolized when President Yushchenko's son success-fully managed to copyright the political brands that were used during what had appeared to be a popular uprising).

WAR AND CAPTURE

The history of warfare explains much about the nature of capture. One conservative sociologist described the state as 'nothing more, basically, than an institutionalisation of the war-making power'.[21] According to one estimate, between 1500 and the present day the leading states were involved in war for three years out of every four.[22] There have been exceptions, like Ashoka, who renounced war after the carnage of his victory over Kalinga in the ninth year of his reign, or the republic of Siena which Lorenzetti celebrated, whose constitution obliged the rulers to 'conserve the city in perpetual peace and pure justice'. A few rulers, like Ashoka, followed the Buddha's warning that 'to the slayer comes a slayer . . . he who plunders is plundered in turn', and when, a few decades after his death, many of Genghis Khan's descendants adopted Buddhism, the genocidal Mongols were almost overnight transformed into peace-loving herders. Many modern states have done all they could to avoid war.

Very early in their history, however, states appeared that were little more than machines for war. They were fuelled by conquest, incapable of standing still, parasitic on their people and even more parasitic on the peoples they conquered. Their example has coloured much subsequent thinking about the state. Churchill wrote that 'the story of the human race is war, except for brief and precarious interludes there has never been peace in the world and long before history began murderous strife was universal and unending.' He was echoing Heraclitus' comments that 'war is common and conflict is justice' and that 'war is the father of all and king of all'.

Yet the role of states in wars is much better understood as a consequence of capture than as a response to human nature, and it is misleading to see humanity as any more inherently warlike than it is inherently peaceful. There are undoubtedly strong drives to defend against threats, and almost as strong drives to acquire desirable things. Violence is endemic in the poorest and least developed communities. Some studies now estimate a death rate in primitive war of at least a quarter of adult males, and very high murder rates persist in the tribal communities of New Guinea and elsewhere.

But full-scale war is not natural: it happens only when there is a material basis for it. There have to be enough people to fight (levels of violence in highly populated fertile valleys were, and are, far higher than in sparsely populated hills), and there have to be things worth acquiring. In simple societies these conditions are less likely. Goods perish and can't be stored. There are fewer positions of rank worth fighting for.

War evolved in tandem with settled, organized power. It is associated with the state, with settled communities, with dense populations and with surpluses. War becomes normal when there are luxuries to win, means of storing them, high ranks to conquer, or no alternative route to achieving growth other than conquest. In medieval Spain, for example, it was said that war was a quicker and more honourable way to wealth than trade. In societies where warriors rule, it becomes common to presume that might is right, and the strong are blessed by the gods. (Thucydides famously reported the Athenians' comment in response to the plea of the Melians for mercy: 'The strong do what they have the power to do and the weak accept what they have to accept.') In extreme cases every part of the state is directed towards predatory war: Genghis Khan and then Timur were so focused on conquest and booty that they cared little about acquiring the skills needed to govern the territories they had conquered. Nazism was a modern form of this pathology, with the subordination of money and politics to conquest, and no vision of domination other than brutal extraction.

Once a state embraces war it succumbs to a logic it cannot control, and to dreams of conquest, domination and expansion (in most empires there could be no greater disappointment for the army than when an ambitious campaign was cancelled). War rarely remains rational for long, and no plan survives contact with the enemy: as Clausewitz showed, wars are fuelled by emotion which always threatens to outrun intent. Hatreds ratchet up in the heat of battle and turn limited engagements into unlimited disasters. Sensible goals succumb to tangled messes. This is why wise leaders treat war as a last resort, and if necessary divert the pressures for war rather than welcoming them. Pericles, for example, ran a succession of minor wars which were enough to satisfy the bloodlust of some of his colleagues without risking escalation. After he died this sense died with him, and Athens plunged into a war in Sicily which led to its destruction.

Groups which capture states turn to war because it serves several purposes at once. The practical demands of war justify expanding their control, from food supplies to information (it must have been apparent to chiefs in the most distant past that as soon as threats had disappeared their authority was likely to wane). War is also attractive because it polarizes: it reinforces people's sense of commitment to the community, and it awakens identities. It is not coincidental that many revolutionary regimes turned quickly to war, diverting the surplus energies they had unleashed – France's many wars after the revolution, the Bolshevik invasion of Poland in 1920, and Iran's promotion of Hizbollah in Lebanon in the 1980s, are all examples of this. The Nazis and Bolsheviks both lived by military metaphors of political war against their enemies, and made the most of a constant sense of threat. Saddam Hussein's ability to survive disastrous wars with Iran and with one of the largest coalitions ever assembled (in the first Gulf War) shows how a climate of war can be exploited to tighten control.

Democracies are not immune to these temptations. One study found that over the last two centuries countries experiencing democratization have been significantly more likely to initiate wars than either autocracies or mature democracies (a tendency that's connected to their hostility to minorities which was mentioned earlier).[23] Mature and stable democracies, by contrast, rarely see the calculus of aggressive war as attractive, and genuinely popular governments rarely feel the need to cultivate climates of fear.

Some states have used their war machines in service to their people. In the Roman Empire the military acted as tax collectors, kept roads open and even built them. The spoils of war supported bread subsidies and work-creation programmes. But these are the exceptions, and more states allowed what should have been a means to become an end, promised too much in order to win their wars, and then had to cope with inflated expectations when the wars came to an end. This is why war so often leads to implosions and revolutions, and why big wars so often consume their makers. The First World War, for example, led not only to revolution in Russia and near revolution in Germany and Italy, but also sowed the seeds for radical reform in Britain (where the promise of 'homes fit for heroes' was reneged on). In the USA it led to acceptance of two of the most important popular demands – prohibition of alcohol and women's suffrage.

The other threat faced by militaristic states is conflict with their own people. Precisely because war so often served the narrow interests of an elite, the allegiance of the people could never be taken for granted. Militaristic states had to inculcate martial virtues and overcome the generally stronger attraction of the quiet life and pleasure. Violence towards strangers had to be encouraged by states, whether through propaganda, force or bribes. Many states used slaves in their armies, and promised them freedom as the reward for service. England in the eighteenth and nineteenth centuries recruited soldiers and sailors through the forced conscription of the press gang. Most modern states used forced conscription; some promised conscripts that if they died they would go to heaven as martyrs; others asked them to make do with the nation's eternal gratitude.

Once conscripted, young men had to be turned into killing machines against their instincts. When firing rates were looked at for men in 400 infantry companies in the Pacific and European theatres of war between 1939 and 1945, it became apparent that no more than 15 per cent had fired even once at the enemy during an engagement, although at least 80 per cent could have fired a shot or thrown a grenade. Bayonet training was one way to overcome this resistance to unnatural killing. Stuffed sacks made realistic imitations of human bodies, and would then be repeatedly attacked until ruthless violence became more of a second nature. Yet even this could carry a high cost. Some soldiers suffering post-traumatic stress disorders from Vietnam turned out never to have fought.

For war to be possible it was equally necessary to cultivate an identity, a firm boundary line between 'us' and 'them' to distract attention as far as possible from the idea that 'us' might be the soldiers and 'them' their officers. The result was the odd geography of hatred found in wars like the First World War. Servicemen who had not left their own country hated the enemy more than those who had fought; women at home were the most ferocious haters of all, and sent white feathers to men they deemed too cowardly to fight. Since it was hard to make the frontline troops hate enough it was better to encourage soldiers to fight for their comrades rather than the nation or a higher cause. This is the common story of real warfare: bravery is more often motivated by friends and comrades than by abstract ideals.

What we see here is a pattern. Wars were until recently generally fought for the few not the many. They happened because states that had been captured by elites sought additional surpluses. But to be won they had to draw on deeper wells of emotion. So hatred built on love, whether love of comrades or family, or love of nation, just as ethnic violence feeds off love of friends and family and the urge to protect or avenge them. In all these cases abstract hate draws on everyday love.

THE DARK SIDE OF THE FOUR RESPONSIBILITIES

In the previous chapter I described the four main responsibilities of the state, and in this chapter I have shown how these have repeatedly clashed with the partial character of real states. But the attentive reader will have noticed that the tension between the state's role as a servant and as a master is more basic than this. For each of the four responsibilities rests on coercion, and can be carried out only by limiting the freedom of the people being governed.

The state's responsibility to protect also gives it rights to conscript or to impose martial law. The responsibility for welfare gives states rights to raise taxes and to intrude into private life. The responsibility for justice gives states rights to imprison and sometimes to execute. The responsibility for truth gives states rights to constrain free speech which fuels hatred or damages children.

It follows that any pure ideal of good power is illusory. Where power is concerned the very things that are good often rest on things that are bad. Freedom, justice and welfare depend on coercion, just as peace rests on violence. This renders any pure identity between the state and people illusory. To serve the people states have to command and constrain the people too, and even if in a wider sense the state is merely the vehicle through which the community polices itself, in the day-to-day work of the state one group necessarily polices another. Much the same is true of any kind of power, including the power of parents in the family who have to discipline their children in their own interests. This ambiguity ensures that no state can ever be wholly good. However pure its ideals its character is bound to be influenced by the coercive means it has to use and by the many ways in which it has to stand against the people it exists to serve.

6

The Self-serving State

'By persuading others we convince ourselves.'

Franciscus Junius

I have become a civil servant three times in my life: in municipal government in London, in the British national government and in the European Commission. Each time I was reminded that in becoming a permanent administrator you have to change the way you think. Ostensibly you become a servant of the public, required to subordinate your political views and your personal prejudices to the greater good. But just like your antecedents in Sumeria and China, Prussia and France you also become part of something altogether subtler: a cog in a machinery that exists in order to exist, a machinery that sees itself as the very basis of an ordered world.

In the last two chapters I showed that all states contain within them a moral purpose of service to the people, and that all are to some degree captured by partial interests. But these two portraits of the state do not yet offer a complete picture. To understand why states behave as they do, we also need to analyse how states serve themselves and how they make sense of themselves.

THE STATE AS UNIVERSAL MACHINE

States are often described as machines. They like regularity and repetition. But they are very peculiar kinds of machines, less like engines or pumps than like computers that were theorized (by Alan Turing) before they were built as universal thinking machines, which could take any input of information and process it in any way. States were made before they were theorized but they have some of the same properties: their common tools of categorizing, measuring, administering and organizing made them an equally universal machine at the service of leaders and communities. They could be used to appease the gods, protect against invasion or to manage food supplies, and over time they have been shown to be adept at a multitude of other purposes, from scientific discovery to global exploration, and from genocide to therapy.

States have done all of these things as ordering machines. This is their inner logic, prior even to their nature as machines of war, and it is the source of their legitimacy, which depends on reducing the risks associated with a capricious environment – channelling irrigation, holding supplies of food to prevent famine, keeping animal predators at bay or reducing HIV infections and flows of illegal drugs.

This ordering mentality is absent from pre-agrarian societies. It seems to be founded in the meeting of the agrarian mind, which in the late Neolithic era was bringing order to landscapes as it learned how to regulate the rhythms of nature, and the literary mind, which was bringing order to beliefs, ideas and stories. The states that thrived were rooted in land, and governed by writing, with rare exceptions like the Inca Empire, which made do with sophisticated means of keeping records but had no script. For most, the ability to write and record in order to collect taxes and reward past loyalties made government possible (and indeed, state bureaucrats can make a fair claim to have invented writing in the records of ancient Mesopotamia). Writing allowed officials to counterpose an abstract law to concrete reality, formal borders to irregular geographies, fixed texts to fluid social facts, and gave states the mission of forcing the world better to approximate to the ideal[1] (while also turning the scribes who had mastered the intricate magic of cuneiform, hieroglyphs and pictograms into a privileged elite).

The main alternative for much of history was nomadism. Nomads often looked in on settled civilizations with a mixture of envy, greed and fear. They were often threatened by the settlers, especially when their population rose (sometimes at great speeds, as in the USA and

Russia during the nineteenth century), but they were also able to threaten; the Goths, Huns, Mongols and Tatars all had military techniques superior to the settled peoples they fought, and they also had a mentality that conferred advantage – the mentality of having less to lose than settled populations whose wealth is stored. Repeatedly the settled tried to buy them off. Huge payments were made by the Roman Empire to keep the Germanic tribes at a safe distance, and by successive Chinese empires to keep the barbarians in their central and north Asian homelands. In England the 'Danegeld' paid to the Vikings at the end of the first millennium CE showed how profitable these protection rackets could be. In the long run, however, the struggle was decisively won by the settled peoples, rooted in the soil and cities, and it was their states that set the pattern for the future. Nomads, both literal and metaphorical, still distrust states, but they have been pushed to the margins and nomadic predatory states survive only in the form of criminal syndicates.

When nomads did conquer states they soon ceased being nomads. Genghis Khan, for example, created the largest empire ever within a few decades but lacked the means to run it. He was advised to invent a Mongol script and to employ a parallel army of scribes and administrators to glue it together. Despite his antipathy to settled civilization he was intelligent enough to understand where his interests lay (and came to rely on the Mongol's highly efficient postal system). After his death, his less capable successors, who had not learned how to read and write, contemplated wiping out all the farmers in northern China as well as the bureaucrats to simplify their task. They were dissuaded by one of civilization's great heroes, Yeh-lu Chu'tsai, who argued that the scribes would be loyal servants of the warrior nomads and would ensure them even more booty and prestige.[2]

So from the earliest times states applied the logic of the written word and number to the messy reality of people's lives. They made sense of their world and their role in it by trying to force the world to fit in with, and abide by, their own perceptions. Those working for states tended to 'see like a state' – mapping, measuring, controlling, planning and perhaps too often seeing people as means rather than ends, and the rough edges of life as problems to be managed or contained.[3] To do this states needed categories. How we describe things is often itself a moral act,[4] and many of the binary categories used by states are unavoidably moral as well as practical: an action is legal or illegal; a person is or is not a citizen; individuals do or don't deserve support. Through these categories states shape how people answer their most simple questions: who am I? how should I behave? what can I become?

Taxation requires inventories of land and wealth and trade; landscapes have to be mapped in terms of their productive potential; the conscription of armies requires lists of young men. Day-to-day order requires that boundaries are settled and not fought over. Citizens need to be squeezed into categories, as taxpayers, welfare claimants, patients or parents, to be assessed and analysed. In this way a complex architecture of knowledge comes to be associated with every state, which in time is internalized by the people who learn to think of themselves as, for example, children or pensioners, deviants or second-class citizens. This architecture is always experienced as at least partly alien by the people being categorized (statistics implicitly claim to represent a deeper truth than anything which people themselves observe), and these categories are contested. For example, the British government created a new category of anti-social behaviour in the late 1990s, with anti-social behaviour orders – ASBOs – to punish such things as drunken violence or graffiti; however, it was a struggle to persuade the police to use this new category, and for some teenagers having an ASBO became a badge of pride.

The categories used by states often draw on pre-existing boundaries – between men and women, adherents to the orthodox religion and others, members of different ethnic or linguistic groups. But they then give them added force.[5] Indeed, it is precisely because states can reinforce these boundaries that battles for state power in societies riven by religious or ethnic divisions can be so intense. There is simply more at stake. In Beirut in 1975, where cars were stopped at random for their Muslim or Christian occupants to be slaughtered, or in Rwanda in 1994, where Hutus launched their genocide on the Tutsis (and on Hutus who were insufficiently compliant), being on the wrong side of a categorical divide could be fatal.

At other times states redefine the ways people think of themselves in more benign ways. The US Servicemen's Readjustment Act of 1944, better known as the GI Bill, provided grants to cover college tuition and living expenses and helped some 16 million people to think of their future in terms of careers and progression, whereas their parents had been content with just a job and a pay packet. In northern Europe, states nurtured profound beliefs in human and social rights. Similarly, the European Union has worked hard (with only limited success) to encourage Europeans to think of themselves as European citizens, though it has also faced immense challenges in defining exactly who should qualify for this status: how to treat short- or long-term residents, expatriates, refugees, relatives and so on.

When states define categories they change what is politically possible. The USA (before the 1960s) and South Africa (before the end of apartheid) imposed rigid rules defining who was black and white, and what votes, rights, schools or homes they were entitled to. In the short-term, these chained black people to lives of poverty and oppression. But in the longer-term these categorizations transformed very diverse populations into well-organized and self-conscious movements with access to a language and statistics which could then be used to fight for their own interests. Brazil's black former slaves were just as oppressed in a society acutely conscious of its gradations of class and colour but were never subject to such formal repression. Arguably they suffered more in the long-run than their US counterparts because they had been denied the categories they needed to mobilize politically.

This ability to order a society and how it thinks is unique to states, although some religions and social movements have aspired to it. It was present in Sumer and Egypt but was greatly assisted by new technologies of communication and administration, which captured the imagination of rulers and philosophers at the time of the Enlightenment. Benjamin Constant wrote in the early nineteenth century that

the conquerors of our days, peoples or princes, want their empire to possess a unified surface over which the superb eye of power can wander without encountering any inequality which hurts or limits its view. The same code of law, the same measures, the same rules, and if we could gradually get there, the same language: that is what is proclaimed as the perfection of the social organisation.[6]

That perfection is usually elusive; states often despair about how little can be easily codified, and thus made sense of. Mussolini reputedly said that governing Italy was not impossible, merely pointless, and de Gaulle once complained: how can one govern a country that produces 246 different kinds of cheese? Mikhail Gorbachev, recalling de Gaulle's comment, asked how it could be possible to govern a country with 100 minorities (and especially, one of his officials muttered, if there isn't any cheese).

In England the greatest pioneer of the all-seeing state was Sir William Petty, whose books the *Political Anatomy of Ireland* and *Political Arithmetic* (both published in the 1690s) promised to bring scientific rigour to the practice of power. This new arithmetic would make 'a par and equation between lands and labour so as to express the value of any thing by either alone'; money would price everything, including art, power, friends and favour. At roughly the same time his friend John Graunt pioneered the study of 'social numbers' and paved the way for future governments' measurement of births and deaths, diseases and crime.

In some cases this work could be benign. The nineteenth-century statisticians who took Graunt's work into the mainstream of public policy were usually on the side of progress. Quételet realized that the social patterns his statistics uncovered were explicable only as the results of social causes, rather than individual choices or moral virtues. It followed that they could only be addressed through social action. Similarly Charles Booth's pioneering survey of London's poor (published in seventeen painstaking volumes in 1902) was designed to help solve the 'problem of problems' that he had uncovered, not just to describe them. In other ways, too, measurement and categorization could be progressive. The penny post invented by Rowland Hill in 1840 required consistent addressing systems for every building in Britain; half a century later the telephone required consistent numbers for every building too, yet amid this radical standardization new scope was given for an infinite diversity of conversation, care and love.

At other times, however, states' involvement in categorization could be brutal. Without memory it is hard to act, and hard to channel raw anger into collective action. So the first step of the systematic conquerer is to control how people are categorized and identified, as when Edward I of England imposed yellow signs on all Jews, and the Nazis forced Jews to wear the Star of David and gypsies the black triangle. The second step is to obliterate that identity, as Edward did in Wales where he tried to wipe out any vestige of indigenous culture. Some colonial governments wiped out local religions, forbade education or even conversation in vernacular languages, and many nation states subsequently did much the same. Thailand, not often seen as a particularly brutal country, launched a very similar categorical offensive on its southern Muslim minorities after the 1930s, imposing the Thai language, requiring public servants to adopt Thai names, abolishing Muslim courts and forcing children to pray to Buddha (actions which spawned half a century of rebellion and murderous repression).[7]

Some states went much further. In China the first emperor of the Qin dynasty (and first emperor of China) in the second century BCE achieved notoriety for burning books and burying scholars alive (and was admired in an essay written by Mao at the age of eighteen, who agreed that such laws were needed to push a stupid and backward people into becoming lions). Mao's teenage views came to matter. Later he described the Chinese people as a potential work of art, a blank canvas that he could draw on. 'China's 600 million people have two remarkable peculiarities', he wrote:

First of all they are poor and secondly blank. That may seem like a bad thing but it is really a good thing. Poor people want change, want to do things, want revolution. A clean sheet of paper has no blotches, and so the newest and most beautiful words can be written on it, the newest and most beautiful pictures can be painted on it.[8]

And to write anew the slate had to be cleaned. 'What', Mao asked, 'is so special about the Emperor of Qin? He only executed 460 scholars. We killed 46,000.'[9]

In the twentieth century states took categorical redefinition to new heights, recasting whole societies (as Atatürk did by banning the Arabic script, the fez and the veil) and seeking to eliminate whole categories of people – Jews, kulaks, bourgeoisie – and remaking social categories from scratch. The Khmer Rouge warning to city dwellers took nineteenth-century revolutionary fervour to a logical conclusion: 'alive you are no profit to us, dead you are no loss.' (The only book that Saloth Sar, later to become Pol Pot, could remember from his student days in Paris was Kropotkin's *The Great Revolution.*)

None of these moves was greeted passively. Instead every action by states to impose their own categories has been met with resistance. Rebellions often directed their energies to destroying the state's measurements and categories. Legal and tax records were the first target of the English peasants in the great revolt of 1381 (and lawyers were murdered as the rebels made their way through the countryside towards London). The Anabaptists under siege in Munster in the sixteenth century burned all written records of contracts and debts, having moved to a communal food system to survive. In 1877 Enrico Malatesta and his band of anarchists went from town to town destroying the records of the Italian state, and in 1917–18 thousands of Russian peasants took advantage of the chaos around them to burn their landlords' estate books.

Local people have little need of formal records to tell them what they already know. Distant power, by contrast, needs as much secondary information as possible (which is why international institutions have an unlimited appetite for secondary data, often of dubious provenance). Yet the rebels were often themselves victims of the state's knowledge and its fictions. Even when the powerless rebelled against the powerful, they often did so guided by concepts that mirrored those of the powerful, or naïvely assumed that a benevolent ruler was being misled by his venal advisers.

As we have seen, truth has always been a central source of legitimation for states, the authority for authority. Monarchies sought legitimacy in the truth of genealogies and religious approbation. Democracies sought it in natural law, and totalitarian regimes worked hard to create their own truths, whether through the science of eugenics in the case of the Nazis or Lysenkoism in Stalin's case. In each instance states have sought what could be termed 'cognitive coherence' – a logic that connects their account of the world, the legitimacy of their power, and the virtuous nature of their actions.

The state's cognitive coherence doesn't float in isolation from the beliefs of the society it rules. In any community the greater the number of shared beliefs there are the more fluent will be a community's dialogue with itself (and the more sophisticated its hypocrisies, the gap between what is said and what is done). Any state that can produce the categories with which people think will function more effectively. The self-creating state, in other words, secures itself not only by making the world in its image but by making people think in ways that reinforce its own view of the world, for example by making Sicilians think of themselves as Italian citizens, or encouraging young criminals to think of themselves as delinquents in need of rehabilitation. As I will show in Chapter 8, the revolutionary struggles launched to overthrow states in France, Russia and, more recently, Iran were also struggles against just this kind of cognitive coherence – denials of the truths on which the states were founded.

Seen in this light much of the behaviour of states becomes more intelligible. Western political theory has tended to see states as tools for achieving things. They can be servants of the capitalist class in the Marxist account, or of a plural public in the writings of American liberals like Robert Dahl. The theory of representation describes the state as a transmission mechanism that turns beliefs and desires into practical actions. But these views underestimate the degree to which all institutions, and particularly states, serve themselves, and the degree to which their primary purpose is their own growth and survival (Cicero's maxim was *salus rei publicae suprema lex* – the highest law is the security of the state). They are not straightforward servants that can be mandated through commands, manifestos and referendums. Their primary concern is their own integrity, which is symbolic as well as real,[10] and to be legitimate they have had to appear as guardians of deeper truths, to present themselves as natural and permanent, with historic roots, even if they were in fact artificial and recent.

This does not mean that states cannot be moral; rather it means that the good they do arises primarily from features of their environment which make it necessary for them to do good in order to survive. The drive for coherence motivates states to appear moral, but they are themselves amoral. In democracies states have to serve the public in order to survive; likewise, business enterprises in a competitive market have to serve customers if they are to survive. In highly unequal societies states have to serve the elites – or crush them – for the same reasons. This is the key to understanding states' virtues: they are determined by context, and states are neither innately virtuous nor innately evil.

The term 'autopoiesis' has been drawn from the ancient Greek to describe the process by which systems adapt themselves in response to a changing outside environment. Rather than focusing on how systems respond with actions, the theorists of autopoiesis have emphasized how the structure of a system can change.[11] This autopoietic quality is what has made states seek cognitive coherence: states need to make sense to themselves and to others, and in a world governed by the written word, written propaganda and written instructions it is harder to explain obvious contradictions and, more important, to supply administrators and agents with justifications for their actions.[12] Cognitive coherence reinforces the confidence of officials, allies and the public, who may be very distant from the heart of the state, and prone to lose faith in it. It helps to align the actions of the many, and often disparate, arms of the state.

This coherence is not the same as consistency – anyone exercising power may need to be able to hold at least opposing truths in their mind at the same time to function. The opposite of a truth is not necessarily a falsehood: it may be another truth (for example, the statements 'all people are born equal' and 'all people are born unequal'). Cognitive coherence simply means trying to make as much sense as possible even in a sometimes senseless world.

FICTIONS AND LEGITIMATION

Long before the advent of states the earliest leaders killed and hunted and literally led their followers across forests, steppes and deserts. Often their physical strength justified their power.

In a world of states many leaders do nothing comparable. Some still literally lead their people, as Mao did in the Long March (albeit carried in a litter), and as late as 1743 Britain's George II led his troops into battle at Dettingen. But most leaders' power derives from their role, not their physical strength or martial prowess. From early on some of the most powerful emperors kept away from the risks of combat. Pharaohs and Chinese emperors alike were insulated from stray arrows and spears. They spoke rather than fought. The Aztec word for king, for example, was *tlatoani*, which meant 'great revered speaker' in Nahuatl.[13] Ever since, the actions of most leaders have been detached, removed from real life and its dangers. They appear in rituals, sit in meetings, make speeches, and issue directives and commands. Control over words matters more than control over anything more material. All their hopes and achievements have come to depend on others: they need others to do the teaching, the healing, the fighting, the protecting and the producing while they become conductors not players. The best that they can do is to persuade others to recognize them and to do their bidding through the authority they inherit, the words and symbols they wield. When the magic evaporates they are revealed as empty vessels, and there is nothing more pathetic than a leader whose power is melting away, vainly gesticulating while officials try to look the other way.

As James Madison put it, 'all governments rest on opinion'. States appear to be solid, backed up by great buildings, constitutions and armies. But they depend entirely on whether people believe in them. They are material and physical only insofar as their psychological foundations are solid. As a result all states constantly legitimate themselves, seeking to create meaning and recognition for their actions rather than just fear of their force (as the British Prime Minister Harold Wilson put it, 'most of politics is presentation and what isn't is timing'). Their officials and leaders can scarcely breathe out without legitimating themselves. This is a practical as well as a psychological necessity. When a state legitimates itself successfully the costs of achieving its goals will be low; if it fails to persuade others, it has to resort to costly force or bribes. If it fails even to persuade itself, it soon crumbles. All power, therefore, rests on its fictions as much as on its material character, and, as a tangential result, all leaders are vulnerable to the trap of confusing fictions and truths – believing that if only they can find the right turn of phrase or explanation they will solve the real-life problem that lies behind it.[14]

Both in everyday life and in the affairs of state the exercise of power begins as a claim: power is taken. The art of using power is to act as if others will play along. The most impressive dominators dominate by acting as if the game has been set, and others will follow, picking up cues from those around them. Likewise the best leaders start with decisive bold moves (the decisiveness may matter more than the content). These are all confidence tricks in the precise meaning of the words. They sometimes falter, but so long as they go with the grain of other structural biases they usually find enough who are happy to be followers, find comfort in that identity, or simply go along because of inertia or lack of imagination. Machiavelli wrote of Julius Caesar, whose genius lay in knowing just how much power could be grasped with sufficient courage, that he had discovered that 'it is possible to blind the multitude so completely that they fail even to notice the yoke they are placing around their own neck.'

Yet for the leader legitimation is more than a means: it is also an end. There is no solidly founded science for understanding the motives of leaders, or of their followers. It is not in the nature of leaders to allow themselves to be tested and analysed in laboratory conditions. But the evidence that exists suggests that recognition, appreciation and being valued are as important as fear and domination itself, or the pleasure to be found in exercising power. Machiavelli wrote of the desire for prestige and greatness as the motive of rulers, with material instruments as only means to these ends. His world of intensive competition for public recognition, which was itself consciously modelled on that of ancient Rome, is not dissimilar to the media-intensive world of modern democracies. The great seventeenth-century Arabic writer al-Yusi wrote that 'men serve kings out of fear or greed, and fear makes love superfluous'; but he also understood that most princes are unlikely to be satisfied with fear alone, and will also want respect and love.

No ruler likes to be seen naked; nor do they like to believe that they have no clothes. Pierre Bourdieu wrote in his classic study of the French administrative elite that 'no power can be satisfied with existing just as power, that is, as brute force, entirely devoid of justification.'[15] The elite officials he studied were not content with status and authority; they also wanted respect and admiration for the good they had done. Indeed, every leader, and often every state apparatus, has an image of itself and an idealized view of its legacy, which determines much of its behaviour. Understanding this is often the key to explaining the otherwise inexplicable things that they do; it can also be the key to persuading them to act differently.

Legitimacy is about more than symbols. The French bureaucrats won prestige in the 1950s because their methods were successful and because their efficient technocracy contrasted favourably with the petty squabbling of politicians. More recently, facts have been as important as symbols in explaining patterns of trust in government. In the later years of the twentieth century declining trust was often attributed to such factors as the generational changes in values that have fuelled individualism, or higher levels of education. But the available evidence on how trust has changed for public agencies and governments suggests that none of these factors is decisive.[16] Where trust has declined there are usually more immediate reasons – poor performance, lack of moral purpose, failure to explain and failure to admit and rectify mistakes – and there are plenty of examples – ranging from governments in Scandinavia to central banks and police forces all over the world – of organizations that have gained trust. Most were competent at carrying out their core task; open; clear about their public and moral purposes; quick to explain or apologize when things went wrong; and good at talking to the public.

The experience of the US military is a good case in point. In 1975, after the traumas of the Vietnam War, only 20 per cent of young Americans (aged 18 to 29) expressed confidence in the people who ran the military. Twenty-five years later, and after a period of military success, active communication, tough measures to root out discrimination, and clearer moral purpose, a Harvard poll found that 75 per cent of young people expressed confidence in the military leadership. These gains are likely to have been lost during the more morally murky intervention in Iraq when American soldiers were seen around the world tormenting and torturing suspects, but they show that trust is made, not given.[17]

THE SEARCH FOR PERMANENCE

The human mind works more easily with things and categories than with fluid relationships. So states try to look more like things, made up of roles rather than people. Indeed, the more developed the state, the greater the separation between people and roles, where the former are transitory and the latter are permanent. In many societies power descends on the powerful as a mantle or mandate that appears to come from elsewhere, often from beyond the world of people. We see this in a pure form in the discovery of the Panchen and Dalai Lamas in Tibet, who as children are marked out by supernatural signs and powers. Evans-Pritchard described how among the Nyikang in Africa it was believed that a spirit of power resided in the temporal king, and that when the king died it returned to its physical form and had to be transported with an army to defeat the new king. In Evans-Pritchard's words this dramatizes the idea that 'kingship captures the king'.

Among the Shaba in Zaire, a very different metaphor is used to think about power. There people refer to an old saying: *le pouvoir se mange entier* (power is eaten whole). Power is something good, something whole, that transforms its holder after the office of chief has been eaten. Jason Sendwe, the Zairian Luba leader around the time of independence in 1960, was reported to have begun a speech with the phrase '*depuis que j'ai mangé mon pouvoir*' ('since I ate my power'). Power was not seen as something to be captured or imposed but rather as something to be internalized, a property that is then held by the eater.[18]

In all of these examples we see the idea of office as greater than any individual. It is permanent rather than temporary, endowed with mystery, grandeur and wisdom. Something of this idea survives in the initiation rites of the democracies: one of the consequences of the inauguration of an American or French President and the royal affirmation of a newly elected British Prime Minister is that the rituals reinforce the distance of the role, making it seem less prosaic and functional. All leaders seem to grow, even if barely perceptibly, when they step into the role: the office makes the man or the woman. (In de

Jouvenel's words, the leader feels 'an almost physical enlargement of himself . . . Command is a mountain top. The air breathed there is different and the perspectives seen there are different from those of the valley of obedience.'[19])

The mystery associated with roles is all the more necessary in a modern society where the people exercising the most direct power, the ones who can arrest strangers, or consign them to a mental hospital, are never found at the top of hierarchies. Generally they are people of middle or low status, working with strictly delegated authority. Those at the top, even the lawmakers, spend most of their time exercising a much less formal type of power, which depends on influence, forging consensus, making people think in a certain way (and paradoxically, the higher the status of a position, the more insecure it is likely to be, and the more likely it is to be limited to a short tenure).

Often newly elected leaders find the pomp and mystery that surrounds roles objectionable. They see it as symbolizing not the eternal virtues of leadership but the indulgent fantasies of the *ancien régime* and many have followed the example of Kao Tsu, who founded the Han dynasty. Born to a family of peasants, and trained as a police officer under the Ch'in, he saw the elaborate court ritual as foolish and wasteful and abolished it when he came to power. But without the rituals to hold them in order he soon found that his court had descended into drunkenness and disorder. Worse, he felt that he was not being given the respect he deserved. So the discredited rituals were reinstated, along with all of the pomp surrounding the role of Emperor – pragmatic actions which led to 2,000 years of magnificence and awe.

All states use ritual, and at one extreme the rituals which are ostensibly the means become ends in themselves. In nineteenth-century Bali there was what Clifford Geertz described as a 'theatre state', where 'power served pomp, not pomp power',[20] and there must have been times when Egyptian pharaohs, Venetian doges and Chinese emperors felt the same, slaves to an elaborate machine of ritual and spectacle. But there is a good reason for the prevalence of ritual, particularly in less democratic societies. Commands are direct and verbal and invite the possibility of disobedience. Rituals, by contrast, are not verbal and therefore have no contraries. They invoke sympathy, feeling and experiencing in tandem with others, so it is sometimes through ritual more than negotiation or law that rulers make harmony and blunt recalcitrant rebellion.[21]

In the modern state visual narratives play some of the same roles – video clips of leaders or broadcasts that tell small vignettes about the leader but work primarily at a subliminal level, associating the leader with deeper emotions of patriotism, care for family or compassion. These achieve their impact not through argument but through sympathy and association.

The extent to which all positions of power rest on fictions – the fictions of roles that are made to appear permanent, and the fictions of legitimations – helps to explain not only why leaders are so often distracted from their duties of service but also why so many succumb to paranoia. Their day-to-day experience may remind them of their very real power to pass laws, order troops into battle, or to confirm or commute death sentences. But this power rests on perceptions more than on material reality. Even an American or French President depends for his real power on the support of Congress or the National Assembly, and risks being a lame duck if he loses it. Prime Ministers in parliamentary systems depend utterly on their parties, and, in coalitions, on other parties. All know that the conditional and immaterial nature of legitimacy makes disbelief and rebellion the natural state of things. The one certainty for every leader is that there are others waiting to show that they can do the job better. Every monarch has feared the assassin, the brother or cousin who might usurp, the lords who might revolt. One historian writes of the long-lived and highly stable Byzantine Empire that,

of the 107 sovereigns that occupied the throne between 395 and 1453, only 34 died in their beds and 9 in war or by accident; the rest either abdicated – willingly or unwillingly – or died violent deaths by poison, smothering, strangulation or mutilation.[22]

This is the point of Hobbes' warning that even the strongest must fear the weakest, and throughout history there have been moments when people stopped going along with habitual obedience, and stopped believing, or pretending to believe. These are the moments when soldiers refuse to fire on a crowd, when they accept flowers pushed into the barrels of their guns (as happened in Lisbon in 1975 when Caetano's wrinkled fascist regime finally crumbled), or the moment in 1989 when Nicolae Ceauşescu, speaking from the balcony of the Central Committee building in Bucharest, realized that the crowd was no longer cowed into synthetic adoration but was baying for his blood: all are variants of the story of the emperor's new clothes. Pascal wrote that 'the power of kings is founded on the reason and the folly of the people, but especially on their folly. The greatest and the most important thing in the world is founded on weakness.' But sometimes that folly dissolves like a fog, and suddenly people see clearly.

Every elected leader fears their equivalent moment, when the voters lose faith or, worse, become contemptuous. At these moments the fiction of their power (and of their character as a winner) begins to unravel, and a spell is broken. Once they have been seen as vulnerable and hunted it is rarely possible to recreate the aura of being a winner. For the same reason once a leader faces an imminent term limit, or an election they are likely to lose, much of their power evaporates: what had seemed solid melts into air.

The conditional character of power explains why rulers have struggled to give their power the appearance of greater stability and permanence through compelling narratives and symbols. Émile Durkheim wrote that 'a collective sentiment can become conscious of itself only by being fixed upon some material object' – the body of the king, a building, a place, a stone or a cross. And so the state, which is by its nature invisible, must 'be personified before it can be seen, symbolised before it can be loved, imagined before it can be conceived.'[23]

When Charles IX took over the powers of the French throne at the age of thirteen, in 1563, he was persuaded by his mother, Catherine de Medici, to engage in a vast tour of the kingdom, taking in a hundred towns and cities over two years, to impress on the people the power and majesty of the new king. Much the same was common practice in Java and in India, where new monarchs toured their kingdoms with huge retinues of elephants, horses and carriages, like animals marking their territory. The modern American President travels with an entourage of well over a thousand, not for utility (they make the business of travel far more complicated) but for effect. Red Square and Tiananmen Square, the huge spaces in the geographical hearts of the Russian and Chinese empires, tell a similar story through their scale. Hitler's Chancellery, built just before the outbreak of the Second World War, was full of vast empty spaces that had to be crossed to reach his office.[24] The mausoleums of Lenin, Mao and Ho Chi Minh are even purer examples of regimes standing in the face of death and decay and proclaiming their permanence. England's Henry III spent two years' royal revenues rebuilding Westminster Abbey. In the ancient world, like peacocks evolving unwieldy plumages to demonstrate their biological strengths, monarchs drove themselves massively into debt by building grand palaces so that others might say: 'if he can afford this degree of waste he must be truly powerful.'

The architecture that results is intended to make rebellion psychologically as well as practically difficult. Power presents itself as beyond the human scale and therefore not subject to resistance by mere mortals: pyramids, temples, triumphal arches, all exist in order to make power appear more enduring, less human. In architecture the ideal was to fashion cities that would perfectly mirror the political order, and thus give it permanence – ancient Rome and medieval Beijing, Luxor and Lahore, colonial New Delhi, modern Brasilia each represented a different vision of governance. In the extreme variants of this logic power becomes wholly other: a dangerous force beyond the world of the human. The ground where the Japanese emperor's shadow had passed was considered dangerous. The crockery he ate on had to be smashed. None could look in the emperor's face. For the same reason once a Spanish monarch had ridden a horse no one else could do so. Touching a Pharaoh or his clothes was thought to risk serious injury unless the right ritual precautions were taken, while in Benin any suggestion that the king did human things like eating, sleeping or washing was a capital offence.

To maximize respect rulers draw on the inherited capital of the past. Napoleon was famously painted crowning himself as Emperor (though he also made clear how little respect he had for the traditions he drew on: 'In no way did I usurp the Crown,' he said, 'I plucked it out of the gutter'). Intelligent leaders have been adept at co-opting whatever they could from previous regimes, using their secondhand symbols and rites to inspire awe and wonder. Stalin portrayed himself as Ivan the Terrible and Peter the Great; Castro adopted some of the character of a classic nineteenth-century Latin American *caudillo* or strongman leader. Mao consciously took on the attributes of the rebel heroes of the Water Margin, then of the poet warrior Chuko Liang, and once in power presented himself as a successor to the first Qin Emperor. Mussolini promised to recreate the Roman Empire, Franco the medieval Spanish crusade for Christ the King; Saddam Hussein likened himself to Sa'd ibn Abi Waqqas, the general who defeated the Persians in 637, and later to Saladin; and Hafez Assad promised a return to the Arab imperial caliphate. The leaders of the Taliban launched their conquest of Afghanistan in 1996 while displaying from the top of a Kandahar mosque a cloak supposedly worn by the prophet Muhammad.

Modern imperialists often co-opted the traditional notions of power and obedience that they found in the territories they conquered. They posed as chiefs themselves and, for example in British India and Malaya, maintained figurehead chiefs and sultans as symbols of continuity. (Paradoxically, this forced the anti-imperialist movements to co-opt the values of their oppressors – those of the Enlightenment, liberty and democracy – and to use these as weapons to dislodge the very people who had brought them, encouraged by imperial dissidents like Allan Hume, the Scot who co-founded India's Congress Party.)

Official language could also help to solidify power, and render dissent impossible and unthinkable. This became particularly important as literacy spread. In the words of the historian François Furet the French Revolution brought a world where 'mental representations of power governed all actions'. Much the same could be said of the USSR in the 1930s or China in the 1960s, where the top positions in the state and party apparatus included specialists in the constant repositioning of signs and words, and an implicit worldview in which it was believed that if only the ideological representations could be perfected, somehow the world itself would adjust in tandem.

The British Empire was less overtly ideological but it too was held together by ideas as much as guns. Like the Soviet empire it rested on a material and military base, but it could not have functioned if millions had not wanted to believe and found meaning through identifying with their official beliefs. These imperial ideologies had many similarities to the civic religion of the US (treating the constitution as a sacred text, saluting the flag), or the national civic religions of nineteenth-century Europe, which tried to ape the physical forms of religions with rituals, parades and great iconic heroes. Like those civic religions the British drew sustenance from strong moral claims. Many of the officials and soldiers who sustained the empire genuinely believed that they were bringing protection, welfare, justice and truth to societies where all of these had been missing. Likewise, many of the leaders and footsoldiers of the Soviet empire passionately believed in the progressive, egalitarian and rationalist ideals they had to espouse. Both groups believed in the inevitability of historical progress in which their state had become a principal actor. Obedience was reinforced by rewards and the threat of punishments; yet to be efficient any hierarchy requires that it is internalized, and becomes subconscious (and over time what starts off as habit and necessity can transmute into rational choice).[25]

The drive for permanence shapes how rulers use their power. Often they appear to hoard it. They fear losing it, and therefore tend to cling on, resisting challengers, real or imagined. They see power as a property, something to accumulate, build up and sit on. Some have an almost infinite capacity to justify why power must be held on to, and usually an almost infinite capacity for rationalizing why what is in their own personal interest is also in the interests of their nation or party.

The reasons for this have to do partly with habit and lack of imagination. But there must also be the fear that, having lost power, they will lose everything else that they value. In the past (and the present in some parts of the world), leaving power means risking your life to the whims of your successor, who may at any moment choose to put you on trial or make you disappear (about the only thing that can be said in favour of Chile's dictator General Pinochet is that he handed power over to a democratically elected government, which was then able to start whittling back the various constitutional devices he had installed to protect himself from any future punishment). Even in hereditary monarchies any signs of weakness could be ruthlessly exploited. A succession of Mughal emperors were forcibly deposed by their impatient sons, and in seventh-century China Empress Wu notoriously murdered several of her own children to preserve her power during a forty-year reign. But even in much more ordered democratic societies, once you have left power you lose control over your legacy and your reputation. Accounts of it are more likely to be written by others and to cast you in an unflattering light (as W. Somerset Maugham put it, 'the prime minister out of office is seen, too often, to have been but a pompous rhetorician, and the General without an army is but the tame hero of a market town'.[26]) And although this will be the case whether or not you are in office, the paraphernalia of office, and the day-to-day respect it brings, provide a reassuring counterweight to even the most barbed comment.

These problems help to explain why succession is among the most difficult tasks for any power holder and yet another distraction from the responsibilities of service. Dynastic succession dominated the hopes and fears of monarchs and empires, and set wives and brothers at each other's throats. In Singapore, Lee Kuan Yew achieved the rare feat of simultaneously manoeuvring his (very able) son into a position of leadership in the 2000s, and retaining a role for himself as emeritus leader. Henry VIII of England's entire reign, and the invention of a new church, the Church of England, was shaped by his need for a wife to produce an heir. Mayan rulers captured in battle were kept for long periods before being killed so that their successor couldn't take over – a crude but effective technique for destabilizing the enemy. For democratically elected leaders the priority is to leave in place a successor who will publicly value their legacy, yet all democratic leaders know that sooner or later their enemies will be in charge and will do their best to disparage their achievements. One mark of great leaders is that their works persist even when their enemies hold sway.

So, paranoia is natural, just as it is natural to try to cling on to power and to hoard it. Yet power is not something that can easily be hoarded. It is not a thing, or a stock, or a capital. It exists in relationships and through use. Storing it up guarantees atrophy.

Many of the strategies used by leaders involve visibility: making what is transient and immaterial appear material and permanent. But rulers can also use an opposite strategy to shore up their power, making what is everyday appear mysterious and untouchable. Elias Canetti wrote that the man who has power 'must be more reticent than anyone; no one must know his opinions or intentions.'[27] The founder of the Medean empire, Deioces, is the earliest example of invisibility as a strategy. Deioces, who had made his name as a scrupulously fair judge, agreed to become king in 701 BCE only if stringent conditions were met: a vast palace had to be built for him at Ecbatana; he was to be communicated with only through messengers, and no one in the court could see him more than once a week, so that, as Herodotus put it, 'he might seem to [his contemporaries] to be of another kind'. During his fifty-three-year reign public reverence turned into worship.

Powerful groups often delegate the job of being visible to others so as to conserve both their own respect and their power. The Shoguns in Japan ruled alongside emperors, formally as regents and backroom advisers, but in truth making all the decisions. In the post-war era the leaders of political factions in Japan's ruling Liberal Democratic Party used prime ministers in a similar way. In modern dictatorships the sons of founding rulers are often kept on as token symbols while real power is exercised invisibly (Bashir Assad in Syria and Kim Jong Il in North Korea are both examples – widely seen, perhaps unfairly, as ciphers for ruling cliques). Invisibility has advantages – it helps states resist frontal assault, making them more like a diffuse network rather than a concentrated army. Invisibility also excludes the public from seeing things that rulers fear they would either not understand or not support. As Bismarck put it, 'men should not know how their laws or their sausages are made'.

Today when the public are allowed by the media to see backstage, and understand the extent to which their leaders depend on artifice, one predictable result is a diminution of respect. Democratically elected leaders have to strike a fine balance between honest accessibility and the contempt that comes from familiarity. Since most have won office in part because of their powers of personal charm, they generally find it hard to imagine that too much exposure will harm them.

In modern democracies power and responsibility are, at least in principle, clear, with a line of authority passing from the public, through elected leaders to officials and agencies. But there is a telling story of an Inuit who came to Ottawa to meet the Canadian government (the same story can be told of any modern government). Over three days he sat through a series of meetings with officials claiming to represent the government; meetings were held on questions of land, education, trade and finance. Yet at no point did he meet the government. Exhausted, he gave up in disgust and despair. The government was all around him but stayed hidden. Presumably it made no concessions.

The arts of legitimation appear to be designed to persuade the public that the state and its rulers are good. But the real life of governments suggests that things are not so simple. As much, and often more, effort is devoted internally to the state itself, and to its own self-confidence. Hannah Arendt wrote that 'even the most despotic domination we know of, the rule of a master over slaves, who always outnumbered him, did not rest on superior means of coercion as such, but on a superior organization of power – that is on the organized solidarity of the masters.'[28] Later she went further, commenting that:

Power is never the property of an individual; it belongs to a group and remains in existence only so long as the group keeps together. When we say of somebody that he is 'in power' we actually refer to his being empowered by a certain number of people to act in their name. The moment the group from which the power originated to begin with (*potestas in populo*, without a people or group there is no power), disappears, 'his power' vanishes.[29]

Keeping the group united demands constant attention. Study the diary of most elected leaders and you will find a parade of banquets, rituals, meetings with elite groups and internal sessions, interspersed with the occasional walkabout or question and answer session with the public. Much of their time is devoted neither to giving commands nor to engagement with the people they ostensibly serve: instead it is devoted to strengthening the relationships in and around the core of the state.[30]

OBEDIENCE AND IDENTITY

The categories provided by the state give people ways to respond to countless existing and new situations. Some of these will be laws, others rules, still others norms. Although the state's power rests in part on the symbolic abstractions with which it legitimates itself, these abstractions become real in its day-to-day work in the thousands of offices, police stations or classrooms where the state's business is done, in things like road signs and markings governing traffic, or the civil laws governing behaviour. Strong norms have evolved to define how individuals should behave with a policeman, a teacher or a judge. In these situations state power is rarely considered or rejected through detached reason by independent citizens applying abstract moral principles. Rather, it is made and remade in the daily situations where people assume given roles, play them out, and sometimes challenge them – for example invoking the state's own claimed morality against its real practices. Most of the time upbringing and habit make people automatically align their beliefs and behaviour with what the state demands. For the rest of the time inertia is enough; in the former Soviet bloc, for example, millions voted in sham elections, took to the streets in sham marches, and hung sham flags out of their windows for the sake of a quiet life, and millions more spied on their neighbours for paltry rewards. The risks of rebellion were simply too high, and its rewards too nebulous.

Sometimes these categories fail, and when that happens people feel uneasy and angry. The New Orleans flood of 2005 was a good example of this, when the US federal government failed to play its expected role as guardian, protector and saviour. This prompted the thousands left stranded to respond in radically different ways, whether as grateful victims, as resentful urban guerrillas shooting at rescue helicopters, as appalled protesters in front of TV cameras or as looters out to get what they could.

People learn from an early age a repertoire of responses for dealing with power. Pierre Bourdieu described how among the Kabyle in north Africa, women are expected to adopt roles of restraint and modesty and a posture oriented towards the ground. Men, by contrast, stand straight and face the sky. Among the Nuer in Sudan, Evans-Pritchard described men who 'strut like lords of the earth, which, indeed, they consider themselves to be [because] there is no master and no servant in their society.'[31] Bodily posture becomes even more important for those at the apex of the social pyramid. The position of monarchs in medieval painting is precisely calibrated, looking down on the viewer with a combination of care and sternness. In many societies the courtiers had to abase themselves physically, with the cringe and the kowtow. The British Lord Chancellor traditionally walks backwards ahead of the monarch at the State Opening of Parliament. Among early democratic leaders the characteristic bodily pose was designed for speeches to large crowds, with an upright back, arms open, eyes fixed on a point just above the horizon (the bright future which they could see better than anyone else). Later democratic leaders opted for a very different stance, designed for domestic consumption: comfortable, intimate but authoritative. (In the age of television these are, as Arthur Miller argued,[32] deliberately flat performances, without the character and drama of the age of oratory: performances that make us feel the leader is present with us in our front room.)

Most citizens learn from an early age the quiet deference that works best with officials, teachers or police. We know in our bones who can hurt us, boss us, stand over us, and, later, whom we can in turn hurt, boss and stand over. We absorb all this as small children, by watching, imitating and learning. Sometimes adults explicitly instruct children how to cope with power. Lord Chesterfield wrote to his son about the subtle tactics he could use:

were you to converse with a king, you ought to be as easy and unembarrassed as with your own valet de chambre; but yet, every look, word and action, should imply the utmost respect . . . the art would be to carry the conversation, if possible, to some indirect flattery; such as commending those virtues in some other person, in which that prince either thinks he does, or at least would be thought by others, to excel.

In later life the ability to defer can be hugely valuable. Bertolt Brecht notoriously showed this in his dealings with the House Committee on Un-American Activities in 1947: a committed communist he was able to show them due deference and humility, in marked contrast to the grandstanding of the American colleagues he had worked alongside in Hollywood. His answers were ambiguous but not confrontational, and he was let off, and even offered help if he had any trouble with immigration officials. Why let personal pride get in the way of the calculation that such an unequal battle was not worth fighting?

But deference is only part of the story. The key to understanding why people serve states, and why others serve the community through the state, is identification. It is through identification – with adults, animals or fictional heroes – that people develop their moral imagination, and learn to calibrate their sense of self: when to assert, when to compromise, when to submit. These skills are all needed for living in any community, yet to truly belong we need to be able to experience vicariously what others are going through, or what members of our family or tribe experienced in the past; to feel the pain, or shame, or pride of past achievements unites a group. If we can do that then we can also find security in becoming part of something bigger than ourselves. In later life this identification defines what we are: the family we belong to, the trade we work in, the religion we worship through, or the nation in which we live, as well as defining what we are not.

Within a shared umbrella of identity, it is natural to serve others. Most communities are held together through rituals of mutual service, and states based on strong identities find it easy to demand service from their people. The corollary of this is that anyone beyond the umbrella has no claims to service or support; they start off suspect, and easily become enemies. The same factors that make it easy for us to bond with others also make it easy for us to differentiate ourselves from strangers.

As identities form they soon mark out moral as well as practical boundaries. Claude Lévi-Strauss described these boundaries starkly:

Mankind stops at the boundaries of the tribe, the linguistic group, sometimes even of the village, so that a large number of so-called primitive peoples give themselves a name which means 'men' (or sometimes 'the good', 'the excellent' or 'the perfect') which simultaneously indicates that the other tribes, groups or villages have no share in their good qualities, or even the nature, of man but, at most, consist of 'the bad', 'the evil', 'the ground apes' or 'lice eggs'. Sometimes the strangers are even denied this last foothold in reality and are regarded as 'phantoms' or 'apparitions'.[33]

What is the source of this kind of identity which so easily justifies monstrous acts, including the worst crimes committed by states? At the height of the romantic era, the German poet Johann Gottfried Herder described national solidarity as a kind of self-love, which is why we lend so much admiration to our scientists, sportsmen and women and artists, bathe in their glory, and share an approbation that does not countenance any disagreement. He also thought that identities grow up from the soil, that they are natural, rooted in history and the landscape. But closer inspection of identities show that they do not derive from inside us; nor are they waiting around to be picked up. They are social rather than natural, made through conversation, observation and reflection, and through action and reaction, including, often, the conscious actions of states and elites. Strangers are called 'lice eggs' because it is useful for some people that they should be so described. It is a notorious feature of human societies that relatively mild preferences or dislikes among individuals can become violent hatreds and fissures in groups: groups do not simply scale up individuals, they change their character.[34]

This becomes quickly apparent in the history of national identities. Until the modern era states made few claims on identity. It was enough for people to pay their taxes or serve in times of war. There were undoubtedly patriotic Assyrians, Romans and Chinese. But before the modern era for most people identification was more likely to be very local, particular to a village or tribe. The great multinational empires were generally tolerant of difference and complexity, and left each community to run itself: third-century CE Rome, for example, gave citizenship rights to all free people within the Empire and, according to one perceptive historian of tolerance, 'Roman proconsuls in Egypt or British regents in India, for all their prejudices and the endemic corruption of their regimes, probably ruled more even-handedly than any local prince or tyrant was likely to do – in fact even more even-handedly than local majorities today are likely to do.'[35]

The role of identity became important to states only when nation states had to mobilize the whole population in times of war. Mass armies required commitment on a mass scale, as did the high levels of taxation that were needed to pay for them. And so a much more emotionally demanding, and morally dangerous, bargain was reached in the nineteenth and twentieth centuries between states and people: identification, love and service to the state in exchange for protection and welfare. Identification with the nation and the state offered to make up for the lost intimacy of the family and community, remaking their bonds of mutual commitment at the level of the society as a whole.

By making the nation meaningful, states legitimated themselves, and made themselves more natural. Some drew on pre-existing national identities (a remarkable number, including Britain and India, adopted the name their invaders had given them).[36] But just as often states themselves shaped cultures, languages and even genes into greater coherence. Imagined community, or, more accurately, imaginary communities were conjured up from the available materials, usually led by intellectuals in the major cities, and later reinforced through compulsory education and mass media.

In this way even the most mythical state became at least partly real, for example when linguistic diversity was reduced through compulsory schooling in a dominant language, or when sharper social and linguistic boundaries came to coincide with jurisdictional boundaries, where previously they had been blurred. Italy made its citizens Italians as much as vice versa, just as France made its citizens French. More recently, Malaysia has defined its national character through the three pillars of language, religion and royalty, partly to exclude the Chinese and other minorities and partly to differentiate itself from its neighbours. The Croatian constitution of 1990 described the nation as the culmination of the thousand-year dream of the Croatian people (neatly ignoring the many Serbs who still lived within its borders), and Israel has always been the state of the Jews, not of the many Arabs who live there. In each of these cases, the rulers hoped that reality would sooner or later catch up with their assertions.[37]

Yet the pursuit of an abstract identity always risks detaching states from any moral anchoring in their duties of service. These dangers are most acute during the early phases of democratization, when newly mobilized public energies can be directed against minorities like gypsies and Jews.[38] Deviants, misfits and minorities can end up being categorized not just as eccentrics but as enemies of the state and enemies of the people. The unlucky ones are portrayed as impure, disgusting and subhuman. In Rwanda, for example, the Tutsis were described as cockroaches, just as in Germany the Jews were vermin, and in India the Dalits were rats.

It is no coincidence that many of the worst genocides have been committed by emerging democracies. These are not the results of state breakdown or a descent into anarchy. Most are overseen by highly organized states and carried out by highly socialized killers. They usually involve high levels of mobilization, intensive politics and lively civil networks (civil society is perfectly capable of cruelty).

A heightened sense of identity can also intoxicate rulers with military overreach (as in the case of Mussolini's ill-fated ventures into Africa and Greece), or with the heady oxygen of culture wars (like Turkey's many attempts to squash an independent Kurdish culture). In a milder version it can simply lead to misunderstanding. When President Chirac declared in the autumn of 2005 'we are all children of the republic' in response to rioting Muslim youth in the urban *banlieues* of France, his solution appeared to them more like the problem – of a piece with a state that had not only condemned them to marginal housing and marginal lives, but had also banned their own cultural freedoms in the name of national identity.

The pursuit of identity encourages politicians with a keen nose for dividing lines to start digging trenches. The son of Oswald Mosley, one of Britain's ablest politicians who transformed himself into a fascist, said of his father that 'while the right hand dealt with grandiose ideas and glory, the left had let the rat out of the sewer'. Not all who deal with grandiose ideas are quite so guilty. But abstractions are often treacherous, often become removed from the emotions and ideas with which they originate, and often mislead.

If you identify with your state or nation you do not serve your neighbour as a neighbour but as an example of a category, and it is you who serves the state, not vice versa (as J. F. Kennedy put it so famously, 'ask not what your country can do for you but what you can do for your country', a saying that has become such a cliché that its moral ambiguity is no longer noticed). The enemies of the modern state are just as capable of being motivated by identity to commit acts of callous hatred: like the Chechen guerrilla celebrating the bombed hospital, or the suicide bomber celebrating the deaths of children, the bonds of commitment override the direct morality of service or humanity.

Amid carnage we learn to make the 'world acceptable by making it intelligible'.[39] But something of the same process happens in times of peace, too. When Japan's Prime Minister Koizumi made annual visits to the Yasukuni shrine, the spiritual focus for Japanese nationalism in the 1930s and 1940s and honoured people seen elsewhere as war criminals, he gave the Japanese public a way of making sense of their history, replacing shame and incomprehension with quiet acceptance. When President Nixon whispered to his aide Haldeman (and the tape recorder) while considering the mass of evidence building up against him in the Watergate scandal, 'they want to believe, that is the point, isn't it?', he meant that the public wanted to believe that a President would tell the truth and that he would retain the benefit of the doubt. He turned out to be wrong, but more because his colleagues in Congress no longer wanted to believe than because the public had deserted him.

The more totalitarian modern states took the cult of abstract identity to an extreme. They demanded total identification and total service, but they also became carried away with the abstractions they themselves had created. Nietzsche's comment that 'madness is something rare in individuals – but in groups, parties, peoples, ages it is the rule',[40] came alive in their hands. In these extreme cases many people came to cope with utter powerlessness through identification: internalizing the beliefs of the conqueror as the best way of making sense of their lives and the hopelessness of their position. Bruno Bettelheim once speculated why, despite experience, people invest dictators with virtues and an almost divine character, and suggested that it must be because of fear that the ruler will use his power against them. Rituals, which transcend the dictator's personal nature, confirm that he must be above petty caprice and vindictiveness. The greater the threat, the greater the need to deny it by believing in his virtue and identifying with him (which is why, perhaps, Stalin and Mao came closer to sainthood in the eyes of the people they ruled than almost any other leaders of the twentieth century). Arthur Miller made a similar point when he wrote that 'few of us can surrender our belief that society must somehow make sense. The thought that the State has lost its mind and is punishing so many innocent people is intolerable. And so the evidence has to be internally denied.'

Kidnap victims sometimes succumb to the Stockholm Syndrome, where the victim comes to identify with his or her captor. This involves the same psychology, and is experienced as oddly empowering. Euripides' play *Iphigenia at Aulis* is the classic account of this pattern in the ancient world, describing how a girl, Agamemnon's daughter Iphigenia, is chosen to be the sacrifice who will appease the gods into giving the navy a fair wind. During the course of the play she moves from anguished horror at the prospect of being murdered by her father to enthusiastic embrace of a heroic role.

In Nietzsche's writings this sort of craven and delusory submission is what lies behind all morality; it reveals morality as nothing more than the external subjugation of the free man who, because of the weakness of his will, internalizes and identifies with the sources of his oppression. Yet somewhere in between these two accounts there is a more benign form of identification in which we pool part of ourselves into a large whole, sometimes symbolized by the state, while retaining a sense of separateness. We may admire the state and learn from it, but we also gain the strength to doubt it. 'A fascinating marker of many future leaders', one of the most acute commentators on leadership has observed, 'is their capacity to identify with a more distant authority figure, an identification which manifests itself both in efforts to emulate the leader and in a willingness to challenge that leader'.[41]

A similar pattern may be occurring as democracy evolves. In its emergent phase democracy was allied to the abstractions of identity – of nation, class and race. Politicians saw advantage in talking these abstractions up, and accentuating divides. At worst these abstractions justified monstrous acts against people who lacked the same identity. At best they provided fig leaves for narrow interests and power-seekers. But in the more mature phases of democracy identity becomes less important; the abstractions seem to drop away and we are left with the prose of service.

Generally identities become most important at times of rapid change, or when people are threatened, and of the many identities that people have it is common for the one that is most threatened to become the most important, whether it is being German in the 1920s, Vietnamese in the 1960s or Muslim in the 2000s. This explains why, amid the peace and prosperity of the West, identities have become more subdued. The pattern is not even, and in some parts of the world the claims of identity may even be getting stronger: in the US, leaders feel impelled to proclaim a nationalist fervour that would seem anachronistic in other developed countries; China is discovering an assertive national pride that is being directed against the US and Japan; and India under the BJP experimented with a vigorous and dangerous assertion of a national identity rooted in Hindu exceptionalism. In parts of Europe, too, extreme nationalist parties have kept the ugly politics of the 1930s quietly simmering. But for the most part identities are becoming less intense, less things to live or die for, and less guilty of overriding other, less partial, notions of right and wrong.

7

Moral Ends and Moral Means

'Our evil is to god not evil but ignorance and imperfection, our good a lesser imperfection.' Sri Aurobindo[1]

Abu Nasr al-Farabi, who lived in the early tenth century in central Asia, and worked in Baghdad, Byzantium, Egypt and Syria, was one of Islam's most influential political philosophers. His work synthesized the extraordinary spiritual energy of triumphant Islam with the legacy of Plato and Aristotle and resonates to this day because of his unusual emphasis on the power of individual reason.

In one of his greatest books, *The Perfect City*, he attempted to define what makes a government good. His answers played down the importance of laws or structures. Instead he wrote that a government could be defined as good only if it was founded on the types of knowledge, character and virtue that lead to true happiness. Means had to be judged according to the ends they contributed to, and the best ends were ones which transcended the base realities of daily life.[2] Bad regimes, by contrast, reflected the imperfect characters of human nature.

Al-Farabi listed six of these types of regime, each of which is easily recognizable a thousand years later. There were the regimes of necessity, focused on nothing more than the bare necessities of life, the 'vile' regimes of oligarchy concerned only with wealth and prosperity, and the 'base' regimes concerned only with sensory or imaginary pleasures. There were regimes of honour, whose citizens aimed only at being praised and glorified by others, regimes of domination, whose citizens aimed at overpowering and subjecting others, and, finally, there were regimes of 'corporate association', or democracy, whose citizens' main purpose is to be free to do what they wish. These last regimes, he wrote, were likely to contain the greatest amount and variety of both good and evil things.

Al-Farabi's list provides a neat framework for judging contemporary rulers living in societies fixated on money, celebrity or hedonism. But his argument also raises far more fundamental questions. In what sense can a government be good if it simply mirrors a population flawed by delusions, greed and hatreds? And should it be defined as good by its guiding principles or by its processes, by its means or by its ends?

If you believe that people are fundamentally good these questions are relatively unproblematic. A few simple laws and institutions may be enough to channel their virtues in the right direction. But these questions become much more difficult if people are as bad as they are good. Indeed, if people are intrinsically evil the sort of virtuous government described by al-Farabi is likely to be a mirage.

Much of western political thinking has been overshadowed by Thomas Hobbes' argument for a political theory based on the dark side of human nature, an argument which shocked his contemporaries as much as it shocks today. Power, he argued, is the primary human urge, overriding everything else. We are all driven, he wrote, by 'a perpetual and restless desire of power after power that ceases only in death.' This drive comes from our frailties and vulnerability, the brute fact that we cannot protect our lives and guarantee our well-being, and even the power we already have, 'without the acquisition of more'. The drive to acquire power is in this sense inseparable from the drive to defend ourselves against threats, and lies deep in our animal nature.

Not all of the effects of this drive for power and recognition have to be bad. It can motivate people to create great art or to be generous with their charity ('there can be no greater argument to a man of his own power', Hobbes wrote, 'than to find himself able not only to accomplish his own desires but also to assist other men in theirs'). Alfred Adler, the contemporary and colleague of Freud and Jung, made a similar argument when he claimed that 'striving for superiority' was the primary human drive, and had as its mirror the 'inferiority complex', which could lead to depression and an inability to act. 'We all wish to overcome difficulties', he wrote, and 'we all strive to reach a goal by the attainment of which we shall feel strong, superior, and complete.'

More recent medical evidence seems to confirm the universal character of this drive to win. High status is strongly correlated with better health (Oscar winners live on average four years longer than Oscar nominees). All that we know from social science confirms that people are deeply aware of their relative position; they suffer without recognition and thrive with it.[3] In this sense Hobbes was right: we really are all trapped in a race in which even the most powerful and successful can never feel completely secure.

But Hobbes' cynicism about human nature was much more profound than this. Beneath the surface, he argued, all of us are potential murderers, harbouring fantasies of revenge and malice. If we could get away with murder, we would, literally. This is the hard truth of human affairs; we live in societies that are not far removed from the jungle, and beneath the surface of sophisticated civilization lurks a world of cut-throats and thieves that comes to the fore when order is temporarily suspended, as in the New York power cuts of the 1970s or in New Orleans in 2005. Social psychology has, rather to its own surprise, confirmed much of this story, showing how easily, with a little prompting from the situation or from figures in authority, people can take on brutal roles as prison sadists or torturers.

For Hobbes the logical implication was that we have no choice but to accept the authority of any sovereign who protects us and holds in check this disastrous struggle for power. Only with a clear structure of authority, judgment and enforcement can we avoid the anarchy of a war of all against all, and the murderous desires that lurk beneath the surface of even the most civilized people (perhaps today we might also need protection from the ecological effects of other people's desires). Seen in this light all of the moral ambitions of al-Farabi and Aristotle, Lorenzetti and Mill, look like unaffordable luxuries. We cannot expect the state to be good to any great extent: the most we can hope for is that it succeeds in protecting us from our enemies.

Hobbes' account of human psychology was deliberately exaggerated. But it contains enough truth to resonate. It accurately describes many of the people involved in power and politics who do indeed act as if driven to achieve power as an end in itself. It chimes with the histories of wars and genocides which show how perfectly decent people can turn into monsters, much as we would like to explain them as the result of some abstract evil. And his account helps to explain why all societies achieve such unequal distributions of power and wealth: given the chance to do so, people accumulate power over others, and given the chance people pass on privileges to others like them – one reason why societies that appear to be governed by laws guaranteeing equal treatment and equal opportunities manage so successfully to reproduce inequality.

To say all of this does not deny people's capacity for generosity, altruism and compassion. The officers who went first over the trenches in the First World War, the middle-class communist revolutionaries who risked their lives to overthrow oppressive governments, and the missionaries who brought Bibles or healthcare to far-flung corners of the world, were each animated by ideals that made them act counter to the narrow interests of their group.[4] A host of civic and religious organizations exist only because people think and act generously towards strangers, and are willing to act as if others are intrinsically benign.[5]

But for institutions that are organized around power it is bound to matter more if some people are motivated primarily to acquire power rather than just to use it. Even if only a small minority acts exploitatively or to accumulate power – perhaps the most cynically ambitious members of a political class – this may be enough to mould the character of a society profoundly.

What follows from this? For Hobbes it followed that a supreme ruler was needed to hold everyone in check. But the claim that we should show mute obedience to the sovereign so long as he protects us does not follow logically from the premise. Indeed, mute obedience could be the best guarantee that the sovereign's worst nature will be given free rein. President Mobutu of Zaire and Chile's General Pinochet did not begin their lives as dictators: they became despots because enough people were willing to treat them as despots and too few were willing to challenge them.

But there is also a more fundamental reason why Hobbes' argument lacks logic. If society really is a war of all against all, one of the likely consequences is that power and wealth will tend to be spread very unevenly, with a few winners and many losers. This is certainly what has happened whenever social order breaks down, as in Germany in the 1920s or Yugoslavia in the 1990s. Where there are such inequalities the great majority are likely to have a compelling interest in any device which can curb the winners' cruelty and greed. If people with power will do whatever they can get away with, the powerless have a matching interest to limit what they can do. This is why there is such a strong common interest in moral rules and social institutions that can protect against arbitrary abuse, violence and injustice, whether by other individuals or by the state itself. An amoral view of human nature leads, paradoxically, to the conclusion that government should be very active in shoring up morality and reinforcing society's norms and rules.

Hobbes' claim that people are driven by murderous self-interest has been mirrored in the idea that selfish material interests are the only motivations that matter. David Hume proposed that 'in contriving any system of government every man ought to be supposed a knave and to have no other end in all his actions than private interest'. Both arguments are vulnerable to the observation that any government which took them seriously would require far more police as well as far higher rates of remuneration than modern governments get away with (most real governments have taken advantage of people's willingness to police themselves and of the very varied motivations that turn people into nurses or soldiers). But to the extent that Hume's claim was true it would also lead, like Hobbes', to a paradoxical conclusion: if human nature really is venal then it becomes even more important for laws and regulations to be highly moral so as to rein in that venality.

How credible, then, are arguments for states to be based on other drives, including the strong drive to bond with others?[6] This bond is as universal, as visible in many settings (including in the behaviour of small children), and as absorbing of our mental energies as the drives for power and recognition. There is also just as much evidence that its absence is bad for people's health, and just as many plausible accounts as to why evolutionary pressures should have favoured it.[7]

It is therefore not surprising that many thinkers have claimed that states should reflect this primal drive to bond with others. For them co-operation is the natural state of society, along with trust, harmony and mutual sympathy. The ideal government is one that reflects and validates this fundamental human nature – that trusts people rather than punishing them.

Unfortunately, once again the idea of a clear logical link between human nature and institutional forms misleads. A state founded on co-operation and bonding depends not just on these being strong drives: they have to be overwhelmingly strong if a small number of ruthless freeriders are not to be able to exploit them. For co-operation to be the basis for government it also needs to be inclusive. Yet in practice the drive to form attachments manifests itself very unevenly: we bond strongly with some, and strongly against others, whom we may then collectively disdain, threaten or attack. It is in our nature to form boundaries around our groups and then to try to exploit outsiders, people on the other side of the categorical dividing lines that matter.

These are some of the reasons for being sceptical of the appealing idea that the structures of political life are rooted in human psychology. The logic of these connections falls apart on inspection. In any case our understanding of human psychology is insufficient to ground any firm conclusions about how institutions should be designed. There are simply too many variables involved. Human nature is selfish and generous, violent and peaceful, territorial and mobile, and the character it takes depends as much on the context as on anything innate.[8]

What then of morality itself? Are eternal moral principles a firmer ground than human nature on which to base conclusions about how government should be organized? I have argued that states are moral creations, comprehensible only through the moral lens of service. But this relationship is not direct. The forms that states should take cannot be deduced from moral principles any more than they can be from assumptions about human nature. The reason is that morals have come down to modern communities through several different routes. Our ideas of right and wrong are rarely definitive because their sources clash. Some of these ideas are biologically shaped predispositions, such as understandings of fairness, justice or compassion, which manifest themselves in early childhood, and across very varied civilizations. These are part of what makes us human and they are slowly coming to be better understood as the divides between psychology and sociology break down. But they are no more than dispositions and can be overridden. We are not in any simple way creatures of instinct.

Other senses of right and wrong come from tradition. Traditional moral principles, for example around incest or diet, originated in obvious social needs. Some still make sense; some are embedded in our very sense of identity; and some have come to feel alien.

Reason both shapes and challenges these other moral sources. Reasoned arguments about morality are not exclusive to modernity. The Buddha placed a high premium on reason as a more reliable guide than experience, just as al-Farabi more than a thousand years later made reason the foundation of his political thought. In all societies people have felt the need to justify their actions, and all societies have called people to account, though generally the powerful have had less need to justify themselves, the poor and weak more (indeed, this might be another good definition of power).

Yet because these sources of morality – biology, tradition and reason – often point in different directions, moral questions are never finally, definitively, answered.[9] This is unsettling for anyone – and especially for philosophers – who would like to find universal moral principles that are applicable in any setting. But the claim that morals are universal and timeless is not accurate as an empirical description of the work that morality does in real communities, where conflicts between these sources are constant.

Take, for example, what happens when a stranger starts to build a new house next to ours. Our predispositions may impel us to react defensively against a move that threatens our sense of territory. Tradition may impel us to receive the newcomer with hospitality (or suspicion). Reason may tell us that, given the pressures of a rising population, everyone needs to be willing to compromise. Or take a parent's role in helping their child with an assignment from school. Predispositions are likely to encourage the parent to do everything they can for the child; traditional morality will argue that too much help is akin to cheating, which dishonours the institution and the authority of the teachers; and reason says that too much help is immoral because no actions should be taken that could not be generalized to the wider good. Examples of this kind could be multiplied without limit: everyday life is full of situations where morality speaks with contradictory voices.

These considerations apply with even greater force to states. It is certainly possible to talk about the state in a wholly deductive way, deriving structures and tasks from apparent first principles or from a few behavioural assumptions. Many recent authors have attempted to do just this, deducing what type of state or constitution would result from a genuine fresh start according to rational design. It is also possible to justify a state solely in terms of tradition and precedent (as Confucians claimed to do), just as it is possible to explain states in biological terms as outcomes of evolutionary forces[10] or, like Hobbes, through the lens of predispositions and drives. But the behaviour of real states cannot be explained in such one-dimensional ways. Instead, all successful ones seek moral arguments and metaphors that straddle these different sources, and all successful ones recognize that their moral universe overlaps with everyday life, but is also at times dramatically different.

THE PECULIAR MORALITY OF STATES

In earlier chapters I argued that all states have a moral core but are diverted from their moral duties because they are captured by partial interests, and succumb to the logic of organization that leads them to devote their energies to themselves. Seen in this light the primary moral task for leaders, or for the public, is to help states to approximate as much as possible to their potential as a servant – to counter tendencies to self-service and capture, and the hypocrisies they bring. But what of the means used by states, and what if good ends are met through bad means?

At first glance the best rational principle that should inform the behaviour of any state, and set limits to the means it should use, is Rabbi Hillel's golden rule: 'do unto others as you would have them do unto you'. This rule has parallels in every other civilization –

for example, Christianity's 'love thy neighbour as theyself' and the *Mahabharata*'s 'let no man do to another what would be repugnant to himself' – and appears as good an example of a universal principle as any. The movement towards a democratic welfare capitalism based on service has forced politicians and officials to abide by a rough 'golden rule', treating their citizens with more respect, and more as they would expect to be treated themselves. In international affairs the UN Charter can be thought of as a golden rule for states.

Yet the golden rule turns out to be of limited use as a guide to the exercise of state power. It offers few insights into how a state should behave on the difficult issues: when a leader should send soldiers into war, remove something the people cherish or punish harshly to deter worse crimes.

The claim that the morality of states is radically different from the morality of individuals has been greatly exaggerated, and used to justify abuses of power. Yet the moral issues faced by individuals and states can indeed be very different in kind. Although there are some universal ethical goods, such as courage, mercy, patience and wisdom, that are prized in all settings, in relation to power many of the Ten Commandments are at most conditional: even the most ethical governments kill (in times of war), lie (to protect life) and steal (for example in pursuit of security). All of them worship graven images (usually their own icons inscribed on buildings, bank notes or flags), and all commit adultery (at least so far as international affairs are concerned).

Some of the differences between day-to-day morality and the morality of states arise from scale. Stalin's infamous comment that one death is a tragedy while a million deaths is a statistic is chilling and inhumane. But every government either implicitly or explicitly makes judgements about life and death on a large scale: on what terms to provide healthcare; what risks to accept in vehicles or drugs. Modern technocratic states are the only institutions that formally value life, trade off one life against another, and act as a mathematical god – for example, deciding what investment in rail safety or medical treatments is justified by the lives that would be saved. Yet they feel very uncomfortable making judgements of this kind explicitly, since these judgements are at odds with the role of being a servant (what servant has the right to determine whether their master lives or dies?), at odds with daily morality (which sees every life as sacred), and at odds with the psychology of risk (which responds much more readily to very visible dangers).[11] The same ambivalence colours the state's power to encourage fertility and constrain it (for example through programmes of forced sterilization or rights to abortion), to control what we can put into our bodies (through prohibitions on drugs) and how we enjoy ourselves (through regulations on drinking or gambling).

Some of the differences between the morality of states and everyday morality arise from necessity. Even the most liberal state has to carry out violent acts, such as bombing and espionage, which no private citizen would ever be justified in doing. Any leader may have to order actions that they would not be prepared to carry out themselves (and it may be better to have leaders who are not too easily prepared to conduct violent actions themselves). Arthur Miller wrote of Roosevelt's guile in bringing the US into the Second World War that 'mankind is in debt to his lies'. In the most extreme cases of war or threat, an overly scrupulous concern with personal ethical purity may be a damaging vice when seen from the perspective of the community's interests.

Some of the differences arise from the consequences of choices. War produces many examples. In July 1944 V1 bombs were falling in large numbers on London, targeted primarily on Charing Cross in the centre of the city. British intelligence controlled all the German agents then operating in the UK and suggested that they should send back reports that the bombs were falling too far to the north. This would lead the Germans to aim further south and shift the burden of the attack to the much less densely populated counties of Kent and Sussex. Casualties could be cut by as many as 10,000 as the bombs rained down on fields full only of cows and grass. Winston Churchill and Herbert Morrison (who was then Home Secretary) refused to accept the utilitarian logic of this argument and vetoed the plan: they would not take moral responsibility for redirecting enemy fire on to their own citizens. The Chiefs of Staff, however, persevered and waited until Churchill was abroad before putting the plan to the War Cabinet chaired by Clement Attlee; the plan was agreed, suitably obscure minutes were written and many lives were saved. But some British citizens died who would otherwise have lived.

Some of the differences arise around secrecy. Immanuel Kant insisted that one should tell the truth even to a murderer who asks where your friend, whom he intends to kill, is hiding. You are responsible for the morality of your own action, and not for how anyone else behaves. This view is hard enough to live by in personal life, but is wholly impossible in public life. Governments will often have knowledge that would be very dangerous if widely known, such as knowledge about how to prosecute biological warfare, as well as ambiguous information that could be dangerous if made public. For example, when a modern government receives unconfirmed intelligence about a possible terrorist attack on an airport, it is far from clear whether it should publicize this information and risk mass panic, or keep it quiet (or, as the UK government did in a similar situation in 2002, flood the airport area with troops and police so as to scare off the terrorists and generate communications traffic from them).[12] There are also many examples where half-truths may in the end turn out to be for the best. Should President de Gaulle have revealed his strategy for Algerian independence, since by revealing it its success would have been doomed, and many more lives would have been lost? Should Mikhail Gorbachev have been honest about his intentions for reforming the Soviet Union in the mid-1980s and so guaranteed the maximum opposition to his plans from his colleagues? As Churchill once said, the truth may be 'so precious that she should always be attended by a bodyguard of lies'.

On a more modest scale it is not always self-evident that openness makes for good politics. Anyone wanting to push through a radical reform needs to be very careful about what they say and when. The rough rule for reformers is that early openness is desirable if it mobilizes the friends of reform more than its enemies, but often the enemies of reform will be better organized. Nor is openness inherently good for decision-making: no institution can make difficult decisions well under the glare of scrutiny; and no group can afford to be honest with itself if there is a risk that its most intimate conversations will appear on the Internet. These considerations apply in daily life too, but public curiosity about what states are considering will be far greater than curiosity about private lives.

Some of the other differences which mark out the realm of government from other realms arise from the nature of the states' interests, which require that an enemy's enemy is a friend to a degree that would never happen in daily life. Churchill once said that if Hitler invaded hell he would say a few kind words about the Devil in the House of Commons. It is because of the peculiarity of states' interests that the result of any victory is the end of the alliance that won the victory. This is what happened with the quickly asserted divisions between the victorious allies of 1918 and 1945; the quickly dissolved alliance of China and the USSR, and of China and Vietnam. All were neatly prefigured by the Austrian Chancellor Metternich, who commented after the Russians had helped the Austro-Hungarian Empire to suppress the uprisings directed against it in 1848: 'the extent of our ingratitude will be astonishing' (by which he meant that life would continue as normal).

States have to act under intense pressures of time. They cannot endlessly deliberate, or grapple with moral dilemmas. They exist to do things, and if necessary they have to suspend moral argument and act. This, and the other differences already described, can justify a flexibility with regard to means that would be less justifiable in daily life. But the odd mirror of these differences is that western democracies expect leaders to abide by far more demanding rules than the rest of us in other respects. They are expected to suspend personal considerations when exercising impersonal power – not to give special favours and not to treat people well just because they like them. Rewards to friends and cronies are commonplace in every polity, but they are always resented, criticized and seen as abuses of trust. Equally, democracies don't let leaders use their power to enrich themselves, or gain sexual favours (Bill Clinton's transgression of this prohibition very nearly brought him down; out of office he earns more from a couple of speeches than from a year serving as President).

With Freedom of Information laws in place, the jobs of political leaders have become transparent to an extent not accepted by any of the other leaders in society, and in some countries extraordinarily stringent standards of behaviour are demanded. In recent years, a Finnish Prime Minister – Anneli Jaatteenmaki – and a prospective Swedish Prime Minister – Mona Sahlin – both had to resign over very petty transgressions with credit cards and expenses that would barely merit a mention in other walks of life. At the same time we expect serving politicians to cope with ambiguities and shifts in position that derive not from any malevolence or dishonesty on their part but rather from the fluid complexities of the societies they represent.

So we try to strike a delicate balance. We want leaders with the character to take difficult decisions often far removed from everyday ethics, but with sufficient strength not to enjoy these decisions, not to get lost in the necessary ambiguities, or to let tough decisions become too habitual. (Lee Kuan Yew once said – of the British, not of his own government, which came to power nearly a decade later – that 'repression is like making love: it's always easier the second time.')

States also face more mundane moral dilemmas that are different in kind from those facing individuals. One of the moral duties of the state is to be a guardian, a trustee for the future. This is sometimes interpreted as requiring states to balance their budgets. There are certainly many examples of states which have sacrificed the future in exchange for present glory. Alexander the Great's campaigns fuelled an inflation that halved the value of money. Hitler financed his wars from an expanding money supply and had an aversion to taxation, printing money almost without limit and using the future to buy the present. Ronald Reagan, elected to balance the budget, helped transform the US from the world's greatest ever creditor nation to the world's greatest ever debtor nation.

Yet almost diametrically opposite fiscal skills to those implied by advocates of the moral clarity of the balanced budget have served western countries well. The ability to raise debt was decisive to the success of the British Empire over the French in the eighteenth and nineteenth centuries, and the Keynesian policies that included debt financing contributed a huge amount to human betterment in the second half of the twentieth century. Reagan went on to be judged responsible for one of the greatest economic booms in American history.

THE DILEMMAS OF LOYALTY

The moral dilemmas of state power often come to a head over the age-old questions of loyalty, and it is here that state morality and personal morality are most likely to clash. Power is shored up by loyalty and destroyed by treason. At its core it rests on the ability of leaders to convince others to obey.

Loyalty matters in every relationship that has any meaning in our lives. We expect shared experiences, love and friendship to count for something, particularly when times are hard, and choices are not easy. Doing things together creates a credit that we expect to be able to draw down, and in this we are helped because familiarity makes us partial to our own family, friends or nation.

The willingness not to betray is the minimal price of belonging to the group, and is asked of any citizen or member. Its absence is punished: treason has always been the most serious capital offence. Its presence is occasionally rewarded with gifts and renewed with rituals – oaths, vows, parades, or toasts. Public holidays, for example, are often presented as gifts of the state or sovereign to a loyal public.

But loyalties constantly conflict and the more complex a society is, the more its members are likely to face conflicts of loyalty. Some of the most compelling drama follows through what happens when people struggle with conflicts between different loyalties. Sophocles' play *Antigone* recounts the struggle of Antigone and King Creon over her brother Polyneices. Creon gives the classic definition of authority when he says that 'whoever this city may appoint, that man must be obeyed, in little things and great, in just things and unjust'. Yet Antigone adheres to another loyalty, to family and gods. Von Stauffenberg, the attempted assassin of Hitler, placed loyalty to nation above loyalty to the Führer, as, more ambiguously, did Rommel towards the end of the war. The British spy Kim Philby chose loyalty to a political movement, and a foreign power – the USSR – above loyalty to his nation. The law may penalize treason but it also recognizes that loyalties conflict: husbands and wives are not required to testify against each other in a court of law. Their loyalty to each other is a higher loyalty than loyalty to the truth.

In Book 9 of *War and Peace*, 'Prince Andrei at Drissa', Tolstoy describes the factional landscape of Russia's ruling group in the midst of the Napoleonic Wars: page after page describes each grouping, its beliefs, prejudices and analyses, all profoundly incompatible with each other. All real governments are like this. What at first glance appears monolithic turns out on closer inspection to be riven with arguments and clashes, loyalties to protectors and factions that are constantly being tested, stretched and broken. Should we be loyal to those close at hand or to our leaders? Should they be loyal to us? Or should we judge instrumentally, moment to moment?

Albert Camus commented, 'I believe in justice but I will defend my mother before justice.' But in the liberal tradition loyalty offends against universal ethics. It is anachronistic at best, corrupt at worst. William Godwin argued that if two children are drowning it is better to save the child with more chance of making a useful social contribution than to save your own child, regardless of instinct and loyalty. Utilitarian and Kantian philosophies are premised on an impartial morality that treats everyone equally regardless of ties, shared experience or commitments. Nepotism and favouritism are seen as moral offences, as well as being marks of backwardness.

The most malign forms of government certainly make the greatest demands of loyalty. In the modern era totalitarian dictatorships brought large swathes of life within their own definitions of loyalty. Anyone whose loyalty was suspect risked discrimination or worse. That is why one of the first acts of the new democracies formed in the 1990s was to sharply circumscribe the reach of laws of treason because of their association with totalitarianism (and in the USA no one has been tried for treason since the Second World War). When, in the absence of war, states start to make more assertive demands for loyalty, this is usually a good sign that something is amiss.

So two radically different views of what is right conflict. According to one, any relationship built up of shared commitments and experiences must bring with it a sense of loyalty that overrides not only selfish instincts but also at least some universal moral rules. According to the other, the moral individual must abide either by a set of impersonal laws and principles, or by an equally impersonal set of strategic goals, untainted by sentiment.

Most people and institutions operate between these extremes. We learn that in all human relationships loyalty arises from shared experience and commitments; is shaped by their intensity; can be damaged by conflicts; and accumulates in an implicit accounting of how much has been put in and how much has been taken out. We expect a degree of loyalty as a mark of good character. The employer of twenty years, or to whom one has committed much, can expect loyalty: keeping secrets, not spreading malicious gossip, caring for the interests of the organization. The party that you joined twenty years ago can expect that it will not be left capriciously. The leader of a faction can expect to be able to draw on at least some stock of capital during hard times. In each of these cases loyalty has a primordial, perhaps even biological root, in that in the distant past the group that sustained and protected its members could also make claims of them. Because these very personal commitments are the seeds from which other moralities derive we do not, and should not, trust anyone who too easily opts for abstract principle over human and personal commitments and obligations. Equally, however, we learn that one of the characteristics of any public institution is that it must be fair and impartial, and suppress personal connections and loyalties.

The harder choices arise when the thing to which we are loyal behaves in an amoral way, or in other ways which we disapprove of. Any thoughtful person working for a government or a company is bound to disagree with some of its policies and practices. They learn how to calibrate their dissent – how much can be said, to whom and when; how long they can sustain a dissenting position which will be experienced as tiresome and indulgent by their peers; how long their presence reduces the risks associated with what they see as a wrong policy; and how far they can live with the assumption that loyalty entails keeping criticism private not public, erring on the side of restraint. For example, at the height of the Vietnam War both Hubert Humphrey and Robert McNamara told friends that they were staying on to contain the pressures towards escalating the war yet further. It is easy to see why they felt more comfortable with this argument, and with keeping their jobs and status. Yet in retrospect, perhaps, they would have been more honest, and served the public better, if they had resigned.

Wise leaders encourage private argument and criticism among their advisers; they seek loyalty not sycophancy, and loyalty sometimes has to mean being honest about unsettling truths. Wei Zheng, chief adviser to the ninth/early tenth century Emperor Taizhong, is a good example. He had previously been chief of staff for the Crown Prince who had been beheaded by the Emperor for treason. On being interviewed by the Emperor, Wei Zheng's only comment was: 'if the heir apparent had listened to my advice long ago to get rid of you he would have been spared his fate.' The Emperor offered him a job: this was the plain speaking he most sorely needed.

Political leaders seem to need more competition and ambiguity around them, and thus more scope to choose between diverse sources of advice, than leaders in simpler fields like business or the military. Few need the extreme internal chaos that characterized the higher echelons of the Third Reich, with its surreal mess of competing agencies, ministers and task forces. But the simple hierarchies and neatly demarcated responsibilities of the typical business corporation are insufficiently flexible and robust to cope with the uncertainties and changes that governments often face in turbulent times.[13]

So flexibility comes with the territory. But for everyone there must be a non-negotiable line beyond which it is no longer possible to remain loyal. This is when loyalty to higher purposes takes over. A person who lacks any such lines or limits has ceased to be a moral agent. This is where the larger community that sustains us makes a claim on us.

THE DILEMMAS OF MEANS

The dilemmas of loyalty overlap with the dilemmas that arise over what means can be used. It is never enough to have had good intentions, or to have followed moral rules, if the consequence is that the community is unprotected or its welfare suffers. So the good servant learns to be flexible about means in pursuit of ends.

This description of a great military commander, the Supreme Commander Hu Tsung-hsien, who led the fighting against the pirates on China's southern coasts in the 1550s, exemplifies the flexibility of thought and technique that is often required of leaders. To secure victory, one historian wrote, he used

imperial prestige, offers of pardon, patronising friendship, subornation of colleagues, poisoned wine, moral principles, false intelligence, procrastination, beautiful women, solemn and fair promises, bribery, banquets, threats, intimidation, lies, cajolery, assassination, and deployment of troops to undo opponents.[14]

In the list moral principles come between poisoned wine and false intelligence. What matter most are the results – in this case protecting the community and its welfare.

The tensions between means and ends, and between the morality of fixed rules and principles and the need for flexibility, are best managed with an eye to context, proportionality and their likely dynamic effects. In times of emergency it may be necessary to suspend rules and freedoms: the US Constitution, for example, explicitly permits habeas corpus to be suspended in emergencies, and allows for martial law to be declared. A senior Republican Congressman, Zell Miller, in 2004 voiced the common response to threats when he said that 'all private plans, all private lives, have been in a sense repealed by an overriding public danger.'

Any claim of this kind raises questions of proportion and historical perspective. The USA had suffered a deeply troubling terrorist attack three years before Miller's comment, in the destruction of the World Trade Center. But the enemy had turned out to be weaker than expected; its command centres and lines of communication had been ruptured; and any threat to the USA was marginal, either by historical standards (compared to the threat posed by Japan in the 1940s or the USSR in the 1960s) or by global standards (many other nations faced far more damaging threats of subversion or invasion).[15] In normal times there are good reasons to be suspicious of rulers who demand the freedom to act flexibly. Too often this will turn out to be a justification for actions that damage the interests of the people, if not in the short-run, then in all likelihood before too long. It is possible to justify suspending almost any principle if the circumstances are extreme enough: against the background of a natural disaster or war, some ends do come to justify some means.

Wise societies try to impose strict limits to protect themselves and their leaders from being tempted too often. Torture is a good example of this. There are many instances in which torture may appear to be justified: the classic instance is the case where a terrorist has planted a bomb which has yet to go off and torture may help to avert many deaths. But we fear licensing the state to use such means because they can too easily become habitual, and once habitual can come to be used against people who threaten the state, but do not in any meaningful way threaten the public. Worse, in time they can morally corrupt their perpetrators, and make them less reliable as servants.

These are pragmatic arguments, not arguments of fundamental principle. In the case of the USA there is no argument of fundamental principle why it is acceptable to drop bombs or to execute citizens, but never to use torture. The reasons why torture of the prisoners captured in Afghanistan and around the world after 9/11 was not justified were arguments of proportionality, and dynamic effect: fears, in short, that the means could damage the ends they were meant to serve.

Flexibility with the truth involves similar issues. There are few roles of authority, including being a parent, which do not involve some deception, and often outright lies. But because almost any lie can be justified through some kind of moral argument, however convoluted, too much tolerance for justification can leave a community unable to distinguish between truth and lies. This is why we attempt to impose some absolute requirements for truth as anchors against moral slippage: in courts where witnesses swear under oath, and in parliamentary inquiries which generally reject utilitarian or consequentialist justifications for deception.

A similar balance has to be struck between efficiency as an end and as a means. In Brazilian politics the phrase 'rouba, mas faz' refers to politicians who are corrupt but get things done. They are proof that there is no automatic correspondence between what fits with moral rules and what works in practice: highly ethical leaders can be wholly ineffective. Moral concerns can sometimes get in the way of necessary action. Rogues can get the trains running on time.

So two meanings of good coexist. One is concerned with effectiveness and competence; the other with ethical principles. Sometimes these may clash, and many of the inquiries launched into government wrongdoings attempt to judge whether the right balance was struck: for example, when an innocent Brazilian was mistakenly shot by police on the London Underground in the summer of 2005, were the police judging correctly the conflicting imperatives of decisive action to stop suicide bombers and the rights to life of innocent people? When governments act quickly and decisively they have less time to listen, and less time to think through the ethical implications of their acts – which is why such retrospective inquiries usually conclude that too little attention has been paid to the ethics.

But effectiveness has a moral dimension too. William Gladstone required his officials to write on both sides of pieces of paper, and believed that money should be left to 'fructify in the pockets of the people' rather than being spent by the state. A government that is wasteful, or that squanders resources that are badly needed elsewhere, or that succumbs to the temptation to serve the provider rather than the person in need, is acting immorally whatever its claimed virtues.

Yet the pursuit of efficiency can bring its own moral traps, particularly when it becomes an end rather than a means. The phrase 'bang for buck' was meant in a literal sense by the Pentagon planners who coined it; one suspects that they were less concerned about the relative moralities of accurate and inaccurate carpet bombing. Systems built to maximize efficiency risk morally castrating the people within them since they so often leave to the people at the top the job of worrying about ends and trade-offs, and leave everyone else in the position of functionaries, there just to obey orders and follow the rules. This is particularly true of an age in which the detailed prescription of 'best practice', and real-time monitoring of performance, are so easy. Efficiency can then become a moral alibi, a way of escaping judgement and accountability, just as it was for the many officials and soldiers who excused their actions in the Second World War on the grounds that they were only obeying orders.

THE DEVIL'S ARGUMENTS

This discussion of power and morality would not be complete without mentioning what could be called the 'Devil's arguments'. These are the temptations which can waylay anyone exercising substantial power, particularly individual leaders. They arise because people with power can get away with more. The temptations are well-documented in literature: they include the temptations to exploit, to bully, to oppress or to lie. They also include the temptations of personal vices – greed, lust, hatred and the ballooning vice associated with the lives of Nero and Goering; and they include the temptations of amoral means, associated more often with the cool cruelty of dictators like Joseph Stalin and Mao Zedong.

Any leaders who genuinely believe in an all-seeing and judgemental deity should be able to resist these temptations (although there is little evidence that believers are any more restrained than non-believers). But why should any holder of power who does not believe submit to a higher morality? Why should anyone with power submit to a theoretical superior – a god that may not exist or historical judgements that will be made long after their bones have become dust? In any case, surely history will respect and remember the decisive, the dramatic and the bold, the monstrous heroes like Alexander and Napoleon, Stalin and Mao, rather than the dutifully benign?

Machiavelli wrote the most influential account of why it is foolish to expect power to be good. States, he argued, can lie, kill and cheat, and have to if they are to survive. He rejected the heart of classical humanism: Cicero's claim that if we act from a thirst for virtue (wisdom, courage, justice, temperance – the four cardinal virtues described by Cicero in *Moral Obligation*) we will also achieve victory and see fortune smile on us. Instead, in Machiavelli's account, virtuous acts may lead to your downfall. The lessons a ruler needs most come from reality, not from abstract principle. Men must either be pampered or crushed, because they can take revenge for minor injuries but not for major ones. Cruelty must be seen to be inflicted, as in his most celebrated example, when Cesare Borgia's execution of a leading minister kept the people simultaneously appeased and terrified. The lessons are presented as pragmatism: inflict necessary pain quickly and early, so that it does not have to be inflicted every day. Be feared in a way that avoids being hated. Never keep your word if doing so places you at a disadvantage and the reasons for the promise no longer obtain; make yourself feared rather than loved if you have to choose. Above all, do not become attached to principles or values: vary with the circumstance because fortune is a violent river.

This is an exhilarating philosophy. It allows for a heady ruthlessness; a sense of agency; and a risky connection with the essence of life, free from the constraints of civilization. No wonder some rulers are titillated by such a naked justification for power, and find it easy to reject the claims of conscience.[16] No wonder, too, that many moralists have looked at governments and experienced the pain Milton felt when the Devil he had portrayed in *Paradise Lost* turned out to be a more rounded and compelling figure than the hard, cold and mean God that he had written about.

Rulers know that they are unlikely to be remembered with gratitude. It is a cardinal rule in democracies that governing parties are rarely rewarded for success; the only thing that matters is what they offer for the future. Ingratitude is inherent to politics. There is a famous story of how a mercenary commander saved the city of Siena: the city deliberated for some time over how to honour him and finally decided to kill him and make him their patron saint. All rulers may be unconsciously aware that this will be their fate: so why hem yourself in with unnecessary restraints?

The modern answer to the temptations of power, therefore, does not lie in individual reason or the persuasiveness of great thinkers, but in the reason of systems – structures, constraints and accumulated habits that blunt the Devil's arguments, shame them, contain them and, ultimately, make them unthinkable. It is these that allow al-Farabi's ideal to be approached, and governments to be founded on the types of knowledge, character and virtue that lead to true happiness.

8

Revolt and Revolution

*'How is freedom gained? It is taken; never given. To be free
you must first assume your rights to freedom.'*

Salman Rushdie

Shortly after the American Revolution, Daniel Shays and a group of
poor farmers in Massachusetts launched a revolt against the new
regime. They were bitter about how they had been mistreated by the
courts, and they resented what they saw as the excessive salaries being
paid to officials and the punitive taxes being levied on farmers. In
September 1786, Shays and some six hundred armed farmers attacked
the courthouse in Springfield. A few months later they stormed the
arsenal, shortly before being routed by government forces, arrested
and sentenced to death.

The victorious revolutionaries scratched their heads with worry.
George Washington interpreted the revolt as confirmation that men
'when left to themselves are unfit for their own government'. Thomas
Jefferson took a very different view: 'a little rebellion now and then'
was helpful he said, and 'the tree of liberty' needed to be 'refreshed
from time to time with the blood of patriots and tyrants. It is its
natural manure.'[1]

His implication was that although states aspire to order, their moral
quality depends on rebellion to remind them of their duties, and to
prevent stagnation and complacency. This chapter looks at revolt and
revolution as moral acts, and the continuing significance of the fact
that so many of the world's most powerful nations – including the

149

USA, China, Russia and France – are governed by states that were born in violent revolutions.

For most of human history revolt has been the only effective response to bad government. In many traditions the likelihood of diverging interests between rulers and ruled has long been recognized, and many thinkers sought to define when it was justified to revolt and overthrow bad leaders. In ancient China, as we have seen, one of the founding principles of Confucianism was that an emperor owed his position to his moral virtue. In the tradition descending from Mencius, once an immoral ruler had lost his heavenly mandate the population had the right to overthrow him. Mencius wrote of the king as sent by heaven 'to serve the people with just rule. If he fails and oppresses the people, the people have the right, on behalf of heaven, to dispose of him' – though the more deferential Confucians believed that they might have a duty to lead him towards morality. In ancient India the *Mahabharata* sanctioned revolt against a king who failed to protect his people or oppressed them, and the *Dharmashastra* described kings as servants, removable if inadequate.[2] Bal Gangadhar Tilak (the 'father of Indian unrest') drew on these traditions to advocate violent political action against the British Empire in the nineteenth and early twentieth centuries: when the order of *dharma* no longer protected them, he argued, people had to act violently and passionately but with detachment (*nishkama karma*) so that when the problem was resolved the passion would cease. These arguments drew on an interpretation of Hinduism's greatest text, the Bhagavad Gita, as a description of a family where the moral order or *dharma* has broken down and is being remade.

Islamic tradition is more conservative and has fewer traditions that justify revolt, since the only model of truly legitimate government is the caliphate, which is, by definition, the successor to the Prophet. Sometimes this led to very conservative conclusions. Al-Mawardi, one of the most influential medieval Muslim thinkers, wrote that 'a thousand years of tyranny are better than one night of anarchy'.[3] Revolt may be justified if the ruler has deviated from Islam, and is tyrannical, for example in the traditions of *khuruj* (literally 'going out' against the tyrant).[4] Shia Islam, in particular, has long celebrated rebels ever since the seventh century when the fourth Caliph, Ali, was murdered at Kufa and a few months later his son, Husayn Ibn Ali, died on the plains of Kerbala in a doomed battle against a vastly larger Sunni army, inspiration for successive generations of Shiites to set out on *khuruj* against the rulers of their time, most recently in the Iranian Revolution of 1978.

Some medieval Islamic theorists recognized that there could be tension between the holders of power around the Caliph, and the ulema, the intellectuals and scholars who were most familiar with the shariah law and could best guarantee its interpretation. But the very idea of popular sovereignty was potentially blasphemous since it implied an alternative to the sovereignty of God. This was why Islamist demonstrators in east London in Britain's 2005 election attacked candidates and argued that the very act of voting was blasphemy. Roman Catholicism has for most of its history been equally conservative, tending to side with order against revolt, suspicious of reason and independent argument and, until recently, hostile to democracy. Their stance at least had the virtue of consistency: if you believe in an all-powerful God it is hard to explain why he doesn't take responsibility for overthrowing bad rulers.

Seen from the vantage point of the twenty-first century, one of the great mysteries of history is why people did not rebel more often against states that were so far from being servants. Wilhelm Reich, who explored the twilight zone between Marx and Freud, sex and politics, wrote that 'what has to be explained is not the fact that the man who is hungry steals or the fact that the man who is exploited strikes, but why the majority of those who are hungry don't steal and why the majority of those who are exploited don't strike.'[5] Why, when there were so many more of the oppressed than the oppressors, did they not rise up and force states to become their servants?

Some of the answers lie in the skill with which intelligent rulers divided their people the better to rule them (for example, using troops from one part of the empire to suppress revolt in another, as the Romans and Chinese did). Some of the answers lie in the ways states bent people's minds to see their oppression as natural, immutable or even deserved, encouraging either passive fatalism or identification with the oppressor (like the Britons who quickly came to see themselves as Roman). But another answer is that people *did* rebel, often using the weapons of the weak – delay, evasions, sabotage, low-level disruption[6] – rather than frontal assault, but also often going further into violent revolt, for which, almost without exception, they paid a horrendous price in lives lost and blood shed. Peasant revolts leave far fewer traces than aristocratic wars, but their ubiquity does suggest that the stress of living without power can become unbearable and that, at least in agrarian societies, systems of power regularly reached a critical point in which all the elements were stretched in such tension that one shock could, at least for a time, unravel them.

The evidence is equally clear that although the sparks often found combustible materials, the people in revolt generally lacked the means to sustain their conflagration or to channel their anger into permanent institutions. Having burned down a few buildings and hanged the worst oppressors, they typically went home to finish the harvest. Faced with wily negotiators trained in statecraft, they rarely stood a chance.

England's Peasants' Revolt in 1381 is a case in point. The peasants of southern England stormed into London, sweeping all before them, and set out a radical list of demands. In their first negotiations they demanded the right to pay rents, free use of the forests and the abolition of laws that restricted their right to hunt game. All of these demands were agreed, and signed and sealed in official royal charters by the young King Richard II himself. The next day, buoyed by apparent success, the demands escalated dramatically. Wat Tyler, the rebels' leader, demanded the abolition of all rank and status under the king. Church holdings were to be taken and divided up among the people. The Church hierarchy also had to be abolished.

Even these demands were agreed, but only as a tactical manoeuvre to disorientate the rebels who could not believe that the king was not on their side. Then, in a scuffle, Tyler was killed. His severed head was raised up on a lance and brought to the king; the rebels dispersed; all the concessions were revoked by parliament; and many hundreds, if not thousands, were executed for treason.

The English state at that time felt no obligations of service to its peasants; all that mattered was its own survival. Later generations of rebels lost any illusion that the man at the top might somehow embody moral virtues that had become corrupted lower down. The Russian Narodniki movement in the 1880s aimed to destroy the most powerful person in government (Tsar Alexander II) to stir up the people's revolutionary spirit. Anarchists shared their view that an inert public was waiting to be galvanized by the force of an event or by violent deeds. The notorious International Anarchist Congress in 1881 called on its members to annihilate 'all rulers, ministers of state, nobility, the clergy, the most prominent capitalists and other exploiters', and in the following decades anarchists were successful in assassinating a fair number of leaders, including the President of France, the Prime Minister of Spain, the Empress of Austria, the King of Italy and the President of the USA[7] (no movement has achieved anything comparable since).

The idea that bad power has to be violently swept away, purged by flames, has proved influential. By comparison with the calm physics of the US constitution with its spheres in balance, the Bolshevik newspaper was named *Iskra*, 'the spark', and most twentieth-century revolutionaries saw violent struggle as morally superior to dialogue and compromise. Like nationalists they often adopted a moral metaphor of purification – eliminating the corrupt and oppressive by whatever means were at hand.

The more successful learned that the metaphor of a combustible society could sometimes prove only too accurate. Rebellions suffer the same dynamic as wars – emotions tend to be ratcheted up, ever more outrageous means are justified in the name of ends, and morality gets tangled in the mess of battle before being discarded. Some rebels have ended up killing many of the people they claimed to serve; others have become intoxicated by the glamour of violence and death, and the imagery of a purifying fire.

Revolutionaries gain energy from the abuses and failings of power. But the objective badness of conditions of hunger, war, injustice or lies has never been enough to prompt revolution. In famines and disasters people lack the energy to survive, let alone to revolt. The German communists in the 1920s and 1930s had an infamous slogan: '*nach Hitler kommen wir*' (after Hitler we will come). By this they meant that the monstrosities of Nazism would pave the way for them to take over. The anarchist Bakunin in the middle of the nineteenth century took a similar line. He advocated letting wicked oppressors live; by their 'monstrous acts they may drive the people into inevitable revolt'. Terrorists have often used atrocities to elicit a repressive response that then reveals the 'true' character of the regime and ignites the people's rage; many states, in turn, have fallen straight into this trap.

But most strategies that have tried to make things worse, to heighten the 'objective contradictions' in order to accelerate change, have backfired on their authors (the German communists paid a very high price for their political folly),[8] or sunk their societies into a low equilibrium of violent actions and violent responses in which neither side could prevail. Algeria in the 1990s is a good example of this sort of deathly equilibrium: after the government denied the Islamist FIS movement victory in elections in 1992 (with the encouragement of western powers), the two sides polarized towards ruthless, but pointless, violence.

The most successful rebellions and revolutions of the last century challenged the moral legitimacy of the current rulers and convinced people that an alternative was possible. None was prompted by acts of terror (terror turned out to be an effect not a cause[9]). Instead they more often came when periods of growing opportunity were blunted or temporarily reversed, like sixteenth-century Europe, Russia in 1917 or Iran in 1978. It is blocked hope, not hopelessness, that brings people on to the streets (which is why large bodies of students can be such a threat to stagnant regimes). And when this coincides with international pressure or divisions within the ruling elites, states can weaken sufficiently for the revolutionaries to gain an edge.

Most profound revolutionary changes result from pressure from both the top and the bottom of society. The Marxist belief that only the bottom, the mass of the proletariat or peasants, has revolutionary integrity is a delusion, repeatedly disproven in the actual history of successful Marxist-Leninist revolutions. The poor and dispossessed are unlikely to have the requisite specialized skills of organization and ideology that are needed to overthrow a large state, and every real revolution has brought together an alliance of professionals and disaffected members of the elite, as well as workers and peasants. Lenin and Mao came from the middle class. Castro was the son of landowners. Pol Pot spent his teenage years in the company of princes. For the people at the bottom self-interest was a sufficient motive; for those at the top, a moral sense of duty was usually interwoven with personal resentments.

Revolutionaries had to first demonstrate the state's excessive strength, encouraging it to show its true repressive face. Then they had to show its true weakness. Actions like the Tet Offensive in Vietnam in 1968 make little sense in military terms – at least 35,000 fighters were lost and no territory was gained. But they do make sense as challenges to the moral claim of the state to provide protection and order. For the same reasons rebels attack essential infrastructures, whether through sabotage or strikes, so as to show that the state is out of control (and these devices, usually associated with the Left, could also be turned against them, as when the CIA financed strikes and sabotage against Allende's Chile in the early 1970s). Huge marches show that the state is out of touch against the united people, and help the rebels to talk themselves up.

The classic examples of these were the demonstrations that led to the overthrow of the Iranian Shah in 1978. In the Shia religion funerals take place after forty days of mourning. Each time the Shah's police shot demonstrators they set in motion a cycle of mourning and revolt. On 18 February, 29 March and 10 May ever larger demonstrations fused tragedy and anger until, during the month of Muharram at the end of 1978, daily demonstrations were shot at until, on 12 December, two million people came on to the streets of Tehran to demand the Shah's overthrow.

Revolt simmers constantly because people find powerlessness painful. But it flares up only when special conditions apply. There have to be some leaders able to exploit openings, as the Ayatollah Khomeini was in the Shah's Iran. There may have to be a faltering of repression, perhaps as a result of a division among the ruling elites, or, as in December 1978 in Tehran, unwillingness on the part of the soldiers to carry on shooting at their fellow citizens. Revolt may also be most likely when the state's repression threatens activities which are vital to the welfare of a significant part of the population, like shopkeepers or traders (this last point has often proven decisive in swinging critical groups against the state).

What of the moral content of revolt and rebellion? All rebellions begin as revolts against injustice, oppression and exploitation. The memories of enslaved ancestors do more to drive people to revolt than any dreams of liberated grandchildren. But true revolutions combine moral fervour with an account of how the state should be different, and a vision, sometimes clear and sometimes blurred, of how the state could become a servant.

This is why most revolutions have aspired to the same four goals that define the service of the state: protection (often a call for peace); welfare (and bread); justice (wrongful imprisonments or deaths often spark the critical riots); and truth. The first two goals dominated earlier revolutions – 1789 started as a rebellion for bread; 1917 was about bread and peace. More recent revolutions have often occurred against a background of relative peace and prosperity. In Prague in 1989 the marchers carried banners labelled 'justice' and 'truth', and many revolutions today are followed with truth and reconciliation commissions, which combine the two goals into a single process.

In all revolutions truth is the commanding height which is fought for most vigorously. Certainly the greatest success for any revolutionary movement is to make the state appear to be what it so often is: a fiction that is self-made, often without roots, and one that is immoral as well as false. This is what happened to the Shah of Iran in the mid 1970s and to Soviet power in the 1980s (though the decisive move there was for the fiction no longer to be supported by tanks). Social truth mutates as one set of conventions dies and another set takes hold.

During revolutionary periods the often unspoken contempt of the powerful for the powerless is starkly revealed and plays its part in this shift of truths. Marie Antoinette's comment that if the people did not have enough bread they should eat cake is infamous. Less well known is Emperor Hirohito's memorandum in 1945 to the American Supreme Commander MacArthur, asking that the occupation of Japan should not be too short, because his subjects needed to be kept firmly under control. They were childlike and their 'low cultural level' made them receptive to dangerous ideas about rights. At roughly the same time Crown Prince Akihito, then a boy and later emperor, noted that the war had been lost because the common people had 'behaved selfishly'. In eastern Europe the ruling apparatchiks regularly under-estimated their population's capacity to organize itself; they appear to have genuinely believed that they were needed.

In revolutionary situations most ruling groups reveal themselves to be prisoners of their own fictions, responding to threats by hardening themselves, following the route that the historian Theodor Mommsen ascribed to Cato, the great conservative of first century BCE Rome, the man who 'basically conserved the republic to death'. Few can handle the politics of retreat: making concessions at just the right speed and with just the right amount of moral contrition to stay ahead of the waves.

Revolutions, in short, are moments when, under stress, the symbolic world of the state collapses and its moral promises are revealed to be empty. As this happens the real gulfs of interest between the state and those it claims to serve are exposed. Often there is nothing ready to fill the space created, no organization with an alternative programme or ruling elite skilled enough to take over. Anarchy and disorder are the first result of a regime's collapse. Older powerholders may try to fill the vacuum, to make themselves indispensable. The revolutionaries themselves may try to mirror the state in their own structures, the better to stabilize turbulent currents, channel energies and impose authority. But even when there is a party with a revolutionary programme waiting in the wings it is bound to lack the sophisticated craft skills needed to govern effectively. That is why there is sense in Orwell's comment that 'all revolutions are failures': revolutions never realize the vision in the minds of the revolutionaries, who are indeed often at best disappointed, at worst consumed. Friedrich Engels wrote that 'the revolution made does not in the least resemble the one they would have liked to make', and Adam Michnik, one of the leading intellectuals of the Polish Solidarity movement, the first mass revolutionary movement to take on a revolutionary party, said that those who start by storming Bastilles end up building new Bastilles (and, in due course, as Aldous Huxley put it, 'what starts as heresy ends up as superstition').

Year-zero absolutism certainly has ugly effects. But the uncomfortable truth for an era of stable governance is that revolution has often worked. It worked in the narrow sense that revolutionary regimes now dominate the world. Four of the five nations on the US Security Council – the US, China, Russia and France – share the unusual characteristic of having been born in the violent overthrow of a hated *ancien régime*. The one exception, Britain, still celebrates Oliver Cromwell, the executioner of its king, outside the gates of parliament. All these states were founded on texts with a strong moral purpose. All believed that they had found a unique secret of good power, and all shared the characteristic behaviour of revolutionaries – the burning desire to universalize the principles that had been crystallized in these texts (even Britain, the rather odd product of two revolutions and one restoration, has felt compelled to export its distinct values and institutions). All thought that they had begun history anew. The French revolutionaries tried to replace the Christian era with the Republican era that began in September 1792. Pol Pot decreed 1975 a Year Zero (rather as German liberals had decreed 1945 a *stunde null*). Ayatollah Khomeini described the birth of the Iranian Republic as 'the first day of a government of god'.[10]

At one point the USSR looked like the paradigm case of an aggressive revolutionary exporter, even though the Comintern had not achieved a single successful revolution when it was abolished in 1943; subsequently the Red Army proved a far more proficient exporter. Arguably, however, the greatest revolutionary power of the last century has not been Russia, or Cuba or Iran, but America, convinced of manifest destiny, believing in the superiority of its system, and engaged for more than half a century in promoting its system worldwide. It exemplifies more than any other nation the feverish desire of revolutionary states to promote truth; truth that they had uncovered but which remained invisible to others; truth which, if shared, would make others' lives richer, more fulfilled and more moral.

Revolution worked in that the world was remade and revolutionary nations vanquished their enemies. But revolution also worked in another sense – the indirect sense that the threat of revolution forced ruling elites to share power, to give voice and respect to their peoples. Much of what is taken for granted today as democracy, welfare and the taming of capitalism would have been impossible without the threat of revolution (and in the words of one political scientist, democracy essentially took 'the conception of the right to resistance to unjust authority' to its logical conclusion).[11] The assumption that powerful groups will oppress or exploit to the limits of what they can get away with is the safest and soundest starting point for politics, and it is only fear that holds this in check.

Revolutions undoubtedly produce their own pathologies. If history repeats itself first as tragedy and then as farce, then so do revolutions repeat themselves, first as momentous shifts of the tectonic plates that lead to the slaughter of millions, and then as theatre. In the backwash of the century of revolution, the Baader-Meinhof gang and the Symbionese Liberation Army looked like children mouthing a script they didn't understand, their fingers caught in the great wheel of history. The Red Brigades' most dramatic action, the kidnap and murder of Aldo Moro in 1978, only proved their political bankruptcy. For others it became enough to adopt opposition as a stance. The slogan of the radicals in Italy in 1969 was '*tutto e subito*' – everything and now – a position that was turned thirty years later into a theoretical stance for the anti-globalization movement. Michael Hardt and Antonio Negri wrote (without irony) in their book *Empire* in favour of 'Being-against', the 'essential key to every active political position in the world' that animates the 'lived experience of the global multitude . . . at the most basic and elemental level'. This is a position of permanent sulk or tantrum that is almost opposite to the hard slog of real change (and is perhaps best described as Groucho Marxism: 'whatever it is, I'm against it!').

Modern democratic societies are built to resist revolution. The procedures for making decisions are broadly legitimate, and voices and interests which are blocked can rarely mobilize against the majority. Most modern states have created stakeholders in order. The interdependence and complexity of modern industrial societies renders narrowly monopolized power too inefficient and illegitimate; so power is usually shared and networked, and because power is exercised through so many disciplines and agencies, a higher proportion of the population is likely to have a stake in the complex order of society and stand to lose out if it is thrown up in the air.

In such contexts revolutionaries become irrelevant. Governments today no longer need the kind of law that the US Congress passed a century ago banning anyone 'teaching disbelief in or opposition to all organized government'. The only revolutions that succeed are ones that take society into order, with the minimum disturbance, rather than out of it, like the velvet revolutions in eastern Europe in 1989 that promised to replace the arbitrary inefficiencies of Communist rule with the prosperous order enjoyed across the borders in western Europe, or the revolutions in Asia which deposed Marcos and Suharto. Apparently revolutionary moments like May 1968 in France may sow the seeds of longer-term social change, but they don't threaten the states' ultimate authority.

Rebellion remains a vital part of what keeps power moral. When young French Muslims rioted in 2005 they weren't trying to change the regime, but their actions forced a neglectful government to respond as nothing else could have done, and earned them more recognition than electoral politics had ever achieved. When Bolivian rioters at roughly the same time forced an ineffective government from office they too showed that democracy isn't solely about polite conversation in parliaments. It needs to be continually refreshed, if not with the 'blood of patriots' then at least with raw passions, anger and ideals.

But instead of revolutionary politics, opposition in mature democracies has become part of the way that the system learns and adapts. Dominant political parties respond to challenges by changing their beliefs and their forms, and states respond to social movements by talking to them, even helping them to take institutional form.[12] This is a great progress; it is the way in which revolt, which revitalizes and restores power's moral sense, is institutionalized and tamed, so that the battles of politics leave behind bruised egos rather than bloodied corpses.

9

Hot and Cold Democracy

*'Democracy is that form of government whose principal rules,
when observed, have as their aim the solution of social conflicts
without the need to resort to mutual violence (heads are
counted, not severed).'* Norberto Bobbio[1]

Before modern times most rulers claimed to derive their authority
from God or nature. Their job was to rule; the people's job was to
obey. Democracy has turned this hierarchy upside down, making the
people sovereign, so that whatever they say, either through opinion
polls or through their representatives, is treated with the deference
that was once due to monarchs. Democracy has formalized the principle that anyone affected by decisions should be able to shape them.

The speed with which democracy has become a global standard,
the measure by which all regimes are judged, is remarkable. It has
swept all before it. It has come to be loosely associated with economic
growth,[2] and with the widening of a zone of peace. Its spread is
confirmation, if confirmation was needed, that the desire for autonomy and sovereignty is not culturally specific. Other things being
equal, people prefer to rule than to be ruled.

Yet, the rise of democracy was neither inevitable nor preordained.
I quoted earlier John Adams' comment of two centuries ago that
'there never was a democracy yet that did not commit suicide'. His
pessimism has been vindicated by more modern history too. Germany
and Spain in the 1930s are prominent examples of democratic suicide,
and Argentina a more extreme one, which passed from the introduction of universal male suffrage in 1912 through a coup in 1930 to

democracy in 1946, a coup in 1955 to democracy in 1973, and through a coup in 1976 to democracy in 1983.

The rise of democracy wasn't smooth either. Where democracy succeeded it usually did so as the result of violence rather than quiet consent. The democratization of England followed (belatedly) after a civil war in which over 200,000 lost their lives.[3] Switzerland's emergence into full democracy happened only after the Sonderbund civil war in 1847. The US Civil War's casualties (between 300,000 and 600,000) prefigured the industrial carnage of the First World War, and Germany and Japan only became modern democracies when it was forced on them after bloody defeat in the Second World War. The spread of democracy in the 1990s was as much a result of a change in the balance of military power as it was a consequence of persuasion. The idea that powerful elites like to share power voluntarily is a comfortable myth that helps societies recover from conflict, but it bears scant relation to the truth. The philosopher and theologian Miguel de Unamuno once wrote that 'always it comes about that the beginning of wisdom is fear.' When it comes to the sharing of power, too, the beginning is fear that the alternatives may be worse.

Democracy is widely recognized as the necessary condition for power to be good. But what it is remains blurred at the edges. The American political scientist Samuel Huntingdon wrote that 'elections, open, free and fair, are the essence of democracy, the inescapable sine qua non.' Certainly there can be no democracy unless rulers can be ejected. But democracy is more accurately understood as a cluster of devices and institutions, some of which point in contradictory directions, and all of which are continuing to evolve. Democracy's apparent triumph, and its claims to represent a morally, as well as economically, superior system to all the alternatives has shone a sharper spotlight on these devices and on their tensions. In this chapter I describe what they are and how they work, and ask what it is about democracy that makes democratic governments good.

To answer this question we need to trace out the different directions in which democracy pulls. Democracy was born in ancient Athens, where it meant self-rule. But its contemporary tensions can all be traced to the English Civil War, which was the first great democratic struggle to make the state into a servant, a complex battle that set the tone for the political history of much of the West over the succeeding four centuries, and which even today provides pointers to democracy's future evolution.

ANTI-DEMOCRACY

The first pole of the argument was staked out by Thomas Hobbes, a scarred and scared survivor of the civil war in England who in 1651 made the modern case for a powerful state, a Leviathan, to hold chaos in check. The ruler might be selected from the people rather than by divine right or birth, and they might even be elected. But once in power they needed untrammelled power. Too much accountability and democracy would dilute their powers, and would inevitably threaten the survival of the community as it grappled with enemies outside and inside.

This was the view held by most monarchs, who in any case believed themselves to be servants of God, not man. For the Church, the idea that the masses might be empowered implied a corresponding reduction in God's power on earth, a view echoed in contemporary Islamist arguments against democracy. But Hobbes' argument was more general, and in some ways simpler: an argument about why order always had to triumph over disorder if it was to hold in check humanity's moral failings.

Until the nineteenth century the arguments between democracy and monarchy were decisively won by the monarchists. Plato provided one source of authority: two of his uncles had been killed trying to avert the return of democracy to Athens, and his teacher, Socrates, had fallen victim to democratic intolerance. Most of the critics of democracy took aim at both the character of democratic rulers and the way they ruled. A popular assembly was bound to be incompetent, too easily swayed by eloquence and emotion, and captured by parties that stood in the way of a collective will. The exercise of power would involve more corruption to satisfy the poor and hungry, more insecurity as special interests were paid off, and there was no guarantee that democracy would promote liberty since demagogues would be likely to prevail.[4] For Montesquieu, Hegel and the other great figures of early modern political thought, democracy lay in the past, as a form of government that had been tried and failed.

Many modern autocrats, including Deng Xiaoping, Lee Kuan Yew and Hosni Mubarak, have advanced similar arguments, presenting the fundamental political choice as one between order and disorder, and justifying their position by reference to a set of values (Asian, Catholic, or African), the divisions of the people or the irresponsibility of political parties. Some autocrats have tried to design polities without anything resembling a political party, or even a professional politician, on the grounds that political competition would destroy their fragile order (Nigeria's military rulers, for example, invented a set of approved political parties in the late 1980s, with near identical manifestos and comically similar identities, and Yoweri Museveni in Uganda successfully presided for two decades over politics without parties, to the acclamation of his western aid donors).[5] Their justification was that ethnic divisions would be amplified by open and competitive party politics and that order had to be paramount.

In most parts of the world these arguments are in abeyance now. But they are likely to return if times become insecure, or if nations' self-respect is sufficiently badly bruised, or if too many democracies do indeed show themselves to be corrupt and incompetent.

THE DEVICES TO CONSTRAIN POWER

The next pole of the argument assumes that any Leviathan will be a danger. Its vices are likely to outrun its virtues. So political progress entails constraining the state's sovereignty rather than building it up. This argument was best described by John Locke. In his *Second Treatise of Civil Government*, published anonymously some thirty years after the English Civil War, he called for a democracy based on property, where the primary task for the constitution and law was to restrain state power from abuses, echoing Montesquieu's words that 'power should serve as a check to power'.

This view was not radically new. Much of ancient Rome's history can be read as the ultimately unsuccessful attempt to achieve a balance of powers against kingship, through an extraordinarily complex division of political roles. The idea that power needed to be balanced could be found in the aristocratic republics of Buddhist northern India, and the republics of early medieval Italy, all of which were models of governance with deliberately divided powers and a wider participation in the affairs of the state. Buddha, for example, recommended 'regular and frequent assemblies' to the Vrijjis people. Susa in south-west Iran in the middle of the first millennium had an elected council, and a popular assembly which elected magistrates. Japan's early seventh-century constitution or *kempo*, introduced by the Buddhist Prince Shotoku, stated that 'decisions should not be made by one person alone. They should be discussed with many.'

In the past many societies went through phases when the monarch's authority waned and was dispersed. In pre-Columbian America, for example, Chichen Itza, a late Mayan centre, had a joint government of nobles. Medieval German towns had the *volksammlung*, the assembly of citizens, and Switzerland's rural areas pioneered *Landgemeinde*, a more direct form of democracy. Many had public trusts vested with powers to govern themselves and guided by ideas about public need and public service.[6]

England's civil war accelerated this current of thinking and brought it to the heart of a rising nation. Like so many revolutions the English Civil War did not follow anyone's plan. Chance and contingency explain more than necessity, and when the republic was declared only a tiny minority were republicans.[7] When Charles I described his enemies as advocates of democracy, no one sprang to democracy's defence.[8] But once the king had been judicially executed, the monarchy could never be the same again. Despite the restoration of Charles II (who sought to be almost as absolutist as his father), from then on power had to be conditional, negotiated and limited.

Much of what we take to be modern democracy has therefore come to be defined through its formal restraints on power (very few of which were present in ancient Athens).[9] The evolution of these designs is the great legacy of the political thought of Locke and his successors, and represents a remarkable story of societal innovation and emulation. A dozen or so devices, all founded on the idea that holders of power cannot be trusted, have evolved from this tradition and are now mainstream in modern democracies. They are 'cooling' devices, there to stop leaders from getting carried away with passions or crimes.

CONTESTABILITY

The most important of these devices makes power contestable. Competition is the handmaiden of virtue. The direct election of leaders, and the power to remove them at regular intervals, is the simplest guarantee that states will work to make a reality of protection, welfare, justice and truth. (The great irony of the English Civil War was that the war for parliamentary democracy left parliament so denuded: elections were repeatedly delayed, parliament became a rump and, in the end, Cromwell gave up even the pretence of democracy.) In itself the election of leaders was not new: many past societies elected leaders and monarchs, and the modern Polish monarchy continued to be elected by the nobility until the country was dismembered in the eighteenth century. Republican Rome was a permanent electoral campaign of argument, festivals and bribes.

But the distinctive feature of modern democracies is that the franchise is so much wider. At the beginning of the twentieth century only one nation (New Zealand) was a democracy in the modern sense of the word – governed by rulers elected by all adult citizens. Less than 5 per cent of the adult population was enfranchised in Athens and in the more democratic Italian medieval republics. Even in Britain after the 1832 Reform Act the franchise reached only around 3 per cent of the population. But by the late nineteenth and early twentieth centuries the franchise was extended to 100 per cent of the adult population, first in New Zealand (which introduced universal male suffrage to the Maori in 1867, and to the rest of the male population in 1879 before becoming the first country to introduce universal adult suffrage in 1893),[10] and then by degrees in every other democracy, so that it is now the basic principle of suffrage in some 120 countries.

The ability to vote governments out at regular intervals is the hallmark of democracy. Yet democracies vary greatly in the extent to which they see election as the best way to fill positions of authority.

Some use election to choose police chiefs, judges and school boards, while others restrict election to political roles. Some limit the power of elections by deliberately rotating roles so that a popular leader cannot use electoral legitimacy to build up a power base. In Rome the consuls were restricted to one year in office. The early Italian republics followed suit and generally had very short periods of office. In contemporary Europe Switzerland holds its federal system together by rotating the role of Prime Minister (and has been judged by the World Bank to be the world's most effective government). The US, like many presidential systems, limits incumbents to two terms, and elects them indirectly through the odd mechanism of the Electoral College (a vestige of distrust of the public). A more radical model that achieves some of the same ends is the use of lot as an alternative to election for the appointment of assemblies, and sometimes of leaders: the Venetian republic's intricate system based on lot to elect the Doge was a classic example.

Majoritarian democracy on its own does not guarantee against states acting abusively towards at least some citizens. In societies riven with distrust, the formula of 'one person, one vote' is a poor basis for legitimacy: instead powers need to be formally divided between groups. Northern Ireland and the Lebanon have had to devise complex formulas to protect minorities from each other, and to cool ethnic passions. Nigeria has a confederal arrangement to guarantee minorities some control, while Belgium's system is 'consociational', guaranteeing its minorities power at the centre. In societies that are divided by other inequalities there may need to be special provision for the powerless (for example, India's quotas for tribal peoples that partially make up for the imbalances of a parliament where half the members come from the Brahman caste, which accounts for only 3 per cent of the population). Societies with overly dominant political parties may need special provisions to promote circulations of rulers and strong oppositions, so that those in power expect to be out of it and vice versa. Gregor Gysi, the leader of the ex-communist PDS in Germany, put it well in the party's slogan for the election of 1994: 'good government begins with good opposition'.

The very factors that make a competitive system work may, however, harm it. If leading politicians spend much of their time deriding their peers, trust in leaders as a whole will tend to decline. Consensus is bound to be harder to forge in systems where parties have to define themselves in opposition to each other. Nevertheless, the principle that prospective rulers should compete for power, and that the prizes of victory should be strictly temporary, has turned out on balance to favour good power. And the idea of contestability runs deep. It means that every victory is ephemeral and every apparent consensus can be challenged, and it is through the clash of ideas as much as the clash of people and parties that democracies learn and evolve.[11]

RULES AND LAWS

In the 1990s a group of Italian magistrates – the *mani pulite*, or 'clean hands' – used the law to destroy a clutch of corrupted ruling parties in the '*tangentopoli*' bribery scandals. Their actions, cheered along by the public, were a striking assertion of the claims made by Locke and his successors that laws, rules and constitutions should reign over individual rulers. As Aristotle had argued in Greece, and Kautilya in India, universal and impersonal rules are better guarantees of virtue and good decisions than individual judgement alone. Ch'en Liang, the influential Chinese political thinker, wrote in the twelfth century that the human heart is 'mostly self-regarding, but laws and regulations can be used to make it public minded. This is why the prevailing trend in the world is inevitably moving towards laws and institutions.'[12] Half a century later, the English jurist Henry de Bracton wrote that 'the king must not be under man but under God and under the law.'[13]

These comments said more about their hopes than about reality. But during the medieval period many cities drew up constitutions to guide and constrain their rulers, paving the way for the English constitution written by Oliver Cromwell in 1654, which can make a fair claim to be the first formal description of powers and duties at the level of a large nation (today there are over two hundred, though not including Britain). Constitutions constrain the power of leaders not just by subjecting them to the rule of law but also by precisely specifying their authority and how it can be exercised.

Few monarchs or even emperors were ever wholly above the law;

conversely many modern leaders have invoked the legal immunity that comes with their office to keep clear of the courts (for several European leaders, including Jacques Chirac and Silvio Berlusconi, remaining as President served as an attractive alternative to the threat of prison). But the idea that executive government is subordinate to law is important symbolically as well as in practice. Permanent constitutions that are hard to change embed the fundamental values of a society, and entrench them against abuses. In the US, the constitution stands at the apex of the system, above the merely law-making legislature, although the executive, with the approval of the legislature, appoints the members of the Supreme Court. In Europe human rights legislation has empowered national and European judiciaries to block legislation they disapprove of, and has undoubtedly protected some citizens from arbitrary or ill-conceived policies.

The ideal of a state governed by law rather than solely by representatives has been realized most fully in the German theory and practice of the *Rechstaat*, or the state under the rule of law – advocated by Hegel as the ultimate expression of reason and then crystallized 150 years later as an understandable reaction against a history of extreme executive autonomy and against a population who went along with it. In the pure theory of the *Rechstaat* the law stands even higher than the people. At one point in 1946 the constitution of the new West German republic was going to include the words 'all power derives from the people'. But the drafters concluded that if popular sovereignty was absolute the people could choose once again to replace the democracy with a dictatorship.[14] There had to be laws and rights to constrain the people as well as the state, and democracy had to be protected from itself as well as from its enemies. Article 20 of the German constitution even gives all Germans 'a right of resistance against anyone who attempts to abolish the constitution', which includes by implication a right of resistance to a government legitimately elected by the majority.

Laws can rein in the people and restrain the bad behaviour of future rulers. Japan's post-war constitution was drafted in seven days by a team working for General MacArthur, who was frustrated by the Japanese government's inability to draft a constitution that involved any democratic rights and wanted to guarantee that there would be no return to the militarism of the 1930s. Treaty commitments to such things as fiscal rigour or human rights can work in the same way. These were unknown before the late twentieth century, but have become commonplace – consequences of a lack of self-trust on the part of leaders and citizens (though big countries generally find it too easy to break the rules imposed by international treaties, so these work best for small countries). Some constitutions (including Germany's and Japan's) can best be understood as anchors against an unhappy past, the constitutional equivalent to Odysseus having himself tied to the mast of his ship to resist the Sirens; others can best be understood as anchors against the pull of an unwanted future (like Canada's, which is designed to reduce the risk of the country breaking up).

On their own constitutions can be little more than façades that do little to cool the malign plans of their leaders. Stalin's constitution of 1936 was a model of progressive democracy (though he admitted that 'those who cast the votes decide nothing. Those who count the votes decide everything.'). Many Latin American countries adopted constitutions similar to the US in the nineteenth century without having to concede the painful uncertainties of democracy. Other constitutions have continuously evolved with adaptations, like buildings gaining extensions and new rooms, knocking down walls or dividing the house when families fall out. Always the relationship between the words and the truth is a fuzzy one: the same constitution that in one period guarantees an inclusive polity, open and progressive, in another supports hardened oligarchies paying lip service to the public. China's current constitution, for example, guarantees an array of human and labour rights, which provides just enough grounds for campaigners to struggle to make these commitments real.

Constitutions are fuzzier than constitutional theory would suggest because they embrace competing expressions of sovereignty: on the one hand, the deeper and more enduring commitments of law and, on the other, the more ephemeral expressions of authority based on election. Because both the law and the politicians claim to derive their legitimacy from the people, systems of this kind are prone to conflicts. However, because ultimately legal authority derives from political power, the latter usually wins. The campaign in the 1990s by Italian magistrates against the corrupt executive was neatly turned around by Silvio Berlusconi when he came to power and portrayed the magistrates as interfering egotists. In the US in the 1960s and 1970s the Supreme Court drove forward civil rights and abortion law far ahead of the elected Congress, but then found its own appointments even more politicized as a result. The same ambiguities apply to unassailable basic rights that are guaranteed by independent courts. The English Magna Carta of 1215 was primarily a deal between a king and his rebellious barons, but it did talk a language of rights to the law – 'to no man will we sell, to no man will we deny or delay justice or right' – and it came to be seen as a first step on the road towards the rule of law, and, ultimately, towards the purer democracy portrayed by Thomas Paine as shattering the crown of royal dominion and giving each citizen a jewelled piece. These equal rights can certainly restrain bad states. But they also give rise to conflicts, since most rights turn out to clash with other rights, and in the end politics determines which rights have priority.[15]

DIVISIONS

If power cannot be trusted it has to be broken up. A divided state should be cool and considered, not hot and tempestuous. Much of the distinctiveness of the European tradition comes from the pluralism of societies in which the church was independent of the state, and towns and cities maintained some independence from nations and empires. The virtues of division can be traced back from Montesquieu through Thomas Aquinas to Plato. Even the most powerful emperors sometimes understood that divisions could make the system they ruled over work better. Basil I in ninth-century Byzantium, for example, paid high salaries to judges to make them independent, and provided subsidies for poor suitors bringing actions against magnates and officials. The virtue of dividing power up was most enthusiastically proclaimed by the framers of the American constitution, who tried to balance the greater effectiveness of undivided power with the greater virtue of divided power, on the assumption that power would become corrupt, or would at least risk attracting the corrupt. For James Madison the answer lay in setting ambition against ambition, interest against interest: 'if men were angels no government would be necessary.' This view of government as a grim necessity, an arbiter between malign human natures, necessitated

the regular distribution of power into distinct departments; the introduction of legislative balances and checks; the institution of courts composed of judges, holding their offices during good behaviour; the representation of the people in the legislature, by deputies of their own election; these are either wholly new discoveries or have made their principal progress towards perfection in modern times.[16]

The result in the USA was a system of government in which the various parts could compete for priority. At times the President might make the running – as when Lyndon Johnson drove through the war on poverty or Ronald Reagan imposed tax cuts. At other times the impetus came from Congress. Often progressive change was driven by neither of these, but rather by the courts: from the advance of civil rights to the progress of public health on tobacco, the use of class actions and court judgments substituted for a temporarily captured or blocked political system.

If the goal is to restrain the power of the state and stop corruption, other kinds of division are also essential. Rules are most likely to be fair and honest if their design is separated from their administration. This allows for diverse interests to be involved in making rules but reduces the incentives for the rulemakers to design rules that favour them. Accountability has to be separated from execution through the principle of audit – the external validation of statements, such as national statistics or company accounts. Some responsibilities, particularly for protecting values, have to be put in the hands of trustees at one remove from executive decision-making: this is a role often claimed for Senates and Presidents on the assumption that the elderly will be less prone to venal corruption and burning ambition.

All of these arrangements encourage the principle that decisions should be depersonalized. In states where the personal will of a leader is decisive, the people with exclusive access gain inordinate power (even if they have apparently marginal titles, like the King's secretary in late medieval England, the cupbearer in Persia or the minister of the pen in imperial Ethiopia).[17] Modern constitutions make many of the equivalent roles impersonal, appointed by neutrals using transparent criteria, and they restrict the powers of personal advisers.

The growth of the state in the nineteenth and early twentieth centuries was generally accompanied by a centralization of power, justified by the needs of warfare, and by the efficiency that would result from common national standards for education and the regulation of everything from language to railway gauges. But as war between states has become less common, in Europe, north and south America, the case for undivided centralization has ebbed in favour of radical decentralization and federalism. Indeed, the idea that power needs to be divided and restrained to be good has been applied to almost every dimension of government.

The most radical way of embedding decentralization is federalism, which was pioneered in Switzerland, Europe's first democracy, and involved a strict devolution of powers both to urban assemblies and rural direct democracies. Switzerland's governing model is utterly unique, run by a seven-member Federal Council representing the main parties according to a fixed formula, but each elected by the whole parliament, alongside cantons which retain substantial powers to pass laws and raise taxes. Over the last few decades the Swiss approach has become ever more mainstream.[18] Many countries have sliced back the power of the centre's agents. France was once the very model of centralized command; the state employed every public official, and its agents, the *préfets*, were all powerful. Yet the Loi Deferre, passed in 1982, devolved power down to departments and some 36,000 communes. In the late 1970s Sweden allowed local areas to opt out of parts of the welfare state and declare themselves free communes, running their own services. Even China has moved away from its highly centralized tax system of *tongshou tongzhi* (unified collection and budget appropriation), in which central government allocated budgets to local administrations, towards one with much more local discretion (even though the centre still controls appointments and dismissals).[19] In Bolivia and Chile decentralization has encouraged more popular participation in the business of government, and redirected resources to meeting the poor majority's needs for education, health, water and sanitation. India's decentralization to village *panchayats* during the 1990s had the additional feature of mandated representation for women (a third of all seats) and low castes and tribal groups. Everywhere decentralization has tended to constrain the predatory character of national governments, which siphon off money intended for local services (one study in Uganda in the early 1990s, for example, found that only 13 per cent of grants for schools actually reached them).[20]

The democratic tradition that we trace back to Athens presumes that government works best when it is closest to the people. But there are many other potential virtues in decentralization. One is that it widens the pool of potential leaders at higher tiers of government, providing a training ground in which they can prove their skills.[21] For countries going through a transition to democracy this is likely to be particularly important. It helps to nurture new leaders, and gives them the confidence to govern effectively and without corruption. It can break the dangerous assumption, common among publics who have lived for long under repressive regimes, that all leaders will only be in it for themselves (a system designed to cope with mistrust helps to build trust).[22]

It is a measure of the success of democratic decentralization that no secession has ever happened in a mature democracy. Secessions have often happened in the wake of wars and revolutions, or in societies without universal suffrage, and many nations have fought to secede from dictatorships. There are also many examples of immature democracies facing successful secession, including the Czech and Slovak republics' mutual secession from Czechoslovakia and Greenland's secession from the European Union (though not from Denmark). But these stand in stark contrast to the successful containment of secessionist movements in Catalonia, Quebec, Scotland or India which can best be explained by the dynamic whereby sufficient concessions are made to the potential new nation to make secession less attractive. In Spain, for example, barely a generation after Franco's dictatorship, the regions now enjoy unconstrained autonomy and virtually subcontract national government rather than the other way around. The same pattern explains the containment of the threats to secede of the Northern League in Italy and of Rio Grande do Sul, the wealthy state around São Paolo in Brazil.

Decentralization does not automatically weaken the central state.

Even in the most federal systems, the power of the centre grew over the last century: as Hannah Arendt noticed, one of the peculiarities of political power is that it can be 'divided without decreasing it'.[23] Nor is decentralization guaranteed to make power good. It can lock in greater inequities and undermine minimum standards. It can be a tool for governments that want to dispose of responsibilities rather than powers – the move to federalism in the US in the 1980s was part of Reagan's strategy for slimming government down, and many more recent decentralizations, from Russia and Kazakhstan to Tanzania, have passed responsibilities down to local governments that lack the tax bases to fulfil these roles. Too much decentralization can make it harder for societies to take difficult decisions involving uneven sacrifices (for example, responding to a threat like climate change). But overall the shift of decision-making downwards over the past twenty years has undoubtedly produced better government, more focused on the things that really matter to people.

While federalism and decentralization counterbalance the predatory tendencies of the centre, another set of devices prevents different kinds of power from linking up. Many societies prohibit politicians and officials from taking payments for services rendered (in 2005, for example, India's parliament, the Lok Sabha, expelled eleven members who had fallen for a sting operation offering them bribes to ask parliamentary questions), and prohibitions on party finance aim to stop wealthy elites dominating the state (and in those societies where these prohibitions are weak, like Italy or Brazil, the wealthy do generally dominate the state). At the beginning of the twentieth century Theodore Roosevelt established an armoury of regulators and trust-busting agencies to force business to concentrate on competition and innovation rather than lobbying for protections and largesse from government. These moves were reinforced three decades later by Franklin Roosevelt in his attacks on the 'economic royalists'. But they have been missing in many other countries. The result can be a pathological short circuit which links big business and the big state, but leads both to stagnate (Argentina is a particularly striking example). Burckhardt wrote of ancient Rome that the political and civic order were the same thing, which made them more brittle because the political could not detach itself from itself. A similar problem afflicts societies where business is too interwoven with politics.

In other societies the decisive separations will be different. The priority may be to keep the military at arm's length from the state (as in Turkey, for example), or the church (as in Spain), or to prevent the state from holding a monopoly over military force. In 1689, the English Bill of Rights recognized the right of English Protestants to keep arms after a Catholic king had endeavoured to disarm them, and the belief that people should be free to own and bear arms for self-defence remains strong in many countries, including Switzerland, the USA, Lebanon and Albania.

A rather different kind of separation insulates decisionmakers from too much short-term political accountability, on the grounds that it leads to bad decisions. Independent central banks are one example, but there are many other areas where some insulation can make institutions work better: curriculum design; setting priorities for health treatments; the oversight of science. All of these benefit from buffers and divisions which cut across the pure theory of democratic authority. They dilute popular sovereignty and the sovereignty of representatives in the name of a more fundamental public interest.

What follows from this remarkably varied list of divisions and separations that modern democracies now accept as commonplace? The French constitution of 1791 declared that 'sovereignty is one, indivisible, unalienable and imprescriptible', and nearly a century later Albert Venn Dicey, the greatest constitutional expert in England, argued that divided powers simply bring forth 'the predominance of the judiciary', which was such an unattractive prospect that it justified the absolute supremacy of parliament. Yet the history of modern democracy tells a story contrary to both views, one in which sovereignty has been made divisible, alienable, prescribable, surrounding its power with walls and moats, weighing it down and reining it in like a wild animal always at risk of turning on its rider.

VISIBILITY

These formal restraints, guided by distrust, have increasingly been joined by measures to make power visible. That which is invisible is taken to be suspect. Many parliaments require ministers to answer questions. The British Prime Minister answers to the House of Commons for thirty minutes each week, and flexible rules allow any subject to be covered, as well as secondary and tertiary follow ups. Many ministers opt to do public 'question and answer' sessions with the public. Officials are cross-questioned in public before their appointment and during their term of office. Much of the practice of accountability becomes a professional performance: how to appear open and confident without conceding ground or making a mistake. Modern leaders are carefully trained to cope with the dynamics of aggressive questioning: how to deny the premise of difficult questions; how to project polite civility while saying very little; when to throw in an apparent revelation. The diffuse power of a committee or assembly is rarely effective against the concentrated discipline of the executive (which is why investigative media are often more effective at uncovering lies). But visible responsibility remains the single best symbol of equality between the leader and the led.

Reinforcing this visibility are the various constitutional guarantees of accountability: the legal guarantees for independent media to investigate and scrutinize; the absence of censorship (except on issues like pornography which have nothing to do with the interests of the state); and citizen rights to government information (which are more than two centuries old in Sweden). The head of one industrialized country's civil service described the advent of freedom of information as like having the curtains pulled back as you are getting dressed in the morning – 'and it's not a pretty sight' (although he recognized that the sunlight is the best protection against corruption). In many societies states have gone one step further and provide direct support for criticism, funded through non-governmental organizations (NGOs) and universities that publish reports on the folly of government policy. The cacophony of the modern media celebrates this freedom, even if it sometimes recalls Shelley's comment on his grandmother: that she had lost the art of communication but sadly not the gift of speech. But the presumption that visibility will improve moral standards has been vindicated. The countries with the strongest legal guarantees of open information (including many Scandinavian governments) are also the ones with the least corruption.[24]

The paradox of open government is that confidentiality is as essential to good governance as transparency – it is hard to have an honest discussion exploring difficult possibilities if there is a serious risk of its being exposed in public (the same would be true of most of our daily lives). The British Government's Central Policy Review Staff, for example, was closed down in the early 1980s shortly after a paper on pensions policy options was leaked; its task had been to think long-term and radically, but once its thoughts were public Margaret Thatcher, who was then Prime Minister, felt that she had no option but to denounce it. Leaks destroy trust, and force decision-making into smaller, more secretive teams, which are bound to be worse informed, and therefore likely to produce worse decisions. Likewise a government in which every second person is keeping a diary will be more like a stage set than a body capable of rigorous deliberation. Too much accountability can also be damaging if the need to service the public or its representatives diverts too much of the leaders' time and psychological energies away from their main duties. As with every aspect of democracy, we are dealing here with questions of proportion, not absolutes.[25]

The general point, though, is this: we have come to believe that power can only be good if it is surrounded by constraints – competition, laws, divisions and visibility.[26] The virtue of these devices is that they help to instil integrity; they make it harder to be cruel, capricious or dishonest. Their vice is that they are often at odds with the state's capacity to act as a servant: they may so constrain power that it becomes ineffective; become so intrusive to politicians that no sane person would want to become one; and they may so balance executive power that in times of crisis it freezes.

EMERGENCY POWERS

This last weakness, which is shared by all restraints on power, explains a common cycle. If communities face a compelling external threat, or a major problem that needs to be solved, the constraints on action come to look like dysfunctional red tape, a costly indulgence. Then, when the crisis is at its peak, the constraints are lifted and power is freed, and recentralized, often under pressure from an impatient or insecure public. Abraham Lincoln, for example, justified his actions at the beginning of the American Civil War in 1861, 'whether strictly legal or not', as having responded to 'a popular demand and a public necessity'. America's decision to suspend the rule of law in its treatment of prisoners incarcerated in Guantanamo Bay after the invasion of Afghanistan was based on a similar justification of necessity and popular support. In the next turn of the cycle, as the threats recede and the risk of powerholders abusing their position mounts, the pressure grows to re-impose rules, and in time, through long periods of relative peace and prosperity, power becomes more rule-bound and more governed.

For ancient thinkers it was an unavoidable character of states that they could escape from legal constraints. Their true character is revealed at times of emergency, and that character is of a power that is not responsible or accountable. The Greek thinker Diotogenes wrote that 'because the king has an irresponsible power and is himself a living law, he is a god among men.'[27] In other words, because kings made the laws they could never be subject to them. Even if they appeared to be bound by laws, they retained the power to suspend the laws or ignore them. In today's constitutions that power is much more tightly circumscribed to extreme circumstances where the duty to protect comes first. But every state reserves for itself the right to suspend its own laws, and may have to if it is to fulfil its responsibility to protect.[28]

Machiavelli advised that even the most stable and successful republics should allow in their constitutions for temporary dictatorships to cope with emergencies. He argued that clear limits needed to be set. The ancient claim that *necessitas legem non habet* (necessity has no law) had to be kept within boundaries, and for temporary dictatorship to be acceptable there had to be a credible threat and a mechanism for monitoring and enforcing the limits independently of the dictator (in Rome the dictator ruled for six months; if he failed to stand down he was declared an outlaw). By allowing for temporary emergencies in which democracy was suspended, the system could become more resilient.

Arrangements of this kind reinforce the paradoxical character of all the constraints I have described. They are all aspects of a system that is governed by restrictions, but which itself makes all of the restrictions, a system which in extreme circumstances suspends itself.

REPRESENTATION

If the devices to constrain power assume that the state risks becoming bad, representation assumes that the state can be good and that the people can be masters of a servant state through the device of electing representatives. Representation formalizes the people's role as principal and the state's role as agent, but with an intermediary – representatives who are commissioned by the people and in turn commission the state to do their will.

The idea of representation is relatively new; it is not self-evident. In ancient Athens the people represented themselves. Until the later Middle Ages the fact that someone was elected did not make them a representative in the modern sense of standing for the people who elected them, or acting as their agent. This idea of representation, which seems so obvious today, is not found in ancient Greece, Rome, China or India. Rather it steadily evolved from the experience of the medieval assemblies, through bodies like the Polish Sejm, the Swedish Riksdag and the German Landtage, and took shape in the distinctive model of the English Parliament which, after the nineteenth century, became the template for most other nation states as they established parliaments and assemblies (and internalized Burke's famous distinction between representatives and delegates).[29]

The impossibility of direct involvement by the public in the affairs of large nations meant that as democracy developed it did so through intermediaries – professional politicians, organized in parties, sitting in assemblies and parliaments and answering to a public who became observers and occasional participants.[30] The Greeks assumed that the right scale for democracy and any form of good power would be very small, a few thousand in the case of Athens. The supporters of modern democracy assumed that its natural scale was the nation state, based on a homogeneous, self-aware people.

For more than two centuries sceptics have questioned whether any system of representation can meaningfully turn the state into a servant. Rousseau wrote that 'it is against the natural order of things that the many govern and the few are governed ... the moment a people provides itself with representatives, it is no longer free.' The democratic paradox is that while in theory the people rule, in practice it is governments that govern. The only solution that Rousseau could imagine was 'the obedience of everyone to the law he has prescribed himself'. But Rousseau was unable to provide a convincing account of how this might occur. The public could not meet and deliberate together, and could not act as a single agent. Rousseau proposed periodic popular assemblies, since 'sovereignty cannot be represented'. He was particularly scathing about the democracy to be found in Westminster: 'The English think they are free but they are quite wrong; they are only free when parliamentary elections come round; once the members have been elected they are slaves and things of naught.' In any case, if sovereignty could be represented, the representative would in time claim sovereignty for himself (and, indeed, Napoleon shouted to the members of his legislature: 'I alone am the representative of the people').

The idea that the state can simply reflect the public's wishes has turned out to be a chimera. Sophisticated theoretical analyses of voting long ago showed that it is impossible to design a voting mechanism that could add together every voter's preferences in a coherent and consistent way.[31] Any real voting system will be used strategically – people use their votes not just to express their preferences but also to help achieve an outcome they want (for example voting 'no' in a referendum to weaken the government, regardless of the question being asked). Even if more perfect voting systems were conceivable, and a great variety have been suggested, it is hard for representatives to act as true agents for the public unless the public are themselves well organized, able to formulate claims and demands and to scrutinize what their representatives do – one example of the problem that political scientists have called 'agency costs', the costs involved in getting someone else to act as an agent for you.[32] So representation has to be more than an attempt to mirror the public; it has to involve some kind of conversation in which diverse views find a synthesis.

The other consistent fear of representation is that elected leaders will represent the worst rather than the best in human nature, because they will find it easier to pander to the people's fears and resentments than to their generosity. Leaders who wanted to represent the people would try to give them an identity – as Italians, or Americans, or proletarians or Shiites – since, without an 'us' to represent, the very idea of representation risked becoming incoherent. But that sense of identity would require enemies, outsiders to blame if things went wrong. So, as the ancient philosophers had warned, democracy was naturally associated with factions and divisions, competing identities and claims, rather than with the common interest. It is not a coincidence that nationalism evolved in tandem with representative democracy, directing energies outwards against real or imagined enemies in the imperialist jingoism of Britain, or the revolutionary fervour of France, or in the USA, which began its life as the antithesis of expansionist nationalism but became one of the world's most nationalistic nations. (George W. Bush in the mid-2000s was alone among major world leaders in wearing an enamel badge of the national flag on the lapel of all his suits and regularly claiming divine sanction for the nation he rules.)

The fear that popular power, whether organized directly or through elected representatives, would bring predictable pathologies – a repression of minorities or a dicatorship of the poor against the rich – dominated the thinking of many early democrats. It encouraged the framers of constitutions to build in safeguards against the very popular power that representatives were meant to embody. The people who drafted the American constitution wanted 'mixed government' rather than democracy for just this reason. There was to be a monarchical element, represented by the President; an aristocratic element, represented by the Electoral College and the Senate; and a democratic element in the House of Representatives.

Montesquieu was an important influence on American thinking at this time. He believed that English government worked well only because the central power of the executive in London was balanced by local aristocratic power in the House of Lords and by the power of the gentry in the House of Commons. Without such a balance, states based on representation would naturally tend to become bureaucratic despotisms, whether they served the monarch or the people. Only if important social interests were committed to a wide distribution of power, with strong bastions of authority well beyond the reach of the state, would good government be possible. Representative democracy without an unrepresentative force to balance it would risk descending into tyranny.

The aristocracy on which Montesquieu pinned his hopes became incapable of fulfilling this role. But the new industrial division of labour of the nineteenth century ensured some of the same effects with the growth of a strong business sector, trade unions to represent the workers, and civil organizations to represent ideals, all of which made it harder for any one majority to exercise power despotically. This new social structure also made it possible to aggregate different interests in a small number of competing parties, like the US Republicans, or the German SPD. Representative democracy worked when people came to identify themselves as part of these larger social blocs – classes, interests, nationalities – that roughly fitted the size of the polities they lived in. But it has run into problems when these conditions were absent or disappeared. Many of the contemporary problems of western democracy reflect the breakdown of the class structure that had underpinned political parties. In some countries politics is a constant struggle against fissiparous social realities. In contemporary India, for example, there are national, class and caste-based parties as well as regional and local ones, and the dominant party, Congress, is still living off its prestige as the agent of independence sixty years ago. In conditions of this kind national democratic politics is likely to be under continual strain (India's solution has been to cede a far-reaching federalism to states, with further decentralization below that level).

Representation also becomes difficult when ideological divisions are too stark. Where a society is riven between competing world views, as de Tocqueville pointed out, 'it must either experience a revolution or fall into anarchy'.[33] Algeria in the early 1990s is a good example. President Chadli Benjedid had legalized the Islamic Liberation Front, FIS, and brought it to the brink of power in 1992 when the military cancelled the second round of an election that FIS was about to win; Chadli was forced to resign, and Algeria descended into a bloodthirsty civil war. The West backed the Algerians in their cynical manipulation of the democratic process, shocking the purer believers in democracy. Others argued, in retrospect, that Islamic militants should have been given the chance to run Algeria, on the grounds that this would have been the best inoculation against Islamism for the rest of the region.

Seen through the eyes of the public the task of representation is to represent. But seen through the eyes of the state its task is to provide legitimation. It is now very difficult to rule legitimately without some legitimation from elections. The few exceptions – like the Saudi royal family or the generals in Myanmar – toy with limited or cosmetic elections. Even Saddam Hussein felt the need to hold a nail-bitingly exciting election a few months before his country was invaded (he won: with a vote of over 99 per cent).

The ancient philosophers generally assumed that democracy would be hot, passionate and unruly. Instead, in its representative form, it tamed politics, and made politics work for the state as much as vice versa. Although parliaments are forums of oral culture, they do their business through written laws, which usually strip away unruly emotions and hatreds. Parties wanting majorities have to rein in their extremes. Politicians wanting to enjoy the spoils of power have to take care not to disrupt the mechanisms that generate wealth.

Most nineteenth-century radicals believed that the states they saw around them were irredeemably flawed. Their character as master was ingrained. They either had to be overthrown or rebuilt from scratch. Democracy was simply incompatible with a state based on command and hierarchy. Yet the radicals' demands were never satisfied. Instead the democrats had to compromise, turning the state into what R. H. Tawney called a 'serviceable drudge', directing its old bureaucracies to the new priorities of public health, primary schooling and welfare.[34] During the nineteenth century British writers wrote of bureaucracy as the 'continental nuisance' from which their democracy was immune. Yet by the early years of the next century bureaucracy was rampant, and George Bernard Shaw was able to justify it on the grounds that whereas before corruption and incompetence had been inherent 'state qualities like the acidity of lemons', the state had become so efficient and meritocratic, that progressives needed to 'gather the whole people into the state'.[35] Soon democracy was serving the state as much as the state was serving democracy, and many of the radicals who were elected to office, like the German Social Democrats and the British Labour Party in the 1920s, turned out to be very conformist, desperate not to offend, and eager to win the approval of the officials they oversaw.

The more confident elected leaders argued that their job was not to reflect the public but rather to lead it. They could serve their people best by challenging them rather than reflecting their wishes, and the most moral kinds of leadership might involve giving the community or the organization what it needed, not what it expected or necessarily wanted.[36] That a decision is popular, or democratically decided, would not automatically make it good, and devices that tried to tie representatives down would be likely to backfire: the British Prime Minister Sir Robert Peel, for example, said of manifestos that they bring 'all the constraints of contracts magnified by the far greater possibilities and uncertainties of government'.

Representation has become normal, yet the arguments about it have not subsided. The more successfully democracy has been tamed the more vulnerable it has become to the claim that the people's interests are no longer being served. Immanuel Kant had warned that 'the people that is represented in parliament by its deputies finds these guardians of its rights and liberty to be deeply interested in the position of themselves and their families'. Strong traditions of distrust feed off the assumption that representatives risk being co-opted or corrupted. Some countries have elected leaders primarily because they have never heard of them (this was just about the only virtue, for example, of Fernando Collor, elected President of Brazil in 1989), and in recent decades many great parties, like the Canadian Conservatives, the

French Socialists and the Italian Christian Democrats, experienced sudden haemorrhages of support when the public lost confidence in their commitment to service. More formal delegation through mandates and manifestos have been proposed as solutions but can simply empower one set of political professionals relative to another. In the US, arguments for term limits and recalls (successfully used in California to replace Governor Gray Davis by Arnold Schwarzenegger) have fed off populist outrage against elected bodies (by the end of the last century only one in ten Americans had confidence in Congress). Almost everywhere referendums have become more common, not as plebiscites to approve leaders, but as complements to representative democracy that can provide additional legitimacy. And many countries have tried to open up recruitment to political and administrative elites, encouraging more lay people to serve as jurors, magistrates and councillors, so as to hold in check the excessive professionalization of representatives or presidents.

Fears that representatives are bound to become detached from the people they claim to serve are unlikely to disappear. Most democracies have tended towards a consumerist model of representation, in which citizens choose between two or three competing parties offering packages of policies that are put together by professionals rather than members. In place of representation this model substitutes a relationship of contained transaction, with nothing like the emotional commitment or identity implied by a party or government that is an expression of the people's needs. Worse, it has tended to freeze politics. After the nineteenth century's burst of innovation, which gave rise to what we recognize as the modern forms of government, including parliaments, parties, manifestos and professional politicians, there has been little innovation in the mechanisms of democracy. Despite scattered experiments with deliberative polls, citizens' juries, open source methods of communication and participative decision-making, the only successful innovations that have taken root are tools of research (the opinion poll and the focus group) and tools for communication (the ministerial statement on television rather than in parliament, and the more sophisticated marketing of the television spot and the Internet). In short, the political class has hung on to its privileges and fixed the rules of the game to make it harder for outsiders to break in.[37]

THE CO-EVOLUTION OF EQUALITY AND DEMOCRACY

Powerlessness is bad for people. It is bad in direct ways, because when you are powerless you are likely to have bad things done to you. It is bad in less direct ways, because low status weakens people's very physiology,[38] and when their identity or self-esteem are threatened their capacity to perform diminishes too (being powerless really does make people lesser people).[39] These are all reasons why any society concerned about helping its members to flourish has to distribute power relatively equally, without great gulfs or imbalances.

Democracy turned the state into a servant, and was founded on the claim that people are fundamentally equal. But when there are deep inequalities of wealth and income, even apparently democratic states are more likely to be captured by the rich. The most radical arguments made at the time of the English Civil War took this problem seriously. The formal apparatus of liberty, and even elections, would count for little if the underlying structures of power were heavily weighted against the poor. For the radicals there seemed little point in replacing monarchy with an oligarchy of merchants and landlords.

Gerard Winstanley's *Law of Freedom* was published in 1651, the same year as Hobbes' *Leviathan*. He was one of the first modern thinkers to grasp that economic equality was essential for political liberty. Hobbes believed that a strong state was needed to curb the drives of men of roughly equal physical strength. Winstanley hoped that a communal, non-competitive equality could achieve the same thing. In a competitive environment the power-hungry leader would encourage 'fears where no fear is; he rises up to destroy others for fear lest others destroy him; he will oppress others, lest others oppress him.' In a co-operative environment without stark gulfs of wealth and power no one would need to behave like this. Winstanley's philosophy built on the old rhyme from the time of the Peasants' Revolt: 'When Adam delved and Eve span who was then the gentleman?' – promising a return to an older primordial equality without ranks or property. 'Kingly power', he wrote, 'is like a great spread tree; if you lop off the head or top bough, and let the other branches and root stand it will grow again and recover fresher strength.' So revolution had to be far-reaching.

Winstanley was not against government as such, but against government that 'gives freedom to the gentry to have abundance, and locks up the treasures of the earth from the poor . . . if they beg, they whip them by their law for vagrants; if they steal they hang them.' Kingly power meant class rule. The task for his generation was to 'make restitution of the earth, which has been taken and held from the common people by the power of conquests.'[40]

Winstanley's ideas failed in the climate of the Protectorate and the Restoration. Cromwell turned the New Model Army against the Levellers and radicals. Colonel Richard Rumbold, the Levellers' leader, was, two decades later, hung, drawn and quartered for his part in the Rye House Plot against Charles II, though not before saying that 'there was no man born marked of God above another and none comes into the world with a saddle on his back neither any booted and spurred to ride him.' But in the following centuries these ideas reappeared repeatedly and became the foundation of the progressive Left and its arguments to extend the meaning of democracy beyond equal rights and equal votes to equality of work and wealth.

James Harrington, the author of the other great Civil War treatise *Oceana*, made some parallel arguments. He was convinced that unfair changes to property had sparked off the Civil War, and that one of the keys to a good constitution was an upper limit on property. His other favoured idea was that offices of state should be rotated: a third of the executive or senate in his model constitution had to be voted out by ballot every year, and could not be elected again for three years. Too much power concentrated in the same hands was a recipe for despotism and corruption.

Both Harrington and Winstanley recognized that whatever the formal claims made by constitutions, the interests of those in power and those they served were unlikely to be aligned where there were big gulfs of wealth and opportunity. They grasped that states are likely to care most about legitimization when the underlying facts of power force them to do so – when they need the people's acquiescence or support. Seen through this lens, history can be read as a story about the changing balance of power between rulers and ruled. In pre-agrarian societies there had been a relative equality of power between them and a low power ratio (although as we have seen, there were still privileged elites), and the memories of such times survived in the traditions of leaders who were themselves sacrificed to the gods. In much of the world agrarianism sharply ratcheted these ratios upwards, with larger surpluses and stored wealth, and so spawned empires with huge concentrations of power and wealth, and cultures around the state that emphasized the gulf between rulers and ruled.

Societies based on farming could still be reasonably equal, so long as there was relatively equal access to the main means of production. In agrarian societies that meant land, and in England the fact that much of the land was owned by independent farmers was critical to the growth of a common law independent of the sovereign, and with it a language of rights.[41] Magna Carta is important not only because of its contents (it is one of the oddest documents to have become an icon of democratic history, a mishmash of details about licences, fines and baronial privileges) but because it recognized an equality of power (at least between nobles and the king), and so provided a restraint on England's kings, who had to give acknowledgement to it at least forty times over succeeding centuries. Once it was acknowledged that the king was only a first among equals, it became easier to imagine how others could be brought into the world of rights and privileges.

Low power ratios also depended on weak armies. All of the early democracies, starting with Iceland, England, America, Australia and Switzerland, were protected from other states by seas or mountains. They were relatively free from the direct threats that would justify a coercive central power; and they lacked the large accumulations of spoils in their capital cities that so often corrupt elites. By contrast, the constant competition of nations on much of the European continent where these conditions were lacking (and where control over the means of production was less distributed) bred absolutism, strong armies and bureaucracies, and weak civil rights. It is no coincidence that Winstanley's most ardent followers came from that very rare phenomenon in early modern Europe – a people's army that had been created to cut the ruler down to size.

Later, when the Industrial Revolution had filled the cities with poor and overworked labourers, the balances of power changed again, and many states discovered that the only way to avert revolution was to expand political and social rights and bring the new working class into the political conversation. The advance of welfare in Germany, Britain, France and Scandinavia is comprehensible only as a historic compromise struck between classes; its consolidation is comprehensible only as the result of democracy.[42] Equality and democracy co-evolved. The power of concentrated and organized labour drove the spread of the franchise and trade union rights; the need for mass armies reinforced the same process and forced states to legitimize themselves; and the power of crowds armed with rifles undercut the advantages of technologically advanced states.

As democracy and equality evolved in tandem poor majorities used democracy to get the things they needed: pensions and schools, homes and jobs. For exactly the same reason elites have resisted democracy, as when Brazil's military took power in 1945 to prevent the heirs of Brazil's great progressive leader Getúlio Vargas from pursuing land reform and democratization. How these battles play out depends both on underlying power ratios and on tactics. Elites which recognize their weakness may make concessions to avert revolution. Even limited welfare can buy off revolt, literally (Bismarck's welfare state remains the boldest example of such a pre-emption from above). In very unequal societies the incentives for elites to resist democracy are high, as are the incentives for the poor to take hold of the state. The result can be erratic long-term instability (as in the case of Argentina, which only a century ago was one of the world's richest countries). Fear of coups may restrain redistributing governments (Lula, Brazil's President in the early 2000s, was all too aware of the fate that befell another democratically elected leftist, Salvador Allende, in Chile thirty years previously), just as fear of popular revolution encourages it. As James Madison pointed out, politics is more likely to be volatile when the economic returns to state control are high. Conversely, in relatively equal societies, repression is likely to be more costly for elites than redistribution.[43] Some of the wiser reformers have understood that redistribution of land and education can give the poor a stake in continuity and order, which in turn makes democracy less costly for elites. For example, the land reform imposed by the occupying

Americans on Japan, Taiwan and South Korea after the Second World War, turned out to be a remarkable piece of luck for those societies, not just because it helped their economies to grow but also because it forced their governments to become better servants. This luck was not matched in South America, where US support for conservative regimes kept land firmly in the hands of the elites, and directly hampered both democracy and economic growth.

So democracy is made possible by greater equality, and in turn promotes equality, forcing states to focus on the mundane prosaic needs of their citizens rather than on glory. Democracies spend 25–50 per cent more on public goods and services than autocracies, and pollution controls are twice as high in democracies as in autocracies once the effects of income are excluded. Strong environmental policies turn out not to be caused by, or associated with, higher income as was once thought, rather they are encouraged by democracy, and the claims of the relatively poor for cleaner air and water.[44] Evidence from Africa shows a similar story – as democracy spreads governments spend proportionately more on primary education while spending roughly the same as non-democratic societies on the university education that benefits the elite.[45] Democracy also has an equalizing effect on power relations between men and women. The best evidence for this is that in the nineteenth century women's life expectancy was about five years less than men's. Since 1900 the trend has reversed and a gap in the other direction is continuing to widen.

It is not inevitable that any of these trends will continue. Most liberal advocates of equal rights still do not extend their arguments into the world of work; democracy usually stops at the office reception and the factory gate.[46] Because so many different factors affect inequalities it would be surprising if there were consistent or predictable patterns. A further distribution of power, and greater reciprocity between states and citizens, might be encouraged by the continuing spread of literacy and the dramatic rise in higher education (from under 5 per cent of the population in developed countries in 1960 to nearer 50 per cent). China's 1978 land reform, which allocated rights strictly in terms of demography, is one of the world's most historically important acts of egalitarianism (and contrasts with India where land is still held very unequally by landlords).

But twenty-five years after its land reforms the unbalanced introduction of markets and regressive taxes have made China one of the world's more unequal societies. Within other market economies the unprecedented economies of scale and scope, and unprecedented levels of market dominance (look for example at Intel or Microsoft) that come with knowledge-intensive economies, have generated concentrations of wealth whose only precedents are the predator empires of the distant past. Around them has formed a more polarized labour market in which the returns available to the few lawyers, consultants, designers and managers who can market their skills globally have pulled ever further away from the average. This may be one of the reasons why some of the world's wealthiest societies are witnessing falling relative social mobility and, according to some evidence, a diminished circulation of elites (for example, in the top US universities, only 10 per cent of undergraduates come from the bottom 50 per cent of the income range).

OLIGARCHY

These tendencies are bound to influence the moral character of governments, pointing in precisely the opposite direction to the equalizing effects described above. A century ago Robert Michels presented tendencies to oligarchy as an 'Iron Law' that would ensure that the new democracies would serve the few rather than the many. His main target then was Europe's socialist parties: whatever their claims to represent the people, in reality they would only favour one of a set of competing elites.[47] His case was exaggerated, and with varying degrees of success many of the parties he criticized succeeded in distributing power to the relatively poor and weak. But he was right to sense how likely it is that power will consolidate beneath the surface of competitive democracy as political parties freeze their original networks of support and patronage. He was also right to sense that in some democracies the ironic result of government by, for and of the people would be the rise of new dynasties (though even he might not have foreseen that all four of the Indian subcontinent's big nations would come to be dominated by political dynasties, or, for that matter, that

American politics would be so coloured by the Bushes and Kennedys).

In the mature democracies tendencies towards oligarchy are particularly associated with the concentrated power of business and the media. Business acquires power both indirectly as a by-product of pursuing profit, and directly, in those industries that depend on governments for their contracts, regulations and privileges (Haliburton, the company whose boss, Dick Cheney, became US Vice President in 2000 is a particularly good example). The media includes organizations that have power thrust upon them simply because they are good at attracting large audiences, and others that actively seek power (like Rupert Murdoch's Newscorp that has aggressively used its power to promote his causes).

Oligarchy may be a universal tendency (if an elite can get away with reproducing itself, it will), but it depends on favourable conditions. It is unlikely where there are barriers in the way of accumulating or passing on opportunities, in genuine meritocracies, or where strict rules make it harder for elites to turn one kind of privilege (like money) into another (like political power). Societies with extensive public provision and fewer elite institutions tend to be less oligarchical (which is why Canada is a more mobile and open society than the USA, and why Sweden is less of an oligarchy than the UK).

Where the tendencies towards oligarchy are strong they reinforce the well-documented links between social exclusion and political exclusion. The tendency of the relatively poor and excluded to opt out of participation is evident not just in election turnout patterns in the UK and US but also in the newer forms of cause-based activism right across the western world, which are more likely to be dominated by wealthier groups than the older activism of parties and civic engagement. The rising use of the Internet in citizen action, for example, appears to be a radically democratizing tool, making it easier for civil society to organize itself. Yet from any global perspective it encourages more communication and co-operation between the relatively privileged rather than stronger connections and alliances between the privileged and the poor.[48] In other words, the underlying dynamics of democratization and distributed power are by no means assured. These are all reasons why social policies to equalize access to human and social capital are inseparable from good governance.

'A BEING THAT GOVERNS ITS OWN ACTIONS'

This chapter has shown, I hope, that democracy is not a single thing. It is an agglomeration of often contradictory devices and principles that is still evolving. It aims towards an ideal of service but can never quite reach it. Within our constitutions we balance and divide government powers to stop them from oppressing us, but in being balanced they can be neutered and rendered useless. The workings of the state are made visible, but they can become so transparent that the confidentiality needed for making hard decisions is undone, or the lives of leaders are so exposed to public scrutiny that few want to countenance taking on a role of responsibility. The state can be broken up, dispersed and weakened. Yet when enemies appear we want a strong power to protect us. We aspire that the state should be direct, immediate and in touch, but then find that it is too hyper-reactive, too emotional, insufficiently grounded, informed or responsible. Democracy depends on equality, but constantly throws up new forms of oligarchy.

The tensions that grind beneath the surface of modern democratic politics have at their core the ambiguous idea of self-rule. Thomas Aquinas' comment, that 'the highest manifestation of life consists in this: that a being governs its own actions. A thing which is always subject to the direction of another is somewhat of a dead thing', is as good a definition of the spirit of democracy as any, and of what people risked revolt for. Powerlessness constricts and constrains; it chills the lifeblood.

Yet in a packed society on a planet of teeming cities this ideal is unreachable: to get by autonomy has to be constrained, and communities survive only if they are able to agree and enforce constant compromises between people and interests. Self-government in any strict sense is an impossibility except on a desert island. It is an impossibility for the individual since so much of what we need for life must come from others. It is an impossibility for small communities since in even the smallest village there will be conflicting interests, and the word 'self' soon becomes incoherent. And it becomes extremely hard at the scale of a nation or a continent with tens or hundreds of millions of minds with differing needs.

What we legitimately want may be something rather different from self-government. We want to be able to exercise power with others, to be part of how decisions are made, and included in at least some of the decisive conversations, even if often that means we are on the losing side. We want to be governed by systems that do not depend on the virtue of rulers. Instead, we want systems that can channel the full gamut of human motivations – from greed and lust for power to altruism and belief in human goodness – into the public good, because their underlying logic forces leaders to behave like servants even if they think like crooks.

IO

Alienation and Cycles

'How long do works endure? As long as they are not completed
since as long as they demand effort they do not decay.'

Bertolt Brecht

Many past religious visionaries, revolutionaries and radicals dreamed
of a perfect end point: a stable and benign order that they imagined
as a city on the hill, or as a utopia where history comes to an end
and the community returns to a primordial state without greed and
division. Democracy has often been portrayed in just this way – a
perfected mechanism that automatically equilibrates itself and guarantees the public good. In this chapter I look at the patterns of decline
that afflict even the best intentioned governments and ask: why do
they decay, and what makes renewal possible?

One of the Arab world's greatest historians was al-Yusi, who wrote
in the seventeenth century about many of the same themes of power,
guile and betrayal as Machiavelli. He told a perfectly sculpted story
which has parallels in every culture, and which stands well for the
experience, as opposed to the theory, of democracy:

After Ibn Abi Mahalli seized Marrakesh, the brothers of his order sought him
out to pay him homage and offer their felicitations. But as they stood before
him congratulating him on his newly conquered kingdom, one of their
number remained silent. The prince pressed him to explain himself. He
replied: 'You are Sultan for the time being. I will not speak unless you give
me leave to tell the truth without fear of reprisal.' 'Granted,' said Ibn Abi
Mahalli. 'Speak up then.' 'In ball games,' said the faqir, 'some two hundred

men chase after a ball and struggle to tear it away from each other, risking blows, injuries and death, all for the sake of the ball. The whole enterprise results in nothing but fear and pain. And if you examine the ball you find that it is nothing but a bundle of rags.' When Ibn Abi Mahalli heard this parable he understood its meaning and burst into tears. 'We intended to restore the faith,' he said, 'but we have gone astray.'

The idea that the holders of power are always liable to forget what it was that they fought for is remarkably common. Morality is rarely stable. Whatever is good has to be repeatedly fought for, and the experience of individual governments and administrations has more in common with the human experience of cycles of birth, maturity and decay than with ideas of progress or cumulative evolution. All too often administrations that start with high ideals and enthusiasm end in failure and corruption. Grand plans shrink back, and promises are forgotten.

This appears to be a natural rhythm. It was first set out, with great sociological insight, by Ibn Khaldun in the *Muqaddima*, written in 1377 and one of the world's first great texts of social science, which described the moral cycles of power in north Africa. The main explanation for government dynamism, Ibn Khaldun argued, is the moral force of outsiders. Every few generations a new wave of nomads swept into the cities and drove out the tired ruling dynasties, bringing fresh energy and idealism. But before long they too were corrupted, prompting another wave of rebellion and renewal. 'Reason and tradition', he wrote, 'make it clear that the age of forty means the end of the increase of an individual's powers and growth ... the same is the case with sedentary culture in civilization ... when elegance in domestic economy has reached the limit it is followed by subservience to desires. From all these customs the human soul receives a multiple colouring that undermines its religion and worldly well-being.'

According to Ibn Khaldun, the herders and mountain people, the people of the 'bled' (the areas beyond the reach of formal state power) were virtuous, full of courage, energy, sobriety, modesty and honesty. Their virtues grew directly from the hardship of nomadic life, which bred an intense solidarity. Repeatedly, however, tribes were drawn into settled areas, sometimes as new dynastic rulers. But the price they paid for their new prosperity was that they no longer relied on their own solidarity. Instead, settlement led to growing inequalities. The solidarity of the tribe became ever more a distant memory, a useful myth rather than a reality, and in time the experience of power destroyed the very thing that had been its source in the first place.

That source was *asabiya*, the subtle concept that lies at the heart of Khaldun's account. It is a complex kind of power, derived from the egalitarianism of the tribe, but ultimately condemned to undermine that egalitarianism. *Asabiya* is in a sense a deception, the feeling of being a group which, in fact, reinforces domination by one family or leader. It supported a simpler moral authority in the desert areas, but mutated in towns that were full of 'immorality, wrongdoing, insincerity, trickery, lying, gambling, cheating, fraud, theft, perjury and usury.' In towns and cities rulers could not contain their greed; officials became rapacious. Excessive taxation undermined the economy, wrecked social order and sowed the seeds for the regime's downfall. And so a cycle was set in motion: barbarian nomads repeatedly conquer the settled communities, inject them with new energy, but then find their energies sapped until the cycle begins again.[1]

Ibn Khaldun was writing about the very particular conditions of north Africa in the Middle Ages. But his comments resonate much more widely. Any settled regime, free from immediate threats, will risk sinking into stagnation. It may become self-serving and complacent, prone to convince itself that its tasks have been completed, and tempted to pay no more than lip service to its originating ideals. The sort of egalitarian ideas that underpinned *asabiya* and inspired radical reform down the ages have, again and again, become little more than cosmetic masks for new kinds of power as passion cools into hypocrisy. These are all, perhaps, examples of what Mark Twain meant when he said that history doesn't repeat itself, but it rhymes.

Why is this such a general pattern? There may be less fear; rulers may become comfortable, more confident that they have the main interests locked in on their side. But perhaps the deeper reason is that any settled regime loses touch with the sources of its moral virtue, the empathy and sympathies which energized it in the first place. Politics draws its energies from dissatisfaction, resentment and unfairness. Inevitably, once the excluded take power these motivating forces falter. Moral ideas that start off close to everyday life – grounded in love of family or community – become more distant and formulaic, and new rulers come to see like a state, making their own survival a priority and turning their exercise of power from a means into an end.

There are obvious parallels between human life cycles and those of ruling groups. Psychologists point out that children make much more use of the right side of their brain than adults: they are more open, creative and willing to experiment. Then, as children mature into adults, more ideas and practices that start in the right brain move to the left brain, where they become hardened as habits, assumptions and routines. These make life simpler because they help us quickly to draw on well-established rules when we face a new situation. But they are also enemies of flexibility and innovation. Analogous processes happen within governments and parties. When young, or challenged, they may be highly creative. But then, sometimes after just a few months or years, sometimes after many decades, stagnation sets in. The powerful become comfortable with their offices and with the paraphernalia and the respect that comes with the job. Ritual takes over from spontaneous affection. The arteries harden. The rhetoric becomes formalized and stilted. Mercy is replaced by cruelty. Pomp leads to arrogance, and the seeds are sown for another turn of the wheel.

Some thinkers have presented these dynamics of decay and decline as unidirectional: just as the ageing of the human body can only be arrested and never reversed, so do all regimes face an inescapable slide. Plato thought that politics was located in the inferior realm of the senses rather than the eternal realm accessible to reason, a world subject to inevitable decline, change and decay. In his, and Aristotle's, accounts even states which begin close to an ideal undergo stages of decay (*pthora*), the philosophical opposite of genesis or coming into being. These ideas were echoed in the twentieth century by Pitirim Sorokin, who suggested that in all societies phases of austere idealism, when people value the social good, are succeeded by phases of individualism and decadence, when they forget the ideals that had made them great.[2]

Such grand accounts can claim too much. But state power does indeed tend to stagnate, to lose touch with its original ideals and to serve itself rather than a higher cause, and this decay always has a moral aspect. In Montesquieu's words, 'the deterioration of a government begins almost always by the decay of its principles.'[3] These are all reasons why stability is never a good in itself, despite its critical importance to human well-being. At the turn of the twenty-first century, the eight countries consistently rated the most corrupt in the world – Congo, Iraq, Myanmar, Sudan, Indonesia, Syria, Pakistan and Burundi – were also among those in which the political leadership had been most secure, measured by the longevity of its tenure (North Korea would be another example). Large areas of the world, notably the Middle East, suffered from an excess of stability and continuity in the last decades of the twentieth century. Before that the Cold War froze much of the world into deadened replicas of Stalinism pitted against stagnant anti-communist autocracies, and earlier still the Pax Britannica propped up the decaying Ottoman Empire in the name of regional stability.

In all of these cases destabilization was a precondition for progress. But how does renewal happen? How is stagnation averted?

There seem to be at least three conditions for any polity to renew itself. First, there has to be some shared acceptance that things are wrong, and that usually means a sense of moral as well as practical failure (for example, national decline, humiliation or defeat). Second, there have to be ideas about what can be done. These may be found among intellectuals, or radical officials, clerics or entrepreneurs. Third, there have to be leaders willing to take these ideas on.

In the cases of Roosevelt in the 1930s or Reagan in the 1980s in the US, or Attlee in the 1940s and Mrs Thatcher thirty years later in the UK, all three conditions were present. But often politics becomes stuck, even when renewal is badly needed. Britain in the 1930s showed that two of the three conditions are not enough. The country faced profound challenges – depression and mass unemployment, combined with a growing military threat from Germany. Many of its greatest thinkers, including Keynes, had developed comprehensive ideas about what should be done to revive the economy, and some of their ideas were already being put into practice around the world, from Scandinavia to New Zealand. But the political leaders who understood what needed to be done, including Lloyd George, the former Liberal leader, were out of power and the political leaders who were in power, led by Ramsay MacDonald and Stanley Baldwin, were oblivious to what needed to be done, utterly imprisoned in traditional economic orthodoxy and a complacent international outlook. The USA (and much of the West) in the 1960s provides a very different example of how two out of three are not enough. This was a time of profound social and cultural change; millions recognized that the old ways of doing things needed radical reform to catch up with the aspirations of women and the black minority, and there was a rare intellectual ferment. But little or none of this was translated into the primary colours of mainstream politics of an era dominated by Lyndon Johnson and Richard Nixon, Harold Wilson and de Gaulle, who found much of what was happening either baffling or repellent.

When movements for reform do triumph, people's capacity for hope, an often underused muscle, twitches into life and even the air that people breathe seems lighter. Something of this quality of renewal accompanied the coronations of kings or the arrival of new dynasties. In ancient Egypt renewal was institutionalized: once pharaohs had been in power for thirty years they went through regular rituals in which they symbolically died and were reborn. This mood of spring after a long winter is experienced with greatest force in the immediate aftermath of revolutions like those of 1789, 1917, 1978 or 1989 when suddenly anything becomes possible. Often it accompanies election victories that throw out long-lived regimes. In 1928 none of the Nazi leadership of five years later appeared among the 15,000 entries of Germany's *Who's Who*; though most of the bureaucracy retained their positions during the transfer of power, just as post-war West Germany maintained continuity with the Nazi regime. Regimes come and go: government carries on regardless.

The actions of a new regime can be rough: sweeping away established procedures, cherished programmes and policies and agencies which assumed they were permanent. Young regimes have relatively few goals, and are good at prioritization. People from outside the state who have been imagining alternatives are suddenly called upon to serve, and experience the vertigo of having their ideas put into effect, and getting lost in the corridors of power. The role of outsiders can be decisive, because 'however arduous, [it] has one great advantage: it enables one to preserve one's integrity, to remain untouched and uncorrupted, to retain the candour and the high expectations of youth.'[4] Outsiders can also bring a rough clarity to bear. The most dynamic civilizations often began with conquest by warriors (Romans, Franks, Ottomans, Mongols, Mughals) who started off well down the cultural hierarchy of their times. Their actions may have been brutal (like Caliph Omar destroying the Library of Alexandria or the Bolsheviks planning to destroy St Basil's in Red Square). But in retrospect settled civilizations benefited from repeated injections of barbarian energy that stripped away their accretions,[5] and on a milder scale all cultures and polities seem to benefit from periodic rough challenges.

Competent political parties try to renew themselves to avoid the rough justice of history. Some have gone to great lengths to lend themselves a fresh veneer. India's BJP, for example, celebrated its 25th anniversary in 2005, a year after losing power, with an extravaganza staged by a film director:

The show . . . was perfectly choreographed. A pulsating techno drum beat from powerful speakers placed across Mumbai's historical Shivaji Park. A dazzling display of fireworks lighting up the night sky. Lotus flowers blossoming across the ground. A giant-sized lotus opening to reveal 14 BJP leaders.

Unfortunately the spectacle did little to hide the fact that the party lacked any coherent strategy, or that the party leadership was passing from one veteran to another.[6] Yet many parties, including Britain's Conservatives, Japan's Liberal Democrats, China's Communists and Sweden's Social Democrats, have succeeded at renewing themselves both symbolically and substantively on several occasions, often while still in office. All managed to internalize the three conditions for renewal: recognition of a major problem; a body of new ideas; and leaders willing to use them. Generally renewal depends on close attention to public hopes and fears and being willing to ditch cherished beliefs and rhetoric if they no longer resonate. Other essentials include the promotion of new blood, vigorous internal competition among potential future leaders and energetic co-option of once-excluded groups. All of this has often required ruling parties to make themselves vulnerable, to admit mistakes and to free themselves from their own past. Yoichi Koizumi in Japan, for example, renewed his own party, the Liberal Democrats, in the 2000s in part by running against it. Margaret Thatcher did the same to the British Conservatives. Tony Blair opted for what was called the 'masochism strategy' – putting himself into situations where the public could vent their anger. In all of these cases, too, there was a sense of renewed moral purpose, of parties remembering what they were for.

Similar patterns of cyclical rebirth can be found in individual careers. Many leaders are brought down by their qualities – the fierce certainty that becomes brittle arrogance; the consensual gentleness that becomes weakness and vacillation; the vaulting rhetoric that becomes hubris – and often the leader is replaced by someone just like him or herself twenty or forty years before.

Some leaders go through deep cycles of renewal within their own careers. Mao lost much of his support base when he was in his thirties; Churchill and de Gaulle seemed like heroic failures in 1939 (and Churchill's career had seen a succession of terrible misjudgements, from Gallipoli and the Gold Standard to his obsessive hostility to Indian independence). Some have experienced many great failures and seem addicted to tempting fate. Political economist Jean Monnet, who experienced more than his fair share of setbacks before becoming an architect of the European Union, said that he regarded 'every defeat as an opportunity'.

More common is a cycle over several lifespans: the revolutionary leaders who are followed a generation later by cautious bureaucrats, with no experience of risk and danger, who nervously celebrate the founding exploits of the regime while all too aware of the distance they have travelled. Past successes can make it harder for subsequent generations to see things as they are. The *Quarterly Review* of the British Admiralty in 1847, for example, wrote of 'intellects becalmed in the smoke of Trafalgar', and in the history of capitalism, too, the pioneer barbarians who swept aside the old order in the nineteenth century were followed by machine men: when Keynes was asked in the 1930s what had happened to people like Morgan and Carnegie, the great pioneers of the new era of industrial capitalism, he said that 'their office boys rule in their mausoleums'.

Behind many of these cycles in politics there is a consistent pattern in which alienation is the decisive factor. Karl Marx argued that under capitalism workers are alienated from the product of their own labour, and that eventually this alienation becomes so severe that the workers turn into a revolutionary force that transforms the social and economic order and moves it to a new and higher equilibrium. A parallel dynamic can be observed in politics, as the people come to be alienated from the parties and governments which had earlier drawn energy and legitimacy from their aspirations and needs. Leaders like Ibn Abi Mahalli, the conqueror of Marrakesh, are transformed by their roles, and as they succumb to the vices of power the gap between ideals and reality widens until in time public dissatisfaction becomes so intense that a new set of rulers is brought to power.

The devices of liberal democracy are necessary conditions for any society to benefit from good power over any length of time. They inject some dynamism and they make it harder for leaders to overstay their welcome too long. But they are not sufficient. In the next four chapters I therefore turn to the other crucial contributors to good power: to the role of knowledge, ethics, civic commitment and a favourable world order, and I show how they can unsettle and energize stagnant systems without the destruction of war and revolution.

I I

Habit-forming Ethics

*'To be master of the world would indeed be supreme felicity
if one were universally loved; but for that one would have to
be at the same time the slave of all humanity.'*

Sri Aurobindo

When I was seventeen, during the year between school and university
I earned enough money cleaning bottles in a hospital to pay for a
flight to south Asia. Wandering around a forest in Sri Lanka a few
weeks later, I sat on the ground for a rest and was greeted by an
elderly fellow walker dressed in monk's habit, who started asking me
questions: where was I from, what was I doing, what was I looking
for? His name was Nyanaponika Thera. I later discovered that he was
one of the sharpest thinkers of Theravada Buddhism, a student of
Jung who had left Germany in the 1930s.[1] He encouraged me to stay
in a monastery and introduced me to the main texts of the Pali canon.
To a modern reader they are repetitive and sometimes even banal, yet
they are shot through with a remarkable clarity of insight.

Over the succeeding weeks we met for daily discussions, disen-
tangling one of the oldest arguments: whether to change the world
for the better we first need to change ourselves, or whether, as I had
been taught, life is too short and the problems too urgent so that
politics has to come first. The arguments were inconclusive. But I
never again saw the world in the same simple light, and I learned to
see how even those who exercise power are themselves often trapped
by it, slaves to illusions of permanence and glory, and condemned to
end their lives disappointed and bitter. I had absorbed the western

assumption that structures are all-important for politics; but after my encounter with Nyanaponika Thera it was obvious that the qualities of the people exercising power are bound to matter just as much.

The historian Lord Acton is best remembered for his comment that 'power tends to corrupt and absolute power corrupts absolutely'. But this was preceded by another sentence, which is of more interest for us here. When it comes to supreme power, he wrote, 'historic responsibility has to make up for that want of legal responsibility'. But what is that historic responsibility? What ethics and rules should the holders of power follow and how should these be encouraged and enforced?

Some of the answers are already clear: we want leaders and officials whose primary concern is the interests of the people they serve, and who avoid self-serving corruption, cruelty and treason. Probably the most important quality to be cultivated in any civilized society is self-restraint, and that is bound to matter most for people in power; indeed, one definition of bad power would be power in the hands of people lacking self-restraint.[2]

However, many of the questions that governments face are not simple choices between right and wrong, but choices between conflicting moral principles. They share this character with the moral dilemmas that are faced by anyone in a position of power and responsibility, even within a small firm or a family: when to keep secrets; whether to use force; how to balance loyalty to those around you and loyalty to higher principles or institutions; how to balance the tensions between justice and mercy, generosity and prudence. The big dilemmas are not between right and wrong but between right and right.

In the ancient world it was generally assumed that the qualities of leaders mattered as much as laws and structures in keeping leaders moral. Plato's *Republic*, Kautilya's *Arthashastra*, and Confucius' *Analects* attempted to systematize what these qualities should be, and to describe how leaders should learn ethics. Good laws needed to be complemented by internal constraints. Kautilya, for example, wrote that 'government by rule of law, which alone can guarantee the security of life and the welfare of the people, is in turn dependent on the self-discipline of the king.' That discipline 'is of two kinds – inborn and acquired . . . self-control, which is the basis of knowledge and discipline, is acquired by giving up lust, anger, greed, conceit, arrogance and foolhardiness.' Leaders, in other words, need to cultivate the right qualities through working on themselves, and in the Buddhist and Confucian traditions they are depicted as living in a constant struggle against the temptations of sin, desire and attachment (ideas mirrored more recently in Gandhi's concept of *swaraj*, self-rule, as the objective of politics, by which he meant both freedom and 'disciplined rule from within').

THE TEMPTATIONS AND VICES OF POWER

Without that work, leaders find it hard to resist the maladies that one Chinese Prime Minister in the T'ang dynasty had observed in emperors: 'preference for winning; embarrassment at hearing of one's mistakes; indulgence in sophistic debates, showing off one's intelligence, increasing one's authority, and failure to restrain one's strong will.' Once they contracted these failings, he warned, they no longer listened to their people, and the seeds of chaos were sown.[3]

There is a longstanding belief that the people who choose political careers are uniquely ill-suited to the jobs they seek. In Plato's *Republic* Socrates takes it as self-evident that those most eager to find power are likely to be the least equipped to hold it. 'Good people won't be willing to rule for either money or honour', he says. 'They approach ruling not as something good or to be enjoyed, but as something necessary, since it can't be entrusted to anyone better than or even as good as themselves. In a city of good men, if it came into being, the citizens would fight in order not to rule, just as they do now in order to rule.' The reason is this: 'anyone who is really a true ruler doesn't by nature seek his own advantage but that of his subjects, and everyone knowing this would rather be benefited by others than take the trouble to benefit them.' Leadership, in other words, is a burden to be imposed on the good, and kept away from the ambitions of the bad. For Socrates the life of the politician was simply incompatible with the pursuit of knowledge, which required the sort of withdrawal from civic life that Epicureans and Stoics advocated.

Usually the psychological makeup of many leaders is far from conducive to good government. In some cases an almost psychopathic pleasure in power appears to be the motivation (and these are the people who crumble when they lose power). Some appear to become leaders to put right a childhood loss. Many lost a parent at an early age (including both Tony Blair and Bill Clinton) and appear to seek affirmation and love in their political careers. Some are shaped by adversity. Franklin Delano Roosevelt at thirty-nine was tall, handsome, charming, ambitious – and superficial. After he was diagnosed with polio he suffered from acute depression, but thereafter was able to empathize with people who had lost or suffered, which may have been the key to his greatness.

Others stumble into leadership without showing any obvious qualities or qualifications. No one expected either Stalin or Hitler at the age of thirty to amount to much at all, let alone world renown. A Captain Mayr, who had known him at the time, described Hitler as like a 'tired stray dog looking for a master, ready to throw in his lot with anyone who would show him kindness' (when in power Hitler said: 'I go where Providence dictates with the assurance of a sleepwalker'). We now know that his father beat him and that he in turn beat his younger sister. For others leadership was the best route to respect. The young Fidel Castro picked fights constantly and carried a gun as a student. 'Never back down,' he said repeatedly, 'it's a question of dignity' (and when the Soviets backed down in the Cuban missile crisis it was against his will). Many leaders have been outsiders seeking recognition: Hitler the Austrian, Milošević the Montenegran, Napoleon the Corsican. For some, power appears linked to sex and virility. Mao's potency was said by his doctor to have varied in tune with his political fortunes.

There are examples of leaders who have won power because of their qualities of character. Haile Selassie of Ethiopia, who came from a minor noble family far from the direct line of succession to the king Menelik II, impressed everyone he met with his grace, patience, assurance and bearing, and combined this with a raw cunning to win power over the other warlords who misread his quiet demeanour. But decades later he had become the deranged despot described in Ryszard Kapuscinski's classic *The Emperor*.

Electorates try to make some rough assessment of the character of their putative leaders, who in turn typically portray themselves as everyday people (even though the very fact that they seek office makes them extraordinary), devoted to family life, unconcerned with personal ambition, thoughtful and respectful. As Machiavelli put it in *The Prince*, the ruler wants people to have the impression that 'he is all gentleness, all faith, all trustworthiness, all humanity and all piety'. Journalists try to uncover the truth, and have to be suspicious in part because no polity has yet introduced methods that could more systematically assess candidates' character, and judge how they would respond under stress or when faced with temptations.[4]

A different variant of the argument that power-seekers will be unqualified for power comes elsewhere in Plato's *Republic* in the story of the Ring of Gyges – a ring that allows the holder to become invisible at will. The moral of this story is that no one can easily resist the temptations associated with either magic or power:

No one would be so incorruptible that he would stay on the path of justice when he could take whatever he wanted, have sex with anyone he wanted, kill or release from prison anyone he wishes and do all the other things that would make him like a god among humans.

So power is like electricity, essential but also dangerous: dangerous both because of whom it attracts, and because it transforms the people who hold it. The characteristic tone of discussions of leaders' ethics down the ages reflects this. Some are plaintively idealistic, like Erasmus' listing of the ruler's virtues in *The Education of a Christian Prince*: clemency, kindness, equity, civility, benevolence, prudence, integrity, sobriety, temperance, vigilance, generosity and honesty (all virtues that, according to Norberto Bobbio, could be termed 'weak'). Reading their words you can sense the anxiety of arguing against the odds. Some (like Confucius) strive almost too hard to persuade the reader (and themselves) that moral behaviour is always in the best interests of rulers. Others make no pretence that this is so, and wallow in cynicism. In hearing the words of the Nazi leaders and their intellectual apologists, for example, you feel their almost visceral pleasure in a world driven by might and physical force, intolerant of losers.

LEADERS' ETHICS

If power attracts the bad and corrupts the good, what is it that makes leaders behave well? Good power is possible because all people have some dispositions to act morally. These will vary in strength, reflecting the complex co-evolution of genetic dispositions and experience. They can be reinforced by social norms (Max Weber, for example, explains that the bureaucrat is compliant because to do otherwise would be 'abhorrent to his sense of duty')[5] and weakened by temptations.

In a democracy the ultimate enforcement of good behaviour comes from the public exercising their votes. The corrupt and evil get their come-uppance at the ballot box, at least some of the time,[6] and most constitutions give legislatures powers to impeach executives, and judges powers to launch investigations. These devices to constrain the abuse of power are one of the West's greatest innovations and exports, but they are not the end of the story and other traditions have richer insights into how moral principles can be internalized into the minds of rulers and officials. Chinese tradition has been particularly concerned with this question.

Confucius' claim that 'to govern is to put right' because 'if you lead the people by being put right yourself, who will dare not be put right?' may have been wishful thinking but over the succeeding centuries his ideas achieved enormous influence on officials' self-image.[7] In one direction lay the bookish learning of the prefect and philosopher Chu Hsi, who saw human nature as perfectly moral but clouded by materiality. Chu Hsi's philosophy guided the Chinese civil service exams until the twentieth century. In another direction the school founded by Wang Yang-ming prescribed meditation as a tool for self-improvement on the grounds that moral laws are universal and innate and can therefore be discovered through cultivating the self. Moral knowledge was seen as intimately connected to social action: together they improved both self and society.

China's strong tradition of meritocratic appointment of officials and its cultivation of learning both derive from Confucian ideas. These did not always lead to clear prescriptions; for example, it was unclear whether officials' pay should be raised to prevent corruption or kept low to encourage humility. But the idea that the emperor's legitimacy depended on his moral virtue gave Confucian officials 'perhaps their only weapon within the imperial system to circumscribe the imperial power and ideally to establish a benevolent government'.[8]

In India there were no traditions of divine kingship or priestly rule; instead the divide between the realm of Brahmans and the realm of state power (which was usually in the hands of Kshatriyas) made it all the more important to define the moral responsibilities of power. Large sections of the Puranas, the *Mahabharata* and *Ramayana* epics and secular literature are concerned with the duties of kings, the *raja dharma*: the duties to promote justice and welfare and stop people taking advantage of others. The king's *dharma* is to be just, impartial and lenient and not to tax too harshly. If weak, he should promote welfare so as to encourage public support; for the same reason he should be kind to newly conquered territories. Protection of life and livelihood through detailed rules on social security are justified to secure the welfare of the people, since (in the words of the *Arthashas-tra*) 'it is the people who constitute a kingdom. Like a barren cow a kingdom without people yields nothing.' Buddhist political thinkers drew radical conclusions from these ideas. Mahavastu advised kings to favour immigration and friendship with neighbouring countries. The Kutudanta Sutra advised kings to provide food subsidies for the poor and investment support for merchants.

In the West the best modern account of leaders' ethics was provided by Max Weber, in a series of lectures given in the grim post-war winter of 1918/19 (published as *Politiks als Beruf*). Weber identified three critical qualities in a politician: passion or commitment to the cause; responsibility towards this cause; and proportion in detachment from things and people.

What is interesting about this list is its studied ambiguity. The starting point is passion: care about the task at hand and about what can be achieved. This is a moral starting point, which draws its energy from the needs of the community, and from the gap between ideals and reality. It is also what enables the leader to communicate and persuade. The second quality overlays this with another sense of morality – responsibility for the results of decisions and actions. It is not enough to have good intentions or to adhere to the Ten Commandments or any other abstract principles: we expect leaders to be able to think through the full implications of what they do, and of the events which happen to them. That sometimes requires leaders to think like chess players, grandmasters who see the whole board and its hidden dynamics and possibilities.

This is perhaps where the gap between everyday service and the service of leadership is greatest. Everyday service requires careful listening and attention. But from leaders we look for a far rarer capacity to understand. A good illustration of this capacity to see the full historical, and moral, implications of a moment in time came just after the attack on Pearl Harbor. Lord Alanbrooke, the British chief of the military staff, who had been worried about a Japanese attack on British positions, wrote in his diary, 'Oh dear, so we have wasted 72 hours of intensive staff work on a false appraisal.' Churchill simply said: 'So we have won the war after all.' He realized the full implication of bringing the USA into the war, and therefore how an apparent disaster could in the wider perspective be a boon.

With the third quality of proportion in detachment come a host of other skills, such as guile, judgement, self-restraint (so that power is not abused) and suspension of personal feelings (so that power is exercised impartially). Detachment makes possible what in Zen Buddhism is called 'beginner's mind', the freshness of thinking that is destroyed by an excessive competence and knowledge.

That flexibility of thought means that statecraft has little in common with science, engineering or scholarship. It is more similar to activities like making music or climbing mountains, where experts improvise within some fixed rules and aficionados appreciate each other's boldest moves. 'Following the book' is unlikely to be a recipe for success. That is why among the Confucians expediency (*ch'uan*) was seen as a vital complement to doing right. It necessarily involved careful listening and observation. Lu Chih, one of the leading officials and thinkers of the T'ang era, frequently advised the emperor to 'understand the changes of the times' and avoid being imprisoned by dogmas and assumptions. Likewise in the writings of al-Farabi, the virtuous ruler combines political science – knowledge of the patterns and rules of power – with political experience, which together give the ruler the necessary flexibility to adapt to uncertain and unknowable events.[9]

Detachment is not the same as the indifference that François Mitterrand advised. It is possible to be detached about means but also passionate about ends.[10] Detachment can also be selfless. Marcus Aurelius advised leaders to 'begin each day by telling yourself: today I shall meet interference, ingratitude, insolence, disloyalty, ill will and selfishness', but the role of the wise man is to 'accept without resentment whatever may befall'. The suspension of ego makes it easier to embrace truths, to be honest about errors, and to take responsibility even when you are not responsible; as Winston Churchill put it after the fall of Singapore: 'I did not know; I was not told; I should have asked.' The Cuban missile crisis was only a crisis rather than a catastrophe because President Kennedy had near him a man willing to tell him he was wrong. Just as the crisis neared its climax, and General Curtis LeMay advocated war (failure to act would be 'as bad as the appeasement at Munich'), the then US Ambassador to Moscow, Foy Kohler, explained that he and his colleagues were misreading the Soviets' bellicose and threatening telegrams; what the Soviet Union most needed was a way out without loss of face.[11]

For a leader to be ethical he or she has to be willing to take responsibility. This is also the heart of the democratic system: ultimate responsibility rests with individuals who must answer to their citizens face to face, and resign when things go badly wrong. Sometimes, however, leaders claim to accept responsibility as a subtle way of avoiding it. It has become common for leaders brazenly to accept sole responsibility for mistakes as a way of claiming moral virtue (by highlighting their willingness to accept the burden of responsibility) when their real purpose is to curtail further enquiries and debate. This habit has some similarities to the syndrome that Michael Walzer described as the 'suffering servant' in a commentary on Max Weber. The suffering servant, he wrote, 'lies, intrigues, sends others to their death – and suffers' but because we cannot be sure of the true motives that lie behind his actions we suspect 'the suffering servant of either masochism or hypocrisy or both'.[12]

Some of the qualities I have set out here are critical to what could be called the inner circle of leadership, the leader's primary duties. These derive from primary accountabilities: who is being directly served, and who can call power to account. In a democracy this will include the party, the parliament and the public; in a business it will include the shareholders first, and then other interests. The more difficult issues arise when we consider a second circle – all those who may be affected by the exercise of power but who have little or no voice or formal claim on leaders. These may include future generations, the citizens of other nations, and the weak and disenfranchised. Because our fundamental moral principles are universal we see the greatest leaders as those who are able to speak to this wider constituency without forgetting the first. These are the leaders who can 'stand in the shoes of the universe' without losing sight of who they serve day-to-day. The wise ones avoid counterposing the interests of the one against the other, but find ways to align them without overburdening their citizens.

As Roosevelt once put it, the public 'cannot, because of human weakness, be attuned for long periods of time to a constant repetition of the highest note in the scale'. Managing these different levels of expectation requires great skill: Roosevelt preparing to enter the Second World War; Ashoka renouncing war; Olof Palme committing his nation to development globally, each is an example of this sort of ethical alignment, of a leader successfully outgrowing his own role and constituency. Akhenaten's futile attempt in thirteenth-century BCE Egypt to create a new religion is an early example of failure, a leader who baffled his own followers at the same time as he riled his enemies.[13]

What of personal qualities? It is often argued that personal behaviour should not be used to judge leaders. What does it matter if they are adulterous, deceitful in private life, or prone to drink too much, and what right do the public or the media have to intrude? It is true that there is no direct causal link between personal virtue and public achievement. Churchill when Prime Minister drank heavily – a bottle of whisky a day – smoked, and quipped that the only exercise he took was as a pallbearer at the funerals of his friends who lived healthily. Adolf Hitler was a teetotal vegetarian. Many of the iconic leaders of the twentieth century turned out to be philanderers or compulsive liars, but their achievements have been little dimmed as a result.

But these arguments against taking personal behaviour seriously are fallacious. Precisely because we usually lack good information with which to judge potential leaders' qualities we have to rely on these other clues as to their self-discipline, their likely behaviour under pressure and their honesty. These clues need not be either relevant or decisive, and they have to be weighed against other evidence that is more directly relevant to the offices they may hold. Bill Clinton's explanation of his misdemeanours with Monica Lewinsky – 'because I could' – did not automatically disqualify him either from office or the approbation of history. (President Mitterrand's response to the allegation that he had fathered an illegitimate child was, 'et alors?') But it is bound to be relevant to any assessment of the character Clinton brought to his role as a leader.

OFFICIAL ETHICS

Officials within the state have different ethical duties from their leaders. Max Weber thought that they were subject to 'exactly the opposite principle of responsibility', since the honour of the official 'is vested in his ability to execute conscientiously the order of the superior authority', whereas the honour of the political leader lies 'precisely in an exclusive personal responsibility for what he does, a responsibility which he cannot and must not reject or transfer.'[14] Taken at face value the implication is that few officials have any moral responsibility so long as they obey orders.

In most regimes the paramount quality needed in officials is loyalty to the legitimate authority (and the ability to switch loyalty instantly if that changes). Other qualities include a pragmatic instrumentality – getting the task done; integrity; distance from special interests; long time horizons; a strong commitment to due process and rules; impersonality; and not exploiting privileged information.[15] The ethics of officials are policed more in terms of whether they have followed procedures than whether they have achieved the desired outcomes, and they are judged more for sins of commission than sins of omission.

The most immediate temptations for officials are power and money; they command both day-to-day and are bound to be tempted to divert some for their own benefit. Most states and empires devised rules to keep officials focused on their jobs rather than on accumulating power or wealth. In China the mandarin principle of appointment based on examinations and merit was designed in part to constrain the formation of permanent elites. In the Byzantine Empire, from the time of Justinian, officials had to swear on the gospel to administer without 'guile or fraud'. They were forbidden to accept presents, to marry among their relatives or neighbours or to build houses where they were serving (this rule was eventually suspended, setting in motion worsening conflict between the civil service and the warrior aristocrats).

Some regimes have used very radical measures to make it harder for officials to pass power and wealth down the generations. The Mamelukes were former slaves imported from the Caucasus to serve as soldiers for the caliphate who later became rulers (in James Harrington's words in his book *Oceana*, written when the Mamelukes were at the peak of their power, they were 'a hardy people, to the Egyptians, that were a soft one'). Each new generation was imported in, and leaders were elected by their peers. The rationale for their existence was that it would prevent the formation of dynasties, ensure that their loyalty was only to the state and hold at bay material temptation (rather like the eunuchs in the Byzantine Empire, who were also unable to pass their privileges on to the next generation). As recently as the 1960s Lee Kuan Yew discussed with his advisers whether Singapore might create a Mameluke-style corps to run the country.

The modern British civil service was explicitly founded on very different ethical principles to protect it from partisanship, and from the caprice, nepotism and inefficiency of the previous system in which sinecures were sold to the incompetent sons of the aristocracy. The two great mid-nineteenth-century reformers who created the modern civil service, Sir Stafford Northcote and Sir Charles Trevelyan, saw that efficiency and integrity were closely linked, and ushered in a deal in which civil servants were given security and prestige in exchange for open, competitive and meritocratic appointment and clear subservience to their elected masters. Politicians lost the right to hire and fire at will, but gained in return loyalty, competence and confidentiality. Civil servants gave up political autonomy and identity, but won indefinite tenure and progression based on merit in exchange. Thereafter the self-image of the civil service was closely bound up with its ethical integrity: resistant to corruption, respectful of the law, committed to public service as a high calling.

Ethical learning retains a place in the formation of many civil services around the world. For anyone who sees themselves as an upright and honourable man or woman, immoral and dishonourable acts will be painful. This may be why many public bodies put applicants through a long and arduous process of recruitment. The mandarinate exams in China; the highly competitive recruitment to ENA in France; the humiliations and rigours of recruitment to the best armies, all help to reinforce a common identity and to make people open to new norms of behaviour.

Behind many of these examples are strong ideas of vocation. Service of this kind must be a lifetime commitment, not something to be dipped in and out of (partly because that would involve being contaminated by other moral syndromes – for example, seeing a spell in government as a good commercial opportunity). There are also common references, as in Max Weber's account, to the importance of detachment. The official should not take pleasure in power. As Socrates suggests, power must be seen as a necessary burden, and in some respects a lonely one, involving detachment from the natural human instincts to help friends and family.

Among officials and advisers distance too plays an important role. To be too closely associated with one regime or ruler makes it harder to serve the next one. During the American Presidential election of 1968 Henry Kissinger offered inside information on the negotiations for peace in Vietnam to both Richard Nixon and his adversary Hubert Humphrey; having successfully won Cabinet office he continued to maintain some public distance from Nixon, which then made it possible for him to serve under Gerald Ford.

HOW SHOULD ETHICS BE LEARNED?

The governments that have cared about ethics have generally followed the Confucians in using traditional methods of pedagogy – setting out rules, using parables and case studies – to instil ethics into officials. A contemporary example is the ethical reasoning taught in the Kennedy School at Harvard University's Masters of Public Administration courses.

But these are not always the best ways to learn ethics. We generally acquire ethics as we acquire other things; they become clear to us as we grow up in society with others, as we are rewarded, punished and observe life around us. Ethics are more akin to language, with grammars, words and scope for limitless improvisation than to the sort of knowledge that can be learned by rote. They include rules but involve far more than rules. Indeed, when we see someone who confuses ethics with rules we speak of 'blind obedience'. In the extreme cases this leads to *kadavergehorsam* – the obedience of corpses – to use the strikingly resonant phrase Adolf Eichmann used about himself during his trial in Jerusalem.

As with language, competence grows out of practice and experience, rather than solely from formal pedagogy. Aristotle wrote that 'one enters the palace of reason through the courtyard of habit': through practice and reflection, ethics become part of the character of the individual, something internal and automatic, rather like all kinds of expert behaviour.

There is a similar view in many eastern traditions. Mencius, for example, understood ethical behaviour in terms of 'extension', applying principles from one situation to others. So we might extend from a situation where we automatically feel compassion to other, more complex situations. Becoming ethical means cultivating the proper dispositions, rather than simply learning rules. Becoming a servant means being a servant, and, through acting as a servant, changing your own nature.

Behind this common-sense outlook lies a radical view of the self, a less unitary self than the western view of a coherent ego consciously making judgements according to a calculus of rules. Instead, it implies that the self consists of processes of which we are unaware, indeed of which we cannot be aware. Our mind creates structures, including ethical dispositions, out of experience as well as out of conscious choices. Experience and action are inseparable; the self is made up of what it has thought and done, and, in particular, what it has thought and done with others, shaped through language and relationships. It is in this sense both private and public, not something pure and standing apart. The otherwise meaningless comment in the *Tao Te Ching* that 'a man of the highest virtue does not keep to virtue and that is why he has virtue' makes sense only if we see it as about learning.

Contemporary psychology confirms this view. As Francisco Varela put it in the lectures on ethical know-how he gave shortly before his death:

Modern western science teaches us that the self is virtual and empty and arises continuously to cope with breakdowns in our microworlds; Taoism, Confucianism and Buddhism teach us that ethical expertise is progressive in nature and grounded in the on-going realisation of this empty self in ordinary life and action . . . ethical know-how is the progressive, first-hand acquaintance with the virtuality of self.[16]

This argument is challenging to many people brought up to equate morality with fixed rules. But as Jonathan Glover points out, many of the twentieth century's most immoral acts arose not from the absence of morality but rather from excessively rigid moral principles. Those who led their countries into the First World War, for example, 'made an absolute out of a morality of national honour, regardless of the consequences of obeying such a morality',[17] and the Communists who built the Gulags believed themselves to be part of an extraordinary moral crusade to remake mankind.

It does not follow that there is no need for clear rules to live by, or that we should all invent our own morality. Rules serve as a shorthand, encapsulating the experience of communities over long periods of time. They help to prevent the corruption that can follow from what philosophers call 'consequentialist' reasoning, which uses ends to justify means. Equally, moral notions need to be reasonably simple if they are to be taught to children and transmitted down the generations. A world in which everyone made up their own moral rules would soon become a hell. In every community there is a layer of ethics which must take this form, and must be taught and reinforced as a set of rules that are not open to negotiation.

Beyond these, however, there will always be scope for argument and fluency. It is in this space, beyond the formal rules, that leaders need not only experience and reflection but also private sources of guidance that are not beholden to them, people who can speak honestly, and sometimes brutally.

MORAL PLURALISM AND INTEGRATION

I've argued that morality should not be conceived as a set of rules that are implanted in people's minds; it lives instead through practice and reflection, and takes on many varieties. Indeed, in some regimes moral pluralism made survival possible. A moral principle could be valid without necessarily being universal. In the Ottoman millet system each community was permitted to follow its own laws and raise its own taxes – subject to loyalty to, and taxation by, the empire. In medieval England the Lombards and Hanseatic League were permitted their own self-governing enclaves, while in China the great fourteenth-century traveller Ibn Battutah found himself at home in the Muslim enclaves in the major cities. Today many societies permit some pluralism; India, for example, respects the laws of many of its minority groups. Certainly for a society to cohere it is not necessary for everyone to share the same beliefs and values, or the same convictions about good and bad.[18]

Indeed, pluralism goes further than this. Close inspection of any society reveals that alongside some common core principles there is a mosaic of distinct moral practices. So, typically, soldiers live in a moral universe of unquestioning discipline and obedience, combined with ruthlessness. Stewards of land and other assets (such as museums) live with an ethic of care and minimal disturbance, respect for nature and tradition. Traders and entrepreneurs value easy acquaintance and weak ties, respect for contracts, straight dealing in relation to commerce, pragmatism, and a disdain for values that cannot be monetized.

The people most directly engaged in knowledge, in universities and laboratories, respect experiment and enquiry, depth and complexity, and work within a discipline. Those living a spiritual life value the immaterial, restraint, humility and tradition. People working in care value modesty, selflessness, sacrifice and a disdain for money. For doctors, the sanctity of life is paramount, though matched by the obligation to engage in triage and judge relative need in times of crisis.

Some of these moral rules are made precise in professional codes, partly to keep out outsiders, and partly to protect clients and the public from the abuse that can so easily flow from asymmetries of power and knowledge. The Hippocratic oath protects the patient from the doctor who will always know more. The teacher is obliged to transmit truth, not to indoctrinate. The soldier is precluded from using his weapons within the community he serves; the martial arts specialist from using his skills except in self-defence. Many of these moral outlooks clash at the margins, for example in arguments over whether doctors or religious organizations should be allowed to seek wealth and fame.

These different moral practices become most visible at times of crisis or failure. When something has gone badly wrong investigators usually probe not whether the right things were done but whether the right procedures were followed. In the wake of 9/11 or Hurricane Katrina which wrecked New Orleans in 2005, for example, a clutch of different investigations probed how each profession had behaved: how the intelligence agencies had suppressed or ignored crucial data; how doctors treated the sick; how public officials provided food and welfare; and how politicians cut essential investments in levees.

Such moments unveil the many different moral worlds that make up any government – the world of officials, valuing integrity, instrumentality, procedure and impartiality; the world of politicians, valuing power, rhetoric, guile and flexibility; the world of the law, seeing the world in binary oppositions of legal and illegal, guilty and innocent, and operating through precedent and principle. Each has its own language and norms with which it refers to itself, and makes sense of its day-to-day practices. Each shares the weakness that it can interpret the others only by translating them through the distorting prism of its own framework.[19]

Two radically different views of government arise from these moral differences. One sees government as just another specialized domain, the source of laws, rules and authority which is limited and bounded like other spheres. The skills associated with governance are therefore seen as specialized ones of administration and negotiation, the drafting of laws and handling emergencies. The professions involved in governance are to be allowed their own worlds: professional politicians specialized in the art of public opinion, electoral battle and position-taking; officials specialized in administration; and a clutch of fellow-travellers in the lobbyists, consultants, campaigners and commentators who together fill out the lived world of political power. But all need to be hemmed in, kept as plumbers and fixers rather than visionaries and prophets ('kings cannot be imams . . . it is impossible to wear the crown and the simple white robes of a preacher at the same time', wrote Makhdum-ul-Mulk to the head priest of Akbar's mosque; the letter was intercepted and led to his execution).

The other view sees government as standing above all other domains, an overarching power, at different times concerned with all of these other practices. It exists to synthesize, to see the whole and to integrate, to make sense of each of these worlds in order to enable the whole to survive and develop. At its worst this view justifies the totalitarian invasion of other spheres, sometimes in the name of religion, sometimes in the name of ideology, and sometimes in the name of the market (Trotsky compared the relative modesty of Louis XIV's claim '*l'état c'est moi*' with Stalin's claim, 'I am society'). But at its best, this view encourages rulers to seek ways to guide the whole of their society with a type of knowledge and understanding that transcends the limitations of each part.

Those engaged in the exercise of formal authority are bound to have some of the attributes of a specialist profession. But more than any other profession they should have at least some of the attributes of a more holistic role – seeing things in the round – and in a world of greater differentiation and interdependence, their ability to take a systemic view that is holistic and integrative may become even more essential.

POWER AS A GIFT

Truly exceptional leaders serve in an unusual way, which casts a different light on the meaning of service. Often they seem to intuit what their community most needs. Their language and behaviour are unsettling; they show that what appears to be a stable order is in fact a disorder, and they set out an alternative order and how to achieve it. Leaders like Mahatma Gandhi, Nelson Mandela or Willy Brandt exemplify the idea that the world can be shaped and is subject to human sovereignty, not just to nature or impersonal big systems. Theirs is the language of action and responsibility, not subservience to necessity, and at their best they raise the level of people's conduct and their ethical aspirations.[20]

Leadership in this sense takes the idea of service to a new level. It is service not to people as they are, expressing a given set of needs and wants; it is service to what they could be. As Bertrand Russell commented, 'most people would rather die than think. In fact they do', and there may be few immediate rewards for leaders who dismantle cherished beliefs. It is far easier to massage ideological erogenous zones than it is to cultivate a new sense of possibility. But the leaders who end up being remembered generations later are the ones who have glimpsed, and served, a possibility rather than the status quo.

These leaders grasp the paradoxical nature of their power, and realize that this kind of leadership is correspondingly more dangerous than its mundane equivalents. As Max Weber pointed out, true conviction politicians are more at risk of mental collapse because of the tendency for messy reality to impede pure ideals. There is a fine line between stretching idealism and hubris; on which side of the line a leader has operated can rarely be judged except in retrospect.

For leaders who believe themselves to have a greater understanding of the dynamics of a situation, self-restraint becomes both difficult and essential. Transformational leaders lead from the front – sometimes so far in front that they become contemptuous of everyone around them. The British satirical programme *Spitting Image* once portrayed Margaret Thatcher dining with her ministers and ordering raw steak. When the waiter asks, 'What about the vegetables?' she replies, 'They'll have the same.' Perhaps it is not surprising that shortly afterwards the 'vegetables' combined to oust her from office.

Even the greatest leaders can do little directly. Their greatest impact comes through changing how people think and see rather than through their direct commands. When Clement Attlee was asked what Churchill had done to win the war (Attlee had been deputy Prime Minister), he said 'talk about it', a comment that is sometimes interpreted as a put-down, but which accurately reflects a situation in which the leader's direct power was less important than his influence on the morale of millions of other people who held the real power to win or lose the war.

Understanding this requires considerable humility on the part of leaders. Yet their daily lives make humility unnatural. They are treated with deference and servility, surrounded by sycophants, lauded with honours, and required to take part in rituals that honour them. Ethical behaviour becomes habitual through repetition. In the same way arrogant behaviour all too easily becomes habitual through repetition, and the accumulated experience of deference may persuade the person with power that they must, indeed, be superior to those they exercise power over. Only leaders with great strength of character resist the temptation to believe the messages of their environment. King Canute famously sat on his throne by the shore to demonstrate the limits of his powers to his courtiers, a story that is remembered today precisely because it is so exceptional.[21] (The story is also interesting as a reminder of the ephemeral nature of supremacy. After a series of brilliant military campaigns the Danish monarchy looked set to rule England for centuries: instead it was soon gone, leaving the role of cultural hegemon to the Normans.) Prime Minister Wen Jiabao of China is said to have to stop his cavalcade at random to urinate so that he can have some unprogrammed conversations with ordinary farmers and their families and break through the blanket reassurance of official propaganda.

The most compelling accounts of the moral duties of power holders see these roles not as possessions but as like a gift. When people receive a gift they are duty bound to reciprocate. If that gift is a talent they are obligated to cultivate their gift, and then, through the pursuit of their vocation, to return the results to the community.[22] These ideas tap into the very ancient idea that gifts grow as they are shared and circulated, and decay without use, at worst destroying their possessor if they are hoarded. Whereas the exchange of commodities leaves the two parties the same afterwards even if better off, a gift transforms both, and the circulation of gifts binds the community closer together.

In the arts this is well understood. Artists give never just for the reward or the return but because they are impelled to share their talent. Indeed, if their artistry is reduced solely to reward, money and prestige, there is always the fear that somehow the gift will be corrupted. Instead, the ideal is to pursue a vocation as if it is a gift to be nurtured through practice and mastery, and then shared as widely as possible. The same idea applies in some of the professions, notably medicine and teaching. It implies an ethic of service and humility, of 'passing it on'. It is nature's nature to find uses for things – soil, water, minerals and intelligence. The idea of the gift suggests that it is against nature not to offer up skills and wisdom for the sake of the community, not to find uses for ourselves. Indeed, in many folk tales the people who fail to pass on a gift they have received end up suffering a cruel fate as the gifts turn on their possessor.[23]

This idea of giving is not automatically virtuous. In the manual that had been used by the al-Qaeda terrorists involved in the atrocities of 11 September 2001, Osama Bin Laden advised them to think of their duty to kill anyone who got in their way as a gift, owed to their parents. The Tamil Tiger or Hamas suicide bombers are told that they are conferring the ultimate gift on their community, just like the officers and troops sent to the trenches in 1914. But this very language confirms how powerful these ideas are and how strongly people want to make sense of their lives as part of a chain of giving.

12

Civic Commitment

'There is existing in man a mass of sense lying in a dormant state and which, unless something excites it into action, will descend with him in that condition to the grave.'

Thomas Paine

When I was a teenager, I drifted into becoming a political activist. I felt angry about the very evident hypocrisies of power and the poverty and misery that still survived in the very rich country where I was brought up. I believed that 'something should be done', even if I was less clear what that something was or whether I really had anything to offer. I wanted government to be on the side of the angels, not just a collection of time-serving bureaucrats tying knots in red tape. Activism became part of my identity, and I misspent my teenage years knocking on doors, standing on street corners, organizing strikes and marches, and reading Mao and Lenin as well as Mill and Jefferson.

Activism had many virtues. Some were obvious (like inculcating the value of good organization), some less so (like forcing me to confront the views of my fellow citizens, few of whom were willing to fit into the roles I had allotted to them). I met many remarkable people with a passion to make the world a better place: veterans of the Spanish Civil War and the Second World War, people struggling against dictatorships in Latin America and the Middle East. Even when their political beliefs seemed confused it was hard not to be impressed by their qualities of character and courage. Dante reserved the darkest places in Hell for those who remain neutral in times of moral crisis: these were people who could never be neutral.

I learned many things from them – how to read power with intelligent suspicion, taking nothing at face value; recognizing what isn't said as well as what is; seeing how lofty ideals can mask low interests, and peeling off the layers of fiction with which every state covers itself. They showed me what it feels like to see power as alien and other, crushing and random, not cool and rational as it believes itself to be. Like William Cobbett, England's greatest radical, who cheered when the House of Commons burned down in 1834, and described government as a 'nightmare' or an 'indigestion', they knew well how to analyse what governments said so as to trace the webs of artifice, bombast and threat.

I was never a very successful activist. But these experiences left me convinced of the virtues of public activism, and of the idea that a society of sheep must in time beget a government of wolves.[1] Democracies exist only because enough people were unwilling to be sheep, and brave enough to fight violent wars to achieve a share in power. States act as servants mainly because they were forced to. But once the public have achieved power, it is not enough for them to be wolves, angrily demanding their rights from the state that is now their servant. Instead, the good things in life – better health, learning, prosperity – depend as much on them as they do on anything the state can do for them.

The best state is one that is a servant to the people. The best society is one where the people are servants to each other. In this chapter I ask what role society plays in good government. Kautilya wrote that good government depends on the ruler's self-control, which depends on him giving up 'lust, anger, greed, conceit, arrogance and foolhardiness'. But if the people have become masters and the state has become their servant, do the same considerations apply to them?

An influential body of thought is deeply suspicious of public activism. It claims that mature democracy works because different elites compete for power, not because the public are actively involved in decisions.[2] The history of democracy, in this view, is best understood as a history of pacification, as messy, loud and unruly movements were tamed into the ordered contests of elections and manifestos. Workers, for example, had to give up the option of smashing machines when their trade unions were recognized and they were allowed to strike; demonstrators had to abide by strict rules in exchange for rights of assembly. This was progress since too much passion, sound and fury could lead to disaster, and the grand political narratives that brought people on to the streets could easily lead them astray. The heightened intensity of strident campaigns and revolutionary moments often left a quiet majority disenfranchised. So why not let people get on with their lives, leaving the state and politics to muddle through with just an occasional steer or prod when things start going awry? And why not let the political world become a specialized sphere sufficient to itself, governed by political professionals, scrutinized by media professionals, in arguments constructed by paid lobbyists, with the citizens left just as consumers, choosing at regular intervals between contending alternatives?

Public apathy in this view is something to be celebrated, a symptom that government is working and that people have no need to waste their energies on activism. Reinforcing this view is the subtler argument for passivity – that progress in civilization has always tended to involve processes becoming more complex while what we would today call 'interfaces' have become simpler, so a more complex market economy can be participated in much more easily now with the help of a few reliable tools like money and credit cards, standardized contracts and legal licences. Sophisticated cars can be driven by much less sophisticated drivers who don't need to understand how carburettors work. Powerful computers can be understood by lazy users who would have no idea how to write a software program. By analogy the greater complexity of state actions makes governance ever less comprehensible to the public. Indeed, for them to understand the complexities of monetary policy or social security would require such an investment of time that it would damage family life or the economy. Yet the democratic device of an occasional vote between three or four alternatives provides a simple interface, a rough and ready but fairly efficient way to keep the state's actions in line with public preferences.

THE INSTABILITY OF PASSIVE POLITICS

These arguments should not be dismissed too easily. Government can be extremely complex. In many countries only one or two people truly understand how the big systems of social security or government finance work, because successive reforms have left behind so many layers of complexity (and it is also sometimes said that anyone who really does understand these systems soon goes mad). We have no choice but to delegate the job of understanding these systems, as well as the job of running them.

The problem is that if too many decisions are delegated in this way democracy becomes unstable. A dynamic of alienation inevitably follows. If people really are less responsible for what is done in their name, they are likely to feel less responsible as well.

In the run-up to a British referendum on a regional assembly in 2004, one voter commented that 'power always seems to end up in the hands of people who have the ability to sit for long periods in stuffy, badly decorated rooms – one reason why I have never been involved in local politics.'[3] Her attitude was a common one. Once politics is seen as an ugly world of lies, deceit and doubtful motives, ordinary people want less to do with it, but by avoiding it they make it even more of a world apart.

A passive public is bound to understand less about what is being done in its name and is therefore more vulnerable to being misled. All of the moral dilemmas described in Chapter 5 are recognizable to anyone who has held a position of public power such as serving in a local authority, a school board, or a parish council. They realize that many of the hardest issues that states face involve contending rights rather than battles between right and wrong. Through the exercise of their freedom they become better able to use their freedom. By contrast, people who haven't had any experience of power are more prone either to identify with their leaders or to dismiss them all as crooks, just as commentators who are detached from the experience of responsibility are likely to find it harder to calibrate their moral judgements. The result is that models of democracy that treat citizens as passive onlookers are liable to fail in fulfilling the most basic tasks of any state – the task of legitimating itself, and the actions that are needed to serve the community's interests.

Perhaps the most serious vice of a passive and pacified democracy is that if the public are detached and unconcerned about what their governors do, except in the broadest brush strokes, it ceases to matter if rulers act immorally. In some polities scandals are uncovered by brave journalists or campaigners only for it to transpire that few really care. Pages of newsprint may be devoted to the details of the scandal, but with a sufficiently detached or cynical public, none of this may count for much, and the guilty can blithely carry on. This is the pattern that has been seen in many recent scandals: President Chirac ignored a litany of evidence of financial misdemeanours; Prime Minister Berlusconi ignored evidence of links to the Mafia and enormous conflicts of interest (and then changed the law, for example on false accounting, to protect himself from further prosecutions); President Bush ignored the detailed evidence of torture at Abu Ghraib. In each case no heads rolled, and leaders carried on as if nothing had happened and as if they had nothing to be ashamed of (and presumably, the next generation of leaders adjusted their behaviour accordingly). The implication was that dishonesty and moral corruption are inevitable, a necessary price to be paid for strong leadership.

The great Italian political thinker Azo, writing in the thirteenth century, described the legacy of Rome as one in which 'the people never transferred power except in such a way that they were at the same time able to retain it themselves.'[4] This is a good description of democracy, and is incompatible with a deskilled and passive public. It requires the people to sustain their own capacity to exercise power, in parallel with the state and sometimes in conflict with it. In a more modest form, Thomas Aquinas took a similar view. While assuming that the best form of government must 'be one in which a single individual is placed in command of everyone else and rules them virtuously', he also recognized that good government depends on 'there being others under him who are also capable of governing virtuously, [so that] all the citizens are involved in public affairs, not merely as electors of their rulers but as potential members of the government themselves.'[5]

A state that can act as a servant requires a people that is also willing to take and use power for itself. The history of democracy is therefore never simply a story of pacification and passivity; instead it is bound up with the histories of social protest and moral persuasion in which social movements have claimed to better represent the interests and spirit of the people than their supposed representatives. Orthodox constitutional theory describes elected governments as the sole repository of legitimate authority. Yet real democracies seem to depend for their vitality on this external challenge to complement the internal challenge of competing political parties. The democratic ideal realizes itself both through politics and outside it. Through politics it seeks to turn the state into a servant rather than an oppressive master. Beyond politics it turns the people into the makers of their own world, inventing and running the economy to meet their own desires, inventing and running the society to reflect their own needs and aspirations. The Ayatollah Mohsen Kadivar put the case for democracy in just this way when he said that (according to Islam) 'human beings are endowed with magnanimity. They are the carriers of the spirit of God, and are therefore entitled to act as God's viceroy or Caliph on earth.'

THE POWER OF THE POWERLESS

The possibility of acting in this way is open even to the least powerful. This is just one example: over two thousand years ago the kingdom of Chu was besieging the capital city of Song. The Chu forces were reduced to seven days' rations. The city of Song was on its last legs. Each ruler needed to assess the state of the other, and sent an emissary to meet the other side with a view to ascertaining how long they could last. The man from Song chose not to conceal the truth. He said that things were terrible. Children were being eaten. Their bones were being used for fuel. He said that he could see the other man was a man of honour and would feel compassion for their plight. In response, the man from Chu replied with equal honesty and said: 'Be tenacious. We have only seven days' supplies left.' When told this the ruler of Chu was at first furious. But on reflection he changed his mind and ordered his army to withdraw.

This example is striking because both emissaries betrayed the most basic demand that any state makes – the demand of loyalty in defence of security. Yet each was clearly acting in accordance with a higher duty of service. This is the irreducible power open to any individual. It is a fragile and risky power, a power of performance and effect, where force of will and sacrifice rupture the norms of expected behaviour, and can briefly turn the world upside down. The Quakers, founded by George Fox in seventeenth-century England, created a movement based on quiet moral power of this kind (and were a direct inspiration for the founders of Greenpeace three centuries later). They pioneered peaceful non-cooperation as the best response to injustice. Mahatma Gandhi made it into a political philosophy. In March 1922, when Gandhi was arrested as leader of the non-cooperation movement in India he refused a lawyer. He pleaded guilty, and even pointed the judge towards incriminating material which had been ignored. The trial ceased to be a trial of him and became a trial of the colonial system, as he explained why he had ceased to be a 'staunch loyalist and co-operator' and become an 'uncompromising disaffectionist'. He told the judge that if the system was right he was duty bound to impose the severest penalty. If he was uneasy, he had a duty to resign. The judge was profoundly moved, described Gandhi as in a different category 'from any person I've ever tried or am likely to have to try', reluctantly imprisoned him for six years, and said that if the government were to release him sooner no one would be better pleased than he. Wisely the colonial government never tried Gandhi again, though it did arrest him on many occasions.[6]

Martin Luther King adapted Gandhi's ideals a few decades later: 'unearned suffering is redemptive', he promised his followers, and like Gandhi went on to prevail over force. This sort of individual courage plays a critical role in every process of change. The sacrifice of figures like Jan Palach in Prague in 1969, or the self-immolating Buddhist monks of Vietnam, awakens the community and reveals power without its wrappings of normality as cruel and cold. Actions of this kind are, through some lenses, highly irrational; they are always a gift or sacrifice made by some in the interests of others. Religious belief can make sense of such sacrifices; for example the East Germans who took to the streets in 1989 were led by Christians who believed in a heavenly reward as well as justice here on earth. But sacrifice from non-believers is just as prevalent.

Why do people sacrifice themselves? They can be motivated by love of those around, the friends and relations who have been killed, imprisoned or oppressed. It can feel intoxicating to throw yourself into the arms of destiny, or historical determinism. Rebellion can be the only way of making meaning out of a meaningless life. In its dark side rebellion can become a cult of death.[7] But the day-to-day rebellion of peaceful challenge, undertaken by people who are willing to suffer punishment, helps to prevent torpor, and returns societies to their deepest claimed values.

If individual moral courage is the seed of radical change, its fruits have continued to evolve as states have imagined themselves more as servants and less as masters. For example, it is only during the last two centuries that it has become legitimate for large bodies of the public to organize themselves in membership-based institutions, to march, shout and make claims. The most visible expression of this activation of the people is the demonstration, in which many people signal their solidarity and their commitment, and make themselves vulnerable to the forces of order. There is no record of a demonstration in the modern sense before the middle of the eighteenth century (and the term did not come into common use until the 1830s), yet demonstrations then spread rapidly, alongside other kinds of activism, as the public was morally awakened. The followers of John Wilkes – the great radical renegade supporter of freedoms who opposed British policy in North America in the 1770s – regularly brought thousands on to the streets of London. At roughly the same time the Quakers launched campaigns against slavery, with petitions and, later, boycotts and a powerful slogan – 'Am I not a man and a brother' – perhaps the first great campaign of social protest. Over the succeeding half century the demonstration spread across Europe until, by 1848, it was an established part of the political repertoire, the favoured tool for the relatively marginalized to make their case in an almost military parade, usually aimed at the symbolic centres of the city. Since then demonstrations have steadily grown in number and become a tool not only for the radical Left but also for civil servants and students, and even wealthy landowners (in advanced industrial societies the proportion of the population taking part in demonstrations in the late 1990s was double what it had been in the supposedly more active 1960s and early 1970s).

In Gdansk, Berlin, Teheran and Manila (overthrowing Marcos in 1986 and Estrada in 2001), revolutions have been made through demonstrations, as the people's confidence grew and the confidence of the state waned. The demonstration serves like the display of a big cat – a show of strength to make the use of force redundant. But it also often has the properties described by Martin Luther King and Gandhi: by making themselves visible and vulnerable the people gain moral force.

The demonstration symbolizes the people becoming performers in the world of the state rather than bystanders. It is an exercise in attraction, which tries to pull in passers-by and, through the media, to demonstrate the cause's worthiness, its unity, its numbers and its commitment.[8] It can even on occasion be a moment that combines celebration and repentance, as when the former Alabama Governor George Wallace took part in the 1995 re-enactment of the 1965 Civil Rights march from Selma to Montgomery which he had so furiously opposed.

But demonstrations stop short of the exercise of power; indeed, they are almost the antithesis of the popular exercise of power because they are claims directed at the state, and depend on how the state responds. They are performances and their very character as a performance risks becoming an end in itself. Todd Gitlin has described how the media coverage of student protesters in the 1960s encouraged their leaders to remain newsworthy through actions that no longer helped their cause. So keen were they to stay in the public eye that they came to judge their success by reference to coverage not results, and prioritized eye-catching symbols over building up the movement. As the leaders became detached from reality, and hungry for validation by the media, they ended up oscillating between despair and hubris. This is the trap for all activists in a media-saturated age.

The demonstration is a device for making claims of others, and of the state. It may involve great bravery, and it may be decisive in forcing states to act morally. But it sits outside the normal machineries of power, and it always risks being no more than a monologue which goes unheard by the people it is directed to, or which, like the huge global demonstrations against the invasion of Iraq in the spring of 2003, is heard but simply ignored.

DEMOCRACY AS CONVERSATION

The better way to share responsibility and keep power moral is to involve the people in the conversations of government. The diaries of ministers and officials are filled with talk – committees and working groups, task forces and lobbies. What distinguishes different societies is the breadth of these conversations (whether they are inclusive or exclusive) and their tone (whether people dare to say what they really think).

Many past societies have valued robust public argument as the best way to get good decisions. Ancient Athens was a constant ferment of ideas and disagreement, and honoured rhetoric. The Buddhist and Jain traditions were famous for encouraging public deliberation, and for their lack of respect for formal authority.[9] One of Ashoka's pillars proclaimed that 'there should be no extolment of one's own sect or disparagement of other sects . . . on the contrary other sects should be duly honoured in every way on all occasions.' Nelson Mandela describes in his autobiography the African traditions of public deliberation which he saw as a child in the meetings in the regent's house in Mqhekezweni: 'Everyone who wanted to speak did so', he wrote, and 'the foundation of self-government was that all men were free to voice their opinions and equal in their value as citizens.'[10] Ming China invented the 'community compact', monthly meetings with food provided, during which people discussed behaviour, rewards and morality, often in response to edicts from the emperor.[11]

Conversation is not just how we decide between competing claims, it is also how we think. It is only by trying arguments out that we learn their strengths and weaknesses. But in most democracies these conversations are still limited; the visible ones take place primarily among elite groups or in newspaper columns subject to the whims of proprietors. Most of the day-to-day business of contemporary government is closer to a monologue, with occasional moments for limited responses in the consultation, the public meeting, and the question-and-answer session. The other conversations that take place in kitchens, bars and offices, blogs and web pages, exist in a somewhat parallel world. These tend to be rather different in ethos – more equal, more continuous, more ragged. The challenge for democracies is whether they can bring more of that vernacular conversation into their deliberations.

Over the last two decades many of the newer democracies have stepped well beyond the eighteenth- and nineteenth-century models that predominate in Europe and north America. Wider conversations have been institutionalized, not just in elections and parliaments (literally 'places of speaking', overseen by 'Speakers'),[12] but also in local councils, panchayats, assemblies and citizen forums (like Indonesia's Forum Wargas). Some nations enshrined these much more broad-based conversations in their constitutions. The Philippines did so in the early 1990s, shortly after Brazil's 1988 constitution asserted that public participation in local services was a democratic right and gave birth to thousands of councils linking service providers, social organizations and government (over five thousand in health alone). In Bolivia citizens' oversight committees won the power to freeze municipal budgets if spending veered too far from plans. In Porto Alegre some 100,000 people, about a tenth of the adult population, attended participatory meetings during the course of the initiative to open up the budget-setting process in the 1990s and 2000s.[13]

In parallel, the new social softwares of the Internet have made it possible to involve far more people in rolling conversations than ever before, pointing to a future in which new consensuses may form more organically from the bottom up as people reason and dispute together. These have moved beyond the hierarchical divide between leaders and led, and also beyond the presumption that everyone's opinions are equally valid. Instead authority and attention are earned rather than inherited, as greater prominence is given to people whose past opinions have been found useful by other participants.

Not all parts of the world hsve embraced the spirit of democracy with quite the same vigour. In Uzbekistan in the mid-1990s only one man, Abdulkhafiz Jalolov, stood against the President, Islam Karimov, and even he refused to vote for himself on the grounds that 'both sides should not forget about being noble to each other . . . it would not be modest to vote for myself'. But in many countries such modesty has been put aside in favour of vigorous argument and struggle as people have learned not to be sheep.

ACTION AS ARGUMENT

The conversations in democracies are usually about what the state should do for people. When we vote we rarely commit ourselves to anything, beyond perhaps a modest rise in taxation. There is, however, a very important tradition in democratic culture, which aims to transcend the limitations of the demonstration and the conversation. It is premised on the idea that when we see a problem we have a responsibility to solve it ourselves, so far as we can, rather than waiting for the state. It is a tradition of creating the new society in embryo through practice rather than argument.

During the nineteenth century, while some were marching in the streets, others were trying to create a new society based on mutuality, reciprocity, freedom and equality. Robert Owen, Charles Fourier, Étienne Cabet and Horace Greeley were among those who inspired, and in some cases created, utopian communes.[14] They were careful to theorize what they did and published pamphlets and newspapers that propounded their ideas. Robert Owen, for example, prefigured all of the characteristics of what came to be called the social entrepreneur in the late twentieth century. A succession of different models of organizing the world caught people's imagination and then spread. Some offered a different way of doing schooling (like the Steiner and Montessori schools, or Froebel's kindergartens), or healthcare (for example, the growth of hospices for the terminally ill). Co-operatives and mutuals spread all over the world, and Israel's Kibbutzim were deliberate microcosms of a radically different possible society. Britain's Michael Young was one of the outstanding examples of this social fertility and entrepreneurship: he helped create over sixty organizations, ranging from the Open University to the Consumers' Association, each of which embodied a radical idea about how the world could be different.

The pure utopias and communes all failed. The strength of their ideals exacerbated the contradictions that, as we have seen, underlie any kind of government. Any community on any scale needs rules, authority and order, and the exercisers of authority can never remain morally pure. Sooner or later the community's survival depends on difficult decisions and compromises, and when that happens the ideals can quickly unravel; the purer and more demanding they are, the more vulnerable they will be. Hegel wrote particularly well on this point, criticizing his predecessor Kant for his moral arguments, which demanded 'such inner purity and self-perfection' that only a hypocrite would claim to act morally.[15]

But a myriad of more pragmatic idealists created new forms of social organization and new ways of living that did not demand complete allegiance, and many of these spread and even became mainstream. An alternative history of social change would show how these were designed, adapted and diffused, often in the face of resistance from existing interests, and how much of what we think of now as the service state was first incubated far away from bureaucracies and politicians.

Such a history would show how hard it is for states to lead profound processes of change. The most ambitious strategies to change societies have usually failed. We know much about the failure of the communist attempts to reshape human nature, but the same failings, albeit on a much more modest scale, affected President Lyndon Johnson's Great Society project to eliminate poverty, or the project to reimpose conservative moral values in the US and UK in the 1980s. Those attempts that succeeded turned out in retrospect to have been working either in tandem with, or in the slipstream of, a social movement. The reasons are simple: fundamental social change always requires people to change their habits and beliefs, and this rarely happens unless people have their own reasons for doing so. States can crystallize the claims of a social movement, and many social movements can never succeed unless they persuade a state to entrench their claims in law. But states can only very rarely initiate change.

This has radical implications for how we think about the role of states in promoting moral virtues. It implies that the state cannot sit outside or above society simply doing things to it. Instead it has to sit within society, responding to a more creative kind of citizenship, which is not solely about scrutinizing or persuading the state but is rather about creating change in and around it. Hubert Dreyfus and his colleagues describe this as 'disclosing new worlds'. Through practice, and reflection about practice, people discover new ways of organizing their lives together, perhaps through a mutual help organization for people suffering from the same disease, or a microcredit organization putting women in charge of organizing loans to their peers, or a network of mentors working with young criminals.

All social change of this kind is highly collaborative; it involves people working together. It is also highly moral, though rarely moralistic. George Gilder, one of the theorists of business in Silicon Valley, offered an intriguing definition of the qualities of the entrepreneur which makes particular sense in the context of collaborative change of this kind. The first quality to be found in any entrepreneur, Gilder wrote, is the ability to give. As an example of giving he described Henry Ford offering low prices to create the market for his cars, a temporary sacrifice for future reward. The second quality, he wrote, is humility, by which he meant entrepreneurs being willing to spend a lot of time in 'the grit and grease and garbage of their business'. He also meant the ability to listen. Entrepreneurs must be 'meek enough and shrewd enough to endure the humbling of self that comes in the process of profound learning from others.' The third quality is commitment, by which he meant people who 'give themselves, their time, their wealth, their sleep', people who 'leverage their lives to their belief in a redemptive idea'.

This description may seem distant from the lives and work of most entrepreneurs in business. But it is an apt description of the service engaged in social enterprise, an ideal of leadership from the bottom if we define leadership as giving the community what it needs, rather than what it wants or expects.

This ideal of an active and engaged citizenship whose energies are directed to society as much as to the state has deep roots. For James Harrington this was the best of the legacy from ancient Rome and Greece, whose liberties had declined because of the rule of barbarians who 'deformed the whole face of the world' with their 'ill features of government'.[16] Only the very active participation of the people in the business of government could restore the liberties of the past, and only if everyone was willing to put their talents and energies at the disposal of the community could the common good be upheld, and with it individual liberty. His book, *Oceana*, describes a utopia of rotating offices, checks and balances and civic participation, imaginatively fusing an idea from Venice here, a tradition from Athens there. The underlying ideal was that 'freedom is a form of service, since devotion to public service is held to be a necessary condition of maintaining personal liberty'.[17]

This ideal of service, like the ideal of state service, begins with practical essentials, not with grand rhetoric. It is nurtured in the day-to-day realities of the local community, of roads and schools, public spaces and deciding how to punish petty criminals. It is through handling these issues that people learn how to exercise civic power, and through these practical essentials that people's direct interests are linked to the higher needs of the community (William James wrote of democratic politics helping to ensure that 'common habits are carried into public life'). And it is through practice that reformers avoid the common risk of being like pilots who know how to get the plane to take off but not where to land it (de Tocqueville was describing a similar danger when he wrote of intellectuals with 'an almost infinite distance from practice' who bring 'all the habits of literature into politics').

The ideal of active service implies a strong sense of responsibility. The state's responsibilities to protect, to provide welfare and to serve justice and truth, should be shared by citizens, and indeed cannot be carried out without the participation of citizens willing to serve in armies, to pay taxes and give to charity, to sit on juries or to educate their children.

CONDITIONAL RIGHTS

What follows from this ideal of service is a radically different view of the nature of rights and responsibilities. The advance of rights has been both a consequence of human progress over the last two centuries, and an encouragement to it. The language of rights has provided a good account of the more inclusive bargains and deals which societies have struck in order to get by. But the theory and practice of rights gives little indication as to what people or organizations should do, as opposed to what they are entitled to do. To talk solely of rights soon leads to a logical imbalance, since all rights are necessarily related to responsibilities. They may not directly imply responsibilities, as is sometimes suggested: a small child has many rights that do not imply responsibilities on his or her part. But they are logically related to responsibilities on the part of others – parents, state agencies and strangers – because if these duties are neglected the rights turn into empty shells.

The idea that active service is a necessary foundation for any free community, and any state that aspires to moral virtue, challenges many of our contemporary ideas about citizenship and rights. The citizenship that was fought for over two hundred years, and is now common in much of the world, is automatic for anyone who meets some fixed criteria – blood and soil in some countries, parentage and location in others. The rights of citizenship are universal within the borders of the nation, but then stop abruptly there. Your rights do not depend on what you have done, how good or bad you are or what you have contributed to your community, but are automatic. Any differentiation of citizenship rights (except perhaps for prisoners) is seen as regressive and at odds with the underlying natural law theory of rights; if equal rights derive from nature then it is perverse to distribute them differentially. Most societies have experienced long and bitter battles over precisely who should be counted and how – what rights should accrue to blood descendants, the relatives of migrants, temporary workers and students. But the basic principle, that anyone passing a certain threshold should be entitled to full rights of membership within the nation, is common, as is the assumption that none of these rights applies to anyone outside the nation.

But if a healthy polity depends on constant active engagement this results in a classic structural problem. The passive become free-riders on the active. They benefit from the work provided by the people who run for election, sit on boards, or scrutinize the successes and failures of government. Yet they contribute nothing to it. In the domain of justice the free-riders are the people who demand their rights to a jury trial but use every lever to avoid jury duty when called; in warfare, they are those people who clamour for war but pull every string to ensure that they or their children are not called on to fight. In politics the free-riders are the people who don't bother to follow what the parties are doing or to vote. In a more connected world, with higher levels of migration and greater mobility among the highest earners, the free-riders are those who benefit from prosperity and good order but who have no commitment to the communities around them, behaving like visitors and tenants rather than stakeholders.

Past societies have resolved these tensions by compelling people to live out their responsibilities: conscription for the military in times of greatest danger, compulsory jury service, and, in some thirty countries, compulsory voting. Yet compulsion of this kind sits uneasily with the self-image of a free society, and goes against the grain of the tendencies to specialization. We more naturally contract out specialist roles to judges, soldiers and professional politicians in place of amateur participation by the people as a whole.

None of this would be a problem if we could be certain that there would always be a sufficient supply of civic energy. But in some societies and at some times this energy will be inadequate. Civic life and politics may become insufficiently attractive as a source of fulfilment and recognition. Albert Hirschmann once described the cycles of disappointment that lead societies through waves of civic activism to periods of quietism, when energies are devoted instead to private life. Big social problems motivate people to form pressure groups or stand for office, but over time the intractability of the problems they come up against leads to disappointment, prompting people to return to cultivating their gardens (both literally and metaphorically) until it again becomes apparent that they cannot lead a good and happy life while the world around them is out of balance. Hirschmann's story is a cyclical one, but he also acknowledged that the cycles can become stuck. At worst a vicious spiral can set in if the few who do engage in civic life become less typical of their fellow citizens (in the UK, for example, the average age of local councillors is now fifty-eight), more extreme, or more obsessive and so make civic life repellent to the people it is meant to serve.

The problem for a rationalist, individualist and instrumentalist account of democracy is that it rests on a contradiction. Democratic power is meant to represent interests that are expressed through voting for contending parties. Yet voting and political activism are in some ways highly irrational. It is very rare for an individual vote to have any discernible effect on the results of an election, and even in an age of instant electronic voting the effort involved in learning about the contending positions and expressing a preference is out of proportion to the influence of the voter. Political activism and standing for office may appear more rational as a way of exercising power. But the paradox is that political activism is only seen as honourable if it is not designed to serve the interests of the activist him or herself: its legitimacy rests on it being a gift, not a transaction.

All the available evidence on voting suggests that most people do not go to the polls as a rational, instrumental way of advancing their own interests. Except in extreme cases, where elections are very close, voting is comprehensible only as an expression of identity or duty, of a relationship between the citizen and the political system. One simple piece of evidence for this is the data on trust: voting levels decline in near perfect correlation with declining trust in government, a result precisely opposite to what you would expect from the rationalist model where dissatisfaction should lead to greater activism. Likewise voting tends to be lowest among the groups who might be expected to benefit most from state action – the poor, excluded and marginalized.[18] What Pierre Bourdieu called 'socially constituted agoraphobia' leads many people to exclude themselves from public life[19] and rising income inequalities are strongly associated with declining civic involvement (and voter turnout), as well as widespread feelings of stress and anger, inadequacy and disrespect (not surprisingly murder and violent crime also correlate closely with levels of income inequality).[20]

The predominant liberal model of citizenship is therefore vulnerable on several fronts. It doesn't explain why people act as citizens, it may undercut the very commitments on which it depends, it may encourage free-riding and, because of resentment of free-riding, much less civic activity than society needs.

A different idea of citizenship would acknowledge that civic life, and good power more generally, depends on a basic equality of respect and recognition and on giving as well as receiving. No community can thrive without the active commitment of many of its members, whether as professionals or amateurs. It would make the rights associated with citizenship more conditional. A basic level of citizenship rights would be open to anyone willing to obey the law and pay taxes. But beyond that level new rights would accrue to those who contribute more to their society – by voting in elections, taking part in jury service rather than avoiding it, or committing time to community service.

In the field of health there has been extensive discussion about whether rights to health treatment should in any way be linked to obligations, which might range from duties to ensure that children are vaccinated against infectious diseases to rules that gave priority treatment to people who committed themselves to more healthy lifestyles. In education it is widely accepted that some rights are linked to behaviours – and not just that more subsidized education is provided to children who do well in exams. These principles could well be extended. For example, judges sentencing criminals, panels making decisions on planning applications and competition authorities ruling on mergers might all explicitly take account of how much the individual or institution had contributed to their community.

In each of these examples the specifics are all-important in determining how legitimate conditions are. There have been plenty of unpleasant arguments for conditionality, usually directed solely to the poor. Beatrice Webb, one of the most influential social and political thinkers of the early twentieth century, proposed to the 1932 Royal Commission on Unemployment Insurance that unemployment benefits should be conditional on 'a prescribed attendance for a Health Course giving a varied day at Swedish Drill and other appropriate exercises varied by lectures, etc.' More recent neo-liberals often went much further, demanding detailed commitments as the condition for receiving benefits. However, the other examples cited demonstrate that it is possible to enhance obligations without impinging on people's freedoms, by leaving them free to choose a lower level of rights and obligations if they so wish.

The idea of conditional citizenship is not wholly new. Many societies grant full citizenship rights to new migrants only after a fairly long period of residence. In the USA volunteers on the Americorps volunteering programme receive credits towards the costs of their higher education, and many societies have given special treatment to military veterans in recognition of their gift to the community. But for the most part the idea that citizen rights should be automatic, and universal, has become deeply entrenched as a fundamental principle, even though it clashes with a more common-sense view of morality as involving give as well as take.

THE STATE AS INFRASTRUCTURE

The argument that good power rests on constant work by society, and service within society, also has radical implications for how the state should be organized. Much of the machinery of the contemporary state is essentially pre-democratic, reflecting its continuities with the state that served kings and emperors (the US is the main exception in that the nation took shape ahead of the creation of a national bureaucracy).[21] The state that was taken over by liberals, social democrats and Christian Democrats was not by its nature democratic. Rather, it was, and still is, designed around command rather than accountability. Authority is concentrated at the top, and is directed downwards through hierarchies in the form of laws, directives and commands. The officials who run the state are usually tightly woven into the circles of the elite, concentrated in the capital. At the heart of the state the officials responsible for security operate in a culture that is instinctively hostile to openness, public activism and discussion.

This is not a model of organization that encourages or can cope easily with intensive public involvement. In no nation has it come close to Lincoln's idea of government of, by, and for the people. Instead we have government chosen by electorates, respectful of the people, and, to varying degrees, committed to their welfare – which is a great advance over what went before but it falls short of full democracy. The command of the state has been transformed but not the state itself. The nineteenth-century French anarchist Proudhon's lifelong denunciation of the perversion of democracy into a mere competition for the '*imperium*' seems vindicated.[22]

So how could the state be organized differently, and better embody the spirit of democracy? How could it be organized so that the people would share power and responsibility with the state, in the way that Azo described ancient Rome: transferring power while at the same time retaining it?

Many nineteenth- and early twentieth-century radicals accepted the ancient view that such a recasting of the state could only happen if it was broken up. Large scale was the enemy of democracy as was the monopolization of power by any one group. And so experiments began, which continue to this day, with local councils and committees, public decision-making forums, communes and soviets, participatory budgeting, citizens' juries and assemblies, and courts made up of the people not judges, all designed to ensure that state power was no longer a specialized monopoly of elected politicians and officials but rather made local and shared with the people. Underlying all of these experiments was an argument that the state could never truly be a servant unless the boundaries between the state and people were torn down. All were realizations of Chekhov's comment about 'squeezing the slave out of ourselves drop by drop'.

These radical models offered a very different exemplar to the unitary, consistent bureaucratic state, in which authority was neatly channelled up from the people to the state and then down again through its hierarchies. They pointed towards a possible, perhaps even probable, future in which the boundaries between society and the state become porous, and in which people exercise their collective freedom in many different ways, sometimes through civil society and sometimes through the state. But they were, even at their best, uneven, and at worst chaotic and cruel. The most radical forms of democracy flickered only briefly, for example in the revolutionary period after the First World War or after 1968. They were particularly ill-suited for the harsher kinds of decision that any state has to make, notably around war and peace. There was also a mismatch between the cool, text-based modes of the state and the heightened oral culture of the public meeting. In the participatory forums of Ken Livingstone's Greater London Council in the 1980s, for example, thousands of people, including many from the most marginalized groups, were brought into the business of government for the first time. The problem, however, was that the most vocal could dominate. The passionately intense could drown out the cautious and uncertain. Responsibility could be dissipated: it is a well-attested fact that the larger the group the less any member of it feels responsible for its actions, or for responding to an obvious wrong. There was no premium placed on consistency or the pursuit of slow, careful strategies. The methods which brought people together didn't bring to the fore the wisdom that was contained in the crowd; often the effect was quite the opposite. Often greater deliberation seemed to widen differences, making people more aware of just how much they disagreed with others.[23] For the people working in the state who were trying to make it a true servant the experience echoed the experience of so many servants down the ages – perpetually being shouted at by an irascible, never satisfied master.

At a very local level the dangers of participation are less because discussion is likely to be more practical. This may be why many of the innovations in local participation, from Porto Allegre in Brazil to radical regeneration schemes in the UK, have worked much better than the larger scale revolutionary councils. They are self-consciously prosaic and everyday, concerned with things like sanitation and waste, and so are less prone to rhetorical capture and distortion.

In recent years much has been learned about how large-scale conversations can be constructive, with fair chances for everyone to express an opinion and transparent methods for arriving at decisions. With the help of the Internet and its successors, the evolution of these methods is likely to transform democracy, since they will allow large populations to deliberate, giving greatest voice to the people who have earned the highest reputations for being wise or useful, and helping to turn debates into decisions. They will, in other words, be steps towards helping whole societies to think in ways that are rather more like human brains. In deliberations of this kind high status will no longer be assumed to lend people unique wisdom. Nor will the simple majorities of referendums, elections or opinion polls look like adequate ways to resolve complex choices. Instead the most successful methods will combine dialectical reasoning, open conversation and the aggregation of opinions in ways that tap the full intelligence of a community – something that the political methods of the nineteenth century so signally failed to do.[24]

The republican tradition of civic activism also has another side, which is less about discussion and more about action, addressing how people can achieve change with the state, and how the state can provide infrastructure in its widest sense – tools and platforms with which people can shape their own society and make their own solutions.

This idea is widely understood in economic life. Some ancient states, and some twentieth-century ones, tried to plan and run the economy in detail. But most modern states instead try to set the rules, enforce the law and provide public goods, so that the people and free-standing businesses can take risks, trade and create for themselves. The 'infra' structures which the state provides support the structures which society itself creates, and the invisible hand of the market translates these many actions into a common prosperity.

This is equally relevant in other fields. Within society laws and fiscal regimes that make it easy to create new organizations help to foster a spirit of self-organization, particularly if the state also provides money, skills and advice. In schooling the state can itself provide schools, or it can provide an enabling environment of law and funding, training and advice, which makes it easy for communities to create their own schools, with the state acting as the default provider (and regulator of such things as curriculum content and admissions policies). Similarly, the state can provide hospitals to cure sick people, or it can provide the tools which make it easier for people to sustain their own health. The same principle applies to individual lives. Many modern states describe themselves as 'enablers', providing the tools with which their citizens can govern their own lives, plan careers, and expand their sense of possibility.

Providing infrastructure instead of structures transforms the nature of the service relationship. It reduces the risk that the state will, with its good intentions, take moral autonomy away from the individual, leaving him or her more dependent and less sovereign. But it also does more. Much of the recent thinking about service in states has adopted models from the private sector, which in turn had largely drawn on industrial manufacturing models favouring speed, standardization, flow and efficiency. Yet many of the services provided by states work only to the extent that the individual helps them to work. No school can provide education unless children want to learn and parents encourage them to do so. Doctors can only make their patients healthy if they are willing to take care of themselves.[25] These services are also radically different from the manufacturing model of delivering a specified thing at a specified time. Instead, they are more like crafts, founded on dynamic repetition in search of perfection (as opposed to precisely identical repetition), and a commitment to maintenance and improvement (rather than disposal). None of these is easy in a structure whose commands run from top to bottom and whose accountability runs from bottom to top.

Industrial models of service are also misleading for another reason. They point in the opposite direction to aspirations. The ideal service for most people is closer to the ones that are available to the wealthy, whether in private hospitals, or from tailors, lawyers and financial planners. These services are human, immediate, personalized and rich in communication, anticipating need rather than just meeting it and 'going the extra step'.[26] In the case of therapeutic services the servant's job is to change the master, to make him or her healthier, fitter, happier. So true service for states implies a profound rethinking of service models towards shared production and responsibility, which are likely to involve smaller-scale units, more co-creation and more personal responsibility, and even a commitment to changing the people rather than simply seeing them as sovereign.

This idea has some very ancient roots. In the Confucian tradition people were seen as potentially morally perfectible, and it was a central duty of the state to provide the education and example that would lead them to right conduct. Aristotle, in *The Nicomachean Ethics*, discusses in some detail the ways in which the state could shape those parts of the human psyche that are malleable so as to achieve a better society. John Stuart Mill later argued, in the same vein, that the most important determinant of the quality of government is the quality of its citizens, and that government therefore needed to promote citizens' virtue and intelligence.[27]

But western liberalism is sceptical about the idea that states should actively shape their citizens' behaviour, even if the intention is that they should take more responsibility for their own lives. For more recent liberalism, procedures matter more than substance; what is right in terms of processes matters more than what is good in terms of outcomes. Any interference in the consciousness of citizens calls forth fears of a manipulative state brainwashing free people, and, paradoxically, the better the state of psychological knowledge (and therefore the more effective the interventions) the greater the fear of how it might be used. Herbert Spencer's forecast that the state would become minimal because 'human nature will have become so moulded by social discipline into fitness for the social that it will need little external restraint, but will be self-restrained'[28] sounds to some modern ears like a travesty of freedom.

Any community has to strike a balance between self-restraint and external restraint, and cannot avoid shaping its members to some degree. To exclude states from doing this consciously and transparently means leaving the ground free for other powerful, but probably unaccountable, institutions to do it instead: media, advertisers, religions. Indeed, precisely because the state's monopoly over ideas and information is now so contested, there is less to fear from an activist state. In any case, it is better to have an open conversation about what good qualities the community wants to cultivate and which bad ones it wants to contain and constrain than for this to happen haphazardly.

Such deliberate evolution of human potential and consciousness may offend some believers in choice and individual autonomy. But if good government depends on the quality of rulers, and if in democracies the people have become the rulers, it follows that progress is bound to depend on some conscious evolution of people's qualities of awareness and self-restraint: growing what's good in people, holding back what's bad, and ensuring the widest possible argument about which is which.

For some utopians the ideal active civil society replaces politics. In William Morris's *News from Nowhere*, one of the characters asks about politics and is told: 'We are very well off as to politics – because we have none.' There are many believers in a world wholly ruled by laws, administration or markets, who believe that these are somehow more rational than the messy realities of politics. But politics reflects humans as they are and all attempts to iron out the warp and weft of conflicts and difference are doomed to failure. What I have described here is therefore not a regime of good power that is guaranteed by perfect rules, but rather a regime of good power that is sustained by continual work, and constant recreation in a more, not less political society. Without a vigorous public, animated and engaged not just in making arguments and claims but also in remaking the world around them, even the most decent democratic regime will risk stagnation. This ideal is an ancient one. Lao Tzu wrote that 'the good leader is the one that the people adore; the wicked leader is the one that the people despise; the great leader is the one the people say, "We did it ourselves."'

13

Unsettling Knowledge as a
Source of Renewal

'An nescis, mi fili, quantilla prudential mundus regatur.' (You should know, my son, with what little discretion and knowledge the world is ruled.)   Attributed to Pope Julius III

In 1967, the US Secretary of Defense Robert McNamara commissioned an extensive study of the Vietnam War, which was then at its peak. He wanted to know more about the origins of the war, about whether the US could win, and about whether the casualty counts that his press officers issued each day were accurate. Forty-seven volumes were prepared by a team of officers and analysts and taken together they amounted to a damning critique of US policy and behaviour – so damning that great efforts were made to prevent their publication.

The leak of these documents, which came to be known as the Pentagon Papers, sparked off a furious debate about the role of the press. The government's call for an injunction came before a Judge Gurfein, who wrote in his adjudication rejecting the government's claim that 'a cantankerous press, an obstinate press, a ubiquitous press' had to be 'suffered by those in authority' for the sake of the higher values of freedom.

Freedom of the press wasn't the only issue in this case, however. It also raised important questions about the moral role of knowledge in government. To govern well governments need outside criticism and scrutiny, but they also need to be able to think and argue in confidence, without a running commentary of doubt and criticism. They need a culture of internal openness and argument that is often at odds with a free and rambunctious media, which will seize on leaks to show that government is divided and uncertain.

In Chapter 4 I showed that governments are good not because of their inherent virtues but because their environments force them to be. I have already touched on how transparency changes their environment, making it harder for rulers and officials to be corrupt or self-serving. But the relationship between power and knowledge goes far beyond this. In recent years government has become enmeshed in the broader shift to societies based on knowledge in ways that have further transformed their moral environment. Responsibility for truth, the authority for authority, has passed beyond the control of states which can no longer tailor it to their needs. Yet as this has happened a host of new difficulties and choices have come into view.

TOLERANCE OF MANY DIFFERENT PATHS TO TRUTH

The first of these is how to be tolerant. Power has always rested on knowledge. Kautilya wrote that 'rulers see through spies as cows through smell, Brahmans through scriptures and the rest of the people through normal eyes.' Their superior knowledge, and their ability to cover up their sins and their errors, enabled rulers to do wrong as well as right.

Past rulers claimed unique insights that were beyond the reach of the people they ruled. But the best modern governments open themselves up to doubt and learning. They acknowledge that there are many paths to truth, and no monopoly of received wisdom.

This does not imply limitless tolerance. The defining characteristic of a free society is not that it tolerates all actions, since it cannot (no democracies tolerate female circumcision, underage drug use or polygamy). Instead its defining feature is that it tolerates many paths to truth, and tries to internalize within itself sufficient challenge and argument to protect it from its own beliefs, with officials and advisers who are willing to speak truth to power.[1]

There is a striking parallel between the first rise of democracy in Greece and the rise of dialectics, the intellectual techniques of logic and argument that we associate with Parmenides and Heraclitus,

Socrates and Plato. The latter presumed that communities could agree on the principles for discovering knowledge, and that these could be stated publicly in ways that would make it possible to distinguish truths from falsehoods. Indeed, without commonly accepted methods for reasoning it is hard to see how any democracy could function. They also presumed that truth was not revealed; that it was not the preserve of the chosen few; and that knowledge was dynamic, not static.

Democracy as both a form of government and as a mentality has always had to fight against enemies in this respect. The religions and states which were founded on written texts often found tolerance difficult to stomach, rationally so if they believed that they already possessed the only authentic truth. Marxism-Leninism reached such extremes of intolerance that students in Maoist China were imprisoned for reading too much Marx and Lenin and not enough Mao. Some of the Communists' pronouncements echoed Caliph Omar's famous justification for the destruction of the Library of Alexandria on the grounds that if it contained books in accord with Allah they weren't needed since he had the Koran, and if they were not in accord with Allah they weren't needed either. More recently the influential Islamic theorist Sayed Qutb hardened his monotheism into an argument for monoculture in which there could be no room for doubt or argument and no separation of the religious and secular, since if God is the only God he must rule everything and every part of life without question.

Christianity has also repeatedly succumbed to the same intolerance. American Evangelical Christians, for example, have demanded that children should use creationist textbooks in which dinosaurs and fossils were created by God only a few thousand years ago. Some have even campaigned to remove from public signs information that the Grand Canyon was formed millions of years ago. Not surprisingly, they applauded when George W. Bush announced that he had received more guidance for his Middle East policies from God than from his earthly father.

All of these claims to uniqueness and exclusive wisdom start with faith. But given what we know of history, they also bring with them the whiff of newly dug graves.

It is an Islamic ruler, Akbar, who remains the best example of reasoned tolerance in a ruler, and from a time – the sixteenth century – when Christian monarchs were rarely if ever so enlightened. Ruling an India that was still predominantly Hindu he decreed that 'no man should be interfered with on account of religion and anyone is to be allowed to go over to a religion that pleases him.' He said we could not rely on the 'marshy land' of tradition, but must use the *rahi aql* or path of reason to guide us. Akbar established the principle that the state should be neutral between religions, ended discriminatory taxes on non-Muslims, and publicly talked to all the different strands of Hindu thought including the charvakas, who were atheists.

Helped by his adviser Abu'l Fazl, Akbar developed an almost secular morality, which transformed the Islamic concept of *sulh-i kul*, absolute peace, from being a mystical idea to a more practical one that described how diverse groups could live together in harmony, with kingship as both divine right and as a contract between ruler and society. There is an illuminating story about how he helped those around him to understand what tolerance meant. Responding to a mullah who claimed that every child was born with an instinctive bias in favour of Islamic principles, Akbar decided to put it to the test. Twenty new-born children were put in the charge of a nurse with no one else to meet or talk to them. Akbar said, 'We shall examine them and see if they are prone to emit sounds even remotely suggestive of Muhammad or any other champion of Islam.' At the end of the year all the children were dumb.

This example appears cruel to modern sensibilities. But it demonstrated an active understanding of tolerance rather than just a passive one, an idea of the ruler and the state as engaged in constant battle against prejudices, misconceptions and intolerance.

The second requirement for a good government is to remain open to many truths, while also accepting that there can be commonly shared ways of reasoning, and of distinguishing truths and falsehoods. It was a cardinal principle for the philosophers of the Enlightenment that whereas an oppressive regime must be based on falsehood and dogma, a free one must be based on objective truths, truths that lay beyond the control of power. It was a mark of an oppressive regime that it would seek to create its own reality, rather than learn from objective truth.

In 2002 a senior White House aide to President Bush gave an interview to a journalist, Ron Suskind, in which he said that the journalist was 'in what we call the reality-based community' made up of people who believe that solutions emerge from the 'judicious study of discernible reality'. But, he commented, 'that's not the way the world really works any more. We're an empire now, and when we act, we create our own reality. And while you're studying that reality judiciously, as you will, we'll act again, creating other realities, which you can study too.'

Power's relation to truth is more complex than either the Enlightenment ideal or its mirror can admit. It is more like the relationship of a magnet to objects. Some it pulls; some it distorts; others it repels. Karl Marx explained this with the greatest clarity, showing how power shapes categories and makes it impossible even to imagine alternatives,[2] giving contingent human relationships the appearance of being facts of nature, immutable realities. So in market economies what appears to be a free exchange between individuals voluntarily selling their labour to private firms is really a deeply unequal relationship of exploitation.[3] In politics, too, the facts of power are made to appear natural; this was the vivid premise of George Orwell's *1984*, where the language of 'newspeak' was designed to render dissident thoughts unnameable and therefore unthinkable.

This can be apparent in the ways that states handle uncomfortable truths. Information is more freely accessible and abundant than ever before and there are fewer secrets any more, and less inside knowledge that doesn't soon dribble out. But it doesn't follow that the public will necessarily be well informed. The White House under George W. Bush, for example, successfully convinced a large majority of US citizens that Iraq was behind the 9/11 attacks on New York. The US government, like other states, could not ban challenging ideas: instead it sought to marginalize them, squeezing them out of the mainstream channels rather than suppressing them. If enough people didn't care, or didn't want to believe contesting ideas, the fact that they were freely available in newspapers or on the web wouldn't matter. If the wider community did little to assert its own dialectics – its own methods for reasoning and distinguishing truths and falsehoods – then power could prevail.

OPEN AND ETHICAL MEDIA

In 1997 Tony Blair was interviewed on BBC radio and talked about his childhood. It was reported in newspapers that he had fondly recalled watching Jackie Wilson playing for Newcastle United football club from the Gallowgate end of their ground. Journalists soon pointed out that Wilson had stopped playing for Newcastle by then and that the Gallowgate end had yet to be built. How could a man who lied so casually about minor matters be trusted on anything else? The story was repeated again and again by journalists, biographers and opposition politicians; once 'on the books', no one felt any need to check whether it was true, and the story provided a useful justification for vitriolic accusations that Blair was a liar. Eventually, eight years later, a journalist checked the tape and found that Blair had in fact made none of these claims.

This example is a minor one. But it illustrates the central importance of truth to the modern state. Truth has become a cardinal value in societies rich with information and knowledge. We depend ever more on secondhand information for daily life, business and politics. A century ago it mattered most what those around us said and did. Daily life was lived with primary sources. Today we look to books or newspapers, websites and TV programmes to know what we can eat, what career to follow, or whom to vote for.

As a consequence the question of who can be trusted, whose facts are reliable, becomes all important, and a critical battleground between journalists and politicians, civil servants, non-governmental organizations and scientists. States have to struggle to demonstrate their ability to contribute to truth and knowledge. Their bona fides are usually in doubt. Those who lie too bluntly are quickly found out. The intelligent ones learn to be smart about what to say and when and how to be 'economical with the truth' (the infamous phrase coined by Sir Robin Butler, head of the British civil service).

In liberal political theory the free media are meant to be the best guarantee that in the end truth will prevail. Seen in this light it is progress that states which used to communicate directly to their citizens now do so mainly through the media, where their messages are reshaped by the logics of news values and commentary. In James Madison's influential vision of the infant American democracy, the media were expected to provide a market place for ideas and truths in which severe competition would promote truth over falsehood. John Stuart Mill argued in similar ways about the value of allowing many partial truths to compete so that ultimately a more complete truth would prevail.

In many parts of the world journalists do indeed remain in the heroic frontline to counter oppression and lies. In the Ukraine, for example, where one of President Kuchma's security men, Mykola Melnychenko, was recorded planning the murder of a critical journalist, Heorhiy Gongadze, or in Bangladesh, where the journalist Sumi Khan has become a symbol of individual courage after being repeatedly stabbed and beaten for revealing the complicity of powerful figures in Islamist violence, the idea of an independent media struggling for truth remains valid. In the developed democracies, too, the private and public media are often the only institutions with the resources needed to investigate official misdemeanours. Organizations like the BBC, the *New York Times*, *Die Zeit* or *Le Monde* have come to be associated with accuracy, and market forces do indeed encourage truthfulness. When they get something badly wrong abject apology soon follows. Thanks to them anyone wanting to find authoritative and independent assessments of what rulers are doing can easily find them. Sophisticated judgements that were once accessible only to the best-connected members of the elite are now freely available.

But although democracy is impossible without free media it does not automatically follow that where the media are free rulers will be adequately scrutinized and assessed. When the French Revolution introduced freedom of speech, the result was not an outbreak of sober judgement but what the historian Simon Schama described as a wave of 'polemical incontinence' that drove the country first to regicide and then to the Terror.[4] More recently free media have proven as well-suited to bile and prejudice as to fearless investigation. Partly this reflects the nature of media markets: they can at times reward accuracy and truth but if information is packaged in with entertainment, and if truthfulness is not a sufficiently high priority for consumers, it can easily fall victim to sensationalism, or the prejudices of a proprietor. If readers and viewers lack independent information on whether particular media tell the truth they may be unable to make wise choices about whom to believe. Worse, in a web environment, the sheer range of sources and facts may overwhelm people (and according to some recent research on health, people were more likely to be well-informed if they relied on their friends and family than if they relied on the web).

Government structures only work to promote good behaviour if they are aligned with the ethics of those working within them. The same is true in competitive media. Market imperfections can be magnified if professionals working in the market are not motivated by a strong ethic of searching for the truth, just as political imperfections will be magnified if politicians and officials lack a strong ethic of service. Yet for many newspapers, magazines and broadcasters it simply doesn't matter much whether what they print is true. Like the worst governments they see reality as something to be created, not interpreted. Nor do they accept the authority of any third party that can validate what they do.

The net result of the way parts of the media work is that the public are often left with systematically incorrect perspectives on the world around them. Derek Bok cites evidence which showed that in 1996 half of all Americans believed that the number of US jobs had fallen over the preceding five years; 80 per cent that inflation had not fallen; 60 per cent that unemployment had either risen or stayed the same; 69 per cent that the federal budget deficit had grown worse; and a majority that the quality of air had deteriorated. All were untrue.[5]

More recently the British pollster MORI has surveyed people's beliefs about their society, providing a perceptual map which shows the consistent patterns of misinformation on issues like migration, Europe and crime. When told the true facts people's attitudes often shifted, showing just how important misinformation can be to the dynamics of politics.[6]

In a climate of pervasive cynicism populism can work for politicians, whereas sober honesty can backfire.[7] The public have been encouraged to follow the advice given to his journalists by Harold Evans (one of the most influential editors in both the US and the UK): when listening to politicians, he warned, you should always have in mind 'why is this bastard lying to me?' I. F. Stone made a similar comment; his most important message to trainee journalists was: 'governments lie'.

With a strong ethic of truth-telling in the media, scepticism of this kind can reinforce all that is best in politics. But without such an ethic this attitude can simply lead to cynicism, and undermine any sort of truth and any capacity for legitimation. Journalists who used to dine with politicians now dine on them, and use them as props for their own aggrandisement. Anthony Sampson, who wrote a regular report on the anatomy of power in modern Britain, commented that the biggest change between his first edition in the early 1960s and his last, published in 2004, was that 'the masters of the media are the new aristocracy, demanding and receiving homage from politicians, big businessmen and the aristocracy.'

Like most aristocracies the top ranks of the media resent any suggestion that they might need to be held to account, or subject to ethical standards. This ethical deficit at the core of the information society is compounded because all communication now competes for time and attention with the vastly increased volume of commercial communication. Commercial communication, like political communication, indirectly promotes the idea that there are no truths, only strategies and claims (a view which has, indirectly, had a vast influence on the academic study of communication).

The public doesn't only need better news and facts. John Stuart Mill was right to say that 'very few facts are able to tell their story without comment to bring out their meaning'. Nor do we live in a world made up of unproblematic objective truths. But we should want institutions – governments as well as media – to place a high value on the search for truth and objectivity, even if this ideal is never quite attainable. And we should want them to be able to calibrate their judgements, since if people assume that every politician is a scoundrel there will be no incentives for the potential scoundrels to rein themselves in.[8]

There are some solutions that several societies have groped towards as they have come to understand the critical role that the media play in making democracy function. One is to enhance and protect parts of the media insulated both from the state and from market pressures, ensuring that these have a strong ethic of truth-seeking and sufficient resources to compete for attention. Another is to apply the principles of validation to the media themselves so that they are publicly judged against criteria such as accuracy. This is not a task which governments can do. But civil society and the universities can play a much more active role in assuring standards, investigating errors, and holding to account individual journalists and media outlets against a strong ethic of truth and accuracy.[9]

STATES' DEPENDENCE ON KNOWLEDGE

The media matter because they are such an important part of the environment in which governments operate. But their importance and scale is not the only way in which governments' environment has changed. Just as important to the moral character of politics has been the growing dependence of governments on knowledge. Shelley wrote that the poets were the unacknowledged legislators of the world at precisely the moment when scientists and engineers were beginning to make a far stronger claim. No society today can function without multiple centres of knowledge – scientists exploring physics or chemistry, businesses exploring consumer behaviour or new materials, voluntary organizations exploring new needs, professions exploring new practices in architecture or healthcare.

Some past states valued this kind of pragmatic knowledge. Francis Bacon's advocacy of a state based on knowledge and reason was mirrored in the Chinese ideas of evidential research in the eighteenth century, which criticized empirically unverifiable moral principles.[10] But the value of independent sources of knowledge has become much more evident in recent years, and has been reinforced by the power of professions, businesses and civil organizations. The dialectical, logical reasoning that lay at the heart of Greek philosophy has now permeated much of the modern state.

As a result, among the senior positions in a modern government are a chief scientist and a chief medical officer, a chief economist and a chief statistician. They are usually as much representatives of their professional disciplines within government as vice versa, and they see themselves as guardians of professional ethics as well as knowledge. They are powerful because an advanced democracy cannot function without the constant production and dissemination of data and know-ledge – about everything from new materials and software to prices or public opinion. Distorted information produced to please vested interests is of little value to anyone. This is why liberalizing societies often start off by freeing the business media, because markets cannot function without accurate and critical flows of information and analy-sis, to tell if a company is overvalued, if its executives are incompetent or if its new product is a dud.

Legitimacy increasingly rests on a thin line of scientific reasoning. When the British government faced an outbreak of foot-and-mouth disease in 2001 its very credibility depended on being able to offer a plausible analysis of what was happening, and the speed with which the disease would spread. The government also needed a credible plan for stopping it. Luckily for its ministers, the then Chief Scientist was able to devise an epidemiological model which accurately predicted the likely pattern of infection and how it could be arrested.[11] A similar situation faced the Chinese government as the SARS outbreak spread in 2004. At first it was met with denial, but it soon became clear to the scientists running the government's policy that this would be more damaging than an admission of the truth, both about the problem and about how it was being addressed.

Keynes famously commented that 'there is nothing a government hates more than to be well-informed; for it makes the process of arriving at decisions much more complicated and difficult.' But in many circumstances governments cannot afford to be ill-informed. Blithe ignorance carries a high cost, particularly when citizens, or the world, are watching. So, for example, healthcare without independent medical trials, evidence and argument is bound to be less effective, and therefore less useful politically, than healthcare based on sound evidence, and those countries where governments have taken an ideo-logical position on medical science have generally cost their people dearly. President Thabo Mbeki's scepticism about the relationship between HIV and AIDS probably contributed to many unnecessary deaths in South Africa, just as half a century ago Trofim Lysenko's influence on agrarian science in the Soviet Union kept millions hungry.

The systems that produce and circulate knowledge rest on devices and values that states can influence but not control – the comments and criticisms of peers working over many decades in a common pursuit of truth; the valuing of enquiry and criticism, novelty and experiment; an ethos that favours profundity and insight rather than only utility; campaigns and advocates that dig out suppressed knowledge. These systems of knowledge have to negotiate the terms of their independence, since often nominal independence coincides with financial dependence on states (typically a majority of research funds come from taxes raised by states, as does some 30–40 per cent of NGO income in developed countries).[12] But governments' dependence on independent knowledge means that they cannot afford to distort it or manipulate it too much, without risking failure or opprobrium or both.

Einstein was once berated by his secretary for asking the same exam questions to his students in two successive years. He replied that it was true that the questions were the same; however, the answers had changed. So it is with modern states. Many of the questions they face about protection, welfare, justice and truth are constant, but the answers are perpetually changing. The result is the mutual dependence of states and a largely independent system of knowledge which is visible in the vast flow of facts, investigations and audits that characterizes modern states in the richer countries. These now learn much more systematically through pilots, evaluations and real-time feedback on what is and isn't working, and they depend day-to-day on networks in which professionals, policy-makers and external experts share data and knowledge – like the health collaboratives in fields like cancer care, or the industry of economists around the monetary policy committee of the Bank of England or the Federal Reserve, or the tens of thousands of environmental scientists and experts who comment on climate change or biodiversity.

There will always be political limits to their willingness to expose ideology and prejudice to real-world tests; few leaders like seeing their cherished pet scheme rubbished by cool evaluators. But governments have found that across large areas of activity it is safer to make use of these devices to seek the truth than it is to pretend that they have a superior insight into how the world works.

Visibility is becoming as automatic as secrecy once was. It used to be said that governments were the only known vessels that leak from the top. Now their leaks have become institutionalized. Citizens can look up details of the performance of their local school or police force on the web, or compare the performance of their national government to others. States make it easier for civil society and the economy to function by providing information, for example reliable information on diet and obesity, currency reserves, weather forecasts and security (and even the once-secretive intelligence agencies put their threat assessments on the web). The consequence is that there are few fields of government activity that have not, at least somewhere, been through a revolution in knowledge, with more conscious experiment, theory and modelling, and more exploration of even the most intimate parts of life. In a sense the Panopticon has been turned inside out: where once, in the picture drawn by Jeremy Bentham and theorized by Michel Foucault, states observed every part of society from a single vantage point of observation, today the opposite is closer to the truth, in that the workings of the state are visible, scrutinized and measured, whereas the daily lives of citizens are private.

The moral quality of this shift is unmistakeable. Bad power is power that refuses to answer for itself, that hides, that believes itself to be its own justification, and demands accountability of everyone else. Bad power is power that seeks to make its own reality. Good power, by contrast, opens itself to scrutiny and accepts that truth is something to be sought, not asserted.

Yet this blurring of the boundaries between the state and society is not quite as automatically good as it at first seems. The knowledge that is produced at one remove from the state is also produced at one remove from the people it is there to serve. Most intellectual disciplines have a far stronger sense of service to themselves than of service to the people, and most assume that the public are incapable of competently interpreting their own lives. Rational, well-meaning experts have been involved in many of the horrors of the last century, from experimental torture in concentration camps to forced sterilization; it is all too easy for knowledge to become detached from humanity and care, and for professionals to see other people as means not as ends. Even more horrific than the bombs and the gas chambers was the sheer banality of administration in totalitarian regimes, the painstaking bureaucracy of identity cards, logistics and regulations that made the killing so efficient, applying the everyday tools of methodical order to an exceptionally evil task.[13] Scientists blind to the uses that will be made of their knowledge, officials 'just obeying orders', and journalists looking on as they witness atrocities, are all examples of the risks of a culture of detachment, in which a professional ethos is defined by its lack of commitment rather than by its commitment.

Yet despite these blindnesses, once states are more closely woven into open systems of knowledge, in which information flows easily and freely, many of their characteristic vices become less sustainable. One is the vice of self-deception. *Homo sapiens sapiens* is not a rational animal but a rationalizing one, highly suggestible, prone to copying the apparently successful, and good at ignoring problematic information. Large bureaucracies are skilled at manipulating their own beliefs – the 'Potemkin villages' designed to showcase the state's genius and benevolence are usually directed to the governors themselves as much as to any visitors. All states risk becoming prisoners of what they have said. People have limited capacities to hear the truth, and the more they have invested of their lives in one truth the less easy it will be for them to discard it. Those who have promised radical change are most vulnerable to their own propaganda. You can't easily tell the Salvation Army that there is no salvation. George Orwell said in 1949 that the ruling Labour Party's biggest problem was its own propaganda – which happened not to be true (he was even more scathing about the truths believed by the opposition Conservatives).

States that reject criticism are helped by people's desire for a quiet life. A common feature of all accounts of states breaking down, and of impending genocides, is the unwillingness of so many of the officials involved to accept what appears in retrospect obvious, and the complicity of much of the public in lies and silence. Yet where there are open media, argument and analysis, and independent sources of knowledge within the state itself, these self-deceptions are harder to sustain. When the media make it possible to *audi alteram partem*, we hear about what is happening to the people on the receiving end of the state's actions, and gain a richer moral understanding than when the affected are mute and invisible.

Open sources, open information and working within networks all protect against these vices; they protect states from themselves. It is no coincidence that states in recent years have made the greatest blunders when reliant on information that is not subject to such systematic processes of external challenge and assessment. Intelligence agencies are notoriously prone to exaggerate threats, not least because they are so rarely subjected to independent validation, and this tendency becomes even more dangerous when political leaders signal clearly which facts they want. The flawed claim that Iraq owned large stockpiles of weapons of mass destruction (WMD) in the early 2000s is just one of hundreds of examples of how dangerous knowledge can be when it is detached from an open system of checks and exposure (and because the Americans in particular were so committed to proving their claim: one of the inspectors charged with finding these weapons described what they were asked to do as 'believing is seeing'). Ironically the only inspector to find hidden WMD in the Middle East was Mordechai Vanunu, the Israeli whistleblower, who languished for years in solitary confinement as his reward.

VALIDATION AND TRIANGULATION

What holds abuses of knowledge in check? What makes it hard for governments to lie or to create false truths? The simple answer is validation. Because the bona fides of the state are suspect societies have come to rely on a distinctive new device to regulate this production of knowledge, and to judge behaviour more generally, a device of validation and triangulation – validation to assess the truthfulness of claims, triangulation because it involves a third party taking a distinct perspective of assurance, inspection and investigation.

The sixteenth-century Ottoman poet Kinalizade Ali Çelebi wrote that 'true friendship means looking at a friend's work with the eye of an enemy'; so, too, do the true interests of the state lie in scrutiny with the eye of an enemy. This is the principle long applied to companies to ensure that their accounts are truthful. It has been applied to professions and public services, particularly where there are big asymmetries of knowledge between citizens and those they depend on. It has been applied to government, for example through Britain's National Audit Office and Audit Commission. In some places (for example in Kerala and West Bengal in India) public hearings on major items of public spending have achieved some of the same objectives. In other cases civic organizations have taken the lead; in Bangalore, for example, a citizens' report card on public services was introduced in the early 1990s, scoring their performance in terms of service delivery, corruption and staff attitudes.[14] In Bolivia the Popular Participation Law established community-based 'Vigilance Committees' in the mid-1990s, with powers over money, including the authority to lodge an official complaint (a *denuncia*) of municipalities that *in extremis* would result in their funding being cut off. These examples of bottom-up validation have often proven more effective than top-down validation, and have certainly changed the balance of power.

Globally, validation has become commonplace. The European Union has adopted what it calls the principle of 'open co-ordination', using peer pressure and transparency rather than laws and directives to encourage better behaviour by governments; for example, reducing the temptations to run up debts for future generations. In effect, public opinion and the opinions of other governments combine to serve as an external validator. Some governments have enthusiastically embraced these soft external constraints rather as smokers are often the strongest supporters of smoking bans. The International Monetary Fund and World Bank act in similar ways, reporting on country policies and making recommendations (often amid controversy). Their role is reinforced by independent initiatives like Transparency International, which monitors corruption levels.[15]

None of these validators necessarily has any better access to the truth than the governments they oversee. Sometimes they can be used to legitimate bad decisions. Experts can be expertly wrong. But they are more likely to be committed to truth than officials and politicians, and taken as a whole the rise of validation and triangulation has tended to make states more accountable, more reflective and better able to make the right decisions (one definition of power is the ability to get away with mistakes – they make it harder to do so). The tendencies of government towards what Churchill called 'terminological inexactitude' have been at least held in check.

Yet the pursuit of 'the truth, the whole truth and nothing but the truth' is not a viable approach to government. Truth can clash with other moral goals, such as security (where saying too much about a new weapons system diminishes its effectiveness) and welfare (where there may be very strong reasons to be reticent about a possible economic shock or a prospective tax change). Truth may offend against justice; for example, should the public have a right to know every criminal's location, or every paedophile's current address? Openness can be almost as much of a vice as secrecy.

Just as in daily life we are all required to make judgements about the relative virtue of truth and other moral principles, this is even more the case with politicians. The heart of the problem is to distinguish those cases where deceit or economy with the truth is in the interests of the government rather than the public, from those where it is in the public interest. The only viable answers locate some of the job of validation within the state itself. Many governments already have quasi-judicial procedures to oversee such things as wiretapping and the interception of e-mails. This same principle can be applied to decisions over how information should be treated – what should be made public, when and on what basis. Lord Acton wrote that 'everything secret degenerates, even the administration of justice'. So long as sufficiently legitimate validators can be found, such devices to internalize validation may just provide a reasonable balance between the vices of openness and the vices of secrecy.

EXPERIMENT AND INNOVATION: THE STATE AS LABORATORY

The great conservative states of the past produced knowledge and then froze it, sometimes almost literally in stone temples carved with decrees, proclamations and legends. Pharaonic Egypt and Imperial China cultivated immutability and deference to tradition. New knowledge was suspect, and could only gain a hearing if it was presented as a recovery of old knowledge.

Modern states have generally been more at ease with innovation, usually inspired by the competitive threat of war and by the moral drive towards betterment. Indeed, some states were far too innovative. Stalin invented a novel system of planning and Gulags.[16] It was radically creative for Pol Pot to empty Cambodia's cities, as it was for the French revolutionaries to invent ten-hour days and ten-day weeks, but very little else can be said in favour of their ideas.

Yet encouraging innovation in and around the state is one way of countering tendencies towards self-service since it keeps to the fore the questions 'what should the state do?', and 'how should it do these things better?' States lack some of the obvious pressures for innovation, such as competition, or the threat of destruction. Big programmes can accumulate a logic of their own – the policy equivalents of the Maginot line: marvellous, complex, elaborate, but beside the point. In big bureaucracies the costs associated with failure (or asking too many questions) have generally been higher than the rewards for successful risk-taking, and states can be a powerful brake on innovation in the economy and civil society if they maintain inflexible regulations, impose excessive taxes, or harass entrepreneurs.

But this is not inevitable. States can be designed to support innovation, and to open themselves out to challenge and scrutiny. Many of the decisive innovations of the eighteenth and nineteenth centuries came from public organizations (mainly armies), and in the twentieth century a high proportion of fundamental innovations were also directly supported by states, from the jet engine to the Internet (the unlikely legacy of DARPA, an arm of the US Pentagon) and the world wide web (the equally unlikely legacy of CERN near Geneva).[17] The Manhattan project and the Apollo space programme were vast examples of successful innovation administered by government. Competitive markets, by contrast, are ill-designed for the long timescales and uncertainties of fundamental innovation.

If state support for research and development in technology is now well-established (and rising as a share of GDP), deliberate strategies for innovation within government are much less common. It takes courage to open up existing programmes to the implicit criticism and challenge of experiment. Likewise, for politicians to admit that a new policy is an unproven experiment asks a lot of them, and of the public they serve: it entails admitting the limits of their knowledge. I have seen ministers trumpet the success of a pilot only a few weeks after it started; in another case unwelcome results were simply suppressed; in a third case their clear findings were brazenly ignored. That pilots and evaluations have spread nevertheless shows that the benefits from more knowledge outweigh the risks of embarrassment and failure. Many governments deliberately create knowledge about themselves. They can overtly commit funding to innovations in their own bureaucratic structures and in services; they can promote flexibility (for example, allowing agencies in some areas to break rules where they believe these inhibit effectiveness, as in Britain's employment and education zones); they can incubate new models (providing protected space in which new ideas are allowed to achieve a critical mass, as Singapore has done); and they can use more radical measures that separate spending and provision and open public money up to competition. The character of the knowledge they produce will vary from the quasi-scientific – for example, evaluations of labour market policies or medical trials – to the speculative: in areas as diverse as the regulation of biotechnology or e-government, their sheer novelty guarantees uncertainty, and mistakes. Yet in all of these fields, the scientist Linus Pauling's comment that 'the best way to have good ideas is to have lots of ideas, and then to discard the bad ones' remains pertinent.

These devices to support innovation and renewal within government have to be kept within boundaries. There can be little tolerance for risk and creativity in much of the state – to experiment with blue and purple traffic lights or novel safety procedures in nuclear power stations would be immoral, and a betrayal of trust. Treating citizens as participants in laboratory experiments is, to say the least, morally problematic. Instead states have to carve out safe spaces where they can create knowledge without too great a risk.[18] The overall aim of these devices is to generate novelty, test it, and then winnow down to the far smaller number of possibilities that will work. But their indirect effect is also to expand the imagination of the political realm, and so to make people aware of new possibilities.

The German poet Hölderlin argued that what made the state a hell on earth was that man tried to make it a heaven. But the mistake has always been to believe that there could be only one way to heaven, and only one vision of what it would be like to get there. This is why openness to competing knowledge is so important. Knowledge can be profoundly unsettling for governments (the knowledge contained in the Pentagon Papers certainly was; as Robert McNamara later said, 'we were wrong, terribly wrong'), but that very unsettling helps them to think and act more clearly, and in the long run the US almost certainly benefited from the leaks, which made it easier for Nixon to withdraw from Vietnam and so saved many thousands of lives.

14

Could a Government Serve the
Whole World?

*'Nothing can ever happen again without the whole world
taking a hand ... there are no questions that can be settled by
being settled at one point.'*   Paul Valéry

Morality doesn't fit neatly into jurisdictional boundaries. But governments do. In this chapter I turn to the global dimensions of good
power. I ask whether states have any duties to protect, or to promote
welfare, justice or truth beyond their borders. I examine why child
soldiers and child labour, small arms and landmines, the drugs trade
or diamond sales have intruded into the polite world of diplomacy,
and how we should think about the many human needs that have
become globally interdependent as never before.

THE TWO FACES OF THE MODERN NATION STATE

Throughout the modern era the starting presumption of both political
theory and practice has been that nations (or societies) are closed,
sovereign islands that are, in moral terms, sufficient unto themselves.
Modern democratic states have sharply distinguished between what
they should do for their citizens and what they should do for people
who are not citizens. Within the nation's boundaries the state's roles
have been shaped by political and moral arguments about service.
Competing classes and parties fought fierce battles over equity, justice
and fairness, but they all recognized that domestic policy had to be
guided by moral considerations. Indeed, at home democratic states

had no choice but to act as servants rather than masters. A state that was genuinely single-minded in its pursuit of power and prestige would soon lose all legitimacy, any prospect of cognitive coherence, and, within a short space of time, any power.

However, externally, even the most democratic states behaved very differently, following a theory in which the interests of states and peoples were identical (and, at the very least, it was no concern of other states if they were not), and power and morality were very distant cousins, barely on speaking terms. Ironically this estrangement was credited to a churchman, the ferociously manipulative Cardinal Richelieu. Henry Kissinger wrote that 'In the world inaugurated by Richelieu, states were no longer restrained by the pretence of a moral code.'[1] Hans Morgenthau, one of the most profound influences on diplomats during the twentieth century, described in sharp detail why the interest of the state is fundamental; why the world is driven by the human search for power and domination over others; and why any attempt to pursue other goals leads to disaster and ultimate conquest by others. 'All history', he wrote, 'shows that nations active in international politics are continuously preparing for, actively involved in, or recovering from organized violence in the form of war.'[2]

These arguments justified a strong but limited external role for the state. It should not preach or proselytize. It should concentrate on a narrow idea of interest, and take all necessary steps to protect it. It should behave as if other states share this fundamental concern, and as if they are untrustworthy. All rhetoric and ideology should be interpreted as masks for self-interest. The job of promoting values, forging friendships or understanding, should be left to civil society. Morality should be seen as a costly, perhaps even fatal, luxury.

This view was shared on the other side of the Cold War divide by many of the Leninists. In their actions, despite the rhetorical and practical support they offered to world revolution, they were often *plus royaliste que le roi* in their ardent realism. Stalin's serpentine tactics in the mid- to late 1940s represented the apotheosis of this realism, flimsily wrapped in an ideological cloak (and like much 'realism' was not always very realistic – most obviously in his refusal to believe that Hitler would invade in 1941).

In a world where political survival and evolution were primarily determined by warfare, this stance of distrust often made sense. The protection of virtue and trust within the community depended on vigorous distrust outside it. Indeed, security might even be better promoted by appearing erratic and unpredictable to intimidate enemies, rather than being consistent and trustworthy. North Korea's rulers have followed this strategy successfully for many years. As Pablo Picasso once put it, 'the best calculation is the absence of calculation'.

The contemporary Chinese government has continued the tradition of realism. More copies of Clausewitz's *On War* are said to be sold in China each year than in the rest of the world put together, and its rulers are relentlessly focused on interests – how through diplomacy to secure raw materials (particularly oil), how through intelligence to keep abreast of the world's top companies' plans, and how through the combination of the threat of force and soft power to sustain a periphery of pliable or cowed allies.

An alternative vision of a world based on international law, shared values and morality was promoted by the theologians Francisco de Vitoria, Francisco de Suárez and Hugo Grotius in the sixteenth and seventeenth centuries. It was rationalized in the secular vision of world peace proposed by Immanuel Kant in his essays *Idea for a Universal History* and *Perpetual Peace*, and many practical people proposed similar schemes. William Penn, the founder of Pennsylvania, for example, proposed a parliament of princes that would set the rules of justice among nations and enforce compliance. The Duc de Sully proposed a European army that would punish renegade monarchs, and Tom Paine suggested a European Republic to be overseen by a General Council which would resolve disputes between nations.

For most of the last few centuries these could be plausibly portrayed as nothing more than fantasies for the soft-headed. The credibility of any of these plans depended on all agreeing to its constraints, in particular the most powerful, and no one could offer a convincing account of how this would happen.

During the twentieth century, however, a time of global wars and revolutions, these fantasies became less fantastic and the gulf between domestic politics and international politics narrowed. Democratic culture turned out to be incompatible with a pure realism. Once the public cease to accept that the state is an end in itself, but see it instead as a means towards ends and a servant of their needs, the frames for thinking about the world have to change too. The question that was addressed by Machiavelli, Morgenthau and others was, how can the interests of the state best be advanced? But the peoples of the world were more interested in asking how *their* needs could best be met.

Seen through this frame many of the old assumptions turned out to be logically incoherent as well as morally dubious. One was an assumption about war – that it would remain the ultimate arbiter of the power of nations, and that the main forms of global violence would be wars between states. Instead, war has quickly been removed from the prerogative of all but the most powerful nation states. The interconnectedness of the world has multiplied the number of enemies any aggressors are likely to face more than the likely number of allies. In the past aggressors who sought to conquer territory had a 50 per cent chance of winning, often much more when, like the imperial powers of the nineteenth century, they benefited from technological superiority. By the mid-twentieth century this ratio had fallen to 30 per cent. By the 1980s (the era of the Iraqi invasion of Iran and the Argentine invasion of the Malvinas/Falkland Islands) it had fallen to 19 per cent, and by the turn of the century close to zero.

Aggressors don't only lose more often; they also implode more often. In the remarkable history of the twentieth century most aggressors were destroyed by their own aggression: Austro-Hungary and Imperial Germany collapsed at the end of the First World War. Nazi Germany was the primary governmental victim of the Second World War. The USSR's engagement in Afghanistan precipitated its own collapse. Europe's states, which in the eighteenth and nineteenth centuries had strengthened each other through competition within the European land mass and then through the great empires, fought themselves to a standstill in the twentieth.

Another assumption which has disappeared is that war to pursue the national interest will generally be legitimate. The need for money to pay for wars forced monarchs to hand power to parliaments. It was a mark of William of Orange's cleverness that he understood that he had to give England's wealthier taxpayers in parliament a say over which wars were fought, but that once they were included in the game they would show just as great an appetite for expansion as any monarch. Yet the wider democracy of the twentieth century constrained the ability of rulers and elites to fight, since the poor knew that they were likely to lose more and gain less. War has also lost legitimacy because its indiscriminate nature has become more visible. In 1900 the ratio of civilian to military casualties was around 10–50 per cent, now it is more likely to be over 90 per cent. In the most recent Iraqi war the ratio has been even higher. For all the talk of smart weapons to avoid 'collateral damage', civilians are more likely than ever to be in the frontline of destruction, and some 25,000 civilians are thought to have died violently in Iraq since the US-led invasion in 2003, 37 per cent of them as a direct result of coalition forces, four times as many as the number who have died as a result of the insurgency.[3]

The history of democracies and republics is far from pacific. Believers in liberal values have rarely been willing to accept that their values should be restricted to a particular place or group of people. Instead, as more people were included in political life expansionist energies were often unleashed. It is no coincidence that so many of the great empires were forged by republics: Rome, Athens, the Netherlands, Britain and the USA all drew a moral confidence and expansionist energy from their own values. Sometimes those energies were directed against highly democratic or popular governments. The term 'khaki election' refers to the jingoistic mood of the British electorate at the time of the Boer War who wanted to suppress a popular uprising of the Afrikaners. Between the eighteenth and twentieth centuries the more democratic settler societies were among the most genocidal: the whites' slaughter of Native Americans, and Australians' treatment of Aboriginals disprove any claim that rights and votes automatically encourage what today are seen as virtuous actions. The invasions by Britain, France and the USA of revolutionary Russia in 1920, the subversions of partially democratic Iran in the 1950s and democratic Chile in 1973, collusion in blocking the election of an Islamic government in Algeria in the early 1990s, and the many failed attempts to subvert and overthrow President Chavez of Venezuela in the 2000s, are all counters to the glib assertion that democracies never fight other democracies. Within countries, too, democracy can exacerbate strife: in India, for example, ethnic conflict rose during periods of democratic contest, and abated under martial law.

But there is for all that a link between service at home and a spirit of service abroad. Contemporary democracies find it harder to legitimate actions except against tyrants. And in their dealings with non-democracies, they generally prefer sanctions and denunciations to force. Because democratic culture is founded on conversation and justifications, its spread has narrowed the space for blunt assertions that might is right. Arguments about just war theory concerned with the causes, conduct and consequences of war (*jus ad bellum, jus in bello* and *jus post bellum*) have been given more airing, despite failing to secure a constitutional home. Even the most warlike democracies find it important to show that they act only in the last resort, that they protect non-combatants and take responsibility for the results of their actions.

The precise meaning of service at a global level remains elusive. It has proven impossible to secure widespread agreement on how the principles of just war theory apply in real life cases, as the many arguments around the invasion of Iraq and intervention in Kosovo proved. Within nations it is never easy to assert principles of justice at times of stress. During the Vietnam War, for example, the American Senator Mark Hadfield introduced a resolution into the Senate calling on the US to repent its war crimes; he was denounced for being unpatriotic even though he had merely quoted Abraham Lincoln's words during the Civil War.

But war has undoubtedly lost some of its lustre, and the shifts in perception against war as an extension of politics have been reinforced by experience. Wars often promise to resolve tensions, to 'bring things to a head'. Where there are long-standing and intractable problems war can appear to be an attractive way to circumvent frustrating talk which leads nowhere. Yet war is rarely so decisive.[4] Just as often the 'problem' simply goes underground, to reappear in other forms; the Israeli–Palestinian conflict and the Korean War are two long-running examples, as were the world wars – each of these promised a decisive resolution, yet the First World War led to chaos, the Second to division, and the third or Cold War to disorder. Again and again, too, terrorism and oppression have become each other's excuse.

If war has become less effective as a means to achieve desirable ends, peace has become more so. Between nations peaceful habits, like warlike habits, can be reinforcing. Measures which increase a people's security without diminishing the security of others are far more effective than any alternatives. This was the lesson of the later stages of the Cold War and of the European Union. More visibility, openness and mutual surveillance can increase the security of both sides. The more these measures are practised the more they become second nature; learning to negotiate, learning to understand the other's point of view, learning to trust or that being open does not mean laying yourself open to attack. These are all examples of the kind of ethical know-how that can only be learned through practice rather than theory.

By most measures the world has become a more peaceful place. In the second half of the last century intrastate conflicts worsened even as interstate conflicts diminished, many of them the bloody price of decolonization and a Cold War fought by proxy. But since the early 1990s the number of armed conflicts has fallen by 40 per cent; the number of deadly conflicts (defined as wars leading to more than 1,000 combat deaths) has fallen by 80 per cent, and even the annual number of mass killings has fallen by a similar percentage.[5]

Many of the habits of warfare look increasingly like a limb left over from a previous period of evolution. What remains is self-respect and pride, which is no longer defined through the zero-sum calculus of the battlefield.[6] Certainly a remarkable pattern has appeared. The ends of wars no longer lead to massacre and retribution. Instead they lead to gifts – the Marshall plan which helped to revive the devastated European economy in the 1940s, the large-scale injections of US finance into Japan (but not into Vietnam, which had made the mistake of coming out of its long war triumphant), and the packages of aid for Afghanistan in 2001 and Iraq in 2003 all confirm this new pattern.

If the main assumptions of 'realism', of a world of competing nation states using war as an extension of politics, have dissolved so have its theoretical underpinnings. One of the foundation stones of realism – particularly in the influential versions promulgated by Morgenthau and his followers – was the idea that people, and states, have a will to power and therefore cannot be trusted. Power could never be good. This was why morality could never be more than marginal in international affairs.

This claim is often presented as universally true. It may be true of some people at some times. But it is not true of all people at all times and is not even true of most people most of the time. (As we saw earlier, Machiavelli was more realistic than the realists when he wrote that among the 'grandi' – the urban elites – there was 'a great desire to dominate others' but among most people 'their sole desire is not to be dominated'.)

Moreover, to the extent that some leaders do have such a will to power, this will almost certainly be in tension with the other main plank of realism, the idea of interests. According to the nineteenth-century British Prime Minister Lord Palmerston, and generations of diplomats since, a state's interests are eternal while relationships are ephemeral. Yet it does not follow that public interests, national interests and the interests of the state are identical and singular. Although there are undoubtedly a few areas in which the interests of a community are unambiguous (for example, the terms of trade or budgetary contributions to transnational bodies), in most real situations interests are not so self-evident.

Even the direct interests of states themselves are rarely singular; most states are made up of competing forces reflecting competing parts of the elite – commercial, military, humanitarian, professional. This becomes obvious in historical retrospect. What, for example, was the US interest in Vietnam, the British interest in Sierra Leone or the French interest in Nouméa? The American ground troops who were baffled about what they were doing in Danang or Hué in the mid-1960s were baffled for good reason.

For all the reasons set out previously there is always likely to be a gap between the interests of the people and the interests of states. This gap is particularly wide in international affairs, since in most countries only a wealthy minority of people and institutions have substantial interests beyond the national borders (the obverse of this is that politics is always far more local and domestic than it appears from outside). State interests are more often the interests of ruling elites, and cliques within elites. Most past wars and expeditions may have been dressed in the national flag, or justified by supposed threats and challenges to honour, but they were about what the rulers could get away with. Most overseas adventures gambled the resources of the state, and of the many, to provide winnings for the few. This was the common story of empire and colonialism, and the same has often been true of more recent international adventures, many of which have imposed huge fiscal burdens on states, almost equally large windfalls for selected contractors, military industries and companies involved in resource extraction, but nothing for the majority. This was why democracies often tried to shackle their rulers, making it harder for them to launch wars, why the framers of the American constitution were so fearful of overseas adventurism and why parliaments and assemblies have continued to struggle to rein their executives in, demanding to know more about what intelligence agencies do in their name, and demanding the right to vote before military action is taken.

The conduct of international affairs has taken a long time to catch up with domestic democracy and still betrays its past as part of the captured state rather than the servant state. This can be seen in the capture of subsidy by exporters, particularly those involved in high technology and armaments (two centuries after Adam Smith exposed the absurdity of export subsidies), and in the fact that most diplomatic services prioritize capital and trade above labour or the interests of individual travellers, not the other way around (which is what would be expected in a genuine democracy). All are symptoms of this characteristic skew of international affairs and of the absence of objective national interests.

In recent times, there have been even stronger reasons for the public to want to rein in their governors. In a more connected world the sins of the past are visited on the present. It may not be wholly rational to blame today's citizens for crimes committed many generations ago. If the claims for restitution not just for the Holocaust, but also for slavery and the Irish Famine, were to be accepted it is hard to know where any line could be drawn. But there is nevertheless a plausible moral logic to some of these claims, which call on a nation or community to make up for past misdeeds. The protracted negotiations during the 1990s and 2000s to reconsider New Zealand's Treaty of Waitangi, which was originally signed on 6 February 1840, are a classic example. Although there was no literal sense in which today's white New Zealanders were responsible for the bad faith that surrounded the treaty and its interpretation, they could not avoid their responsibility to put it right if they wished to live in harmony with the Maori with whom they shared the country's two small islands. It is almost as if modernity has rediscovered the ancient Indian idea of karma – that moral and immoral acts create their own effects, a calculus of action and reaction that works itself out over decades and centuries.

The problem with founding diplomacy solely on interests goes deeper still. In its etymology the word 'interest' comes from a Latin verbal expression meaning 'it makes a difference'. So interests are the things which make a difference, which are valued. Interests are simply the things that matter to people and for which they are willing to fight and to make sacrifices. Most people's sense of identity includes both material interests and symbolic values, and much that has been defined as the national interest is more meaningful as a symbolic value than as something tangible and material. So the fight against communism in Vietnam (or the promotion of communism by Cuba) had as much to do with moral purpose as with any clear material interests, as did the promotion of Islamic revolution by Iran in the 1980s, or the promotion of Christianity in Russia by powerful groups in contemporary America. If in their domestic affairs states valued human rights, equity, environmental improvements and freedom, they could not easily discount all of these abroad in the name of national interests.

THE LIMITS TO STATE ACTION BEYOND ITS BORDERS

The underlying theory of morality adopted by the USA, France, Britain and other western nations treats morals as universal.[7] It follows that one vision of the servant state is that it might spread its service ever wider beyond its borders, in line with its capacities. Having met its own citizens' needs for protection or welfare a good government might find ways to serve others.

Something of this idea animated the generous politics of the northern Protestant countries in the 1960s and after. Canada and Sweden, in particular, pioneered policies of aid and development that shared their money and skills in ways that were quite different from the post-imperial policies of France or Britain, or the Cold War manoeuvrings of the USA.

But the idea that any state can spread its service beyond its borders meets obvious limits, and not just because of the gap between near infinite needs and limited resources. The most basic limit is that any such action impinges on others' autonomy – and this is the main objection today to past attempts to spread virtue and particular ideals of service, like the Christianization of Africa. But there are also subtler limits. A state cannot act impartially between its own citizens and others without ceasing to be a state or ceasing to be a servant to its own citizens. And it cannot act beyond its boundaries without running the risk of disturbing some basic moral precepts, in particular about reciprocity, fair entitlements and freeloading, since even if the state could spend money blind to borders it cannot raise money from people who are not its citizens, any more than it can be answerable to them.

The same is true of the law. There continue to be strong arguments for the principle that laws and their enforcement should be non-territorial, justified in part by the idea that morals are universal. Eichmann's trial in Jerusalem for crimes committed in Nazi Germany established the precedent. More recently Belgium has recognized the principle of universal jurisdiction, and convicted four Rwandan citizens for their involvement in the genocide of the early 1990s. In 2005 a UK court convicted Faryadi Sarwar Zardad, an Afghan warlord, under the UN torture convention for crimes committed in Afghanistan in the 1990s.

These energetically pursued cases – Zardad's case cost the UK government some £3 million – have undoubtedly discouraged torture and genocide. But the scope for abuse of this principle of non-territoriality is vast. The decisions are likely to lack legitimacy (what right does a foreign judge have to rule on my country?) and, except on rare occasions, it is not practical for one nation's justice system to take on the world.

Similar problems arise in relation to the use of war as a tool for justice. Can a state act impartially in relation to people who are not its citizens, protecting them from threats, including threats from their own state? Some interventions of this kind are widely acknowledged to have been for the greater good: Tanzania's invasion of Uganda to depose Idi Amin, India's intervention in east Pakistan which led to the creation of Bangladesh and Vietnam's invasion of Cambodia to oust the Khmer Rouge each broadly met the claims of just war theory. It could reasonably be claimed that there was an imminent threat and all the other options had been exhausted (these examples also met the less often remembered principle that you should die rather than kill if you are under attack; self-defence does not justify war, except when other innocent people are under attack).[8] These examples also met Michael Walzer's condition that humanitarian intervention is justified when it is a response (with reasonable expectations of success) to acts 'that shock the moral conscience of mankind'.[9] In other words, in each of these cases the state that was attacked had become criminal as judged by the informal court of global opinion. In each case, too, the invading nation extricated itself reasonably quickly, and left behind a functioning state answerable to its own people.

But all actions of this kind have dangerous consequences. As Clausewitz warned, all wars risk ratcheting out of control. Within their borders states impose strict limits on people's capacity to take the law into their own hands because of what it leads to – at worst anarchy, at best encouragement for habits of precipitate action and a corrosion of the state's authority. For the same reasons, within the international system strict limits have to be imposed on how states can respond to what they see as threats to their interests and security. When there is a dispute we look to third parties – courts and other international institutions – to arbitrate and to act dispassionately. Like states these third parties may be imperfect, and sometimes unable to act even when they should. But only in extreme cases of direct and imminent threat is there ever any moral, or practical, justification for unilateral action to bypass legitimate common institutions, since any such action provides justifications for others to abandon self-restraint.

Here we come back once again to Weber's admonition about the only two mortal sins in politics: lack of realism and lack of responsibility for the consequences of decisions. In a world of weak common institutions realism may be a spur to unilateral action; but responsibility for the full consequence of decisions should be a powerful constraint on actions that otherwise appear pressing and self-evidently good. In the *Persian Letters*, published in 1721, Montesquieu observed that while it is sometimes necessary to change certain laws, one should do so only with 'a trembling hand'.[10] The same applies to any use of war as an instrument either of interests or of principle, and we should distrust any leader who is too eager, or too oblivious to the ambiguities that surround any use of force.

These self-restraints matter because in international affairs, even more than within nations, there are bound to be many more morally repugnant situations than it can be feasible or legitimate to respond to. In relation to distant nations our knowledge about the complexities lying behind conflicts and our sensitivity to unintended consequences is likely to be diminished. Moreover, once another state is seen to be on the wrong side of a struggle between good and evil, it becomes hard to negotiate or compromise, or to recognize the moral compromises being made in the name of good.

A 'trembling hand' is even more necessary where pre-emptive or preventive actions are being contemplated. Pre-emptive actions in advance of an attack, or a disaster, can be justified if the quality of intelligence is sufficiently high and the risk of harm sufficiently grave. But pre-emptive actions slide on a slippery slope towards moral confusion, because there is rarely sufficient knowledge available either about what is being pre-empted or about the efficacy of the action taken to prevent it. (How would Britain's moral standing have suffered if it had carried out its plans to invade Norway pre-emptively during the Second World War, plans which were themselves pre-empted by Hitler?) Any pre-emptive or preventive action entails the obvious flaw that it has no inherent limits, either in time or in space: just how far should we go to prevent a possible attack, or, closer to home, a possible criminal act? For most people, there is also a more basic moral problem, which Francisco de Vitoria pointed out several centuries ago when he wrote that 'it is unacceptable that a person be killed for a sin he has yet to commit.'[11]

Many communities will at times want to intervene in situations which do not directly affect them – to help for humanitarian reasons, or to promote the overthrow of an oppressive regime. Our moral sensibilities are not bounded by constitutional limits. We respond to other people's needs as people, not as legal categories, and when states are unable or unwilling to protect the welfare of their citizens there are powerful motives for action. When Ethiopia faced famine in the 1980s and Somalia descended into violence and Serbia intensified its occupation of Kosovo in the 1990s, the publics of the world clamoured that something must be done. To do nothing in the face of highly visible problems is psychologically, and morally, unsettling. To have the power to act, and not to act, is to become at least partly complicit in the wrongs being done.

But any action changes the balance of sovereignty, and any far-reaching action must impinge on the sovereignty of the state in whose territory the disaster or crime is taking place. Where an evident wrong is being committed by a state or with its connivance there may be strong moral grounds for coming to help the victims. But for another sovereign nation to assume this sovereignty invariably causes problems, however well-intentioned the action.

The example of Pancho Villa should have served as a warning for many others. Pancho Villa had been a hero to the Americans in the early stages of the Mexican revolution at the beginning of the twentieth century. But when Venustiano Carranza emerged as the victor, Villa returned to a life of banditry in his home region of Chihuahua. In 1916, his gang raided Columbus in New Mexico, across the border in the USA, and opinion turned against him. President Woodrow Wilson sent a force to capture him, which grew to over 100,000 men supported by air power, and tracked him through the deserts and mountains. Mexican opinion then turned in a mirror fashion: the peasants who had tired of Villa's antics now saw him as a heroic rebel standing up against foreign bullying. Over many months Villa harried and mocked the US forces until the next year they eventually withdrew, humiliated. The rights and wrongs of the action mattered little. What mattered was that the Americans' actions offended against the pride of sovereignty.

Woodrow Wilson had already adopted a vigorously aggressive foreign policy. 'I am going to teach the South American republics to elect good men', he said, justifying interventions in the Dominican

Republic in 1914 and Haiti in 1915. But the lesson of these and countless other flawed interventions is that it is inherently hard for any state intervening in the affairs of another to be seen as a servant. They will not be accountable to the people they are meant to serve; they are likely to carry too much historical baggage; and precisely because they are likely to be neighbours they cannot be seen as impartial. Actions by powerful nations, especially superpowers, bring these risks to an overwhelming degree. It is as natural to resent your liberators as to praise them, and it is natural that the habits of empire, however benignly intentioned, will affect the minds of the imperialists, since they will never submit to becoming servants in a formal sense. Even America's actions in Europe after 1945, rightly described by Geir Lundestad as 'empire by invitation', fall into this category.[12] Again we return to the general lesson, that whenever one of the identities that we value is threatened it becomes more important to us.

More neutral vehicles have some advantages. The African Union, global bodies like the United Nations, or organizations whose business is not sovereignty but rather solving a problem at a particular time, can each act with less charge around them. But even they will risk coming to seem alien and oppressive, and even they may leave less capacity behind because the very fact of acting like a state in another country reduces the space for its own people to act like a state. The sharp decline in governance capacity in Africa over the last thirty years, which has coincided with massive flows of aid, is a case in point: 'capacity sucking out' rather than capacity building, as Michael Ignatieff put it. Powerful nations find it almost impossible to resist the temptation to direct and act, rather than to allow poorer and weaker countries the sovereign freedom to make mistakes or do things differently.

The appetite for interventions and for the risks they involve will always be limited. Liberal ethical theory is universal but moral sentiments are uneven. The claim that people should behave precisely equally to others, regardless of whether they are family or distant strangers, is bound to be ignored in practice: as a claim it therefore condemns people to failure. The pain of people who are closer to us and more like us may be felt more directly than the pain of distant strangers. The pain of people who are visible will be felt more directly than the pain of people who are invisible (which is why the collateral damage of an intense war is felt more keenly than the mundane murder and oppression that may have preceded it). This unevenness also affects the countries providing help. Where the imperative to act is humanitarian, the impulse to intervene is likely to be felt most intensely by one part of society, while the obligation to act is likely to fall on another (including soldiers often drawn from the most marginalized and disempowered parts of society).

These considerations take us once again to questions of service. The heart of the problem is the tension between the service that is about meeting needs for protection, welfare, justice and truth and the service that is about accountability and power. There is no doubt that service is possible without accountability and shared power. Many autocracies have also acted as servants; paternalism (or maternalism) is generally morally preferable to oppression. Where there are pressing needs and weak local institutions it would be perverse to refuse to act simply because there are no legitimate mechanisms for answering to the people being served. But service without accountability tends to be unstable. In time conflicts and problems arise and then there is little to restrain self-interest masquerading as service, wrapped up in rationalizations and half-truths.

The same applies to non-governmental organizations motivated by altruism. The imperative of service has to come before politics when there is an emergency. But the insight of democracy is that service is never sustainable without power in the hands of the people being served. For all of these reasons the halfway position between a realist world of competing nations and the ideal of a global government with the means and legitimacy to act globally is uncomfortable, morally compromised and hard to sustain.

GLOBAL GOVERNMENT

Global government, in its widest sense,[13] has long offered a possible answer to this dilemma: by internalizing the potentially contradictory meanings of service it offers a way to solve them. The European Union's enlargement to the east achieved something of the same effect, transforming poor supplicant countries into common owners of the European institutions.

As we have seen, the earliest states grew up in response to both necessity and opportunity. The densely interdependent populations that made some kind of state necessary 5,000 years ago are now being replicated globally, with worsening pressures on water supply, climate change, declining biodiversity and imbalances between those parts of the world that can barely help producing vast surpluses of food and those that struggle to feed themselves. Where states grew up in response to the problems of other people, global government is slowly growing in response to the problems of other states and other peoples: the escalating conflicts over water and poisonous emissions into the air, civil wars and genocides, the promotion of terrorism and organized crime. These problems precisely mirror the many problems of protection, co-ordination, externalities and prisoners' dilemmas that justified the early states, but on a much larger scale. They are questions of survival – acute challenges to human beings' capacity to make their own history rather than be victims of it.

It is no longer possible for nation states to pretend that they can be the sole vehicles for their people's hopes and interests, and the wiser ones have learned that they cannot carry out their duties without the help of others. Their citizens cannot be protected without the help of other states, cannot be made prosperous without trade with others, and cannot be kept healthy unless others remain healthy. In a world where people are mobile, justice can no longer be contained, and truth has never recognized any borders. The result is a well-documented crisis of the nation state that has been ably summarized by Philip Bobbitt:

No nation state can assure its citizens safety from weapons of mass destruction; no nation state can, by obeying its own national laws (including its international treaties) be assured that its leaders will not be arraigned as criminals or its behaviour be used as a legal justification for international coercion; no nation state can effectively control its own economic life or its own currency; no nation state can protect its culture and way of life from the depiction and presentation of images and ideas, however foreign and offensive; no nation state can protect its society from transnational perils, such as ozone depletion, global warming and infectious epidemics.[14]

But it doesn't follow that all states are equally powerless to act. Instead a new geography of power and morality has taken shape in the wake of the Cold War. First, there are the lawless regions where national governments are weak. These are the areas, such as east Timor, Abkhazia or Bosnia, into which the UN has been pulled most often, to act as protector, feeder and peacekeeper. Second, there are the regions where nations are reasonably at ease submitting to the rule of international law; Europe is the clearest example. Third, there are the nations that are uncomfortable with such external constraint. They include 'rogue nations' like North Korea, but also the most powerful nations of all – the USA and China – whose relative strength may grow in the years ahead.

In one possible future these two nations will take the lead in solving the new problems of interdependence. They will reinforce their position as the poles of a connected world, claiming rights to act that they deny to others, and protecting the interests of clients and allies.

Both can be described as 'imperiums', since they are not empires in the classic sense of seeking territorial control over others. But they do seek power, and power to command others, and they seek a world where the rules are very different for big countries and small ones, lucky citizens and unlucky ones. Not for them Harry Truman's comment (about post-war America) that 'no matter how great our strength we must deny ourselves the license to do always as we please'. Imperiums want power that is unbounded, exclusive, and opportunistic about rules. If Hobbes' *'homo homini lupus'* (man a wolf to men) is the starting point for politics, in the imperial view *'princeps principi lupus'* (the prince is a wolf to princes) is the starting point for the affairs of states. In this view might is not always right. But right needs might, and cannot rely on weak moral claims, or the promise of the rule of law.

The fundamental mark of imperium is that it challenges the moral idea that has become central to western civilization and to the global community: the categorical imperative, first articulated by Immanuel Kant, according to which for any principle to be valid it must be universally applicable. The mark of imperiums is that they demand and assert rights which they believe should be denied to others. These may be rights to hold nuclear weapons, to protect favoured industries, to use military force, to pre-empt threats, or to deal brutally with dissenting nations within their sphere of influence. For them morality is asymmetric.

America and China are the only two likely imperiums in the current era, though Russia and India are also candidates, and the European Union could potentially develop in this direction. The USA and China are inheritors of world views that have been sustained over 2,000 years on a very large scale, as well as both being revolutionary nations (China is still ruled from the precincts of its imperial palace, while Rome has been displaced to Washington).[15]

Neither nation is willing to be constrained, except tactically, by global government, though both find advantages in collaboration (and in the US, as a democracy, debates on international affairs are far more robust and visible). Both seek to negotiate their own compromises with it, knowing that global government cannot afford to ignore them. Both see themselves as exceptional – the US as a chosen nation, uniquely endowed with moral purpose, uniquely paramount in its wealth and technology, oscillating between isolationism and seeking to remake the world according to an ideal. China is unique in different ways, as the world's most populous nation (until India overtakes it), with an unmatched continuity of civilization and state power and a powerful sense that history is now on its side.[16]

As great powers they are radically different. The US is, as a vivacious democracy, far more open and at ease with dissent than China. It is also far more powerful, possessed of a nuclear capability so much greater than any other nation that it no longer needs to fear 'mutually assured destruction': if it wanted it could destroy any other nation's nuclear weapons without the risk of retaliation. But the early years of the twenty-first century will probably turn out to be a high point of its hegemony, and already we can see signs of what is likely to become a vigorous competition to mobilize world opinion and institutions. For both the USA and China the gambits will include bilateral, partial settlements with other nations, offers of special privileges and tied aid. Military coercion and threat will be used for the more problematic states, with weak potential enemies picked on both to maintain morale at home and to 'encourage the others' abroad without too much risk or cost. (For twenty years the US has fought wars against small, and sometimes tiny enemies, from Grenada and Panama to Afghanistan and Iraq.) Much will be invested in moral and cultural argument and legitimation, in television channels and websites, curriculums and news (and, less visibly, in demonstrating the incapacity of global government, through forcing it to fail to make decisions).

But the likely imperiums will also be radically constrained as to what they can do. The US has shown that it can win conventional wars, but not unconventional ones against forces with popular support, such as in Somalia, Colombia and Vietnam. Its 725 military bases around the world are a source of vulnerability as well as of power. Its remarkable nuclear supremacy has simply confirmed why other non-nuclear powers, like Iran, should want to play the nuclear game so as to preserve at least a shred of national military autonomy. Meanwhile China's only recent military excursion, in Vietnam, was a humiliation. Both imperiums depend on others for food, energy flows and market access. Their dependence will intensify the struggle to control resources, particularly oil. But it may also make possible a continuing accommodation between the imperiums and a global government. Such an accommodation may be morally complex, but no more so than the settlements that initiated most states. It requires a convergence of interests of the imperiums and the global bodies, a convergence that is likely to take shape around a limited number of decisive tasks, and common interests in co-operation.

A POST-IMPERIAL WORLD

How possible is a truly post-imperial world, which recognizes the equal rights of peoples, communities and nations? Past visions of global governance and the rule of law remained just that: visions with little prospect of realization. Democratic nation states remain far more capable of managing the circuit of coercion, taxation and legitimation than any transnational bodies, and they lay claim to a superior moral standing because their leaders are directly elected by the people.

But the idea that moral duties drawing on the fundamental needs of human communities need to manifest themselves on a global scale is not a fantasy. Nor is it new. The Catholic and other Christian churches trying to realize Christ's teachings in the world were always global in ambition; so were the Islamic *umma* or community and its associated organizations of welfare and teaching promoting compassion, Buddhist *sanghas* promoting the way to well-being, and the Communist Party and Comintern striving for utopia. All institutionalized a universal, global claim. But none managed to build institutions that could meet human needs consistently, and over wide distances, and none was able to exercise much lasting influence on the morals of states.

Most of the early thinkers about a more benign global order feared global government, even if they longed for the peace it might deliver. Kant thought that it risked becoming a 'horrible despotism'. More state-like forms of global government are historically unusual. But they have been quietly evolving for some 150 years, building on the agreements to regulate trade and customs on rivers like the Danube, and the arrangements for regulating postal services in the mid-nineteenth century and, later, telegraphy. These were founded on necessity and common interests. But the greater ambitions of global government also benefited in the long-run from public activism – the emergence of a global civil society from the anti-slavery campaigns of the mid-nineteenth century, through the Balkans campaigns in the 1880s to the twentieth-century campaigns for human rights, the protection of the world's ecology and humanitarian intervention.

Like national power, much of the power associated with global government was taken or agreed first, and then legitimized afterwards. This is certainly the story of the United Nations in 1945, the creation of a small bold group who seized a historical moment. The growth of the European Union shows the same characteristics. Strong-willed pioneers, acting well ahead of public opinion (though legitimized by national parliaments) and gambling that in time it would catch up, succeeded in creating not only a common bureaucracy but also much of the paraphernalia of a national state – a currency, legislature, courts and even an embryonic army. The UN, too, has had its own assembly, its own military forces (albeit always on loan), its banks and health services, alongside an International Court of Justice and an International Criminal Court.

The motives that produced global organizations were as mixed as the motives that gave rise to nation states. Powerful nations, naturally, used transnational bodies to serve their own interests. During the Cold War the USSR and USA each had its own family of dependent states, and its own neighbourhood for which it claimed responsibility. Their greatest risk was that a feud would arise in which some transgression would force them to respond. Like weak governments trying to hold together order in nations with multiple centres of power, they feared that small problems would escalate or that over-belligerent relatives would pull them into war. For them, the UN was an insurance policy against small problems becoming unnecessarily amplified. In Europe, too, progress was only possible because of the range of motives involved: France seeking a new outlet for hegemony as its empire collapsed; Germany seeking to protect itself from itself; the smaller countries seeking larger guarantors; business, more prosaically, seeking larger markets.

But all governments, once established, have a logic of their own that is greater than any causal explanation based on interests. The European Union maintained a momentum of enlargement and integration despite public scepticism and conflicting national interests. Similarly the embryonic global government around the United Nations has aspired to cognitive coherence – to the creation of its own fictions, its own symbols of permanence and a structure of values that protects it from the manipulation of nation states.

It is meaningful to talk of global government because these agencies do govern: they impose and police rules; they are recognized as legitimate; and they are universal. Yet they lack the money, the people or the technology to do very much. They have potentially limitless duties but no powers to raise taxes, no powers to conscript soldiers, and no independent means of developing technology. Even the most widely accepted international rules, like the Geneva Protocol of 1925 banning chemical warfare, have been breached with impunity (in that case by Saddam Hussein in the 1980s). Global agencies have yet to find effective ways to translate legitimacy into power. They have no rights to exploit the world's commons – geostationary orbits, oceans, Antarctica or cyberspace – as new tax bases, and their structures are better designed for the risks of half a century ago than contemporary ones like organized crime, climate change and terrorism. Meanwhile the agencies which do have some power, like the World Trade Organization, have found it hard to turn that power into legitimacy.

Contradictory design principles make these institutions resistant to reform. Some mirror raw power: military power in the case of the UN Security Council (made up of the victors of 1945), and economic power in the voting rights in financial institutions (which favour donors over receivers). Some mirror principles of citizenship, the idea that anyone is entitled to equal membership by virtue of being there. So any nation can join the UN (or the Olympics or many other world bodies), regardless of its behaviour, its constitution or its values. The result is a constant tension between the accumulating moral principles encouraged by the global community (for example, the principles that unprovoked aggression should be reversed, that polluters should pay or that all people are entitled to human rights) and the lack of means to enforce them.

The very weakness of global institutions has forced some constructive innovation. Global governance has evolved in part as an open system, held together by communication and knowledge rather than coercive powers, and aided by informal and formal networks for making decisions, including some 25,000 international NGOs. These can work well at aligning thousands of players (just as some nations have prospered without very visible leadership – Japan has often been analysed by political scientists as more of a network than a hierarchy), and they can create climates of opinion which strongly influence decisions. But such loose networks are poorly designed for hard decisions and sacrifices, for the management of resources or legitimation, or for fostering common values.[17]

THE FOUR RESPONSIBILITIES AND
GLOBAL GOVERNMENT

Why, then, is global government a possibility rather than a fantasy? Humans have the often marvellous and often maddening ability to be animated by the merest glimmer of a possibility on the horizon. Yet here we are dealing with observable currents of change rather than just aspirations. Global government is more than a fantasy both because of common interests in an ever more interdependent world and because there are widely shared values of service, peace and freedom to be found in every political tradition and every religion (admittedly alongside the calls for murder and revenge which litter the Bible, Koran and the Bhagavad Gita).

There have been many attempts to imagine what a global government might look like if it was deduced from first principles, and if there was a contract (John Rawls called it a 'Law of Peoples') between the peoples of the world and new global bodies. These all confirm that governments at every scale have to grapple with similar problems. It is not a coincidence that both the UN family and the family of institutions joined together in the European Union share the same moral structure of legitimation as nation states. Like them they draw their moral strength, and their cognitive structure, from the fundamental needs of all human communities for protection, welfare, justice and truth. Each of these now has a global dimension, overriding in the case of protection, less so for the others. How global institutions respond to these needs is bound to be different from nation states, let alone small communities; the latter have moral arguments that are rich, contextual and shaped by history. For global bodies serving diverse cultures the universal shared morality has to be more limited.[18] But the shape of these responsibilities is identical.

GLOBAL PROTECTION

The first duty of any global government has to be protection – establishing rules to prevent and contain war, capacities to make peace and keep it, and powers to avert threats and disasters. For three centuries the optimists have hoped to achieve protection through the law. Hans Kelsen, who did much to provide the intellectual thinking for the founding of the United Nations, put the argument in its clearest form. Nation states, he said, were inherently inadequate vehicles for the achievement of a society based on right. A higher order was needed – a global one – from which the laws of national regimes could derive. This alone would guarantee that strong states did not dominate weak ones. It would be 'a universal community superior to the particular states', enveloping them all within itself, and a transcendent *'tertium super partes'* would govern the system and put an end to the anarchy of competition between states.[19]

Kelsen believed in the supremacy of law over politics. He wanted law to be purified of all ideology and freed from any reliance on natural science or evidence.[20] The purpose of the UN was not just to transcend national sovereignty: it was to transcend the very idea of a sovereign political order and replace it with law. Against the odds something of this vision has been achieved, in that international law has raised the costs of aggressive war even for the most powerful states. Disregarding the United Nations carries a price – as the US discovered after the invasion of Iraq when it was unable to secure sufficient allies to help it achieve a successful peace. There are still no formal laws to define the global community's duties to protect people from their own states, but there has been intensive argument and debate about how to formalize this responsibility, along with limiting conditions to ensure that intervention does not become too habitual.[21]

But Kelsen's vision of the rule of laws is inadequate to deal with the most serious threats. At the level of the world as a whole, laws that are detached from sovereign power can be both too passive and too inflexible, too limp and too rigid. Sometimes what is morally right is legally wrong. Equally, legal rightness may not in itself legitimate actions in the eyes of the global community. Without the political authority that comes from a dynamic relationship between rulers and ruled the international laws of the UN lack teeth. Hence the argument that what is needed is something more like a global leviathan, with overwhelming but limited powers to deal with the small number of civilization-threatening dangers of an era when vastly powerful technologies are within the grasp of individuals as well as states, or where collective actions threaten the survival of the species.

The principles of protection agreed by the UN's founders assumed that the main threats came from other nation states, not from small bands, networks or systems. Yet for most of the world's population the threats of financial collapse, terrorism or climate change are now more pressing than the threat of invasion. By the third decade of the century CO_2 levels in the atmosphere may be reaching levels that will be impossible to reverse; both China and the USA will be contributing some quarter of the world's total; and rising sea levels will already be threatening very large populations in countries like Bangladesh. Precisely because the actions needed to arrest climate change will have a very uneven distribution of costs and benefits it is unlikely that consensus will be possible. Yet no power at present exists that could penalize the nations or industries doing most to threaten future security.

The ability of humanity to alter the ecosystems on which it depends, and to tip them, perhaps dramatically, out of equilibrium, changes everything and makes it even less likely that law will be enough. It creates a need for government in its purest sense: a power able to steer people away from disaster.

Almost as compelling are the threats to security from weapons. The dramatic destructive power of weapons justifies far more powerful policing to hold them in check. The eighteenth century was coloured by the destruction of Lisbon in an earthquake in 1755, which was taken to confirm the power of God in an age of scepticism. The destruction of Moscow in 1812 confirmed the power of man in a new era of mass warfare. The destruction of Dresden, Hiroshima and Nagasaki ushered in the age of deterrence: its emotional power kept peace on track even during the most hysterical phases of the Cold War. Soon, perhaps, the destruction of another city through nuclear weapons, this time at the hands of terrorists, or perhaps a natural disaster that is indubitably associated with climate change, will confirm to the world that a new era of statehood is needed.

GLOBAL WELFARE

The second responsibility of a global government has to be welfare. As within nations, much of the job of government is to set the rules. Rules for trade are reasonably established, although always vulnerable to a backlash if powerful interests in the richer countries decide that the terms of trade no longer work in their favour.[22] Concern for welfare has long been institutionalized in the World Bank and the World Health Organization, although the resources spent are a tiny fraction of what has been spent through nation states. The Millennium Development Goals (MDG) have given welfare more prominence (though even if the MDGs were met, to take just one example, some 1.6 billion people would lack toilets and 900 million would go without easy access to drinking water[23]).

The harder task for any global government will be to define and enforce property rights for the new commons, the shared goods on which life depends. These include water rights, which will be a matter of survival in much of the world; rights to emit pollution; and rights to use space or the oceans. By standing for equity in a dramatically unequal world any credible global government is bound to challenge the richest and most powerful states. But in an interconnected global community the combination of enlightened self-interest and the force of shame can powerfully shape behaviour (as has been seen, for example, in agreements to limit European and American pharmaceutical companies' property rights in relation to vital drugs for HIV/AIDS).

GLOBAL JUSTICE

The third duty of global government has to be justice – establishing principles of international law alongside courts with powers to convict, and in some cases powers to overrule national jurisdictions as, for example, in the European Court of Justice, the International Court of Justice and the International Criminal Court. Some nations have chosen to exempt themselves from these courts or to ignore their findings. Many states have acted illegally without any penalty; for example, US support for terrorist paramilitaries in central America in the mid-1980s and French terrorist actions against Greenpeace in New Zealand at the same time went unpunished.

The efficacy of global justice remains partial, and its future direction and scope is unclear, again because it is detached from sovereign power. A maximalist approach would tie the benefits of membership of the global community to acceptance of common principles of justice, which would go beyond trade and war to encompass harm to the environment, or anti-social behaviour (for example preventing dictatorships from selling off finite resources). A minimalist approach would at least secure agreement to common judicial treatment of the most flagrant crimes.

GLOBAL KNOWLEDGE

The fourth duty of global government has to be to promote knowledge and truth. The informal systems for promoting knowledge, including the global system for peer review of scientific claims, have generally fared better than the formal systems supported by the UN and the EU. Reason, argument and dialogue have become, de facto, the legitimating truths of the international system. The thousands of scientists in the International Panel on Climate Change (the IPCC) working to reach a consensus on climate change exemplify a global community seeking truth. At times the UN has toyed with highly politicized notions of truth, as for example in the discussion of a New World Information Order (which would have been tightly controlled by states) in the 1980s. But in the practice of global institutions, the lack of day-to-day political control has allowed a stronger commitment to evidence and the pursuit of truth than has been possible within national polities.

These four sets of goals have emerged for the same reasons that they did in nations: they reflect the fundamental needs of human communities that cannot be met adequately by individuals, families or small groups on their own. There is no guarantee that these goals will be acted on, and at any one moment there may be as many signs of retreat as advance. But they provide a way to think about what needs to be managed globally, and what pressures and requirements may need to be imposed on lower-tier bodies, in this case nation states and regions, making it easier to be good, and harder to be bad.

The public base for global government remains underdeveloped. According to surveys only some 6 per cent of the world's population identifies more with the world than with their region, country or locality. But the figure is much higher in some places, including the US (where it reaches 20 per cent), and among higher earners (9.2 per cent), and 48 per cent of the world's population views the results achieved by the UN as very or somewhat satisfactory, including 65 per cent in North America.[24]

For the European Union much the same structure of legitimation applies. Its institutions are legitimate because they have delivered peace, prosperity and an emerging architecture of justice (and some fairly half-hearted attempts to cultivate a European approach to knowledge, with funding for pan-European culture and science). Europe's successes have all been ones of practical, quiet service. Its failures have all come from the pursuit of grandiosity and styles of decision-making that are the opposite of service: secretive, closed, elitist.

That there is a global need for protection or welfare does not of itself imply that these should be direct responsibilities for global government. Indeed, there is a good general rule that the larger the entity, the more it should work through alignment and co-ordination rather than direct action, because of its greater capacity for false information and error. This implies that the direct roles for a global government should be tightly limited to interventions to protect where national and regional bodies are unable to do so; actions to promote welfare where others have clearly failed; justice for only the most extreme crimes; and, wherever possible, time-limited, specialized vehicles for action rather than permanent bureaucracies.

Nor is it necessary for these different functions to be brought together within a single structure. Europe has shown how government can be organized in a network. Its institutions both compete and co-operate, and include a directly elected parliament that does not appoint the executive, independent judiciaries, and a complex set of relationships between the Commission, the Council of Ministers and the Parliament.

At a global level each of the four main duties could be carried forward by very different institutions. For protection what is needed is a powerful executive (perhaps a Global Protectorate, built out of the experience of the UN Security Council) with very strong powers to act in response to short-, medium- and long-term survival threats, but also very strict rules on how those powers can be used. For many other functions common rules are needed – for trade, exchange, flows of information, intellectual property, contagious diseases – with a smaller subset of problems requiring task-based agencies (for example to deal with acute poverty, water shortages or the development of essential new technologies). For justice, independent judicial arrangements operating in a clear relationship with lower-tier bodies are essential. All of these roles may evolve far beyond the structures associated with national states, towards more open systems of co-ordination that rely on information, argument and scrutiny rather than formal direction. By the same token more international laws may be made enforceable by local or national courts. The traditional apparatus of states – with public assemblies of a few hundred representatives, common armies and currencies – is likely to appear ever less appropriate to the tasks ahead.

A complex geometry of this kind is both possible and desirable. But for any global institutions to act as true servants of billions of people, very special constraints as well as powers will be needed. I listed earlier the many requirements – for contestability, the rule of law, division and visibility – that have been imposed on national governments to prevent abuses of power. For global bodies far more stringent constraints will in the long run be essential. The greatest weakness of any global organization is that it is likely to lack contestability. A powerful and monopolistic global government could easily, as Kant worried, become an oppressive monster: hence the virtue of plenty of divisions, and even some internal competition, using open systems to achieve co-ordination rather than explicit lines of authority.

There is also another reason why global agencies need special constraints. I have argued that all states are built on an ambiguous relation to law. They make constitutions and are also subject to them; and they retain the right to suspend laws if necessity demands it. For nations the risks of abuse of this power are contained in part by the presence of other nations. But for a global government the risks could be much greater. A global leviathan, like any government, must be able to declare an emergency and even to suspend its laws – but even more than national governments it must be severely constrained in exercising these rights. This is why any global government must remain in some respects subordinate to lower tiers.

The other additional restraints on global government have to come from the ethics of the people in its agencies and bureaus. So far global institutions have paid little attention to their own ethics and how these are perceived. Professional formation has been a low priority. Over many years the European Commission resisted audits and inquiries, and sacked whistleblowers, until the whole leadership of the Commission was forced to resign in 1999 in the wake of a report detailing fraud, nepotism and irresponsibility. The investigator had written of 'a growing reluctance among the members of the hierarchy to acknowledge their responsibility'. It had become difficult 'to find anyone who has even the slightest sense of responsibility'.[25]

In the UN, too, despite the remarkably high motivations of many of its employees, the culture of professional ethics is weak. This has not been helped by recruitment methods that give quotas to different parts of the world and manage performance only loosely. These quotas may have been necessary to legitimate the UN, and the makeup of any global body needs to look like the world it services. But rigid application of quotas harms legitimacy if it undermines ethics and effectiveness. A survey in 2004 showed that staff believed that 'integrity and ethical behaviour' were not taken sufficiently into account in selection, promotion and assessment. Staff complained about the geographic quotas for recruitment and promotion; the lack of clear codes of conduct; promotion by seniority; and the lack of protection for whistleblowers, or of any external oversight of disciplinary procedures.[26]

Direct accountability from global bodies to the world's public is impossible: there is no simple way for six or eight billion people to elect, dismiss or scrutinize rulers and bureaucracies in distant locations. Nor is contestability easy to build into institutions that must be highly monopolistic. But the very impossibility of accountability and contestability makes strong ethics all the more important: they have to carry more of the load in building trust. It is hard to imagine a more inspiring and motivating ethos than duties of service to the world's population. For global power to be trusted, these values, and the broader skills needed for global action, need to be consciously inculcated in a cadre of officials, who are rigorously overseen, and made visible to the people being served.

CONDITIONAL GLOBAL CITIZENSHIP

In a possible future, global institutions would evolve on several tracks simultaneously. Some would remain as they are, largely unconditional, offering nations both big and small rights without responsibilities – the de facto right to protection against invasion and humanitarian assistance without corresponding duties beyond small financial contributions.

But the weaknesses of unconditional citizenship are as obvious in international affairs as they are within nations. If the rights of membership come without any linked responsibilities, free-riding is inevitable. Worse, the moral claims of the community are bound to be compromised if there are no shared values, and no agreed minima of acceptable behaviour.

This has already become clear in the United Nations. A system in which Libya could chair the committee concerned with human rights and Saudi Arabia advises on the position of women is bound to lack legitimacy. The alternative is to make membership of the parts of global government more overtly conditional (rather as membership of the World Trade Organization already is), and more directly tied to stated values. Rights to service from the global community would depend on demonstrable service to citizens within the nation. The benefits of membership would depend on behaviour that contributed to the global good. Global government organized in this way would grow through the power of attraction, just as the EU has done, and would be overtly founded on values. Like the Europe of the European Union it would achieve security through mutual transparency and use open systems of co-ordination and benchmarking to empower people to demand more of their states; the power of shame would substitute for formal penalties, allowing governments at all levels to evolve in tandem with social movements organized around new threats and moral duties – from poverty to climate change and health.

In this scenario the United Nations organization would be paralleled by a United Democracies organization. Membership would be conditional, at first on the presence of democracy, human rights and so forth, and in time on more demanding conditions, the most important of which would be willingness to pool military forces and give up the right to wage war independently. The organization would aim to embody the ideals of service – ranging from conflict prevention to disease control – in its work, at first as a large faction within a still-functioning United Nations but in the long-run absorbing more of the latter's functions.

Whether the greatest nations could join more conditional, values-based international bodies is unclear. They would have to suspend their claims to uniqueness and asymmetrical powers. They certainly risk becoming trapped in the position that Livy described in ancient Rome: 'we can bear neither our shortcomings nor the remedies for them.' But their citizens might see more to be gained from joining in with other like-minded countries, ceding sovereignty in exchange for an environment with less risk and uncertainty. Recent survey evidence clearly points in this direction. According to one large poll of global opinion in 2005, covering 24,000 people in 24 countries, nearly two-thirds (64 per cent) favoured a more powerful United Nations, and roughly the same proportion (63 per cent) an elected UN assembly. Large majorities also favoured a bigger role for non-governmental organizations and Europe, with its postmodern approach to power and change had, to a striking degree, become the world's preferred model of governance, with dramatically more favourable perceptions than the USA.[27]

A world order more overtly founded on shared values has precedents. In medieval Europe, for example, the surface picture of nations pursuing their own narrow interests concealed the large measure of civilizational consensus that constrained and guided national actions. That consensus lacked anything like the institutional form of a European Union or United Nations, but ruling groups were joined by ties of marriage and powerful institutions, above all the Catholic Church, operated across national boundaries and challenged the legitimacy of nation states. For global government a parallel course is possible.

'Realism' was realistic in the past because the penalties for amoral behaviour were so slight. A world in which there are strong common institutions founded on shared values, and distributing rewards and penalties, would, by contrast, build morality into the world's very fabric. It would render realism unrealistic and bridge the gulf between

a domestic realm where politics and morality are automatically interwoven and an international one where they are at best distant cousins.
Such a world remains elusive, and acutely vulnerable to the machina-
tions of aggressive supernation states, but it is now possible as never
before.

15

Service to the Future

'What has posterity ever done for me?' Groucho Marx

Throughout the preceding argument I have described the moral duties
of governments, both national and global, in terms of humble, and
often prosaic, service to the people. But states should be guardians of
interests that transcend those of today's citizens. Any state which only
tried to maximize the well-being of today's citizens would be betray
ing its deeper responsibility to the interests of the community (and to
the ecological systems on which human life depends). Most societies
recognize this and their ideals of service overlap with ideals of
guardianship towards people or things that cannot easily represent
themselves, and ideals of trusteeship that require us to leave the world
better than we find it.

These ideals run up against the many compelling pressures that
governments face in their day-to-day business. When I joined the
British government in 1997, these pressures had become so intense
that the future had effectively been put on hold. Public capital spending had been sharply cut back; budgets were managed year to year;
investment in preventing crime or disease had been squeezed. The
nearer one came to the centre of power in the mid-1990s the shorter
the time horizons were, so that the Prime Minister's closest advisers
were rarely looking more than a few weeks or months ahead. Their
highest aspiration was simply to survive in power. In other countries,
too, governments have been all too willing to build up debts, to run
down public assets and to sell off scarce resources.

How governments think of their place in time greatly influences how they behave. In the case of Britain in the mid-1990s a government with a small majority sensed that its future had collapsed and that it owed little to its successors. In other cases, including the governments of 1906, 1945 and 1979, there was such a strong sense of responsibility for the future that high risks were taken to leave behind a legacy of lasting change.[1]

Good government should be illuminated by the future. But many governments live with their eyes on the rear-view mirror, refighting ancient battles and reigniting ancient enmities. For Slobodan Milošević, Serbia's President in the 1990s, the most pressing priority was not the welfare of the Serbian people, but how to relive in the present the supposed meanings of the battle of Kosovo in 1389 so as to ensure his survival in power. In a climate dominated by past passions any sense of possibility or obligation to the future can all too easily be crowded out. Having no sense of historical depth can be very damaging for a nation, and increases the risks that it will repeat its errors ('that's history' is a statement of dismissal in the US). Ibn Khaldun advocated 'lifting the veil' because 'the pasture of stupidity is unwholesome for mankind.' But there are also few things more debilitating than knowing too much. Leaders without much sense of how to serve the public in the present all too easily fetishize victimhood in the distant past, or glory, or empire, to make sense of themselves and of their failures. Faced with the vices of bad history, distortion and myth, the cure is likely to involve more and better history, which is why it is so important to have a symbolic confrontation with the past in societies moving beyond dictatorship, along with deliberate forgetting of the kind that Cambodia's Hun Sen recommended twenty years after the killing fields of the Khmer Rouge, when he asked his fellow citizens to 'dig a hole and bury the past'.

For a minority of regimes it is not history, or short-termism, which encourages evil but rather a hallucinatory future – the future of utopian communism, which justified the Gulags, or the future of a thousand-year Reich, which justified genocide. Yet the most common vice of states is a truncated future rather than a hallucinatory one: leaders act as if future generations had no claim on them. They respond urgently to dramatic events but ignore slow, cumulative trends. The dominant forces in modern democratic societies encourage them

– competitive electoral politics attends to welfare and prosperity now, not in the distant future (pollsters have yet to devise a way to ask the unborn for their opinions). Competitive consumer markets attend to current desires not future needs, and competitive capital markets generally demand immediate returns in which the future is, literally, heavily discounted. If the most pressing concern for a ruler is the state of the opinion polls, or the bond or currency markets, the needs of the next generation are likely to fade into insignificance (hence the colossal rise in debt under Presidents Ronald Reagan and George W. Bush, which in immediate political terms made absolute sense).

Given uncertainty about the future, and rapid change, governments can easily rationalize living in an eternal present. Pandolfo Petrucci, who was the lord of Siena a century after Lorenzetti's time, wrote to Machiavelli a classic description of the exercise of power in the present. 'Wishing to make as few mistakes as possible', he explained, 'I conduct my government day by day and arrange my affairs hour by hour; because the times are more powerful than our brains.' It is easy to rationalize such short-termism as an unavoidable response to the pressures of turbulent events, or of the media and daily politics. Faced with profound, long-term and intractable problems like climate change, it is natural to wish to avoid necessary sacrifices (hoping that something will turn up), and it takes a lot of bravery on the part of any leader to tell people that they have to give up things that they value in the name of the future.

These are just some of the reasons why so many past states and civilizations disappeared, not through conquest but through their inability to act as a guardian of the scarce resources – water, forests or soil – they depended on. The mind of the state is much more easily consumed by immediate processes and struggles than by the patient, arduous work of protecting against possible long-term threats. Even highly sophisticated societies can wreck themselves by losing sight of the long term: California, for example, managed to turn the US's finest schools into some of the worst in the space of a generation through ill-conceived if popular policies for cutting taxes.

These tendencies may be magnified in an environment awash with information, with 24-hour news channels hungry for a running commentary that gives the daily life of governments some of the properties of an eternal present, without depth, or past or future. More attention comes to be paid to performance and activity rather than slow change, breeding an impatience for immediate results, which, if real results are unobtainable, substitutes symbols and spectacles.

Plato in *The Statesman* suggested that the main job for rulers was 'weaving the future', by which he meant responsibility for what would be left for future generations. Given the strong counter-pressures this ideal is elusive; leaders often only turn to it when their term of office is nearing completion, by which time it may be too late. Perhaps every society, including the emerging world society, needs a party for the future, institutions devoted to countering these tendencies and caring for the community's survival needs. In the distant past the elders played this role; they preserved the community's memory but also stood sufficiently apart from the day-to-day pressures of the community to see when far-reaching changes were needed.

In modern states these roles have to be distributed. They are needed at the heart of the government machine providing confidential advice to rulers (like Britain's Strategy Unit or France's Commissariat de Plan), as well as in and around it in independent institutions scanning the horizon, thinking through complex chains of cause and effect and unintended consequence. Further out, conversations are needed that bring the main professions and the public into contact with the systemic nature of change.[2] Some North American states have pioneered new methods for doing this. From 1989 onwards, for example, the state of Oregon involved tens of thousands of people in discussions about the future that led to targets being set on topics such as workforce skills, health and welfare. Oregon also pioneered new models of community engagement that helped them avoid the declining social capital and trust that afflicted the rest of the US. More recently, in 2002 Alberta in Canada held a grand 'Future Summit' drawing on hundreds of local meetings, again to forge a consensus on what needed to be done.

Attention to the future is easiest to instil in the parts of the state that are most insulated from immediate pressures, such as central banks, scientific funding agencies, and some regulators. But it is most needed in the parts of the state that are closest to politics, like public health or crime, since otherwise difficult decisions cannot be explained to the public and legitimated.

The mental models required for this sort of work are very different from those needed for quick decision-making, rationalization or, for that matter, for scholarship. They require openness to the unexpected, the time it takes to become immersed in and conversant with a complex system, familiarity with many disciplines, and the mental toughness needed to escape the tyranny of the status quo.[3] They require counterbalances to the tactical and contingent – the fear of leaks that crushes honest debate, the insecurity that prevents rigorous self-scrutiny, and the wishful thinking that prefers not to contemplate unpleasant possibilities.

What governments need is not a firm forecast of what the future will bring but rather methods that prepare them for both more and less likely possibilities. No one can know the future. But it is possible to better understand the present and the possibilities that it contains. Few in the early 1990s expected that the coming decade would bring a civil war in Europe with hundreds of thousands killed, half a billion users of the Internet, a long stagnation in Japan and a long boom in the United States, or the complete mapping of the human genome. Few in the run up to 2000 anticipated thousands killed in a terrorist attack on New York or the partial collapse of the California electricity system. No government can predict the unpredictable, but wise ones avoid being trapped by their own assumptions.

Smaller countries appear to find this sort of work easier, perhaps because they are more realistic about the environment they operate in. Singapore, for example, puts its senior managers through regular exercises in which they work through scenarios in which the country faces war, water shortages or economic crises. North European countries, including the Netherlands and Finland, have also institutionalized a capacity to imagine alternative futures. In larger countries the pull of illusions is stronger, just as in the past so many empires clung myopically to their own delusions rather than face up to forces that would kill them. But in an era when populations are ageing and when the most pressing survival challenges cannot be solved within the span of a single generation, the cultivation of a party for the future has become essential for good government.

Borges in one of his stories describes an animal – the hidebehind – which is always behind you when you walk in a forest, which you can never see, however quickly you try to turn around. This creature is posterity; it stalks you but you can never see its judgement, only glimpses and shadows. Where politics and government are concerned, nothing is permanent, fixed or certain and government and politics 'give rise to settlements, not solutions'.[4] It is in this spirit that any service to the future needs to be framed – humble, flexible and none too certain about the twists that change will bring.

16

The State as a Work of Art

'Knowledge has two extremes which meet: one is the pure
natural ignorance of every man at birth, the other is the
extreme reached by great minds who run through the whole
range of human knowledge only to find that they know nothing
and come back to the same ignorance from which they set out,
but it is a wise ignorance which knows itself.'   Pascal

Hegel described the state as 'a work of art' and believed that it had
reached its final form in Prussia in the early years of the nineteenth
century.[1] As works of conscious design the greatest constitutions and
states do indeed stand comparison with the finest achievements of
civilization in visual arts, music, philosophy or poetry. They, too, are
manifestations of the human imagination, and surpass them in the
extent to which they have transformed people's lives.

Unlike most other works of art, however, they usually have many
makers and they involve trial and error, and ceaseless response to
changing circumstances (which is why Hegel was wrong to presume
that states had reached anything like a final form). They were then,
and are now, works in progress, evolving through trial and error,
observation and learning.

In the preceding chapters I have set out an argument about their
evolution. I have presented states as inescapably moral because they
depend on loyalty, commitment and legitimacy, and can justify themselves only through their service in meeting the needs of others. I've
shown that morality is not something to be considered as marginal to
the business of power. It is wrapped up in every relationship of service,

domination or trust. It is the currency in which human affairs take place, and all efforts to squeeze it out of politics (or, for that matter, out of business or science) have in the past proven futile.

The ideas of service which I describe have a very long ancestry and they are not inherently modern. But the modern world has learned much that is new about how the devices of democracy, when combined with an active public, open knowledge and a favourable global environment, can make governments more focused on their practical duties of service, less self-serving, and less distracted by delusions.

Perhaps the most important lesson the world has learned is that alignment is all-important in shaping the relationship between rulers and ruled. Good government does not result solely from wise constitutions, or from appointing good people to positions of power. The world is full of progressive constitutions that coexist with reprehensible behaviour, and of corrupt leaders who started out full of promise and ideals. Good government results from the alignment of the many vital forces that reward the good and punish the bad, including laws and constitutions, the personal ethics of politicians and officials, the vigour of the media and critics, and the moral voice of the outside world. Everything that we know from social science confirms the counter-intuitive conclusion – people's behaviour depends greatly on the environment they are in, and the subtle messages that encourage or discourage good behaviour. Governments are good when they have to be good, and when these factors are aligned it becomes hard for politicians and officials not to act morally.

I have repeatedly emphasized that government, and democracy, will continue to evolve. I don't discount the scope for the resurgence of aggressive nationalism, theocracy or fascism. But I've also suggested some of the ways that a more positive evolution might take place. In one direction lies the possibility of rapid evolution in how communities and societies reason, argue and agree, helped by the new social software technologies. These may in time make the formal apparatus of voting and binary debate ever less important; they certainly have the potential to radically deepen what we mean by democracy. In another direction lies a more deliberate evolution of consciousness so as to inculcate, through practice, habits of mutual respect and personal responsibility, deeper awareness of others, and the ability to reason collectively. I've also suggested how states may dissolve further into their societies, becoming ever more like infrastructures and platforms rather than structures, and I've indicated the forms that new global authorities could take.

These may leave our governing systems looking very different. But if I'm right their tasks will change relatively little. They will still focus primarily on their four critical tasks of protection, welfare, justice and truth. And they will still be unable to avoid the dilemmas and tensions that inevitably surround the exercise of power.

THE SEVEN AMBIGUITIES OF SERVICE

The critic William Empson described the seven types of ambiguity that make literature and poetry effective. During the course of this book I have described seven ambiguities that mark the nature of service even in the most advanced democracy. In literature ambiguities give words some of their power to move us. In government they are rather more unsettling, because most of us want to believe in an ordered and meaningful world. But appreciating these ambiguities is a necessary starting point for anyone who wants to be a politician, an official, an activist or a journalist.

First, governments (in the broadest sense) create the rules they operate by, and can, *in extremis*, suspend them.

Second, in order to be good servants governments have to act as masters, issuing commands and often overriding the wishes of the people they serve.

Third, every ruling group serves some more than others, and no one has yet designed a way of appointing a government that does not leave them at least partially captured by some groups at the expense of others.

Fourth, every real or imaginable government has its own interests, which will often be different not just from the people it serves but also from the people who nominally lead it.

Fifth, the business of governing involves ordering, categorizing and controlling – the opposite of any ideal of personal, attentive service (and much of the daily life of government has to be indirect, run through intermediaries, agencies and networks; again, the very opposite of the direct intimacy and accountability of service).

Sixth, to get good government the people themselves have to work hard, scrutinizing, complaining, arguing and engaging. A society of sheep begets a government of wolves.

Seventh, the outcomes of good government depend on people's willingness to serve themselves and to serve their community. Relatively few of the important tasks of government in protection, welfare, justice and knowledge can simply be done to passive recipients. In this sense, too, good government is a joint creation.

Recognizing these ambiguities and paradoxes is essential for any grown-up politics that gets beyond the cycles of illusion and disillusion that have been so common in the past. We can contain and treat these ambiguities but they render impossible any notion that a pure ideal of good government could ever be achieved.

JUDGING GOOD POWER

So the moral position of government is necessarily ambiguous. But despite these ambiguities it is possible to judge how good states are and how much they approximate to an ideal of service. States are moral through what they do, not what they say; through their service rather than their procedures. Their greatest virtues are practical and tangible, and their worst vices arise from the lure of abstractions and inflated rhetoric.

These virtues can be observed and assessed. The basic moral claims made by states across thousands of years and many different civilizations provide a universal benchmark by which they can be judged. They include how well the state has protected its citizens (from war, crime or ecological threats); how it has advanced their well-being and welfare (as measured, for example, by incomes, happiness or health); how well it has promoted justice and fought against injustice; and how well it has encouraged the pursuit of truths and knowledge (as measured by what they know).

To judge any particular administration we have to look at how well it has performed these tasks in the circumstances it inherits, how it compares with other governments in similar countries, and whether it has enhanced or run down its inherited stock of financial, human, social and natural capital.[2] The same frameworks for judgement are applicable to the emerging forms of transnational and global government. At the same time we also have to watch out for the typical ploys of bad power: encouraging fear, hate and division; running down assets; pursuing war as an end in itself rather than a last resort; giving privileges to oligarchs and special interests; and allowing moral standards to slip by accepting dishonesty, corruption and misinformation.

Any judgements about governments are bound to be subject to argument. But there is a surprising amount of consensus across the political spectrum as to the key criteria by which governments should, at least in principle, be judged, even if there is less agreement about how different priorities should be weighted.

Senator Daniel Patrick Moynihan once described the process whereby governments reposition the goalposts to give themselves the appearance of success even when they are failing. He called this 'defining deviance down'. In the case of nation states the recent experience has been one of defining deviance up, thanks to the pressure and knowledge of the public – setting ever higher moral levels by which to judge the performance and acceptable behaviour of states.

MORALITY AND CHANGE

To some extent we get the governments we deserve. Good power is a co-creation; it is something done with the people, not done to them, and publics who contribute nothing to their democracy, and free-ride on the efforts of others, lose the moral authority to complain when things go wrong. It is in the nature of politics that the choices we are given are never ideal ones; but the imperfections of real regimes do not provide an excuse for inaction or cynical detachment. Samuel Finer wrote pointedly in his great history of government about the people of the Roman Empire who moaned about high taxes, and then failed to stand up in its defence:

If a peasant in Gaul or Spain or northern Italy had been able to foresee the misery and exploitation that was to befall his grandchildren and their grandchildren, on and on and on for the next 500 years, he would have been singularly spiritless – and witless – if he had not rushed to the aid of the empire.[3]

Perhaps some future historian will write similar words about detached majorities standing on the sidelines as governments grapple with an unravelling ecology.

Where power is concerned we are all potential participants as well as observers. If we only observe, we don't just run the risk of ending up as impoverished slaves. We also run the risk of accepting too easily the self-image of the state as more permanent and fixed than it is. The great virtue of activism is that it shows us what is hard and what is soft, the plasticity of power as well as its resilience. It reminds us of the power of collective sovereignty, and of how much we depend on common knowledge and shared reasoning. And by challenging power it makes it better.

William Morris wrote in *A Dream of John Ball* that

men fight and lose the battle, and what they fought for comes about in spite of their defeat, and when it comes turns out to be not what they meant, and other men have to fight for what they meant under a different name.

This is perhaps the essence of radicalism. At its best it tirelessly re-energizes societies without being disheartened by the twists and turns of history. It strips away the accretions so that we can see clearly what is essential, and it enables us to imagine how things could be different and better, even in an imperfect world.

Summary of the Argument

1. Human needs are infinitely varied, but not random. There is a consistent pattern of human needs across history and across widely divergent cultures: these include needs for safety, health, material goods, family, community, spiritual fulfilment and comfort. These have translated into a consistent set of demands that communities have made of their leaders, and of states. These demands, which also mark out the moral duties of governments and their nature as servants of the people, encompass four main areas: the responsibility to protect (from wild animals, the elements, other people and other states); the responsibility for welfare (the provision of food, water, shelter and care); the responsibility for justice (the fair resolution of disputes and punishment of wrongs); and the responsibility for truth (knowledge of the world, the cosmos and other people).

2. These roles are fulfilled by parents in every family and are fulfilled by leaders in even the smallest communities. But the advent of large, densely populated communities producing surpluses necessitated new forms of social organization. A host of new problems emerged as people had to cope with large numbers of strangers and with the problems of externalities, co-ordination and trust – some of which were later theorized through the framework of social contracts.

3. States emerged in part because they were necessary for the survival and well-being of densely populated communities. But because control of the state was also immensely valuable, all states were prone to capture by small groups and vested interests, and they have repeatedly been turned into predatory devices for exploiting

and dominating the people they might otherwise serve. Much of the history of warfare is a direct result of this history of capture. All states are in some respects captured. Even the most democratic state is built around some inequalities of power and most contemporary democracies are better understood as oligarchies than as 'government of the people, by the people, for the people'. Most governments have deviated, deceived, and served themselves, behind an often very thin façade of service to the people. To understand how states behave, we have to recognize that they also serve themselves – they exist in order to exist, and devote a high proportion of their energies to maintaining themselves, and to maintaining what I call their cognitive coherence. Officials have interests different from political leaders and from the people. But this self-service goes deeper into the very logic of state administration, which at times is willing to change anything, and sacrifice anything, for its own survival. So all states have three characters – that of a servant, that of a captured master, and that of a servant of themselves.

4. Through most of history, violent revolt was the only weapon available to people to force states to live up to the first of these characters, and to fulfil their duties as servants. But over time the peoples of the world have discovered many devices that force states to live up to their roles as servants. These devices fall broadly into four groups: contestability through election; divisions of power; the rule of laws; and visibility, free media and free access to information. These devices do not arise from natural laws, or God, or historical inevitability. They have been learned, and the most important lessons have been learned from seeing the enormous suffering caused by governments that were free from these devices. An important recent example is the growing use of devices for 'triangulation' and 'validation': the use of third parties to check and corroborate the claims and actions of states.

5. The diffusion of these various devices has greatly enhanced the moral character of governments. However, truly good power is likely only when these structural devices are also aligned with other things – an active and vigorous public, wise critics and commentators, and high ethical standards among leaders and

officials. In the past, ethical standards had to compensate for the lack of structures to make states act as servants; today they can reinforce each other, and make manifest the idea that having knowledge or power is a gift that also brings with it obligations.

6. Democracy, like all forms of governance, is prone to decay and alienation. Power corrupts, as do inequalities. Once-benign regimes inevitably harden and become detached from the values that inspired them. So the pursuit of good power is a constant struggle to renew and revitalize ideas and institutions. Much of that struggle involves countering the universal human tendency to naturalize ideas and relationships – making human-made constructs appear natural, permanent and immutable. This happens to moral ideas and to political ones; often they become distanced from the tasks they were intended to undertake, and come instead to stand against people. The characteristic vices of power include not only the familiar sins of oppression, arrogance, deceit and theft, but also subtler vices like the use of abstraction. The main currencies of politics are words, images and fictions, the stories and claims which lend legitimacy to power. In democratic politics, perhaps even more than in non-democratic politics, these fictions can become traps. Abstractions override realities; vague rhetoric about values or identities masks failures, and leaders all too easily come to confuse announcements with reality, laws passed with outcomes achieved, believing that so long as they can solve a problem through a turn of phrase the problem will go away. Good power is at heart very practical and prosaic: poetry can inspire it but is also often its enemy.

7. Democracy is in part about turning the state into a true servant. But it is also about releasing the energies of the people to make the world for themselves, free from the state. To make this possible states can be moved away from their traditional role of creating and running structures towards roles which are more about creating infrastructures – underlying capacities that support people to make their own worlds. In the economy, these infrastructures are provided by laws, rules and monies; in society, they include the legal, financial and practical supports for social movements, enterprises and activism; in personal life they include

the educational, financial and advisory help that enables people to plan and manage their own lives and careers.

8. A dynamic civic culture stands as an alternative to the drift towards a pacified democracy, made up of passive observers choosing between competing elites. It also stands counter to the claim that law and rules can somehow displace moral argument and action. The popular idea that governance is gravitating towards amoral technocracy is incorrect as an observation, and quite at odds with the tide of laws, regulations and codes with which states try to make moral sense of the world around them. More importantly, to the extent that any polity does move in this direction it also condemns itself to decline, since it cuts off the very sources of commitment and renewal on which it depends. The alternative is to question the fundamental premise of modern constitutional societies, which grant automatic rights and privileges to all members of the nation, and move instead to more conditional models of citizenship in which privileges are more closely tied to contributions.

9. Good global government is becoming essential in a densely populated, interdependent world. In the past, imperial power often shored up oppressive regimes. More recently, global institutions have acted where states are visibly failing to meet the needs of their people. When they do so there is an unavoidable tension between the duties of protection, welfare, justice and truth which may fall to other states, and ideals of autonomy and self-government. In the long-run these tensions can be contained only through progress towards a global government. The same factors that led to the creation of states – including threats to security and the problems of providing common goods – are now mirrored on a global scale. The design and evolution of new structures of government beyond the boundaries of nation states, informed by an ethos of service, and committed to the same tasks of protection, welfare, justice and truth as national states, is the greatest task of the new century, and essential to human survival. These designs will draw on the many devices for good power invented within cities and nation states, but will also be novel in form. Just as within any community the public good depends on public

commitment, so, globally, the rights of belonging to international clubs need to become more conditional, and more overtly based on values.

10. The duties of service to today's citizens need to be matched by duties of service to the future. These duties are bound to be in tension with day-to-day pressures from electorates and markets. They need to be consciously given institutional form, in and around government, as well as outside, in a 'party for the future'. Otherwise the lesson of many past societies and civilizations is that they can easily ignore even the most fatal threats.

Notes

1. Quoted in 'Why is Any Nation a Democracy?', Professor James Q. Wilson lecture to the Manhattan Institute, 1999.
2. In our daily lives most of us routinely overestimate the importance of what psychologists call dispositional factors, such as individual characteristics or behaviours, and underestimate the importance of the situational factors of the wider context. When someone loses their job they are more likely to attribute it to dispositional factors like bad luck, personal failings or a mal-evolent boss than to larger macroeconomic forces. And when genocide is committed we find it easier to look for an evil pathology in the individuals carrying it out than to accept that, in some circumstances, even the most ordinary people become ruthless killers. This is known as the fundamental attribution error.
3. See Felicia Huppert et al., *The Science of Well-being*. Oxford: Oxford University Press, 2005.
4. Recent claims that ecological conditions and, in particular, the presence of certain domesticated animals and crops shape economic and social develop-ment have much to commend them, and explain well the relative advantages of the Old over the New World. By contrast, claims that climate (and disease) explain global patterns of wealth and poverty clash directly with the fact that for long periods of history the centres of civilization and population were to be found in hot, and often tropical, regions, while the temperate regions tended to be backward and barbaric. The reasons why countries in temperate areas have for the last century been so much richer than those in hot areas has much more to do with the specific histories of European imperialism, and the different character of colonies which imported large numbers of settlers.
5. Recent work by John Helliwell has confirmed this statistically. Comparing happiness rates in some fifty countries he found that 80 per cent of the

variation could be explained with six variables, including the quality of government, trust and corruption. An improvement in the quality of government in Belarus (–.76) to that of Hungary (+.87) would increase the average well-being of a citizen of Belarus by almost as much as moving from the bottom to the top decile of the income distribution. There are likely to be many more studies of this kind, increasing in sophistication as more data becomes available. John Helliwell, 'How's Life? Combining Individual and National Variables to Explain Subjective Well-Being', National Bureau of Economic Research, Working Paper 9065, July 2002.

6. This book contains two pairs of overlapping words that are often used interchangeably, but have at least partially distinct meanings. The first pair – 'morals' and 'ethics' – is distinguished by their origins (the first Latin, the second Greek) and a general presumption that the first refers to the principles of ought and should in a community, built up by tradition, while the second refers to more universal principles derived from reason. The other pair – 'state' and 'government' – consists of words both of which are Latin in origin and even 'more' closely interwoven. The state is the more abstract entity: the people living in a territory, recognized by others and sharing allegiance. It is usually assumed that a state has a monopoly claim on people's loyalty. The government is the administrative authority which serves it, and which steers a community of people in a given territory, setting and imposing rules. In recent times the two words have been virtually synonymous, but at many times in the past, and in all likelihood in the future, the two will diverge in meanings and some states will have more than one government (Europe is already in this position).

7. Jeffrey Sachs and Andrew Warner studied 97 developing countries in the 1970s and 1980s and concluded that natural resources were associated with economic failure; the countries experiencing the fastest growth generally had few natural resources. Jeffrey Sachs and Andrew Warner, *Natural Resource Abundance and Growth*. Cambridge, Mass.: National Bureau of Economic Growth, 1995.

8. Gunnar Myrdal's *Asian Drama*, which explained how religion and culture held back Asia's prospects for economic development just as much of Asia was, in fact, beginning several decades of rapid growth, is the classic example of how misleading attempts to establish a causal link between culture and economics can be. Gunnar Myrdal, *Asian Drama: An Inquiry into the Poverty of Nations*. London: Allen Lane, 1968.

9. Helliwell, op. cit.

10. The other guarantee of good power in the eyes of many ancient philosophers was the quality of the class from which the rulers sprang (preferably

aristocratic for most of the ancient Greek philosophers). All of these different factors were considered a few centuries later by a group of scholars who worked full time in the great library at Alexandria to study and assess the lessons of kingship, governance and legitimacy for their rulers. We have no record of their conclusions.

11. Much of the political theory produced in the last half century by such eminent figures as Friedrich Hayek, Karl Popper, Václav Havel and John Rawls reacted against the gross abuses of power by totalitarian states. For them the central problem of political philosophy was how to limit the excessive strength of states, through divisions of powers, constitutional constraints, and the encouragement of a free market and civil society as competing centres of power.

12. Visiting my counterparts in other countries also showed me that the more you know about any polity the more it seems uniquely inseparable from its history (and one mark of the most powerful nations is that they even persuade others of their uniqueness). Yet this is to some degree an optical illusion: seen from a wider vantage point the tasks facing governments look very similar.

13. Jean Dunbabin, *France in the Making, 843–1180*. Oxford: Oxford University Press, 1985, p. 277.

14. Marxists were equally dismissive of evidence and experience, although for them the inexorable laws of history replaced God and nature. They argued that because the world of appearances was so profoundly distorted by exploitation and unequal power, the theorist and the activist had to look behind them to find the hidden dynamics of change. In the marketplace people might appear to exchange goods and money on an equal basis, yet behind the equality of exchange lurked profound inequalities of power and worth. More recently some modern economic theorists, coming from a very different ideological starting point, have deduced the proper roles of the state from theories of the market and state failure built up from first principles. One justification for using deduction rather than observation is that the participants in political life can never see clearly the system in which they live; the job of the theorist is to reveal the hidden realities (rather as the modern novel allows the reader to see things which the characters cannot and relies on the reader not taking at face value what they read). Thus the illusory coherence of capitalism was a deception, through which Marxian political economy tried to break by taking the side of the historic mission of the proletariat. Freudian psychoanalysis revealed the delusions of the patient through the method of therapy. Neoclassical economics revealed rational bases for behaviour that might be quite different from people's own understanding of their motives.

15. However, his great work appears to have taken shape over many centuries, with additions by many hands (and its final form is dated at the earliest to the second century AD, half a millennium after Chandragupta).

16. Even as pre-eminent a theologian as Thomas Aquinas, in his great work *De Regno*, based his arguments on experience, not revelation.

17. Arguably the only way of achieving any distance is to detach ourselves not only from power but also from human intercourse, as in mystical traditions of religion – to reject the world and dissect its illusions from a distance. Yet the knowledge achieved through mystical detachment is not easily used in human society. For those who wish to remain engaged, the only option is to be thrown into the maelstrom of life and accept that every perception will be shaped, compromised and bent by your position within it, and that while knowledge can be gained it must be self-aware knowledge, conscious of its own limits.

18. There are also theories which emphasize the singularity of the state and others which emphasize its complex pluralism, theories which see the state as a space for others to fight their battles and theories which emphasize its autonomy, and theories which highlight the international political economy in which states operate and others which, to all intents and purposes, see them as closed systems. Alongside the neat theories there are also theories, or non-theories, which emphasize chaos and messiness and absence of logic. Mark Haugaard, ed., *Power: A reader*. Manchester: Manchester University Press, 2002, provides a useful overview.

19. A reference to Machiavelli.

20. Many of these goods are also incommensurable in the sense given by Isaiah Berlin, which is why no single calculus can encompass them.

CHAPTER 2

1. Antarctica is the only exception.

2. How much is this inequality either natural or inevitable? The great apes certainly live in hierarchical communities, with strict divisions of domination and subordination, enforced by the greater physical prowess of males over females, and of dominant males over weaker ones. A fair proportion of their everyday social drama comes from struggles for position. In human societies some inequalities are even starker. A human baby is utterly dependent on its parents for longer than any other animal (though if the parents value the child it soon discovers how much power it has over them). But humans have fewer physical differences than the great apes and fewer physically obvious

leaders. Without a naturally dominant source of leadership, human groups may have had to talk and listen more and to work harder at resolving problems. Perhaps argument, rebellion and assertion to gain respect are the natural states of an intelligent, communicative species without huge discrepancies in physical strength: a raw and rough equality, based on the resentment that the powerless have of any domination.

3. David Lewis Williams, *The Mind in the Cave: Consciousness and the origins of art*. London: Thames and Hudson, 2002, p. 80.

4. The classic dispute between Robert Carneiro and Elman Service over whether war or trade did most to shape societies may well be repeated. Robert L. Carneiro, 'A Theory of the Origin of the State', *Science*, New Series, Vol. 169, Issue 3947 (21 August 1970): 733–8; Elman Service, *Origins of the State and Civilization*. New York: Norton, 1975.

5. Some of the best recent books include Robert McCormick Adam, *The Evolution of Urban Society*. Chicago: Aldine, 1966; Henri Claessen and Peter Skalnik, eds., *The Early State*. The Hague: Mouton Walter de Gruyter, Inc., 1976; Deborah Nichols and Thomas Charlton, eds., *The Archaeology of City States*. Washington, DC and London: Smithsonian Books, 1997; and Gary Feinman and Joyce Marcus, eds., *Archaic States*. Sante Fe, N.Mex.: SAR Press, 1998.

6. Bruce Trigger, *Understanding Early Civilisations*. Cambridge: Cambridge University Press, 2003, p. 201.

7. These can also be found in contemporary anthropological evidence from those parts of the world where people have lived without the active presence of a central state, which shows what it may have been like to be a chief trying to weld competing groups into something more coherent. But this evidence is at best suggestive rather than definitive.

8. The idea of the meek inheriting the earth could be interpreted in conservative ways as a reason for the poor to accept subordination in this life, but it was also interpreted by some in more revolutionary ways, from the times of the Gnostics to modern liberation theology.

9. Trigger, op. cit.

10. Petr Charvat, *On People, Signs and States: Spotlights on Sumerian Society c.3500–2500BC*. Prague: Oriental Institute of the Academy of Science of the Czech Republic, 1997.

11. The *Shu Jing* or *Shang Shu*.

12. The absence of any comprehensible written records from the Indus civilizations means that we may never know whether there was a single empire, separate cit- states, or some hybrid.

13. Xenophon described the chief virtue of the *polis* as being that it allowed

'citizens to act as bodyguards one to another against slaves and criminals so that none of the citizens might die a violent death'. Xenophon, *Hiero*, IV, 3.

14. The prisoners' dilemma describes any situation with the logical structure T>R>P>S, where T is the temptation to defect, R is the reward for co-operation, P is the punishment for mutual defection, and S is the sucker's payoff – what happens if you co-operate and the other player defects.

15. Rational individuals will tend to underproduce public goods left to their own devices.

16. Robert Wright's book *NonZero* provides an excellent account of human evolution through the lens of games theory's contrast between zero-sum and positive-sum games. Robert Wright, *NonZero*. London: Vintage, 2001.

17. This task of creating trust reaches deep into culture. It can be encouraged by shared beliefs and symbols, and by the music, shared rituals and dancing, which all played a part in making early communities feel and act like a single organism, united in feelings as well as in interests. It is not a coincidence that in contemporary Europe membership of choirs remains a good indicator of civic health. See R. D. Puttnam, *Making Democracy Work: Civic Traditions in Modern Italy*. Princeton: Princeton University Press, 1995.

18. For example the work of John Nash showed that in prisoners' dilemma-type games, if the game is finite the rational strategy is to defect each time, since both parties will be bound to defect on the final turn and, by extension, on each previous turn. For co-operation to be sustainable, the future must be uncertain and open-ended. J. F. Nash, 'Equilibrium Points in N-Person Games', *Proceedings of the National Academy of Sciences of the United States of America*, 36 (1950): 48–9.

19. Bertrand Lemenicier, 'Fallacies in the Theories of the Emergence of the State', *Journal of Libertarian Studies*, 2003; Etienne de la Boetie, *The Politics of Obedience: The discourse of voluntary servitude*. Montreal: Black Rose, 1976; James Buchanan, *The Limits of Liberty*. Chicago: University of Chicago Press, 1975; Douglass North, *Structure and Change in Economic History*. New York: Norton, 1981.

20. 'A compulsory political association with continuous organization will be called a state', he wrote, 'if and insofar as its administrative staff successfully uphold a claim to the monopoly of legitimate use of physical force in the enforcement of its order.' Weber's definition covers states that he saw as historically succeeding looser political power over a territory backed by the threat of force. Max Weber, 'Politics as a Vocation', speech, 1918.

21. Aristotle argued that there was a necessary link between the dominant forms of military force and the character of the state. He linked the cavalry to oligarchy, the hoplite to a yeoman republic, and the navy to democracy.

22. Mark Edward Lewis, *Sanctioned Violence in early China*. Albany, NY: State University of New York Press, 1990.
23. Michael Mann, *The Sources of Social Power*, 2 vols. Cambridge: Cambridge University Press, 1986 and 1993.
24. Charles Tilly, *Coercion, Capital, and European States*. Oxford: Blackwell, 1993.
25. Karl A. Wittfogel, *Oriental Despotism*. New Haven, Conn.: Yale University Press, 1957.
26. *Analects*, XIII, 7.
27. In a democracy the people commission the government, which has different interests from them, to carry out certain tasks; politicians commission the bureaucracy, which also has different interests; central bureaucracies commission outlying agencies; outlying agencies commission professionals, who in turn often commission ancillary staff. At each step various devices are used to keep control: written commands and contracts formalize what is expected; surveillance tracks whether promises are kept; powers of redress punish agents who renege on their commitments. In some countries armies of inspectors and auditors try to keep track of who has done what. But all of the devices that are used to control delegated power have the paradoxical effect of undermining this trust, since they are premised on the idea that the person exercising delegated power cannot be trusted. Moreover success and failure are rarely unambiguous. The relations between principals and agents may be straightforward when the tasks are simple, easily specified and cheaply monitored. The public can know reasonably well whether their government has delivered higher economic growth than their neighbours; and a ruler can know reasonably easily if a regional governor has or has not built the roads he promised. But many of the tasks that governments carry out involve multiple goals that are ambiguous in nature, such as cutting crime or improving the environment. It is rarely clear precisely who is responsible for successes and failures, even where it is possible to monitor reliably what has actually happened.

A recent analysis of delegation is a report written for the World Bank, which describes modern democracy in terms of three sets of delegations. 'First, the sovereign people delegate decision-making power (usually via a written constitution) to a national legislature and executive. The primary tools that the people retain in order to ensure appropriate behaviour on the part of their representatives are two: the power to replace them at election time; and the power to set the constitutional rules of the political game . . . A second step in the delegation of power occurs when the details of the internal organization of the legislative and executive bodies are settled. A third step in the delegation of power takes the legislature (or its political chiefs) as principal and the various bureaus and agencies as agents.' Gary Cox and Matthew McCubbins, in Matthew McCubbins and Stephen Haggard, eds., *The Structure of Fiscal and Regulatory Policy*. New York: World Bank, 2001, pp. 2–3.

28. Michael Mann has provided the most comprehensive account of these sources of power in his magisterial book *The Sources of Social Power*, op. cit.

29. Battles are won through decisively concentrating forces at the right points. Modern warfare transforms the nature of this concentration, whether in the form of nuclear weapons or through guerrilla warfare that seeks to bypass concentrations of troops and to create a countervailing political concentration of popular power.

30. Movements and interests that want to influence states have to learn how to concentrate their forces on ruling groups' pressure points – threatening their electoral majorities or tax receipts; disrupting party funding; or calling into question their international credibility or the state's ability to maintain order.

31. Each of the sources of state power has its origins in human relations with the rest of the natural world. Pastoralists depended on their ability to command the bodies and lives of animals: understanding their needs, their risks and their idiosyncrasies. For agrarian societies, command over the seasonal rhythms of crops was essential for survival in an economy made up of investment and returns guided by close observation of the climate. For hunters, command over the thoughts of the hunted through guile, deception and intimidation was the key to survival.

32. Thomas Barfield, *The Perilous Frontier: Nomadic Empires and China*. New York: Blackwell, 1989.

33. The power of thought is also central to the story of social development, since civilization is at root the accumulation of thoughts and habits of thought that frame how we see the world and how we think about behaviour, and progress can be understood as the growing relative weight first of money relative to violence (the dominance of merchants relative to warriors) and then of self-conscious knowledge relative to both money and violence.

CHAPTER 3

1. Quoted in Robert Nozick, *Anarchy, State and Utopia*. Oxford: Blackwell, 1974.

2. Samuel Finer, *The History of Government from the Earliest Times*, Vol. 2. Oxford: Oxford University Press, 1997, p. 727.

3. Douglass North's recent book, *Understanding the Process of Economic Change*, Princeton: Princeton University Press, 2005, provides a useful account of how knowledge and institutions have shaped economic growth.

4. H. G. Creel, 'The Beginnings of Bureaucracy in China: The Origin of the Hsien', *Journal of Asian Studies*, 23 (1964): 155–84.

5. Laurence E. Lynn, Jr, 'Public Management: A Brief History of the Field', in E. Ferlie, L. Lynn and C. Pollitt, eds., *Handbook of Public Management*, Oxford University Press, forthcoming. Frederick William I had started training officials and had established two university chairs in administrative subjects in the 1720s (by the end of the eighteenth century there were 23 such chairs), while Frederick the Great instituted examinations and a civil service commission. The greatest advocate of cameralism was Johann Justi.

6. Annual murder rates in England fell from over 20 per 100,000 in the thirteenth and fourteenth centuries to around 1 per 100,000 by the end of the twentieth century. Manuel Eisner, 'Modernization, Self-Control and Lethal Violence', *British Journal of Criminology*, 41 (2001): 618–38.

7. Anthony Giddens, *The Nation State and Violence*. Cambridge: Cambridge University Press, 1985, p. 309.

8. Like many fiscal innovations, income tax spread so quickly because the health of the tax base has such a profoundly important bearing on states' ability to survive (VAT followed the same pattern a century later). Perhaps surprisingly, greater connectedness made it easier for states to raise taxes because it made economic activity so much more visible (states have always found it easier to tax trade passing through ports and border posts than production). The common assumption that globalization will undermine nation states' tax base has not turned out to be accurate. It may be harder to tax very mobile factors of production – tax havens may make it possible for the rich and global corporations to avoid tax – but so far tax collectors have maintained their edge in the arms race with tax avoiders.

9. Charles Tilly, 'Stories, Identities, and Political Change', *International Social Science Review*, Spring/Summer (2002): 255.

10. National identity has always been a galvanizing force for oppressed peoples and for powerful states (from Rome and Persia to China), but until

the nineteenth century national self-determination had never been a general principle.

11. The only emperors are either not rulers (as in Japan) or not real emperors (as in the case of the Emperor Bokassa in central Africa in the 1970s).

12. As measured by outcomes – health and prosperity for example – as well as their governing arrangements, this list would include not only the EU and OECD countries but also some in Africa, including Mauritius and South Africa, many in Asia, including Taiwan and South Korea, and some nations in Latin America, including Chile.

13. Most of these are in temperate climates, just as most of the world's wealth now lies in temperate zones, freer from debilitating diseases, though the reasons have as much to do with history as ecology.

14. Richard Rose estimated figures for 1985 of 1,056,000 for the UK (including employees of the armed forces, hence the discrepancy); 855,000 for Germany and 3,797,000 for the USA. Richard Rose, *Understanding Big Government: The programme approach*. London: Sage, 1984, p. 130.

15. Vito Tanzi and Ludger Schuknecht, *Public Spending in the 20th Century*, Cambridge: Cambridge University Press, 2000, also attempted an analysis of the relative value of spending by the state.

16. The definitive recent overview of these tools is Lester Salamon, *The Tools of Government*. Oxford: Oxford University Press, 2002.

17. By any historical standards democratic welfare capitalism was remarkably successful. This is the message of the most serious attempt to assess the performance of developed countries, conducted by the Australian political scientist Robert Goodin and his collaborators. Their main concern was to analyse how different kinds of system, conservative, liberal and social democratic, performed in delivering results to their citizens. The work drew on long time series data from the US, Germany and the Netherlands (the only countries for which adequate data is available), tracking people's lives year after year between the late 1970s and early 1990s: Robert Goodin et al., *The Real Worlds of Welfare Capitalism*. Cambridge: Cambridge University Press, 1999.

To avoid ideological bias the researchers looked at the criteria that the advocates of each system deemed to be the most important, and then observed what actually happened, for example to the relationship between security and competitive enterprise. The conclusions of the research were clear: all of the systems performed well, but social democracy scored better on all of the morally desirable outcomes of welfare systems than the other two. This research was limited to a handful of countries and one particular period, but it does suggest a useful avenue for future research to test the claims made by political advocates – for example, looking at whether there are clear patterns linking political systems to success in social mobility, stable families or economic growth. A longer time series and more countries might have shown a different picture, but at the very least this research confirms that neutral academic research can provide insights into how well states perform as servants.

18. By Adam Przeworski and Fernando Limongi, in Adam Przeworski, Michael E. Alvarez, Jose Antonio Cheibub and Fernando Limongi, *Democracy and Development: Political Institutions and Well-being in the World, 1950–1990*. Cambridge Studies in the Theory of Democracy. Cambridge: Cambridge University Press, 2000.

19. Robert Barro, *Determinants of Economic Growth: A cross-country survey*. Cambridge, Mass.: Harvard University Press, 1997.

20. India and China provide the world's most important contrasting examples. These had once been the richest, most urban and most civilized societies on earth, but experienced a huge reversal of fortune when between 1600 and 1900 their lands were eaten up by the ravenous empires of Europe. Their once great governing traditions, every bit as rich and sophisticated as the West that caricatured them as despotisms, were dismantled and demoralized, and only very recently have they been able to stumble back towards models of government that learn from the rest of the world's experience but also make sense of their own history – in India's case through a strong federal democracy with a strong free media; in China's through strict, often ruthless, party rule. Both have strong traditions of concern for the moral conduct of power, which contrast with the West's common assumption for much of its history that might is right (and its more recent assumption that only structural counterweights to sovereign authority can make good power possible).

21. According to a Gallup international survey in 2005, 79 per cent believe democracy is the best system of government, but 65 per cent do not feel that their country is ruled by the will of the people.

22. Gallup International Millennium Survey, 2000.

23. The work of Pippa Norris at Harvard provides the most comprehensive mapping of these broad trends in activism and political engagement. Pippa Norris, *Democratic Phoenix: Reinventing Political Activism*. New York: Cambridge University Press, 2002.

24. Philip Bobbitt, *The Shield of Achilles*. New York: Alfred A. Knopf, 2002, p. 230.

25. This is one of the meanings that Bobbitt gives to the idea of the market state.

CHAPTER 4

1. Al-Yusi, *Rasa'il*, edited by F. al-Qabli (Casablanca, 1981), quoted in Rahma Bourquia and Susan Gilson Miller, eds., *In the Shadow of the Sultan*. Harvard Middle Eastern Monographs, 1999.

2. Other examples of the relationship between sages and kings can be found in Leo Strauss, *On Tyranny: an interpretation of Xenophon's Hiero*. New York: Political Science Classics, 1948.

3. This is a temptation that must at times have been shared by most Presidents and Prime Ministers.

4. Jane Jacobs described the morals of protection as a guardian moral syndrome, concerned with care for land and territory, taking the long view, anticipation as well as response, vigilance, and a degree of paranoia. These values are common among armies and aristocracies, civil services and police forces, and can also be found in parts of the modern environmental movement. Jane Jacobs, *Systems of Survival*. London: Vintage Press, 1994.

5. Adam Smith wrote, in the same vein, that 'those exertions of the liberty of a few individuals which might endanger the security of the whole society are, and ought to be, restrained by the laws of all governments . . . which have a duty of protecting, as far as possible, every member of the society from the injustice or oppression of every other member of it.' Adam Smith, *On the Wealth of Nations*, ed. Edwin Cannan. London: Methuen and Co. Ltd, 1904.

6. It is not hard to speculate about many other, far less happy, states in the past. But national happiness is not something on which data has been collected for very long. Bruno Frey's work on the economics of happiness is one of many sources on this. Bruno Frey, *Happiness and Economics: How the economy and institutions affect human well-being*. Princeton: Princeton University Press, 2002.

7. Stuart Hall, Chas Critcher, Tony Jefferson, John Clarke and Brian Roberts, *Policing the Crisis: Mugging, the state, and law and order*. London: Macmillan, 1978 is one classic account of the construction of moral panic for a political end.

8. This argument is expanded in John King Fairbank and Merle Goldman, *China: A new history*. Cambridge, Mass.: Belknap Press, 1998.

9. Muhsin Mahdi, *Alfarabi and the Foundation of Islamic Political Philosophy*. Chicago: University of Chicago Press, 2001, p. 128.

10. Hoyt Cleveland Tillman, *Ch'en Liang* on Public Interest and the Law. University of Hawaii Press, 1994, p. 2.

11. H. C. M. Michielse, 'Policing the poor: J. L. Vives and the 16th century

origins of modern social administration', *Social Service Review*, 64, 1 (1990): 1–21.

12. Howard Glennerster, 'Poverty Policy from 1900 to the 1970s', in *One Hundred Years of Poverty and Policy*. York: Joseph Rowntree Foundation, 2004.

13. In the century after 1870 there is only a weak correlation between left of centre governments and public spending. R. Middleton, *Government versus the Market: The growth of the public sector, economic management and British economc performance, c.1890–1979*. Cheltenham: Edward Elgar, 1996.

14. This data is collected in Nick Donovan and David Halpern with Richard Sargeant, 'Life Satisfaction: the State of Knowledge and Implications for Government', Prime Minister's Strategy Unit, 2002.

15. Seen through a moral lens the appeal of materialism often seems suspect. Yet, as the great English poet W. H. Auden warned, as a rule it was the pleasure-haters who became unjust. W. H. Auden, 'Voltaire at Ferney', *Another Time*. London: Faber and Faber, 1997 (first published 1940).

16. Joseph Stiglitz, *The Economics of the Public Sector*, 3rd edition. London: Norton, 2000, p. 81.

17. Alesina and others have used detailed statistical analyses to argue that the basis for welfare deals is likely to be undermined by mass migration. Racial divisions provide a device for politicians to exploit, and undermine the basis for substantial spending on social security. However, more detailed work shows that the picture is not as simple as this. In those European countries where the Left has traditionally been strong, the impact of race disappears. A. Alesina and E. Glaeser, *Fighting Poverty in the US and Europe*. Oxford: Oxford University Press, 2004; Peter Taylor Gooby, 'Is the future American; or can left politics preserve European welfare states from erosion through growing racial diversity?' *Journal of Social Policy*, Vol. 34, 4 (2005).

18. A. Atkinson and J. Stiglitz, *Lectures in Public Economics*. New York: McGraw Hill, 1980.

19. One of the best recent symbols of the responsibility for welfare is the recovery of Cheongyecheon River in Seoul from underneath an urban highway to provide a 6-km trail of walkways and fountains, waterfalls and sculptures through the city centre. Strikingly designed, it combines nature and urbanity in equal measure as the showcase for the aggressive leadership of the city's mayor Lee Yung Bak.

20. The word in Greek was *nomos*. It is usually translated as meaning 'law', but here it means something prior to law, the imposition of rules by force.

21. Benjamin Schwartz, *China's Cultural Values*. Arizona State University Center for Asian Studies, 1985.

22. This expansion of justice has provided a parallel route for citizens to exercise power alongside the procedures of democracy, and it has ensured that the idea of justice remains dynamic, reaching forward to fairer ideals, as well as referring backwards to precedents. Justice has become in this sense more political, and more tied into the conversations of society, even as it has become more independent from formal structures of representative governance. Even John Rawls, author of the most comprehensive theory of justice in liberalism, came to recognize that any viable conception of justice needed to be 'political not metaphysical', by which he meant that people might more easily agree on the applications of justice than on the fundamental principles from which they derived.

23. This has been the powerful drive of Ronald Dworkin's work through many books, including *Taking Rights Seriously*, Cambridge, Mass.: Harvard University Press, 1977, and *Law's Empire*, Cambridge, Mass.: Belknap Press, 1986. It was also the stance taken in English law, most recently by Lord Denning.

24. See Nikolas Rose, *Powers of Freedom*. Cambridge: Cambridge University Press, 1997.

25. Dictatorships are rarely very comfortable about the truths they rest on, which may be why their secret policemen and torturers usually make motive rather than truth the issue, so that behind every question, every point of view, their priority was to ferret out the purpose rather than the facts.

26. Some possible candidates have been excluded from this list of consistent duties. To modern eyes one of the defining roles of the state is that it marks out people's identity. Yet this was not an important role for pre-modern states, which made little claims on people's sense of themselves, and none saw it as essential to their legitimacy. The idea that states should be based on the boundaries of nations is a modern one. So is the notion that all individuals have identical rights. These are undoubtedly important ideas that are constitutive of many modern states, and whose genealogy can be traced back to the ancient world. But they too cannot be claimed as fundamental duties that stretch across time and space. Samuel Finer, *The History of Government from the Earliest Times*. Oxford: Oxford University Press, 1997.

27. Aristotle, *Politics*, III, 7, 28–32, quoted in Richard Mulgan, 'Aristotle on Legality and Corruption', private paper.

28. Cicero, in Book 1 of *De Officiis*, p. 86.

29. The word for the common good – *kung* – had originally referred only to the imperial realm. This dichotomy between the common good and private

good was in turn related to that between what is right and what is advantageous (*i* and *li*) and between the good king (*wang*) and the strongman (*pa*).
30. To be more precise, good servants do not seek to capture economic rent:
they accept fair reward but refrain from predation.
31. Amelie Kuhrt, 'Usurpation, Conquest and Ceremonial: from Babylon to
Persia', in David Cannadine and Simon Price, eds., *Rituals of Royalty: Power
and Ceremonial in Traditional Societies*. Cambridge: Cambridge University
Press, 1987, p. 33.
32. Three decades of reform at the end of the twentieth century, particularly
in the English-speaking world, promised to put the customer or citizen first,
reshaping government around the needs of the people rather than the con-
venience of bureaucrats. Lessons were taken from private-sector services such
as retailing and finance, to foster speed, responsiveness, politeness and choice
instead of sullen inertia. Canada even set itself targets to improve customer
satisfaction. Of all the many fashions, fads and gimmicks that have been
associated with public-sector reform since the 1960s, this is the one that has
stuck.
33. Richard Easterlin, 'How beneficent is the market: a look at the modern
history of mortality', *European Review of Economic History*, 3, 3 (1999):
257–94.
34. Referred to in Vito Tanzi and Ludger Schuknecht, *Public Spending in
the 20th Century: A Global Perspective*. Cambridge: Cambridge University
Press, 2000. Original source: *Traité de la science des finances*, 2 vols. Paris:
Guillaumin, 1888.
35. One of the great books on presidential leadership, for example, described
it as the 'art of building and sustaining cultural coalitions', solving cultural
dilemmas of a complex and diverse society. Wildavsky and Ellis, *Dilemmas
of Presidential Leadership*. New Brunswick, NJ: Transaction Publishers,
1989.
36. Jean-Jacques Rousseau provided another hugely influential metaphorical
framework for explaining the state. Man is good by nature, but made bad by
institutions (born free but everywhere in chains). Society needed to remake
the contract, restoring popular sovereignty over institutions in order to
become good again. More recently, John Rawls, the pre-eminent liberal
theorist of the twentieth century, argued that the only fair and legitimate
social contract was one which would be agreed by anyone acting behind what
he called the 'veil of ignorance' – ignorant of what social rank or endowments
they would end up with.
37. James Buchanan and Gordon Tullock, *The Calculus of Consent*. Ann
Arbor: University of Michigan Press, 1962. Bruce Ackerman and Jürgen

Habermas drew parallel conclusions from their work on ideal speech situations. Bruce Ackerman, *The Future of Liberal Revolution*. New Haven, Conn.: Yale University Press, 1992; Jürgen Habermas, *The Theory of Communicative Action*. London: Beacon Press, 1981.

38. In Hegel's argument, this creates over time a society of self-aware, truly autonomous individuals, respecting each other's needs.

39. Ronald Dworkin, for example, wrote that we want to decide for ourselves, and we should therefore be ready to insist that any honourable constitution, any genuine constitution of principle, will guarantee that right for everyone. He was writing about abortion and euthanasia, but these comments on ultimate issues of life and death apply in his writings to every other domain of life too. Ronald Dworkin, *Life's Dominion*. London: HarperCollins, 1983, p. 237.

40. The ideal of pure self-rule would also make more sense if most people did create themselves on a blank sheet of paper. But most accept the family, the religion, the culture and often even the politics that they are born into, and these, as much as the other choices that they make, define what they really are.

41. Much of the evidence is collected in a report on life satisfaction published by the UK Government Strategy Unit (and available on the website *www.strategy.gov.uk*): Donovan and Halpern, op. cit. More recently Richard Layard has summarized the evidence in his book *Happiness: Lessons from a new science*. London: Allen Lane, 2005.

42. There has been much debate about how reliable surveys of happiness are. Cultural and linguistic differences (*satisfait* and *zufrieden* not being equivalent to 'satisfied') make direct comparisons between countries difficult, while changing expectations make it inherently hard to compare levels of happiness in 2005 and 1955. But most observers have concluded that these surveys are reasonably robust pointers to people's real states of mind. For example, studies of differences across linguistic sub-groups within nations have shown that linguistic differences alone do not account for the marked national differences that have been repeatedly found. German and French speakers living in Switzerland are found to report uniformly high life satisfaction, and significantly higher satisfaction than their German and French neighbours over the border. Similarly, French speakers in Belgium show a closer match to their Flemish neighbours than to French speakers in France. Nationality is a stronger predictor of life satisfaction than language. Other studies have addressed how well survey answers on life satisfaction correspond to more detailed accounts of psychological well-being and, again, found a close fit.

43. Studies have consistently found that on average married people are

happier than those who were never married, and than those who are divorced, separated or widowed (although divorcees may be happier than when they were married). This relationship holds across cultures and even when income and age are taken into account. The effect is strong: studies suggest that marriage is equivalent in its impact on happiness to very large increases in income. Conversely, divorce, widowhood and separation all reduce life satisfaction. For all its radical changes in form in the last generation, the family, both as an ideal and as an everyday social unit, has proved resilient, remaining, as Christopher Lasch termed it, a 'haven in a heartless world'. Christopher Lasch, *Haven in a Heartless World: The Family Besieged*. New York: Basic Books, 1997.

44. Each of these categories of need has always existed alongside its shadow. In most recorded societies there have been movements to reject the family, community and the pursuit of material things. Hermetic, monastic and ascetic societies have served as a challenge, a mirror in which the mainstream could see itself. Yet none of these rejectionist movements has ever co-opted more than small minorities. None has ever become part of the mainstream, although they have often grown during periods when the moral drive of the state has been in abeyance, like the final centuries of the Roman Empire.

45. Sceptics ascribe this to the communal support provided by a church, temple or mosque, rather than to any intrinsic virtue in a spiritual life.

46. Michael Marmot's book *Status Syndrome* provides a definitive description of the evidence. Michael Marmot, *Status Syndrome*. London: Bloomsbury, 2004.

47. Bruno S. Frey and Alois Stutzer, 'Happiness, Economy and Institutions', *Economic Journal*, Royal Economic Society, Vol. 110, 127 (October, 2000): 918–38.

48. '. . . in communist society, where nobody has one exclusive sphere of activity but each can become accomplished in any branch he wishes, society regulates the general production and thus makes it possible for me to do one thing today and another tomorrow, to hunt in the morning, fish in the afternoon, rear cattle in the evening, criticise after dinner, just as I have a mind, without ever becoming hunter, fisherman, herdsman or critic.' Karl Marx, *The German Ideology*. Moscow: Progress Publishers, 1964.

49. Emmanuel Todd, *The Explanation of Ideology: Family Structures and Social Systems*. Oxford: Basil Blackwell, 1985.

50. The links between family forms and social or ideological effects are not directly causal. Instead there are paradoxical results. For example, countries with primogeniture, a model of inequality in which all of the inheritance goes to the first-born male, may have ended up more equal as a result of having a

reasonably prosperous farming community compared to societies in which the land was divided into ever smaller parcels. Another paradox is that societies based on the authoritarian family are often more prone to anarchy and discord rather than the order they crave.

51. George Lakoff, *Moral Politics: How Liberals and Conservatives Think*. Chicago: University of Chicago Press, 2002.

CHAPTER 5

1. Douglass North, *Understanding the Process of Economic Change*. Princeton: Princeton University Press, 2005, p. 67.

2. In medieval England, for example, Henry III built up his own secretariat in his 'wardrobe' to redirect money to his own personal needs.

3. Nikolai Karamzin, *History of the Russian State*, first published in St Petersburg, 1818–24. The idea that states were, and still are, to a degree criminal enterprises is expounded in Mancur Olson, *Power and Prosperity: Outgrowing Communist and Capitalist Dictatorships*. New York: Basic Books, 2000.

4. Quoted in Tzvetan Todorov, *Hope and Memory*. Princeton: Princeton University Press, 2003, p. 202.

5. John King Fairbank and Merle Goldman, *China: A new history*. Cambridge, Mass.: Belknap Press, 1998, p. 48.

6. Charles Tilly, *The Politics of Collective Violence*. Cambridge: Cambridge University Press, 2003, p. 177.

7. Jessica Williams, *50 Facts that Should Change the World*. London: Icon Books, 2005.

8. According to an IMF economist, one standard deviation in his corruption index was associated with a 0.5 per cent difference in the annual growth rate and a 4 per cent difference in rates of investment. Paolo Mauro, George Abed and Sanjeev Gupta, eds., *Governance, Corruption and Economic Performance*. Washington, DC: International Monetary Fund, 2002. But the elimination of corruption is not simple: the usual bureaucratic response is to increase policing, and regulations, but these can simply drive costs up. The better solutions usually involve simpler processes and more transparency.

9. Carl Schmitt, *The Concept of the Political*. Chicago: University of Chicago Press, 1996; Bertrand de Jouvenel, *On Power*, New York: Viking Press, 1949; Ludwig von Mises, *Die Gemeinwirtschaft: Socialism. An economic and sociological analysis*, trans. J. Kahane. London: Jonathan Cape, 1936.

10. Quincy Wright, *A Study of War*. Chicago: University of Chicago Press, 1964.

11. For the same reasons it may be highly risky to implement transparent economic policies aimed at protecting and promoting property rights, the rule of law, a broadly educated population, low taxes and free trade (fortunately some enlightened despots were willing to take the risk).

12. Abiola had won the previous election, which was suspended by the military.

13. Gallup International, February 2005.

14. The so-called 1978 Gallo Wine Amendment.

15. Bent Flyvbjerg's study of the siting of a bus station in Aarhus. Bent Flyvbjerg, *Rationality and Power: Democracy in Practice*. Chicago: University of Chicago Press, 1998.

16. Presidents with term limits are in a different position, but are usually preoccupied with who will succeed them and whether their work will be continued.

17. Quoted in *Changing Times*, a collection of essays on the civil service, published by the Civil Service Commissioners in 2005.

18. G. D. H. Cole, *Self Government in Industry*. S.I.: Bell, 1917.

19. This was the metaphor used by Sir Richard Wilson, British Cabinet Secretary (head of the civil service) in the early 2000s. His successor, Sir Andrew Turnbull, turned the metaphor upside down and argued that civil servants should amplify and channel politicians' demands.

20. There are exceptions: the use of the American National Guard to protect civil rights in the southern states in the 1960s, or the role of the British army in protecting Northern Irish Catholics in 1969. But these roles are rarely stable and are themselves justified by reference to a higher level of order.

21. Robert Nisbet, *The Twilight of Authority*. Indianapolis: Liberty Fund, 1975.

22. Jack Levy, *War in the Modern Great Power System: 1495–1975*. Lexington: University Press of Kentucky, 1983.

23. Jack Snyder and Edward Mansfield, 'Democratisation and the Danger of War', *International Security*, 20, 1 (1995).

CHAPTER 6

1. M. T. Clanchy, *From Memory to Written Record: England 1066–1307*. Oxford: Blackwell Publishers, 1992.

2. He was remembered by a later emperor, Chien-lung, who wrote: 'although

we were born in different dynasties I respect him for his honesty to his emperor. As emperor myself I hope my ministers take him as an example.'

3. James Scott, *Seeing Like a State: How Certain Schemes to Improve the Human Condition Have Failed*. New Haven, Conn.: Yale University Press, 1999.

4. Julius Kovesi, *Moral Notions*. London: Routledge and Kegan Paul, 1967.

5. Within any society there are what some feminist writers have called the unmarked categories, those attributes that are unthinkingly treated as natural, the measure against which everything else is judged, and states can reinforce their boundaries against the marginal and the deviant.

6. Benjamin Constant, *De l'esprit de conquête*. Neuchâtel: Éditions Ides et Calendes, 1942.

7. Chris Baker and Pasuk Phongpaichit, *A History of Thailand*. Cambridge: Cambridge University Press, 2005.

8. Mao, quoted in Phillip Short, *Mao: A short biography*. London: Hodder and Stoughton, 1999.

9. Mao, in Simon Leys, *Essais sur la chine*. Paris: Robert Laffont, 1998.

10. An extreme version of this argument was made by Michel Foucault in his famous lectures on governmentality. In his account, as states grew they so embraced their societies that the very idea of a sovereign people controlling the state became illusory. Instead power itself governed, disciplining, measuring, policing; government was replaced by governance. This argument tends to drift into circularity; it cannot be tested and gives no criteria by which it could be assessed, and it leaves little space for human action. But it contains some grains of truth in that it accurately hints at the way in which a state can follow an inner logic that is different from the interests around it, or from anyone's intentions.

11. Humberto R. Maturana and Francisco J. Varela, *Autopoiesis and Cognition: The Realization of the Living*. Boston Studies in the Philosophy of Science, Kluwer Academic Publishers, 1979.

12. There is a growing, and fertile, literature on how people make sense of themselves and of their organizations. Karl Weick, *Sensemaking in Organisations*. London: Sage Publications, 1995 is one of the classic texts.

13. The king shared power with an official called the *cihuacoatl*, who oversaw the palace administration (the title literally meant 'snake woman', although the post was always filled by a man).

14. General Rommel was said by his son (who later became mayor of a German city) to have warned him: never believe your own thoughts (let alone your words), a comment that applies with particular strength to politicians and officials.

15. Pierre Bourdieu, *The State Nobility: Elite schools in the field of power*. Cambridge: Polity, 1996, p. 265.

16. Some of this evidence was reviewed in a BBC radio programme on trust: 'Honest Politics', BBC Radio 4, October 2005.

17. A very different example is the handling of food safety in the UK. Confidence in the government's ability to guarantee food safety collapsed in the early 1990s when ministers and government scientists promised that beef was safe even as scientific evidence accumulated on the fatalities associated with BSE, or 'mad cow' disease. Yet later that decade, the combination of a new institution to oversee food safety, open decision-making, and visible use of science with all its ambiguities restored a more reasonable level of trust.

18. Fabian goes on to explain the surprisingly complex origins, or non-origins, of the saying. Johannes Fabian, *Power and Performance: Ethnographic explorations through proverbial wisdom and theater in Shaba, Zaire*. Madison, Wis.: University of Wisconsin Press, 1990.

19. Bertrand de Jouvenel, *On Power*. New York: Viking Press, 1949, p. 116.

20. Clifford Geertz, *Negara: The Theatre State in 19th Century Bali*. Princeton: Princeton University Press, 1980.

21. J. A. Pocock, 'Ritual, Language, Power: An Essay on the Apparent Meanings of Ancient Chinese Philosophy', in Pocock, *Politics, Language and Time: Essays on political thought and history*. Chicago: University of Chicago Press, 1989.

22. C. Diehl, *Byzantium: Greatness and decline*. New Brunswick, NJ: Rutgers University Press, 1957.

23. Michael Walzer, 'On the Role of Symbolism in Political Thought', *Political Science Quarterly*, 82 (1967): 191–204.

24. Charles Goodsell, *The Social Meaning of Civic Space: Studying Political Authority Through Architecture*. Lawrence, Ka.: University Press of Kansas, 1988.

25. The control of history has been another critical battleground in the states' efforts to appear permanent. Without an orthodox account of the past, states risk looking like temporary interlopers. So history has to present an organically evolving community, forged through struggle and oppression, which eventually became sovereign through the state. Renan famously said that nations are communities of shared forgetting as well as shared memory (and that to be a Frenchman it was necessary to 'have forgotten the St Bartholomew's Day massacre').

26. W. Somerset Maugham, *The Moon and Sixpence*. New York: Doran, 1919.

27. Elias Canetti, *Crowds and Power*, trans. C. Stewart. London: Penguin Books, 1981.

28. Hannah Arendt, 'Communicative Power', in Nancy C. M. Hartsock, ed., *Money, Sex, and Power: Toward a Feminist Historical Materialism*. Evanston, Ill.: Northeastern University Press, 1985, pp. 59–74.

29. Hannah Arendt, *On Violence*. New York: Harcourt Brace Jovanovich, 1970, p. 44.

30. Rodney Barker cites the example of the almost invisible set of carvings high up on the Emperor Trajan's column celebrating his victories in Dacia: only a handful of officials would ever come close enough to see them, confirmation, he says, that they were aimed inwards not outwards: Rodney Barker, *Legitimating Identities*. Cambridge: Cambridge University Press, 2001, provides an excellent account of the self-legitimating character of states.

31. Edward Evan Evans-Pritchard, *The Nuer*. Oxford: Clarendon Press, 1940, p. 182.

32. Arthur Miller, *On Politics and the Art of Acting*. New York: Viking, 2001.

33. Claude Lévi-Strauss, *Choses dites*. Paris: Minuit, 1987.

34. Thomas Schelling's work in *Micro-motives and Macro-behaviour*. New York: Norton, 1978, showed how small changes in housing preferences could lead to highly segregated cities.

35. Michael Walzer, *On Toleration*. New Haven, Conn.: Yale University Press, 1997, pp. 16–17.

36. Anthony D. Smith, *Chosen Peoples: Sacred Sources of National Identity*. Oxford: Oxford University Press, 2003.

37. Bhikhu Parekh, *Rethinking Multiculturalism: Cultural Diversity and Political Theory*. Basingstoke: Macmillan, 2000, p. 235.

38. Michael Mann, *The Dark Side of Democracy: Explaining ethnic cleansing*. Cambridge: Cambridge University Press, 2004.

39. Michael Rosen, *On Voluntary Servitude: False Consciousness and the Theory of Ideology*. Cambridge: Polity Press and Cambridge, Mass.: Harvard University Press, 1996, p. 272.

40. Friedrich Nietzsche, *Beyond Good and Evil: Prelude to the Philosophy of the Future*. Edinburgh: Foulis, 1907, section 256.

41. Howard Gardner, *Leading Minds: An Anatomy of Leadership*. London: HarperCollins, 1996.

CHAPTER 7

1. Sri Aurobindo, *Essays Divine and Human*. Pondicherry: Sri Aurobindo Ashram, 1994

2. Muhsin Mahdi, *Alfarabi and the Foundation of Islamic Political Philosophy*, Chicago: University Press of Chicago, 2001, p. 131.

3. Michael Marmot, *Status Syndrome*. London: Bloomsbury Press, 2004.

4. And are only rather lamely explained by reciprocal altruism and the other devices of evolutionary psychology.

5. Michael Ignatieff's *The Needs of Strangers*. London: Chatto & Windus, 1984, remains one of the outstanding accounts of human generosity.

6. A good recent survey of this is Roy Baumeister and Mark R. Leary, 'The Need to Belong: Desire for Interpersonal Attachments as a Fundamental Human Motivation', *Psychological Bulletin*, 117, 3 (1995): 497–529.

7. Robert Trivers developed the concept of reciprocal altruism, further refined by Elliott Sober and David Sloan Wilson, *Unto Others: The Evolution and Psychology of Unselfish Behaviour*. Cambridge, Mass.: Harvard University Press, 1998.

8. Max Weber identified four main types of human action: instrumentally rational, habitual, affectual (or emotional) and value-rational. He tried to think through how certain situations, like wars, move people from one to another. His typology was a helpful corrective to naïve theories that give primacy in human affairs either to raw emotions and identities or to rational self-interest, but it only reinforces just how many different types of behaviour, motive or personality are likely to be found in any population, and often in the same person.

9. For some philosophers this is also why the words 'moral' and 'ethical' are not strictly interchangeable: the first refers to customs and traditions, the second to reason. See Chapter 1, n. 6.

10. Robert Wright's book *NonZero* is one attempt to explain the nature of government through the lens of evolutionary psychology. Robert Wright, *NonZero*. London: Vintage, 2001.

11. Attempts to bring rational consistency to valuations of life generally fall apart, partly because of the political difficulty of acknowledging any risk of death as acceptable, and partly because of the complexity of public attitudes; for example, deaths from road accidents are treated as much more acceptable than deaths from rail accidents because of the greater perceived control of the driver.

12. This action was greeted with scepticism by the media, who assumed it

was a stunt to distract attention from domestic problems the government was facing.

13. What are sometimes described as 'realist' conservative views of how leaders should behave justify a ruthless pragmatism in relation to advisers. According to the realists the leader should never be trapped by loyalty to subordinates. The preservation of power should be the highest goal, and requires utter flexibility and lack of sentiment (this was the view echoed in Mitterrand's advocacy of indifference for leaders).

14. John Fairbank, E. L. Dreyer and F. A. Kierman, eds., *Chinese Ways in Warfare*. Cambridge, Mass.: Harvard University Press, 1974, p. 23.

15. Proportion is all important, and during all but the most total wars many civil liberties, and many restraints on states, can remain in place. Churchill, for example, imprisoned the fascist leader Oswald Mosley during the Second World War, but released him well before its end because he thought that the threat Mosley posed had passed.

16. Gerhard Ritter, in *The Corrupting Influence of Power*. Hadleigh: Tower Bridge Publications, 1952, argued that the utopian tradition of Thomas More and the realist tradition of Machiavelli diverged in the sixteenth century, and did not converge again until Nazism was followed by the Nuremberg trials.

CHAPTER 8

1. Quoted in James MacGregor Burns, *Transforming Leadership*. New York: Atlantic Monthly Press, 2003, p. 80.

2. The *Mahabharata* also rejects the idea that the people have any right to overthrow a ruler: there is no injunction on great epics to be consistent.

3. Al-Mawardi, *The Laws of Islamic Governance*. London: Ta-ha Publishers, 1996.

4. Hasan Hanafi, 'Alternative Conceptions of Civil Society: a reflective Islamic approach', in Sohail Hashmi, ed., *Islamic Political Ethics*. Princeton: Princeton University Press, 2002, p. 60.

5. Wilhelm Reich, *The Mass Psychology of Fascism*. New York: Orgone Institute Press, 1946, p. 53.

6. Described very well in relation to Malaysia in the 1950s and 1960s by James Scott. James Scott, *Weapons of the Weak: Everyday Forms of Peasant Resistance*. New Haven, Conn.: Yale University Press, 1985.

7. President Sadi Carnot, Prime Minister Canovas del Castillo, Empress

Elizabeth, King Umberto and President McKinley were all killed between 1894 and 1901.

8. Although in eastern Germany they did come after Hitler, albeit thanks to the Red Army rather than indigenous revolution.

9. The Bolsheviks and many others did commit some acts of terror, but these did nothing to create the conditions for revolution.

10. Eviatar Zurabel, *Time Maps*. Chicago: University of Chicago Press, 2004, p. 91.

11. It also involved the growth of the notion of the immunity of certain groups and persons from the power of the ruler. Barrington Moore, *Social Origins of Dictatorship and Democracy*. Boston, Ill.: Beacon Press, 1967, p. 414.

12. States like nothing less than inchoate networks, so when, for example, Britain faced a grassroots protest against fuel prices in 2000, one of the government's concerns was to turn the loose network of agitators into a formal organization that could be talked to, and secretly monitored.

CHAPTER 9

1. Norberto Bobbio, *Democracy and Dictatorship*. Polity Press: Cambridge, 1997, p. 84.

2. The links between democracy and growth are complex and not causal. See Darren Acemoglu and Jim Robinson, *Democracy and Autocracy* (forthcoming).

3. Plus another 600,000 in Ireland, a huge proportion of its then population, according to Charles Carlton, *Going to the Wars: The Experience of the British Civil Wars, 1638–1651*. London: Routledge, 1992.

4. Fareed Zakaria, *The Future of Freedom*. New York: W. W. Norton and Co., 2003, is a particularly interesting recent investigation of the subtle relationships between democracy and liberty, and echoes some of these earlier warnings in its advocacy of liberties ahead of full democracy.

5. Museveni preferred instead a politics in which some individuals were allowed to run for election, rather than formal parties. The success of his main opponent, Kizza Besigye's Forum for Democratic Change, in the 2001 election confirmed his doubts.

6. Hans Rosenberg, *Bureaucracy, Aristocracy and Autocracy: The Prussian experience 1660–1815*. Boston: Beacon Press, 1958.

7. Austin Woolrych, *Britain in Revolution*. Oxford: Oxford University Press,

2002, provides the most up-to-date narrative account, and graphically shows how much history was driven forward by unintended consequences.

8. John Dunn, *Setting the People Free: A history of democracy.* London: Atlantic Books, 2005, p. 142.

9. Alois Riklin listed six main innovations to counter the abuse of power. I have added quite a few to the list. A. Riklin, 'Politische Ethik', in H. Kramer, ed., *Politische Theorie und Ideengeschichte im Gesprach.* Vienna, 1995.

10. Adult male Maori won universal suffrage before non-Maori in 1867. The reason is that voting was then still based on property ownership and the Maori held property communally, therefore all had to receive the vote. To avoid being swamped by Maori voters, the government sequestered the Maori into only four seats (a number that remained fixed until electoral reform in 1990s). This is a unique example of a subordinate group gaining rights ahead of others.

11. Michael Wohlgemuth, 'Democracy as an Evolutionary Method', in P. Pelican and G. Wegner, eds., *The Evolutionary Analysis of Economic Policy.* Northampton: Edward Elgar, 2003.

12. Hoyt Cleveland Tillman, *Ch'en Liang* on *Public Interest and the Law.* University of Hawaii Press, 1994, p. 16.

13. Henry de Bracton, *On the laws and customs of England,* c.*1258.* Cambridge, Mass.: Belknap Press, 1968.

14. Heinz Krekeler, who helped to draft Germany's post-war constitution in 1946, is credited with leading the argument against popular sovereignty. See John Lukacs, *Democracy and Populism.* New Haven, Conn.: Yale University Press, 2005.

15. In strict form, concepts of equality are an invention of the modern era, but they have a long ancestry. In Greek, the concept of *isonomia* means literally 'equality of law' and Euripides wrote that 'when the laws are written down the weak and the wealthy have equal rights'. In many other societies too there are norms that are akin to rights (Malinowski wrote of the Melanesians, 'there is a strict distinction and definition in the rights of everyone'). Both cited in Alan Gewirth, *Reason and Morality.* Chicago: University of Chicago Press, 1978, p. 101.

16. James Madison, *The Federalist Papers: Writing of the science of politics.* Harmondsworth: Penguin, 1987.

17. Ryszard Kapuscinski's *The Emperor* describes in detail the strange workings of the court of Emperor Haile Selassie. Ryszard Kapuscinski, *The Emperor.* London: Quartet, 1983.

18. Wallace E. Oates, *Fiscal Federalism.* New York: Harcourt Brace Jovanovich, 1972, is the classic account.

19. In the old system, state enterprises had to submit all their surpluses to the centre; the result of central control was a rollercoaster of incoherence as subsidies lurched up and down with no obvious rationale, whereas local control has proven much more stable (albeit during a period of huge redistribution from poor rural areas to richer urban ones).

20. Quoted in Pranab Bardham, 'Decentralization of Governance and Development', *Journal of Economic Perspectives*, Fall, 2002.

21. The theoretical justification for decentralization is that powers should be held at the level that allows externalities to be internalized (this is known as the 'encompassing principle'). The state's unique role is to see things in the round, but if power is divided into excessively small pockets, the result will be beggar-my-neighbour actions and damaging competition. So in this view local government should be responsible for activities and spending that do not impose any externality on others – waste, water, education, fire – while responsibility for public research, infrastructures, pollution or epidemics should be held at a higher, probably national level. This dividing line is rarely easy to define precisely: some healthcare involves no externalities at all, while some aspects of the containment of infectious disease spread across all jurisdictional boundaries; likewise organized crime can be simultaneously very local in a big city and global in form. Further complicating the issue is the fact that there are often economies of scale in design but not delivery (for example curriculum materials for schools, or training for doctors), just as there are economies of scale in the generation of energy but not in its distribution. Moreover, even when a local authority is acting solely on tasks that do not involve any externalities, its debts can become a burden on the centre.

22. Charles Boix demonstrates that federalism improves the chances of democratic survival. Charles Boix, *Democracy and Redistribution*. Cambridge: Cambridge University Press, 2003.

23. Hannah Arendt, *The Human Condition*. Chicago: University of Chicago Press, 1998, p. 201.

24. The rankings of corruption produced by Transparency International correlate well with rankings of openness. The top places are held by Finland and Sweden. Singapore, which comes fairly near the top, is the one exception that has successfully contained corruption while also maintaining a culture of secrecy.

25. Another paradox of visibility is that the devices designed to weaken central power can have an opposite effect. New knowledge often gives people grounds for making claims because it reveals inequalities and unjustified differences. So federalisms that were intended to lock in decentralization can instead produce demands for greater power at the centre, as poorer

regions make claims for roads or schools, fiscal transfers and universal rights.

26. These principles have come to be so mainstream that they are now applied in other fields as well, including in the economy, where good governance rests on forced competition (the election of directors of public companies), the rule of law, enforced divisions sometimes (when companies grow too big), and requirements to be visible.

27. Quoted in Giorgio Agamben, *State of Exception*. Chicago: University of Chicago Press, 2005, p. 69.

28. The famous tract by Emmanuel Joseph Sieyès, *Qu'est-ce que le tiers état?*' stated this fundamental contradiction most precisely: the constitution presupposes itself as a constituting power.

29. Samuel Finer, *The History of Government from the Earliest Times*. Oxford: Oxford University Press, 1997.

30. Political parties, for all their flaws, have come to do the hard work of synthesizing programmes that have to be consistent, and assembling governing majorities, and they provide a moral discipline that is lacking in polities solely based on individuals, because politicians know that the party as a whole will have to account for any transgressions and corruption.

31. In the eighteenth century Condorcet demonstrated the conditions in which voter preferences may not lead to a stable outcome; two centuries later Kenneth Arrow, in his book *Social Choice and Individual Values*, set out the famous 'impossibility theorem', which showed that whenever there are more than two options voting procedures cannot reliably determine a rank order. Kenneth Arrow, *Social Choice and Individual Values*. New York: John Wiley & Sons, 1963.

32. Jensen and Meckling pioneered the academic work on agency costs, within the broader tradition of work on principal–agent problems. *Democracy in Crisis*. Sydney: The Centre for Independent Studies, 1983.

33. Alexis de Tocqueville, *Democracy in America*, Vol. 1. New York: Alfred A. Knopf, 1945, p. 260.

34. Fear helped these pragmatic conclusions. For countries evolving into democracy, such as Germany or Spain in the early twentieth century, it was too risky to reform or dismantle a state well designed for war. So each new democracy found an accommodation with the military, and compromised with the bankers and the diplomats.

35. George Bernard Shaw, *Transition*, Fabian Essays in Socialism. London: Fabian Society, 1889.

36. In business a crude, but popular, stance says that the only duty of managers is to maximize shareholder value; its parallel in politics says that

the only moral duty of leaders is to do what electors want and to follow public opinion.

37. I have written extensively about this in G. J. Mulgan, *Politics in an Antipolitical Age*. Cambridge: Polity Press, 1994.

38. *Status Syndrome* by Sir Michael Marmot is an excellent up-to-date synthesis of the growing research on the links between inequality and powerlessness and poor health. Michael Marmot, *Status Syndrome*. London: Bloomsbury, 2004. The World Health Organization's commission on the social determinants of health will undoubtedly deepen knowledge in this area.

39. This has been shown by Claude Steele and the theorists of stereotype threat in research conducted over many decades, for example showing how white males' performance declines if, before tests, they are told that white males do worse than Asians. There is roughly the same – substantial – gap in IQ between American whites and blacks as there is between majorities and oppressed minorities in India, Japan and Israel. For a summary see *Scientific American*, February 2005, p. 22.

40. Having started out as what we would today term an anarchist utopian, believing that the state would wither away, Winstanley came to believe that laws would be necessary against the spirit of unreasonable ignorance.

41. Alan Macfarlane, *The Origins of English Individualism*. Oxford: Blackwell, 1978.

42. Dietrich Rueschemeyer, Evelyne Huber Stephens and John D. Stephens, *Capitalist Development and Democracy*. Chicago: University of Chicago Press, 1992, provided the definitive account of the role of the organized working class in the spread of democracy.

43. Daron Acemoglu and James Robinson, 'A Theory of Political Transitions', MIT Department of Economics Working Paper No. 99–26, SSRN, 1999.

44. Robert T. Deacon, 'Dictatorship, Democracy and the Provision of Public Goods', Department of Economics, University of California Santa Barbara, Departmental Working Paper, 2003.

45. David Stasavage, 'Democracy and Education Spending in Africa', Discussion Paper DEDPS/37, London School of Economics, 2003.

46. The pressure for rights at work has generally come from labour movements. These include the European Union's attempts to formalize workers' rights to consultation, and Germany's long-standing representation for workers on supervisory boards.

47. Robert Michels, *Political Parties: A sociological study of the oligarchical tendencies of modern democracy*. New York: Free Press, 1949.

48. Charles Tilly, *Social Movements 1768 to 2004*. Boulder, Colo.: Paradigm

Publishers, 2004, includes a good analysis of the advances and limitations of the Internet as a tool for civic organization.

CHAPTER 10

1. Some environments seem particularly well suited to breeding this charismatic power. Clifford Geertz described a Morocco in which 'charismatic adventurers were constantly arising on all sides', where the 'power of god appeared in the exploits of forceful men'. Other parts of the Muslim world did not fit Ibn Khaldun's picture so well. Clifford Geertz, *Islam Observed: Religious development in Morocco.* New Haven, Conn.: Yale University Press, 1968.

2. Sorokin's argument, which drew on the arts rather than politics, recognizes that different art forms may be moving in opposite directions at any one point in time.

3. Charles de Montesquieu, *De l'Esprit des lois* VIII, chapter I, 1748.

4. Christian Meier, *Caesar*. London: HarperCollins, 1995, p. 133.

5. Some have cast this cycle as one of demoralization. Every civilization, so the argument goes, is born out of a search for oneness and transcendence – the burning passion of the nomads in Ibn Khaldun's account who were often in north African history inspired by a purer, more traditional version of Islam. In maturity, every civilization becomes attached to the search for material things, things in this world: territory, goods and power. Those within it become split between their inner world, from which they draw their energy, and an outer material world that is equally compelling in its claims for obedience. Modern western civilization finds itself at just such a point: separated from a religious world, a world where people felt free in submission and obedience to something larger than themselves – a demanding, stern, but honourable God – and, instead, in a corrupted and mature civilization, where the only measure is the self and the self's own pleasure.

6. *www.outlookindia.com*, 16 January 2006.

CHAPTER 11

1. Nyanaponika Thera's best-known book is *The Heart of Buddhist Meditation*, which sets out in detail what is probably the purist and most rationalist account of Buddhist practice. Nyanaponika Thera, *The Heart of Buddhist Meditation*. Sri Lanka: Buddhist Publication Society, 1992.

2. Norbert Elias' work constitutes the most powerful sustained argument for the idea that civilization is a process whereby people learn to contain emotions and angers, and to restrain the tendency to use violence.

3. Josephine Chiu-Duke, *To Rebuild the Empire: Lu Chih's Confucian Pragmatist Approach to the Mid-T'ang Predicament.* SUNY Series in Chinese Philosophy and Culture. Albany, NY: State University of New York Press, 2000, p. 78.

4. The various kinds of psychometric testing, simulations and role plays used to screen people for senior positions or positions of responsibility in other sectors remain absent from politics.

5. Max Weber, *Economy and Society*, Vol. 1, trans. Guenther Roth and Claus Wittich. Berkeley: University of California Press, 1968, p. 31.

6. Occasionally moral infractions are decisively punished, as when Indira Gandhi was dismissed by the Indian electorate in 1979 for the excesses of the emergency, including the forced sterilization of thousands of men. The Italian Christian Democrats also disintegrated at the ballot box, as scandal piled upon scandal. Yet Mrs Gandhi was soon returned to power, and often the most ethically dubious triumph, especially if the public never learn about their infractions from a pliant media.

7. These ideas begin with Confucius' prescriptions of duty based on the fundamental relationships of ruler and minister, father and son, elder brother and younger, husband and wife, friend and friend, but extend far beyond.

8. Chiu-Duke, op. cit., p. 92.

9. Muhsin Mahdi, *Alfarabi and the Foundation of Islamic Political Philosophy.* Chicago: University of Chicago Press, 2001, pp. 86–7, provides a detailed account of his rather complex views on the links between experience and science.

10. A good example of the difference can be found in Robert Greenleaf's account of servant leadership. Greenleaf sees Jesus in the story of the adulterous woman as an example for all leaders. Confronted by the angry crowd Jesus drew in the sand, detaching himself from the situation and finding himself some time for the creative insight to come: 'let him that is without sin amongst you throw the first stone.' Robert Greenleaf, *Servant Leadership.* New York: Paulist Press, 1977.

11. As Robert McNamara, who was then US Secretary of Defense, has shown this was a classic example of how the ability to empathize with the enemy can make the difference between success and disaster. Cited in the film *The Fog of War.*

12. Michael Walzer, 'Political Action: The Problem of Dirty Hands', *Philosophy and Public Affairs*, 2, 2 (1973): 177.

13. Nagouib Mahfouz's novel *Akhnaton* is a particularly good imagination of what it felt like to see an all-powerful pharaoh attempt a revolution from above, and then succumb to failure. Nagouib Mahfouz, *Akhnaton: Dweller in Truth*. Cairo: Amir University Press, 2000.

14. Dennis Thompson, *Restoring Responsibility*. Cambridge: Cambridge University Press, 2005.

15. David Hume wrote of 'artificial virtues' that are defined by their fit with the functions of a profession or institution, and officials' virtues are very much of this kind. David Hume, *A Treatise of Human Nature*, eds. David Fate Norton and Mary J. Norton. Oxford: Clarendon Press, 2000.

16. Francisco Varela, *Ethical Know-how*. Stanford, Calif.: Stanford University Press, 1999.

17. Jonathan Glover, *Humanity: A Moral History of the Twentieth Century*. New Haven, Conn.: Yale Nota Bene, 2001.

18. Bhikhu Parekh, *Rethinking Multiculturalism*. Cambridge, Mass.: Harvard University Press, 2002, p. 205.

19. The consequence of this moral pluralism is that all functioning societies turn out to depend on institutions in their midst that carry radically different values and moral syndromes while sharing some more basic rules and values. Most functioning liberal societies include, and perhaps even depend on, institutions that are radically illiberal, including religions of revealed truth, families within which the majority may have minimal rights, and hierarchical corporations that make no pretence at democracy. The most ardent theocracies turn out to rest on pockets of scientific reason, as in the case of Iran's programme for nuclear power.

20. James MacGregor Burns, *Leadership*. London: HarperCollins, 1985.

21. That King Canute's story is usually misremembered as an example of royal hubris only reinforces the story's unusual character.

22. If they saw their skill as a gift, perhaps leaders would be more willing to learn, to practise and to train in order to enhance it. The most gifted musicians do not assume that they are born fully competent; yet most rulers and officials are remarkably under-prepared for their roles – the former lacking even the most elementary formal training and reflection, the latter rarely kept up to date with the interdisciplinary knowledge needed to steer complex systems in states that are much larger and much more demanding in their accountabilities than the states of the past.

23. Lewis Hyde, *The Gift*. New York: Vintage, 1983.

CHAPTER 12

1. Bertrand de Jouvenel, *On Power*. New York: Viking Press, 1949.

2. Thinkers as diverse as Gaetano Mosca, Joseph Schumpeter and Richard Posner have made arguments of this kind.

3. Julia Darling, quoted in the *Guardian* newspaper, 11 September 2004.

4. Quoted in Quentin Skinner, *Visions of Politics: Renaissance Virtues*. Cambridge: Cambridge University Press, 2002, p. 16.

5. Thomas Aquinas, *De Regno*, in *Aquinas: Selected Political Writings*, trans. J. G. Dawson, ed. A. P. d'Entrèves. Totowa, NJ: Barnes & Noble, 1981 (originally published Oxford: Blackwell, 1948).

6. There is an uncomfortable parallel in Hitler's life that confirms that compelling rhetoric and moral virtue are wholly unrelated. After his first speech to the People's Court in Munich during the trial in March 1924 for his disastrous attempted *coup d'état*, one of the judges said, 'What a tremendous chap this Hitler is.'

7. Albert Camus, *The Rebel*. Paris: Gallimard, 1951, and Paul Berman, *Terrorism and Liberalism*. W. W. Norton & Company, 2004, explore the often-strange psychologies of rebels who turn towards death and suicide.

8. Charles Tilly, *Social Movements 1768 to 2004*. Boulder, Colo.: Paradigm Publishers, 2004, describes these as the four main messages that social movements seek to communicate.

9. The Jain philosophers famously said to Alexander the Great: 'You are but human like the rest of us and will soon be dead and then will own just as much of the earth as will suffice to bury you.'

10. Cited in Amartya Sen, 'Democracy and its global roots', *New Republic*, October 2003, p. 28.

11. These were not in any way democratic, but they are interesting for our purposes precisely because they were concerned with the conduct of the people.

12. Even James Buchanan, the leading advocate of public choice theory, wrote of the definition of democracy as government by discussion and pointed out that this implies that individual values can and do change in the process of decision-making.

13. John Gaventa, 'Strengthening participatory approaches to local governance: learning the lessons from abroad', *National Civic Review*, Winter 2004, p. 16.

14. Rosabeth Moss Kanter, *Commitment and Community: Communes and*

utopias in sociological perspective. Cambridge, Mass.: Harvard University Press, 1972, provides a good comparison of the communes of the 1840s and the 1960s.

15. Quoted in Dennis Thompson, *Restoring Responsibility.* Cambridge: Cambridge University Press, 2005, p. 211.

16. James Harrington, *The Commonwealth of Oceana,* 1656.

17. Skinner, op. cit.

18. David Halpern, *Social Capital.* Oxford: Polity, 2005.

19. Pierre Bourdieu and Terry Eagleton, 'Doxa and common life', *New Left Review,* 19, 1 (1992): 111–21.

20. Richard Wilkinson, 'Commentary: liberty, fraternity, equality', *Int J Epidemiology,* 3, 1 (2002): 538–43.

21. The French Revolution, for example, 'did not destroy, but consolidated the administrative organization of the old regime by sweeping away its feudal inconsistencies and uncovering its logical structure', which was a rationalized hierarchy of command and allocation of duties and responsibilities. State administration under the Code Napoléon 'was to learn to govern France without ever losing continuity through successive periods of revolution'. Judith A. Merkle, *Management and Ideology: The Legacy of the International Scientific Management Movement.* Berkeley: University of California Press, 1980.

22. De Jouvenel took this argument a step further. In his account of the growth of the power of states he suggested that governments grew by offering to relieve individuals from burdensome social obligations (such as educating their children or taking care of their parents in their old age). In other areas they intervened on people's behalf where they were the weaker party (for example, siding with employees in recasting the relationships between them and their employers). The deals that resulted made people feel loyal to the state in exchange for being empowered against others and released from traditional obligations. According to de Jouvenel this process ultimately created individuals who were free from all social ties – solitary figures who relate to everyone else only by and through the state. A very similar argument could be made about the capitalist market (one of the many flaws of de Jouvenel's account is that it ignores other kinds of power and domination). As such the servant state becomes morally strengthened by its greater activism and the people, who are in principle the masters, become weakened. De Jouvenel, op. cit.

23. Richard Posner makes a similar argument in *Law, Pragmatism and Democracy.* Cambridge, Mass: Harvard University Press, 2003.

24. See Geoff Mulgan and Tom Steinberg, *Wide Open: Open source methods and their future potential.* London: Demos, 2005.

25. David Halpern, Clive Bates, Geoff Mulgan and Stephen Aldridge with Greg Beales and Adam Heathfield, 'Personal Responsibility and Changing Behaviour', Prime Minister's Strategy Unit, Cabinet Office, 2004.
26. James Hillman, *Kinds of Power*. New York: Doubleday, 1995, pp. 66 ff.
27. John Stuart Mill, *Considerations on Representative Government*, 1861, p. 390.
28. Herbert Spencer, *Essays*, Vol. III. London: Williams & Norgate, 1863, pp. 72–3.

CHAPTER 13

1. Aaron Wildavsky, *Speaking Truth to Power: Art and Craft of Policy Analysis*. New Brunswick, NJ: Transaction Books, 1987.
2. Marx's impatience with evidence on the grounds that appearances are likely to be systematically distorted also sits uncomfortably in a culture eager for facts and analysis. Some would say it was also not wholly unconnected with Lenin's infamous order: 'Shoot more professors!'
3. Competitive commercial markets, for example, can appear as natural as the competitive struggles between creatures in a pond or a jungle. But they are very much human creations, governed by conventions, laws and regulations. They can appear to give each worker or trader a fair price for such things as forty hours spent cleaning floors, or a kilo of coffee beans. Yet these prices reflect deeper-rooted relationships of power and exploitation.
4. Simon Schama, *Citizens*. New York: Viking, 1989.
5. Derek Bok, *The Trouble with Government*. Cambridge, Mass.: Harvard University Press, 2001; Derek Bok, *The State of the Nation*. Cambridge, Mass.: Harvard University Press, 1996.
6. Mori.com.
7. Proposition 184 in California, for example, enshrined the rule that mandated long prison terms for third-time offenders ('three strikes and you're out'). This was a classic instance of the mutually amplifying distortions of populist politics and irresponsible media. The idea helped the politicians who promoted it. But early applications of this rule included a 25-year sentence for a man whose third offence was the theft of a slice of pizza, and a similar term for a third-time offender who stole a pack of cigarettes; very few of the people who had voted for this proposition knew that these would be its likely effects.
8. As important as the media are the other art forms. Within literature and film it is rare to find realistic portrayals of politics and government. Far more

common are cartoon caricatures, usually of scheming duplicity. In American culture, Presidents are generally portrayed either as uncomplicated heroes – from *Independence Day* to *The West Wing* – or as villains. In British culture the gamut has been run from *Yes, Minister*, which presents officials as cynically manipulative and politicians as vain and stupid, to *House of Cards*, in which politicians happily murder to advance their careers. Otherwise sophisticated people sometimes conclude that this is what politics is really like.

9. Factcheck in the USA, which assesses the claims made in Presidential elections, is a good model of how this can be done – based in a university, funded by foundations, and beholden to no one but the truth.

10. *'Kaozhengxue'*.

11. In retrospect it would have been preferable to have followed a different policy of inoculation; however, at the time powerful farming interests were set against it.

12. J. Best, ed., *Images of Issues: Typifying Contemporary Social Problems.* New York: Aldine de Gruyter, 1989; H. Blummer, 'Social Problems as Collective Behavior', *Social Problems*, 18 (1971): 298–306; J. I. Kitsuse and J. W. Schneider, 'Preface' in J. Best, ed., *Images of Issues: Typifying Contemporary Social Problems.* New York: Aldine de Gruyter, 1989, pp. xi–xiv; D. R. Loseke, *Thinking about Social Problems.* New York: Aldine de Gruyter, 1997; M. Spector and J. I. Kitsuse, *Constructing Social Problems.* New York: Aldine de Gruyter, 1977.

13. Jonathan Glover provides the best recent account of the moral ambiguities of mass bombings and concentration camps. Jonathan Glover, *Humanity: A Moral History of the Twentieth Century.* New Haven, Conn.: Yale Nota Bene, 2001.

14. Samuel Paul, *Holding the State to Account: Citizen monitoring in action.* Bangalore: Books for Change, 2002.

15. The partnership between states, companies and NGOs, which has formed around the Extractive Industries Transparency Initiative to reduce the temptations for resource-rich states to line their own pockets at the expense of their citizens, is a possible harbinger of a new method of validation.

16. The Gulags continued the Tsarist tradition, but their scale and models of organization were of a different order.

17. Most of the key innovations of the twentieth century resulted from work in universities. See John Kay, *The Truth about Markets.* London: Allen Lane, 2005, pp. 260 ff.

18. See Geoff Mulgan and David Albury, 'Public sector innovation', Cabinet

Office, 2003. This paper was prepared both to describe new approaches to innovation that had been introduced into the UK government, and to fill a gap: we could find no written synthesis setting out a theoretical framework and practical examples of innovation in public organizations.

CHAPTER 14

1. In Henry Kissinger, *Diplomacy*. New York: Simon & Schuster, 1994.

2. Hans Morgenthau, *Politics Among Nations*, 5th edn. New York: Alfred A. Knopf, 1978, p. 42.

3. According to the UK-based Iraq Body Count and Oxford Research Group.

4. Rupert Smith, *The Utility of Force*. London: Allen Lane, 2005, is a good recent overview.

5. 'The Human Security Report', Human Security Centre, University of British Columbia, 2005.

6. As Richard Rorty put it: 'National pride is to countries what self-respect is to individuals: a necessary condition for self-improvement. Too much national pride can produce bellicosity and imperialism just as excessive self-respect can produce arrogance.' Richard Rorty, *Achieving Our Country: Leftist thought in twentieth-century America*. Cambridge, Mass.: Harvard University Press, 1998.

7. Alan Gewirth takes this argument several steps further, suggesting that the very step of acting in any way entails a set of assumptions about the universal nature of morality. Alan Gewirth, *Reason and Morality*. Chicago: University of Chicago Press, 1977.

8. Stanley Hoffman, *Duties Beyond Borders: On the Limits and Possibilities of Ethical International Politics*. Syracuse, NY: Syracuse University Press, 1981.

9. Michael Walzer, *Just and Unjust Wars*. New York: Basic Books, 1977.

10. Montesquieu, *Persian Letters*. Harmondsworth: Penguin, 1998, p. 235.

11. Francisco de Vitoria, in Anthony Pagden and Jeremy Lawrance eds., *Vitoria: Political Writings*. Cambridge: Cambridge University Press, 1991, pp. 315–16.

12. Geir Lundestad, *'Empire' by Integration: The United States and European Integration, 1945–1997*. Oslo: University of Oslo, 1997.

13. I talk of global government rather than a global state, since it cannot credibly claim a monopoly.

14. Philip Bobbitt, *The Shield of Achilles*. New York: Alfred A. Knopf, 2002, p. 228.

15. Washington presents itself as Rome's successor, superseding the various other cities, from Constantinople to Moscow, which have laid claim to this role in the past. Washington shares with ancient Rome a Senate, an admiration for Cicero, and the strange admixture of intense Christianity and hedonism that marked Rome in its later years. Both empires were founded on distinctive ideas of morality and power. The Chinese model was, even at an early stage, intensive and almost totalitarian (the Han, having replaced the competing states that preceded it, employed 20 times as many civil servants per head of the population as Rome, which survived without anything resembling a modern permanent bureaucracy). China was founded on rituals and behaviour, and woven together in a tapestry of duties, obligations and behaviours with the emperor at the top. Rome's formative experience was very different. Like the USA it was born out of resistance to monarchical power.

16. Its strategic goals are captured by the concept, developed by Chinese political thinkers, of Comprehensive National Power (CNP), a single number that brings together various indices of military, economic and cultural power, whose maximization is a national priority.

17. The work of the World Values Survey and Ronald Inglehart suggests that values are becoming more, not less, diverse, even though there are some common directions of change associated with economic prosperity and peace.

18. Michael Walzer, *Thick and Thin*. Notre Dame, Ind.: University of Notre Dame Press, 1994.

19. Hans Kelsen, *Peace Through Law*. Chapel Hill: University of North Carolina Press, 1944 (reprinted 2001 by The Lawbook Exchange); Hans Kelsen, *The Law of the United Nations: A Critical Analysis of Its Fundamental Problems*. New York: Frederick A. Praeger, 1964 (reprinted 2000 by The Lawbook Exchange); Hans Kelsen, *General Theory of Law and State*, trans. Anders Wedberg. Cambridge, Mass.: Harvard University Press, 1949.

20. Martin Loughlin, *The Idea of Public Law*. Oxford: Oxford University Press, 2003, p. 90.

21. 'The Responsibility to Protect', Report of the International Commission on Intervention and State Sovereignty, International Development Research Centre, 2001.

22. It would be remarkable if such a backlash did not occur at some point, led by the citizens of the rich north.

23. Easy access to drinking water is defined by the WHO as being within 1.6 km.

24. Gallup International Survey, 2005.

25. Committee of Independent Experts, 'First Report on Allegations regarding

Fraud, Mismanagement and Nepotism in the European Commission',
15 March 1999.
26. These comments come from Deloitte's survey of UN staff in the summer of
2004. 'United Nations Organizational Integrity Survey', prepared by Deloitte
Consulting LLP, 2004 (*www.un.org/news/ossg/sg/integritysurvey*).
27. 'How The World Sees Europe: Who Will Lead The World?' A 22-nation
public opinion poll by Globescan, April 2005.

CHAPTER 15

1. Avner Offer, *Why Has the Public Sector Grown so Large in Market
Societies?* Oxford: Oxford University Press, 2003, provides an original
interpretation of the shifting balance between prudence and visceral spending.
2. Yehezkel Dror has been the most consistent advocate of more strategic
government, including in his book *The Capacity to Govern: A report to the
Club of Rome*. Frank Cass, London, 2001. My book, *The Art of Strategy*, to
be published by Oxford University Press in 2007, sets out in more detail how
and why governments should try to improve their ability to think and act
strategically.
3. The phrase was used by Milton and Rose Friedman as the title of their
book *The Tyranny of the Status Quo*. New York: Harcourt, 1984.
4. Bertrand de Jouvenel, *The Pure Theory of Politics*, New Haven, Conn.:
Yale University Press, 1963, p. 211.

CHAPTER 16

1. Hegel's confidence that the state had reached its evolutionary end point is
a helpful warning to the many writers who have convinced themselves that
their lifetime happened to coincide with the end of history and evolution.
2. Far more evidence is now available on how different nations and governments perform. Sweeping generalizations that attribute to any group of causal
factors a set of social results are risky. Another turn of the wheel can turn
one decade's winners into the next decade's losers. But there are some broad
correlations between performance across a wide range of indicators and
features of system design. Those nations which are performing best in economic, social and environmental terms tend to be smaller nations with very
open systems in their economy and in politics, that is to say systems that
reward performance and innovation; deeply entrenched democratic cultures;

very low levels of corruption; and high levels of human and social capital. These nations, including Finland, the Netherlands and Singapore, have found ways to align internal capacities with the external environment. Interestingly, too, they are often nations that have experienced traumatic crises and have had to renew themselves. The UK Government's Strategic Audit (published in November 2003 and January 2005) brought together a summary analysis of relative performance across many nations and an explanation as to why some countries were doing so well.

3. Samuel Finer, *The History of Government from the Earliest Times*, Vol.1. Oxford: Oxford University Press, 1997, p. 14.

Index

Abacha, Sani 82
accountability 172, 177, 213–14
accuracy, media 261
activism 193, 226–7, 233, 242, 243, 292
Acton, Lord 206, 268
Adams, John 12
Adler, Alfred 128–9
advisers 9, 143
Africa 191, 286
Akbar 57, 255
Akhenaten 214
Akihito 156
al-Qaeda 225
Alexander the Great 139
Algeria 154, 184
alienation 204, 229
altruism 130
America *see* US
anarchy 157
anti-democracy 163–4
anti-social behaviour (ASBOs) 98
apathy 228
Aquinas, Thomas 194, 230
architecture 112
Arendt, Hannah 117, 175
Argentina 161–2
Aristotle 4, 9, 55, 60, 199, 249
asabiya 198

Ashoka 29, 49
Assad, Hafez 113
Athens 4, 235
Attlee, Clement 136, 224
authoritarianism 40
autocracies 82, 164
autopoiesis 104
Azo 230

bad government, allegory 2–3
Bakunin 153
Basil I: 171
Beckett, Samuel 1
Belgium 167
Bentham, Jeremy 50, 68–9
Berlusconi, Silvio 84, 230
Bettelheim, Bruno 124
biases, state actions 88–9
Bimbisara 9
Bin Laden, Osama 225
Blair, Tony 84, 203, 257
Bobbitt, Philip 41, 288
Bok, Derek 259
Bolivia 173, 236, 267
bonding 131–2
Booth, Charles 100
Bourdieu, Pierre 106, 118
Brandt, Willy 223
Brazil 190, 236
Brecht, Bertolt 119–20

Britain
  18th century 34
  1930s 200
  bureaucracy 32, 185
  civil service 216–17
  foot-and-mouth disease 262
  revolution 158
  see also England
British Empire 113–14
Buddha 4, 9
bureaucracy
  actions 87
  Britain 32, 185
  innovation 269
  Prussia 32
  public opinion 41
  Sumeria 19
  totalitarian regimes 265
  US 32
Bush, George W. 86, 182, 230,
  254
business 175, 183, 193
Byzantine empire 110, 216

Cabet, Etienne 237
cameralist movement 31
Camus, Albert 141
Canada 282
Canetti, Elias 115
Canute, King 224
capitalism 37, 38, 73
Castro, Fidel 113, 154, 208
categories 98–9
categorization 100–102
cause-based activism 193
centralization 173
Chadli Benjedid 184
Chandragupta 9
Charles IX 111
Ch'en Liang 49, 168
Chesterfield, Lord 119

Chile 173
China
  ancient 150
  Confucius 30
  constitution 170
  deaths 47
  Han dynasty 25
  imperium 289, 290, 291
  land reform 191–2
  leaders' ethics 210–11
  Mao 101
  Ming dynasty 235
  modern state 14, 173
  officials 216
  realism 274
  ritual violence 23
  rulers 3
  SARs outbreak 262
  Shen Pu-hai 30
  traditions of power 5, 24, 46–7,
    80, 157–8
  welfare 37
  Zhou dynasty 19
Chirac, Jacques 230
Chosroes I 87
Christianity 254
Chu Hsi 210
Churchill, Sir Winston
  career 203
  Hitler 138
  miners 47
  Pearl Harbor 212
  personal qualities 214
  Second World War 136, 224
  Singapore 213
  truth 137
  war 89
Cicero 60
citizens 240, 249–50, 272
citizenship 241–5, 303–5, 321
civic activism 242

civil services 216–17
Civil War, English 162–3, 165
climate change 296–7, 299
Clinton, Bill 215
co-ordination 22, 301
Cobbett, William 227
cognitive coherence 102–3, 104
Cold War 293
Cole, G. D. H. 87
commons 21, 298
communes 237
communication, commercial 260
communism 36, 72–3
communities 22–3, 318
community 70, 309
conditional global citizenship 303–5
conditional rights 244–5, 321
Condorcet, Marquis de 52
confidentiality 178
Confucian tradition 249
Confucius 9, 26, 210
conscription 92
conservative politics 75–6
Constant, Benjamin 99
constitutions 57, 168, 169, 170,
    182, 236
consumerist model, representation
    186
contestability 166–8, 301
conversations 235, 247
corruption 81, 200
corvees 25
Cromwell, Oliver 168, 188
cultural traits, societies 15
cycles 196–204
cynicism 13, 260

de Gaulle, Charles 47, 100, 203
de Tocqueville see Tocqueville,
    Alexis de
debt financing 139

decentralization 173–4, 175
deductive reasoning 8, 9
Deioces 116
democracy
    contradiction 243
    as conversation 235–7
    disadvantages 6
    disillusion with 41
    early 19, 189
    equality 187–92
    evolution 313
    happiness 71
    history of 227, 231
    ideal 231
    interests 82–3
    leaders 86
    mature 40–41
    mechanisms 186
    moral advantage 6
    nature of 227–8
    newer 236
    passive 229–31
    people 251
    radical forms 246
    representative 37
    rise of 161–2
    scale 181
    self-government 194–5
    service 38, 287
    sustainable 40
    wars 35–6, 91
democratic welfare capitalism 36–9
Democrats (US) 83
demonstrations 233–5
detachment 212–13, 265
dialectics 253
Dicey, Albert Venn 176
dictatorships 33, 46, 86, 180
Dionysius 9
Disraeli, B. 46
distribution 52, 53

divisions 171–6
Durkheim, Emile 111

early states 18–20
Ebert, Friedrich 47
Eisenhower, Dwight 67
elections 78, 166–7, 184
emergency powers 179–80
emperors 18
empires 19, 276
Engels, Friedrich 157
England 24, 25, 51, 162, 189
  see also Britain
English Civil War 162–3, 165
English Parliament 180
entrepreneurs 237, 239
environmental polices 191
equal rights 171
equality 36–7, 187–92
Erasmus, Desiderius 209
ethics
  leaders 4, 210–15
  learning 218–20
  media 257–61
  officials 215–17
Europe 24, 25, 33, 304
European Commission 302
European Union 99, 267, 292, 293,
  300
Evans, Harold 260
Evans-Pritchard, Edward Evan 108,
  119

Fa-Hian 29
families 70, 72
  as metaphor 73–7
Farabi, Abu Nasr al- 49, 127,
  212
Fascism 37
federalism 173
Finer, Samuel 29, 316–17

First World War 92, 93
foot-and-mouth disease 262
Fourier, Charles 237
Fox, George 232
France 24, 25, 157, 158, 173
franchise 166, 190
Franco, Francisco 113
fraternity 36, 37
Frederick the Great 31, 56
free-riders 241–2
freedom
  exercise of 229
  good life 68
  human needs 69
  of information 177
  limiting 93–4
  press 252
French Revolution 34, 36, 258
Frey, Bruno 71
Fuentes, Carlos 5
fundamental attribution error 4
future 306–11, 322

Gandhi, Mahatma 223, 232
Gaulle see de Gaulle
GDP (gross domestic product) 38
generous politics 53
Genghis Khan 97
genocide 40, 77, 123, 265
Germany 35, 47, 82, 162, 169
Gilder, George 239
Gitlin, Todd 234
Gladstone, William 146
global government 287–305
global institutions 7, 293–4,
  301–2
global issues 6–7, 272–305
Godwin, William 141
Goebbels, J. 46, 57–8
Goering, H. W. 46
golden rule 134–5

good, meanings of 145–6
Gorbachev, Mikhail 100
government
 bad, allegory of 2–3
 complexity 229
 darker side 5–6
 evolution 313
 global 287–305
 good *see* good government
 knowledge 252–3
 morality 5, 221
 roots 15–17
 service 7–8
 tasks 4–5
 tools 39
 trust 107, 243
 truth 268
 views of 222
 well-being, effect on 2
 see also states
Graunt, John 31, 100
Great Britain *see* Britain
Greater London Council 246
Greeley, Horace 237
Gysi, Gregor 167

Hadfield, Mark 277
Haile Selassie 208
Hammurabi 55
happiness 1–2, 45, 49–50, 53,
 68–71
Harcourt, Sir William 37
Harrington, James 188, 239–40
health 244, 248
Hegel, Georg 66–7, 238, 312
Henry VIII 25, 115
Henry de Bracton 168
Heraclitus 90
Herder, Johann Gottfried 121
Hirohito 156
Hirschmann, Albert 242

Hitler, Adolf 35, 67, 139, 208,
 214
Hobbes, Thomas 9, 64–5, 128, 129,
 163
Holmes, Oliver Wendell 51
Hotta Masayoshi 35
Hu Tsung-hsien 143–4
human nature 129
human needs 69–73, 318
Hume, David 62, 131
Hun Sen 307
Huntingdon, Samuel 162
Hussein, Saddam 91, 113, 184

Ibn Khaldun 197, 307
Ibn Saud 67
ideas, emulation of 33–5
identification 120–26
imperial identity 35
imperialists, modern 113
imperiums 289–91
income inequalities 243
income levels 40
income tax 33
India
 ancient 150
 Ashoka 29
 decentralization 173–4
 democracy 167
 famine 52
 Guptan Empire 29
 politics 183
 rulers 3–4, 20, 211
 traditions of power 5
innovation 268–70
intelligence agencies 266
interests 83, 279, 281
international affairs 274, 279–80,
 281–7
International Anarchist Congress
 (1881) 153

international law 7, 296
International Monetary Fund
 267
International Panel on Climate
 Change (IPCC) 299
Internet 193, 236, 247
Iran 155
Iraq 276
Islam, Shia 150–51
Islamic caliphate 29
Islamic tradition 150–51
Ivan IV 64

Jalolov, Abdulkhafiz 236
Japan
 constitution 169
 deaths 47
 democracy 162
 Koizumi 124
 leaders 116
 occupation of 156
 strategy 35
Jefferson, Thomas 149
Johnson, Lyndon 238
judgements, life and death 135
just war theory 277, 283
justice 55–7, 298–9, 301, 318

Kadivar, Mohsen 231
Kant, Immanuel 137, 185, 274,
 289
Kao Tsu 109
Karamzin, Nikolai 79
Kautilya 9, 58–9, 206, 253
Kelsen, Hans 295–6
Kennedy, John Fitzgerald 213
Keynes, John Maynard 262
Khomeini, Ayatollah 158
King, Martin Luther 232
kings 18
Kissinger, Henry 217

knowledge 30–32, 57–8
 architecture of 98
 global 299
 in government 252–3
 independent sources 261
 states' dependence on 261–6
Kohler, Foy 213
Koizumi, Yoichi 124, 203

labour, organized 190
laissez-faire 51
Lakoff, George 75
land reform 190–91, 191–2
Lao Tzu 251
larger countries 310
Latin America 170
laws 4, 55, 168–71, 296
Laws of Manu 55
leaders
 advisers to 9
 behaviour 138
 ethics 4, 210–15
 great 214, 223–5
 interests 81
 legitimation 106
 personal qualities 214–15
 power 104–5, 110–12, 114
 predatory 18
 qualities 206–8
 renewal 203
 respect 112
 salaries 61
 states' evolution 34
 survival 86
 temptations 147–8
 transformational 223
 understanding 212
leaks 178, 264
Lebanon 167
Lee Kuan Yew 115
Legalists 44, 56

legitimation 58–60, 105–7, 117
LeMay, Curtis 213
Lenin, Vladimir Ilyich 79–80, 154
Leroy-Beauliey, Pierre Paul 63
Levi-Strauss, Claude 120–21
liberal societies 48
liberalism 36, 73, 249–50
liberty 36, 37
limits, state's actions 282, 283
Lincoln, Abraham 179
Livy 304
lobbyists 85
local participation 247
Locke, John 9, 65, 164
Lorenzetti, Ambrogio 2
lot (appointments) 167
Louis XIII 24
Louis XIV 31
loyalty 140–43
Lu Chih 212
Lundestad, Guneir 286
Lytton, Lord 52

MacArthur, Douglas 169
Machiavelli, Nicollo 9, 17, 106, 147, 179
Macmillan, Harold 4
Madison, James 47, 171–2, 258
Magna Carta 171, 189
male suffrage 33
Mamelukes 216
Mandela, Nelson 223, 235
Mao Zedong 101, 113, 154, 203
Marcus Aurelius 213
market 248, 308
market economies 73, 256
Marx, Karl 73, 80, 204, 256
Marxism-Leninism 73, 154, 254
Maugham, W. Somerset 115
Mawardi, al- 150

McNamara, Robert 252, 271
media 84, 177, 193, 234, 257–61
meditation 210
Mencius 150
Metternich, Clemens 138
Mexico 285
Michels, Robert 192
Michnik, Adam 157
migration 53
Mill, John Stuart 28, 249, 258, 260
Millennium Development Goals (MDG) 298
Miller, Arthur 119, 125, 136
Miller, Zell 144
Milosevic, Slobodan 307
minds, influence over 26–7
minorities 123
misinformation 259
Mitterrand, Franc[,]ois 12–13
mixed government 182–3
monarchies 86, 163
money 25, 27
Monnet, Jean 203
Montesquieu, Charles de 183, 200, 284
moral courage 233
moral pluralism 220–21
moral practices 220–21
moral progress 41–2
morality 5, 132–4
  20th century 219–20
  cycles 197
  differences between personal and state 135–8
  of power 13, 206
  states 32, 33, 134–9
Morgenthau, Hans 273
Morris, William 317
Morrison, Herbert 136
Moynihan, Daniel Patrick 316

murder 21, 90
Murdock, George 15
Murray, Sir George 87
Mussolini, Benito 100, 113
mutual dependence 33–4, 66–8
Myanmar 33

Nagarjuna 51
Napoleon Bonaparte 112
nation states 37, 288
national identities 35, 121–2
nationalisms 37, 86, 182
nations 6, 39–40, 241, 272–3
Nazism 35, 37, 90
neoliberalism 73
Netherlands 34
new regimes 201–2
New Zealand 166, 280–81
Nietzsche, Friedrich 124
Nigeria 82, 164, 167
Nightingale, Florence 31
Nixon, Richard 124
nomadism 96–7
North, Douglass 79
North Korea 33
Northcote, Sir Stafford 216
Northern Ireland 167
Nozick, Robert 68
nuclear power 32
Nyanaponika Thera 205

Oakeshott, Michael 63
obedience 65, 118–19
obligations 244
official language 113
officials 87–8, 215–17
oligarchy 192–3, 319
Oregon 309
organized crime 62
organized interests 83
organized labour 190

Orwell, George 157, 265
Owen, Robert 237

Paine, Thomas 52, 274
Parliament, English 180
participation 247
Pascal, Blaise 8, 111
passive democracy 229–31
Paterson, William 31
Pauling, Linus 270
payments for services 175
Pearl Harbor 212
peasant revolts 152
Peasants Revolt (1381) 55, 152
Penn, William 274
Pentagon Papers 252
permanence 108–117
personal data 32
Peter the Great 24
Petrucci, Pandolfo 308
Petty, Sir William 31, 100
Philippines 236
Picasso, Pablo 274
Pindar 55
Plato
  anti-democracy 163
  decline 199
  dialectics 254
  Dionysius 9
  future 309
  service 60
  Socrates 207, 209
plunder 17
Pol Pot 154, 158
police forces 88
political activism 243
politics
  conservative 75–6
  funding 83, 84
  generous 53
  international 274

motivation 198
paradoxical truths 9
power 27
progress 30
progressive 76
renewal 202–3
poor relief 51
post-imperial world 291–4
power 8–11
  access to 83
  attitudes to 40–41
  bad 206, 264, 316
  constraining devices 164–78,
    210, 319
  drive for 128–9
  as gift 224–5
  good 66, 94, 210, 264, 315–16
  leaders 104–5, 110–12, 114
  morality of 13, 206
  people 230
  political 27
  retaining 85
  temptations 147–8, 207–9
  thoughts, influencing 26–7
  truth 256
  vices of 6, 320
powerless, power of the 231–5
powerlessness 187
pre-emptive actions 284
prisoners' dilemmas 21
privileged groups 80–81
problems of other people 21–3
professional codes 221
professions 59, 222, 225
progressive politics 76
prosperity 50–51
protection 44–9, 295–7, 300, 318
Protectorate 188
Prussia 31, 32
public activism 193, 226–7, 233,
  242, 243, 292

public goods 21
public opinion 6, 32, 304

Qin Shi Huang 68
Quakers 232, 233
Quetelet, Lambert 100

radicalism 317
Rashid, Harun al- 43–4
re-election 85
Reagan, Ronald 139
realism 13, 278–9
rebellions 16–17, 102, 149–60, 233
recognition 128–9, 208
referendums 186
regimes see states
Reich, Wilhelm 151
religions 2, 254
renewal 200, 201–3
representation 180–86
republics 19
research and development 269
resources, surplus 16, 17, 19, 25,
  38, 81
responsibilities 211–12, 213, 235,
  241, 242
restitution 280
Restoration 188
revolutionaries 153–60
revolutions 149–60, 234
Richard II 152
rights 240–45
ritual 109
Roman empire 60, 92
Roman law 55
Rome 4, 20
Roosevelt, Franklin 84, 136, 208,
  214
Roosevelt, Theodore 175
Rousseau, Jean Jacques 10, 181
rulers see leaders

rules 168–71, 172
Rumbold, Richard 188
Russell, Bertrand 223
Russia 24, 35, 47, 157, 158

sacrifice 232–3
Sampson, Anthony 260
Sayed Qutb 254
scandals 230
Schmitt, Carl 81
schools *see* education
science 9, 30, 262
secessions 174
Second World War 136
security 48, 245, 274, 278
seeing like a state 97
self, view of 218–19
self-deception 265
self-defence 176
self-organization 248
self-restraint 62, 63, 206, 250
self-rule 71, 194–5
self-service 95–126, 319
Sen, Amartya 52
servants, qualities of good 61
service
    accountability 287
    ambiguities 314–15
    democracy 38, 287
    global level 277
    government 7–8
    ideal of 34, 42, 240
    industrial models 249
    leadership 223
    meaning of 60–64
    states 248–9
    systems 37
settled peoples 97
Shaw, George Bernard 185
Shays, Daniel 149
Shen Pu-hai 30

Shia Islam 150–51
short-termism 307–9
Siena 3
Singapore 310
slavery 25
smaller countries 310
Smith, Adam 28, 73
social change 238–9
social contracts 64–5
social entrepreneurs 237
social movements 231
social security 33
Socrates 49, 163, 207
Soderini, Piero 9
Sophocles 140
Sorokin, Pitirim 199
South Africa 33
Spain 174
Spencer, Herbert 250
spiritual needs 70–71
Stalin, Joseph 113, 170, 273
Stalinism 35
state terrorism 47
statecraft 212
states
    actions, bias in 88–9
    break down 265
    bureaucratic 246
    capture of 17, 78–94, 318–19
    change 238
    character 319
    citizens 272
    competition 34
    complexity 228
    early 18–20
    evolution of 28–42
    external role 273
    good 315–16
    human happiness 2
    human needs 71–3
    infrastructure 248, 320

knowledge 261–6
limits 282, 283
morality 32, 33, 134–9
need for 21–3
order 15
ordering mentality 96
organization 245–6
predatory rulers 79
self-serving 95–126, 319
service 248–9
size 63
tasks 4
truth 256
types 19, 36
violence 24
see also government
statistics 31, 100
Stone, I. F. 260
succession 115
suffrage 33, 38, 166
Sufyan 43
suicide bombers 225
sulh-i kul 255
Sully, Duc de 274
Sumeria 19
Sungir burials, Russia 16
surplus resources 16, 17, 19, 25, 38, 81
survival needs 309, 321
Sweden 34, 38, 173, 282
Switzerland 48, 162, 167, 173

Taliban 113
Talleyrand, Charles Maurice de 13
taxes 19, 25, 26, 33
temporary dictatorships 180
terrorism 45, 47, 144
Thailand 101
Thatcher, Margaret 178, 203
Tilak, Bal Gangadhar 150
Tilly, Charles 25, 80

Tocqueville, Alexis de 87
Todd, Emmanuel 74
Tojo-ism 35
tolerance 253–6
Tolstoy, Leo 141
tools, governments 39
torture 145
totalitarian states 19, 124, 265
trade unions 183, 190
tragedies of the commons 21
transformational leaders 223
Transparency International 267
treaty commitments 170
Trevelyan, Sir Charles 216
triangulation 266–8
Trotsky, Leon 47
Truman, Harry 289
trust 22, 26, 27, 107, 243, 302
truth 57–8
devices for seeking 263
flexibility with 145
government 268
legitimation 102
media 257–8, 261
need for 318
open to 255
power 256
revolutions 156
tolerance 253
Tyler, Wat 152
Tyndale, William 56

Uganda 164
Ukraine 89
Unamuno, Miguel de 162
unhappiness, nations 39–40
United Nations (UN) 292, 293, 296, 302
universal ethical goods 135
universal jurisdiction 282
universal male suffrage 33

Ur-Mannu 58
US
  1960s 201
  bureaucracy 32
  civil war 162
  constitution 169
  divisions 172
  founded 157, 158
  imperium 289, 290–91
  military 107
  nationalism 182
  presidential system 167
  Supreme Court 171
  terrorism 144
USSR *see* Russia
utilitarianism 50
Uzbekistan 236

validation 266–8
Varela, Francisco 219
velvet revolutions 160
Vietnam War 142, 252, 271
Villa, Pancho 285
violence 17, 21, 23–6, 27, 40, 90
visibility 115–16, 177–8, 264
Vitoria, Francisco de 284
vocation 217
voting 181, 228, 243

Wallace, George 234
Walzer, Michael 213, 283
wars
  assumptions 275–6
  best intentions 77
  casualties 276
  ends of 278
  Germany 82
  history 89–93
  just war theory 277, 283
  knowledge 30
  move to democracy 40
  on problems 39
  world 92, 93, 136, 277
  weapons of mass destruction
    (WMD) 266
Webb, Beatrice 244
Weber, Max 13, 23, 211, 215, 223
Wei Zheng 143
welfare 37, 38, 49–54, 190, 297–8,
  318
Wen Jiabao 224
Wilkes, John 233
William of Orange 275
Wilson, Woodrow 285
Winstanley, Gerard 187–8
Wittgenstein, Ludwig 317
World Bank 267
world wars 92, 93, 136, 277
writing 19, 96, 254

Yeh-lu Chu'tsai 97
Young, Michael 237
Yusi, al- 106, 196

Zaire 108
Zardad, Faryadi Sarwar 282
Zimbabwe 33